The Joy of Cooking

IRMA S. ROMBAUER

A Compilation of Reliable Recipes
with a Casual Culinary Chat

Illustrations

MARION ROMBAUER

SCRIBNER
1230 Avenue of the Americas
New York, NY 10020

Copyright 1931 by Simon & Schuster Inc.
Copyright renewed © 1959 by Simon & Schuster Inc.
Foreword to the Facsimile Edition
copyright © 1998 by Edgar R. Rombauer

All rights reserved, including the right of reproduction in whole
or in part in any form.

SCRIBNER and design are trademarks of Simon & Schuster Inc.

THE JOY OF COOKING is a registered trademark of The Joy of Cooking Trust

Set in Excelsior

Manufactured in the United States of America

5   7   9   10   8   6   4

Library of Congress Cataloging-in-Publication Data
Rombauer, Irma von Starkloff, 1877–1962.
The joy of cooking : a compilation of reliable recipes with a
casual culinary chat / Irma S. Rombauer : illustrations, Marion
Rombauer.
p.   cm.
Includes index.
TX715.R7499   1998
641.5973—dc21   98-4832   CIP

ISBN 0-684-83358-1

Foreword to
the Facsimile Edition

Mother once confessed that when she was first married she could not cook, so Father, an experienced outdoor camper, was her first teacher. In 1910, when on a visit to Bay View, Michigan, she attended classes taught by Mrs. Ray Johnson, a fabulous cook from south of the Mason-Dixon line, who presided over the culinary department of the summer college campus located there. Mrs. Johnson had a national reputation and was most famous for her rich pastries. Our family favorite, a chocolate cake, appears in this book on page 235, labeled the *Rombauer Special*, and has been carried as such in all the Bobbs-Merrill editions.

Going on from those early lessons, Mother became known citywide as a talented cook and hostess. She had compiled recipes for a church bazaar sale, taught some cooking classes, and as a former art student had given many demonstrations in the art of cake decorating. For the benefit of her children she had lists typed of the ingredients of our favorite family recipes, but without directions because my sister, Marion, and I, having grown up in the kitchen at Mother's elbow, knew how to prepare them. I remember sitting on a high stool at a very tender age, using a cutting board and an old-fashioned cleaver to chop cooked spinach leaves to the consistency now reached with a blender so she could make creamed spinach, another family favorite.

After Father's death in February of 1930, Mother found herself with their lifetime savings in stocks, which were almost worthless following the New York stock market crash of October 1929, plus some nine thousand dollars of liquid assets and income from a mortgage that provided her with adequate living expenses but from an asset that would soon be depleted.

Mother was looking around for some means to supplement her income. She had no business experience, though she had been very active in club and civic affairs, such as the symphony support group, the grade school penny lunch program, and the PTA. She had served successive terms as president of the Wednesday Club, which brought to the city for readings or performances the world's outstanding writers and musicians. (The members were the crème de la crème of St. Louis society and were described in a later *New Yorker* featuring Mother's background as "vultures for culture.")

She was inspired in 1930 by her purchase of a small book entitled *Choice Menus for Luncheons and Dinners,*[1] by Gladys Taussig Lang, which was written to benefit one of the St. Louis children's homes. It was sold for $5.00 a copy and several thousand were sold. Mrs. Lang was a very wealthy socialite with a citywide reputation as a great cook and hostess. On perusing the contents of this work, Mother discovered that the menus contained in it could be served only by a person of Mrs. Lang's economic stratum. The success of this book, however, gave Mother her idea: Why couldn't she, with her local reputation, produce a practical cookbook to be sold at a profit for her own benefit?

If Mrs. Lang was the local "Julia Child," Mother was more like today's "Frugal Gourmet." Many of her best recipes she created to serve tasty leftovers. One of the family favorites, *Chicken Soufflé,* appears on page 85 in this book and is in every subsequent edition through 1975, although by then it had lost its identity as a leftover dish.

Once motivated, she drafted her materials and made inquiries of a local printer as to the cost of producing a book in the form she wanted. It must have a washable cover to withstand cleaning off the gook that ordinarily attaches itself to well-used cookbooks. All the ingredients must be listed at the head of each recipe so the cook wouldn't dis-

---

1. St. Louis, Missouri, Main Library, Reference Department.

cover halfway through preparation that the main ingredient was still on the grocer's shelf.

When the printer told her he could produce such a book for one dollar a copy and she was sure she could sell it for three, she approached my sister and me for our approval of the investment of one-third of the family's capital account, which we readily gave. She asked my sister, Marion, an art teacher at the time, to do the cutout illustrations for the book, and thus began their association of working with the book, which lasted until Mother's death in 1962.

Never having ordered a printing job before, Mother was surprised when she received an overrun of some thirty copies. These she sent off to family members and friends. Most fortunately one happened to land in the home of an Indianapolis cousin, Ina Vonnegut. On that Saturday night Ina happened to have a dinner guest, a Mr. Chambers, president of the Bobbs-Merrill Company Publishers. During the evening the subject of new books arose, and Ina, having perused her copy of *Joy*, mentioned it. When she said it was a cookbook her guest asked to see it.

In retrospect one could honestly say that this request was the spark that produced the "Big Bang" creating the universe of modern cookbooks.

Mother told me that the Sunday night following this incident she had gone to bed with toilet paper curlers in her hair. Monday mornings at eight o'clock her regular cleaning service came to clean up her apartment, so on this Monday morning when her doorbell rang, she threw on a ratty old Japanese kimono and went to let in her cleaner. Instead, to her horrified surprise, she found on her doorstep three very well dressed gentlemen who had come to St. Louis from Indianapolis on the overnight Pullman train to discuss a business proposition with her. Mother showed them into the parlor, set about making her appearance respectable, and then heard the following.

The unexpected visitors represented Bobbs-Merrill. They told her that the biggest sleeper in the publishing world would be a new nationally sold cookbook. Now, in 1998, it is inconceivable that in 1931 there were only two outstanding nationally sold cookbooks—the White House and the Boston Cooking School—neither of which had been revised or updated in years.

Furthermore, Bobbs-Merrill, they said, had been looking for an author capable of producing an up-to-date product, but had not found a prospect until they came upon Mother's *Joy* and decided she should be able to do it for them. They asked her to prepare a manuscript from which they could produce the final product. I never knew what compensation Mother was to receive, if any, for doing this preliminary work.

In the summer of 1932 Mother visited me in Seattle. While here, she spent most of the time testing dessert recipes. As always, when a new recipe comes on the scene there are a dozen different variations circulating. One reason for the great success of Mother's book was that she would prepare all variations of each recipe to be tested by a panel of her friends and acquaintances. When she had a consensus of which was best—that one went in the book. This routine was done with every recipe that ever went into a copy of the *Joy* that bore Mother's name.

Another reason for its success, I believe, was Mother's sense of humor, manifested by the anecdotal introductions to a number of the recipes contained in this book and many early Bobbs-Merrill editions, which added the spice and flavor of Mother's personality to the book. A good sample appears on page 60 of this book, where Mother tells about their Swiss cook: "While she was certainly not born with a silver spoon in her mouth—although it was large enough to accommodate several—I am convinced she arrived with a cooking spoon in her hand."

Mother submitted several drafts to Bobbs-Merrill, but before an acceptable work could be agreed upon, the depression of the 1930s once again changed the course of events. In February of 1933 Mother received the following letter:

February 23, 1933

Dear Mrs. Rombauer:

After studying your cookbook and the additional new manuscript with the greatest of care, we have regretfully come to the conclusion that it would be a mistake for us to attempt to take over its publication now. It is a most humiliating confession to make, but we feel that you yourself have done well with the book and that we would only disappoint you with our efforts.

The new manner of arranging the recipes found much favor with our readers, especially with those who were experienced cooks. And all of them, after trying out a few recipes, agreed that the arrangement was a convenience and help. I had hoped that with this selling point in our favor, we could see our way clear toward undertaking the new edition, for there is no question about the quality of the recipes themselves. But the true fact of the matter is that the book trade is in such a low state that we could not get any wider distribution for The Joy of Cooking *than you are doing without our help.*

It is a disappointment to us all that we cannot have the book on our fall list and I return the manuscript with our most cordial thanks for your courtesy and patience, and my sincere personal regards.

Cordially yours,

FLC;JM[2]

Following the receipt of this letter, Mother submitted her manuscript to a number of other publishing companies, all

2. Bobbs-Merrill mss. Manuscripts Department, Lilly Library, Indiana University, Bloomington.

of whom rejected it. She became discouraged, believing that all her efforts were wasted, but fate once again intervened in the form of a letter from Julia Chapman, a sister of Ina Vonnegut. Julia wrote Mother in the summer of 1934 suggesting a visit to her summer home in Ogunquit, Maine. Julia told her that Ina and Mr. Chambers, Bobbs-Merrill president, also had summer homes there, and that Chambers was a frequent dinner guest in their homes. If she came they would take her to him to convince him Bobbs should publish the book. She came — they did — and the rest is cookbook history.[3]

The first contract Bobbs-Merrill offered Mother, her lawyers and author's agents told her to reject because it offered her minuscule royalties until the book had sold a large number of copies. Once that goal was reached she would receive a much larger royalty percentage than ordinarily given to authors. Bobbs-Merrill's position was that they wanted to pour all the initial profits back into promoting sales for their mutual benefit.

I well remember the promotion. It was in the early days of radio and there were very few stations — Seattle had only three — but everyone who had a radio had it on most of the

---

3. In December of 1935 Mother received the following letter:

December 7, 1935

Mrs. Irma S. Rombauer,
5712 Cabanne Avenue,
St. Louis, Missouri.

Dear Mrs. Rombauer:
    Enclosed is form of assignment of copyright on the former edition of THE JOY OF COOKING in duplicate. Please fill in the exact date of publication from your receipt card from the Library of Congress and the number of this card, sign and return one copy to us. The other copy is for your files.

Cordially yours,

THE BOBBS-MERRILL COMPANY

day. For weeks after *Joy* came out, all stations across the nation carried a plug several times a day advertising *Joy,* and within a year it was selling as far away as the capitals of Europe. By 1940 it was number one on the nonfiction bestseller list for two years running.[4]

Despite everyone's advice, the gamble Mother took paid off and she was handsomely rewarded.

Edgar R. Rombauer, Jr.
Seattle, Washington, 1998

---

4. As the old saying goes—the proof of the pudding is in the eating. In 1962, upon Mother's demise, it became my burden as residual legatee of Mother's estate to pay the inheritance tax. I was furnished the figures I needed from Bobbs-Merrill who stated by then over 26 million copies had been sold—which did not include the figures of the plagiarized copies sold by a Chinese company whose plant was located in Hong Kong. Bobbs-Merrill mss. Manuscripts Department, Lilly Library, Indiana University, Bloomington.

Whenever I leave home and begin to move about, I am appalled to find how many people with a desire to write feel impelled to share their emotions with the general public.

Time and again I have been told with modesty and pride, or with both, that I was entertaining a literary angel unawares, until one day, recognizing the glint of authorship in a man's eye and anticipating his imminent confidence, I forestalled him by saying rapturously, "Oh, do you know, I am a reader!"

And now, after all, I am a writer—of a kind.

For thirty odd years I have enjoyed cooking as an avocation, and as I moved about from place to place I found myself encumbered with an ever increasing supply of cook books—domestic, foreign, published and unpublished.

The result of this encumbrance was an anthology of favorite recipes, which disposed for all time of my ambulant library. These recipes have been developed, altered and created outright, so that the collection as it now stands may make a claim for originality—enough, it is hoped, to justify its publication, and to hold the interest of those who encouraged me to put it into book form.

In this practical outgrowth of a pleasant experience, I have attempted to make palatable dishes with simple means and to lift everyday cooking out of the common-place.

In spite of the fact that the book is compiled with one eye on the family purse and the other on the bathroom scale, there are, of course, occasional lapses into indulgence.

Good cooks at home and abroad have contributed to this collection, and many a recipe is coupled in my mind with a grateful thought of the friend who gave it.

General Rules

The recipes in this book call for standard measuring cups and spoons.

The majority of these recipes will serve from four to six people.

All the measurements given are level, unless indicated otherwise.

A standard measuring cup equals ½ pint.

TABLE OF WEIGHTS AND MEASURES

1 salt spoon	=	¼ teaspoon
3 teaspoons	=	1 tablespoon
1 rounding tablespoon	=	2 tablespoons
2 tablespoons	=	⅛ cup
4 tablespoons	=	¼ cup
16 tablespoons	=	1 cup
2 gills	=	1 cup
1 cup	=	½ pint
2 cups	=	1 pint
2 pints	=	1 quart
4 quarts	=	1 gallon
8 quarts	=	1 peck
4 pecks	=	1 bushel
16 ounces	=	1 pound
16 liquid ounces	=	1 pint (2 cups)
4 cups flour	=	1 pound
2 cups granulated sugar	=	1 pound
2-2/3 cups powdered sugar	=	1 pound
2-2/3 cups brown sugar	=	1 pound
2 cups solid meat	=	1 pound
8 egg whites	=	1 cup
16 egg yolks	=	1 cup
2 cups butter	=	1 pound

Butter the size of an egg	=	¼ cup
1 square bitter chocolate	=	1 ounce
1 ounce chocolate	=	1/3 cup cocoa
1 cup raisins	=	6 ounces
1 cup shelled walnuts	=	¼ pound
1 cup shelled pecans	=	1/3 pound
1 cup shelled almonds	=	¼ pound
3 cups of macaroni	=	1 pound
1 cup grated cheese	=	¼ pound
1 pound green peas, hulled	=	1 cup
1 cup macaroni, cooked	=	2 cups
1 cup rice, cooked	=	3 cups
1 cup noodles, cooked	=	1¼ cups
1 lemon, juiced	=	Approximately 3½ tablespoons
1 orange, juiced	=	Approximately 6 tablespoons

The following chart is sometimes helpful:

No. 1 can contains ..... 1½ cups	No. 2½ can contains .... 3½ cups
No. 2 can contains ..... 2½ cups	No. 3 can contains .... 4 cups

Condensed Milk.

Substitute ½ cup condensed milk and ½ cup of water for 1 cup of fresh milk.

Sour Milk.

When substituting sour milk for sweet milk, allow ½ teaspoonful of soda and deduct 2 teaspoons of baking powder for every cup of sour milk used.

To scald milk put it in a saucepan over slow heat, or in a double boiler. When small beads appear around the edge, the milk is scalded.

To blanch almonds: Pour boiling water over shelled almonds, permit them to stand until the brown skin is loosened, then blanch the almonds by pulling it off.

To clean a burnt or a greasy pot quickly: Place an inch of water in the pot, add 1 teaspoonful or more of soda and heat the water to the boiling point.

Granulated gelatine must be soaked in cold water for five minutes, or more, and dissolved in a hot liquid, or over heat.

½ teaspoon gelatine calls for 2 teaspoons of cold water.

1 teaspoon of gelatine calls for 4 teaspoons of cold water, etc.

Use 1 teaspoon of gelatine for thickening 1 cup of Mayonnaise, or whipped cream.

Use 1 level tablespoon of gelatine for thickening 2 cups of liquid, if a light jelly is desired.

Use 1½ tablespoons of gelatine for thickening 2 cups of liquid, if a firm jelly is desired.

To Sauté—is to cook food in a small amount of fat.

To Fry—is to cook food immersed in deep fat.

To Marinate—is to moisten food with French dressing, or vinegar.

Steaming. See Rule for Steaming—Page 309. When steaming food in individual cups, or in muffin tins, cover the tops with buttered paper to retain the heat and to keep the steam from penetrating.

For Baking, Broiling, Stewing, Sautéing and Frying see the chapter on Meats.

CONTENTS

Index

A

B

The Joy of Cooking

Cocktails

Most cocktails containing liquor are made today with gin and ingenuity. In brief, take an ample supply of the former and use your imagination. For the benefit of a minority, it is courteous to serve chilled fruit juice in addition to cocktails made with liquor.

GIN COCKTAIL

½ cup gin
½ cup orange juice

¼ cup lemon juice
A few drops of bitters

Apricot or other fruit syrup to sweeten and flavor the cocktail as desired. These proportions may be varied.

Serve the cocktail iced, with hot Cream Cheese Canapés— Page 6, or with some other appetizer—or prepare ¼ cup of cocktail for each person, chill it in the refrigerator and pour it over skinned, chilled and slightly sweetened grapefruit sections, in fruit cocktail glasses—Page 2. Use chilled orange juice over prepared grapefruit for those who do not like liquor in cocktails. Serve the fruit cocktail as the first course of a dinner with, or without, some kind of appetizer.

TOMATO JUICE COCKTAIL

1 can of tomatoes (No. 2½
    can)
½ cup water
1 slice onion

1 stalk celery
1 bay leaf
3 sprigs of parsley

Boil these ingredients for one-half hour. Season them well and strain and chill them.

NOTE: Good tomato cocktail may be bought bottled or canned.

CLAM JUICE COCKTAIL

Season bottled clam broth with salt, paprika, horseradish, and a few drops of Tobasco Sauce, or a little lemon juice.

CRABMEAT COCKTAIL
6 Servings

1 can crabmeat (6½ oz.) flaked.

Sauce:

½ cup mayonnaise
½ cup catsup
¼ cup horseradish
1 green pepper, chopped

1 pimento, chopped
3 tablespoons chopped celery may be substituted for the pimento or pepper

OYSTER COCKTAIL
4 Servings

24 small oysters
8 tablespoons Sherry

Salt
Cayenne

Pour seasoned Sherry over the oysters 15 minutes before serving them. If cooking Sherry is used, omit the salt.

OYSTER COCKTAIL WITH CATSUP
Individual Service

7 small oysters
1 tablespoon tomato catsup
½ teaspoon lemon juice
⅓ teaspoon Worcestershire Sauce

Salt
A few grains of cayenne
½ teaspoon grated horseradish

GRAPEFRUIT IN COCKTAIL GLASSES

Pare chilled grapefruit and skin the sections. Place the sections (intact if you can keep them so) in cocktail glasses. Fifteen minutes before serving the cocktail sprinkle the fruit with powdered sugar. Immediately before serving it, add a tablespoon of Sherry to each glass, or fill it three-fourths full with chilled orange juice.

GRAPEFRUIT COCKTAIL

Chill the fruit, cut it crosswise and loosen the pulp from the peel with a sharp knife. Remove the seeds and cut out the tough fibrous center with a pair of scissors, or a patent cutter. Sprinkle the fruit with sugar and set it aside for 15 minutes. Add 1 tablespoon of sweet Sherry to each half just before serving the fruit.

OYSTERS IN GRAPEFRUIT

Prepare grapefruit as for grapefruit cocktail, omitting the sugar. Place several small oysters in each center and season them with lemon, salt, horseradish, Tobasco Sauce, or with Sherry. (Omit the salt if cooking Sherry is used).

SHRIMP IN GRAPEFRUIT

Prepare grapefruit as for grapefruit cocktail, but instead of sprinkling it with sugar, season it with salt and paprika. Fill each center with three or four shrimp that have been moistened with French dressing. Serve the grapefruit garnished with a sprig of parsley.

FRUIT COCKTAIL

Use combinations of fresh fruits sliced, sugared and chilled. Flavor them with lime juice, lemon juice, or Sherry.

Seedless grapes, watermelon, green and yellow cantaloupes (cut into balls with a French potato cutter), Queen Ann cherries (stoned and stuffed with filberts) and fresh pineapple make good cocktails. Chilled ginger ale may be poured over the fruit immediately before serving it.

PINEAPPLE COCKTAIL

Peel and dice a fresh pineapple. Make a syrup of ¾ cup of sugar and 1 cup of water. Pour this over the fruit and chill it for several hours. Shortly before serving the pineapple sprinkle it with chopped mint leaves.

PINEAPPLE BOATS
(This is a very attractive looking cocktail)

Trim two-thirds from the leafy top of a chilled pineapple and cut the fruit into six or eight lengthwise parts. Cut off the core and place each part so that it will resemble a boat. Pare the skin in one piece, leaving it in place and cut the pulp into five or six downward slices — retaining the boat shape. Serve each boat on an individual plate with a small mound of powdered sugar and a few large, unhulled strawberries.

HONEYDEW MELON OR CANTALOUPE

Cut the melon in sections. Remove the rind. Serve the peeled sections on lettuce leaves with lime or lemon juice, or with French dressing.

STRAWBERRY COCKTAIL

Place large strawberries (hulled or unhulled) on lettuce leaves and moisten them with French dressing to which a little sugar has been added.

PINEAPPLE AND ORANGE MINT COCKTAIL

1 cup sliced fresh pineapple   1/4 pound After dinner mints
3 oranges

Cut the pineapple into pieces, divide the oranges into sections and remove skins. Crush the mints and combine them with the other ingredients. Chill the fruit for one hour or more. Serve it with a sprinkling of powdered sugar.

Canapés and Sandwiches

Serve the following canapés and sandwiches very hot:

CREAMED OYSTER CANAPÉS

Follow the recipe for Creamed Oysters on Page 76. Place the pan containing the oysters over hot water. Toast small rounds of bread, butter them lightly and put on each round a creamed oyster sprinkled with chopped parsley.

OYSTER AND BACON CANAPÉS

Place one large oyster, or three small oysters, on a round of lightly buttered toast and cover it with a thin strip of bacon. Place the canapés on a broiler and broil them until the oysters begin to curl.

SHRIMP, OYSTER OR STUFFED OLIVE AND BACON CANAPÉS

Surround shrimps, oysters or stuffed olives with small strips of bacon and secure them with toothpicks. Broil them quickly.

CRABMEAT CANAPÉS

1 cup crabmeat (6½ ounce can)	2 teaspoons butter
1 tablespoon green peppers, finely chopped	2 teaspoons flour
	½ cup scalded cream
1 tablespoon chopped pimento	Salt, pepper, a few grains of cayenne
	Grated cheese

Combine the crabmeat, peppers and the pimento. Make a cream sauce of the butter, flour and cream, season it and add

5

it while hot to the above ingredients. Mix them well and place them on pieces of toast. Sprinkle the tops with grated cheese and heat the canapés on a broiler or in a hot oven until the cheese browns.

PASTRY SNAILS

(If the approval of guests is to be taken as a criterion of excellence, this is the prize winning Canapé).

Roll pie crust—Page 209, until it is very thin. Trim it into an oblong about four inches wide. Spread the surface with a filling and roll the dough like a jelly roll. Chill the rolls, cut them in half inch slices and bake them on a greased pan in a quick oven.

FILLINGS FOR PASTRY SNAILS

1. An equal amount of cream cheese and anchovy paste, or deviled ham.
2. Grated American cheese seasoned with cayenne.
3. Cottage cheese, or cream cheese, seasoned with salt and paprika.

TOASTED CANAPÉS OR SANDWICHES

For canapés, spread one of the four following fillings between trimmed slices of bread—cut the slices into small attractive shapes or roll them and secure the rolls with toothpicks.

For sandwiches, serve more generous portions.

These canapés may be prepared in advance, if wrapped in a damp cloth, or in waxed paper, until toasted. They must be toasted on both sides immediately before they are served.

TOASTED CREAM CHEESE CANAPÉS

1 cream cheese	1½ tablespoons butter
½ tablespoon or more fish paste	½ teaspoon Worcestershire Sauce

Spread the filling between thin layers of white bread.

TOASTED MUSHROOM CANAPÉS

Spread sautéd and creamed mushrooms, well minced and seasoned between thin layers of bread. See Page 123 for preparing mushrooms.

TOASTED ROQUEFORT CHEESE CANAPÉS

1 cream cheese
3 tablespoons, or more,
  Roquefort cheese
¼ cup walnut or pecan
  meats, chopped
Seasoning

Spread the filling between thin layers of white bread.

TOASTED LIVER SAUSAGE CANAPÉS

Thin Braunschweiger sausage with canned tomato soup and a little cream until it is a good consistency to spread. Spread it between layers of dark, or light bread.

TOASTED CHEESE ROLLS

2 cups soft sharp cheese
½ teaspoon salt
A few grains of cayenne
1 teaspoon prepared
  mustard
3 tablespoons cream

Stir these ingredients into a smooth paste. Remove the crusts from a loaf of bread and cut it into lengthwise ¼ inch slices. Butter the slices lightly and spread them with the cheese mixture. Roll them lengthwise like a jelly roll. Wrap them firmly in a damp cloth and chill them for several hours. Cut the rolls into thin slices and toast them on both sides.

HOT TOMATO CANAPÉS WITH CHEESE

Place slices of tomatoes on rounds of buttered toast. Season them with salt, paprika and a little mustard. Cover them with grated cheese and place the canapés in a pan in a moderate oven — 375° — until the cheese is melted.

GRILLED TOMATOES AND MAYONNAISE

Tomatoes
Bread crumbs
Salt, pepper
Mayonnaise

Combine bread crumbs with mayonnaise, making a rather thick paste. Cut tomatoes in halves, season them and cover them with the paste. Place them in a buttered pan and broil them for ten minutes in a quick oven.

TOMATO CANAPÉS WITH BACON

Place thick slices of tomato on rounds of buttered toast. Season them and cover them with thin slices of bacon. Broil the canapés under a broiler until the bacon is crisp.

PEANUT BUTTER AND BACON CANAPÉS

Toast rounds of bread on one side. Spread the untoasted sides with peanut butter, cover them with very thin strips of bacon and broil them under a quick flame until the bacon is crisp.

LINK SAUSAGES IN PASTRY

Roll link sausages in small squares of pastry dough. Bake them in a hot oven.

CRAB CANAPÉS

Toast large rounds of bread on one side. Combine crabmeat with mayonnaise and place it on the untoasted side of the bread. Cover each canapé with a heavy coating of grated cheese. Place the canapés under a broiler until the cheese is melted.

CLUB SANDWICH

A club sandwich consists of 3 slices of bread toasted on both sides, spread with the following ingredients:

Slice I. is covered with a lettuce leaf
3 slices of crisp bacon
Slices of tomato
1 tablespoon mayonnaise and Slice II.

Slice II. is covered with a lettuce leaf
Slices of cold chicken
1 tablespoon mayonnaise

Slice III. is placed on top of Slice II.

Serve the following Canapés and Sandwiches cold:

PRETZEL AND CHEESE CANAPÉS

Use small crisp pretzels. Place soft, well seasoned cheese in the hollows and press the pretzels into rolled pretzel crumbs. Chill them until ready to serve them.

SWEDISH WAFERS

Steam Swedish Wafers in a double boiler. When they are pliable, roll them into cornucopias. When they are stiff, fill them with a cheese or sandwich filling.

STUFFED PECANS

Spread large pecan meats with Roquefort cheese that has been moistened with a few drops of lemon juice or cream. Press two halves together.

POTATO CHIPS AND CHEESE

Spread crisp potato chips with cream cheese or Roquefort cheese to which a dash of Worcestershire Sauce has been added, or spread the chips with cream cheese combined with fish paste.

FILLED CELERY

Combine: 1 tablespoon butter
              1 tablespoon Roquefort cheese
              1 package cream cheese and season this with salt.
              Fill dwarf celery ribs and sprinkle them with paprika.

RIPE OLIVES, GARLIC AND PARSLEY

Rub a bowl with a clove of garlic. Put a small amount of olive oil in the bowl and toss the olives about in it until they are well covered with oil. Put the olives on ice until chilled, dust them with chopped parsley and serve them at once.

CHEESE CRACKERS AND FISH PASTE CANAPÉS
(A quick canapé)

Place a small dab of butter in the center of a crisp cheese cracker and next to it, or over it, a small dab of anchovy or sardelle paste.

TOMATO AND SHRIMP CANAPÉS

Place a slice of tomato on a round of toast and put one or two marinated shrimp in the center. Cover the shrimp with a dab of mayonnaise.

TOMATO CANAPÉS WITH CAVIAR AND SHRIMP

Cut thick slices of tomato. Cover them with a mixture of caviar and the yolks of hard cooked eggs, chopped, seasoned with lemon juice. Garnish the slices with the whites of hard cooked eggs chopped, and serve them with a fresh shrimp in the center of each canapé.

9

CAVIAR CANAPÉS

Sauté rounds of thin toast in butter, add finely chopped onion to caviar, spread it on the toast and garnish the edges of the canapés with the yolks of hard cooked eggs that have been put through a ricer. Serve the canapés with thin slices of lemon.

PICKLE CANAPÉS

Remove the crusts from a loaf of bread and cut it into lengthwise 1/4 inch slices. Spread the slices with a paste made of Roquefort or cream cheese, thinned with cream, colored pink with paprika. Roll each slice around a jumbo pickle. Wrap the rolls in waxed paper. Chill them well and when ready to serve them cut them into 1/4 inch slices.

ROLLED TONGUE OR CHIPPED BEEF CANAPÉS

Moisten soft cream cheese with cream, season it with Worcestershire Sauce, finely chopped onion and paprika. Spread the cheese on very thin slices of smoked, boiled tongue, or on chipped beef (put up in glass) and roll the canapés.

ROLLED ASPARAGUS CANAPÉS OR SANDWICHES

Spread thin slices of bread, from which the crusts have been cut, with a little butter and mayonnaise and sprinkle them lightly with chives. Place an asparagus tip at one end and roll the bread about it, or place well drained asparagus tips in French dressing for half an hour, drain them and use them as directed, omitting the mayonnaise. Wrap the rolls in waxed paper until ready to serve them.

CUCUMBER SANDWICHES

Chill cucumbers well, pare and slice them. Season them and place them between layers of bread spread with butter and mayonnaise. Serve them at once.

TOMATO SANDWICHES

Peel and cut tomatoes into thick slices. Sprinkle them with salt and place them between layers of bread spread with butter and mayonnaise. Chopped fried bacon may be added.

PECAN SANDWICHES

Spread chopped pecans, moistened with mayonnaise, on thin

slices of white bread and cover them with slices on which washed nasturtium leaves or nasturtium blossoms have been placed.

MOCK CHICKEN SANDWICHES

Place the contents of a can of Tuna fish in a strainer and pour 2 cups of boiling water over it. Drain the fish well and chill it. Combine it with well seasoned mayonnaise and spread the mixture between layers of bread on which lettuce leaves have been placed.

RIPE OLIVE SANDWICH FILLING

½ cup ripe olives, chopped   1 cream cheese
½ green pepper, chopped

Combine these ingredients and moisten them with French dressing seasoned with onion or garlic.

TUNA FISH, SALMON, OR CRABMEAT
SANDWICH FILLING

½ cup Tuna fish, flaked   2 tablespoons sweet pickles,
1 hard cooked egg, chopped   chopped
½ cup celery, chopped   ¼ teaspoon salt
2 tablespoons pimento,   ¼ teaspoon paprika
  chopped   ⅓ cup mayonnaise

Combine the ingredients lightly, using a fork.

STUFFED OLIVE SANDWICH FILLING

1 cream cheese   ½ cup finely chopped
Enough cream to make it   celery
  the right consistency to   ½ teaspoon salt
  spread   ¼ teaspoon paprika
¼ cup stuffed olives,
  chopped

Garnish the sandwiches with stuffed olives.

ALMOND SANDWICH FILLING

1 cream cheese   ½ cup shredded salted
Enough cream to make it   almonds
  the right consistency to   Paprika
  spread

Garnish the sandwiches with salted almonds.

11

ALMOND AND EGG FILLING

¼ cup almonds, blanched
and finely chopped
Salt, paprika

4 hard cooked eggs, finely
chopped

Enough butter, mayonnaise or French dressing to make the filling a good consistency to spread.

EGG SANDWICHES

Season hard cooked, chopped eggs and make them into a paste with a little cream and a few drops of Worcestershire Sauce Add fried, chopped bacon and spread the filling between thin layers of bread.

PINEAPPLE SANDWICHES (Open)

Cut rounds of bread and spread them with cream cheese. Cover each piece with a thin slice of pineapple and garnish it with a maraschino cherry.

HAM SANDWICH SPREAD

½ pound of ham
1 large sour pickle or 2
small ones

4 eggs, cooked hard

Grind these ingredients and season them with salt, pepper and mustard, moisten them with vinegar until they are a good consistency to spread.

Hors D'Oeuvre

So many combinations of fruits or vegetables take the place of the Hors d' Oeuvre that it is advisable to consult the chapter on Salads before deciding upon this course. The chapter on Eggs and Luncheon Dishes too, has a number of recipes that might rightly come under the heading of Hors d' Oeuvre.

Aspic Salad

CHICKEN, VEAL OR FISH, ETC.

Any clever person can take a few desolate looking ice box left-overs and glorify them into a tempting Aspic Salad.

2 cups stock
1½ tablespoons gelatine
¼ cup mild vinegar, or juice
    of 1 lemon

Salt, paprika, celery salt
1 or 2 tablespoons sugar
    (optional)

Soak the gelatine in ½ cup of cold stock for five minutes. Dissolve it in ½ cup of boiling stock. Combine the gelatine with the remaining stock and add the vinegar or lemon juice and a generous amount of seasoning, if the aspic is to cover unseasoned food. Chill the aspic and when it is about to set, combine it with the salad ingredients. Take 3 cups of solids to this amount of aspic. Meat diced, fish flaked, eggs cooked hard and sliced, cabbage chopped, pickles, cucumbers, celery, green peppers, nut meats, cooked beets, sweetbreads, grapefruit, stuffed ripe or green olives, raw carrots ground or cut into thin strips, etc., may be used in any good combination in aspic salads.

EMERGENCY ASPIC I.

Use the foregoing recipe, substituting beef cubes or Savita dissolved in boiling water for stock — 1/2 teaspoon Savita, or 1 cube to 1 cup of boiling water.

EMERGENCY ASPIC II.

2 cups canned bouillon
1 tablespoon lemon juice
1½ tablespoons gelatine

¼ cup cold water
Salt, pepper or paprika

Soak the gelatine in the cold water for 5 minutes. Dissolve it in the hot bouillon, add the lemon juice and seasoning and chill it until it is nearly set. Add the solid ingredients, about 3 cupfuls, and chill the aspic until it is set.

TOMATO ASPIC WITH CHEESE CENTERS

Prepare Tomato Aspic — Page 173. When it is about to set fill individual molds one-third full. Combine soft cream cheese with anchovy paste (or anchovies mashed) add a dash of Worcestershire sauce and roll it into balls. The amount of anchovy used is optional. Drop a ball into each mold and cover it with aspic. When cold, unmold the aspic and serve it with or without mayonnaise.

TONGUE IN ASPIC
6 Servings

The following is a fine looking dish, as well as a palatable one:

1 — 3 lb. smoked beef tongue
Cold water to cover
1 onion

1 stalk celery with leaves
6 bay leaves
1 teaspoon pepper corns

If the tongue is salty, soak it in cold water from two to twelve hours. Cover it with fresh cold water, add the other ingredients and simmer it gently until tender. (From two to four hours.) Leave it in the stock until it is slightly cooled and when cold enough to handle, skin it and remove all the dry hard portions and the roots. Have a mold or bread pan ready that has been moistened with cold water. Prepare the aspic and when it is nearly set, place a small amount in the bottom of the mold. Then put the tongue into the mold and pour the remaining aspic around and over it. When well chilled unmold the aspic on to a platter and garnish the dish with deviled eggs and parsley, or with slices of lemon and lettuce leaves. Serve it with mayonnaise. The rule for aspic is on the following page.

Aspic for Tongue:

1½ envelope Gelatine
½ cup cold tongue stock
1 teaspoon Savita, or 2 beef
cubes dissolved in
1½ cups boiling tongue
stock
¼ cup vinegar
Juice of 1 lemon
1 tablespoon sugar

A few drops of Kitchen
Bouquet (for color)
1 teaspoon Worcester-
shire sauce
1 medium sized sour sweet
pickles chopped
1 cup celery chopped
½ cup green peppers,
chopped

Soak the gelatine in the cold stock for 5 minutes and dissolve it in the boiling stock. Add all but the last three ingredients and chill the gelatine until it is about to set. Then add the remaining ingredients and the aspic is ready to be combined with the tongue.

CHICKEN SALAD OR FISH SALAD IN ASPIC

Prepare aspic jelly. When it is nearly set half fill individual molds. Place a small ball of rather dry chicken or fish salad in each mold and cover it with aspic jelly. Chill the salads until they are set, unmold them on lettuce leaves and serve them with mayonnaise.

DEVILED EGGS

Place eggs in boiling water and cook them under the boiling point for 30 minutes, then place them in cold water to prevent the yolks from discoloring. Shell the eggs, cut them into halves and remove the yolks. Mash the yolks with a fork and moisten them with French dressing, with mayonnaise, or with cream, and season them with salt, vinegar and a little mustard. Refill the whites and serve the eggs garnished with chopped parsley, chives, or paprika.

DEVILED EGGS DE LUXE

(But no longer living up to their name since Woolworth
has taken to selling caviar at ten cents a tin.)

Prepare cooked eggs, shell them and cut them in halves. Take out the yolks and crush them with a fork, and combine them with chopped onion, caviar, lemon juice and enough cream to make them palatable. Refill the white shells and garnish them with capers or sliced olives.

15

DEVILED EGGS IN ASPIC

Prepared deviled eggs — Page 15. Place half an egg (sunny side up) in one-half cup of well seasoned aspic, that is about to set. Chill and invert the contents of the cups on lettuce leaves. Serve the eggs with mayonnaise.

WATER LILIES

Cut five or six gashes in a hard-cooked egg from the small point down. Press out the yolk, devil it and replace it in a ball with chopped parsley sprinkled on the top. Garnish the eggs with radishes and olives to represent buds, and serve them with French dressing.

EGGS STUFFED WITH SHRIMP OR CRABMEAT

Moisten Shrimp (or crabmeat) with French dressing or lemon juice. Cut hard cooked eggs in halves, remove the yolks and put them through a ricer. Add mayonnaise dressing to the shrimp and a dash of Worcestershire sauce. Fill the whites of the eggs with the shrimp and place them on pieces of toast garnished with the riced egg yolks.

MAYONNAISE EGGS

4 slices of bacon
6 hard cooked eggs, riced
4 tablespoons mayonnaise
½ teaspoon grated onion
1 teaspoon prepared mustard
1 tablespoon parsley chopped
2 tablespoons green peppers, chopped
1 teaspoon salt
½ teaspoon white pepper
Grated cheese

Broil the bacon and mince it. Combine it with the other ingredients. Form them into balls or into egg shapes, roll them in mayonnaise and then in grated cheese. Chill them and serve them on shredded lettuce.

ARTICHOKES STUFFED WITH SHRIMP OR CRABMEAT

Cook artichokes — Page 119. Chill them and cut them in halves. Remove the inedible choke. Moisten shrimp with French dressing, or with lemon juice and fill the hollows with them. Serve the artichokes very cold with mayonnaise.

TOMATO EGG AND CAVIAR

Cover a round of toast or bread with a thick slice of tomato. Place half a hard cooked egg on top, from which the yolk has been removed and which has been filled with caviar seasoned with lemon juice. Use the grated egg yolk as a garnish. Or, skin a tomato, hollow it and place the egg filled with caviar in the hollow, cover it with mayonnaise and use the grated yolk as a garnish.

TOMATOES AND COTTAGE CHEESE

Skin and hollow large firm tomatoes. Salt them, invert them to drain for 20 minutes and chill them. Fill the hollows with cottage cheese. Blanched, shredded almonds and finely chopped celery may be added to the cheese, and the tops may be garnished with chopped chives. Serve the tomatoes with mayonnaise.

MOLDED FISH SALAD
6 Servings

1 cup of cooked flaked fish, or	1/2 teaspoon mustard
1 cup of canned salmon (8 oz.)	A few grains of cayenne
	2 egg yolks
3/4 tablespoon gelatine	1 1/2 tablespoons melted butter
2 tablespoons cold water	3/4 cup milk
1/2 teaspoon flour	1/3 cup vinegar (1/4 cup if
1 1/2 teaspoons salt	vinegar is very strong)
1 tablespoon sugar	

Pour 2 cups of boiling water over the salmon, drain it and flake it. Soak the gelatine in the cold water for 5 minutes, then place it over boiling water until it is dissolved. Combine the dry ingredients and add the yolks, butter, milk and vinegar slowly. Cook them over hot water, stirring them constantly until the mixture thickens. Add the dissolved gelatine and fold in the salmon. Place the salad in a mold and chill it thoroughly. Unmold the salad on lettuce leaves and serve it with cucumber sauce — Page 159.

CREAMED OYSTERS WITH CRABMEAT AND CHEESE

2 tablespoons butter	1/2 teaspoon Worcester- shire sauce
2 tablespoons grated cheese	
1/3 cup tomato catsup	1/2 cup crabmeat chopped
1/2 cup cream	1 cup oysters (1/2 pint)

Melt the butter in a double boiler and add the cheese. When

17

the cheese is melted, add the catsup, Worcestershire sauce and cream. When the sauce is very hot add the crabmeat and the oysters. Cook the oysters until they are plump and serve them at once on toast.

OYSTERS AND SWEETBREADS ON SKEWERS

Surround raw oysters with strips of bacon secured with toothpicks. Place the oysters on small skewers, alternating them with pieces of boiled sweetbread. Heat the filled skewers in a very hot frying pan, cooking them just long enough to crisp the bacon. Serve them very hot.

BAKED OYSTERS ON TOAST

Place small rounds of toast in a shallow pan. Put an oyster on each piece of toast. Sprinkle them with salt and paprika and bake them in a moderate oven—375°—until the oysters are plump. Cover each oyster with ½ teaspoon of:

Lemon Butter:

3 tablespoons butter   Dash of cayenne
½ teaspoon salt   1 tablespoon lemon juice

Cream the butter, season it and add the lemon juice very slowly. Chill it before using it.

OYSTERS AND BACON

Drain large oysters and season them with salt and pepper. Wrap them in very thinly cut slices of bacon and secure them with toothpicks. Heat a frying pan until it is very hot, add Serve them at once on rounds of toast. the oysters and cook them just long enough to crisp the bacon.

OYSTERS IN SPINACH

Half fill oyster shells with creamed spinach. Place an oyster in each shell and sprinkle the oysters with salt and grated cheese. Put the shells in a good oven—425°—until the cheese is melted. Bulk oysters may be placed in ramekins half filled with spinach, sprinkled with grated cheese and baked.

Soups

Soups are given many enticing names, but they fall into one or the other of the following general classifications:

White stock, made with white meats and light-colored vegetables.

Brown Stock, made with dark meats and vegetables.

Bouillon, made with beef (part of which is browned in marrow) and vegetables.

Consommé, made with beef, veal, chicken and vegetables.

These four soups are served clear:

Vegetable Soup, made with stock in which fresh vegetables have been cooked, or to which diced, cooked vegetables have been added.

Cream Soup, (Purée or Bisque), made with strained cooked vegetables, or strained cooked fish, to which a thin cream sauce (made with butter, flour and milk or stock) is added.

Cereal Soup. Stock or cream soup and cereal.

Recently, the French Government conferred a decoration upon the cook who prepares Campbell's soup. It is regrettable that this distinction could not be made to include all soup manufacturers who have brought to us this good and nutritious product at so low a cost.

It is advisable to keep a can of tomato and a can of asparagus soup on the emergency shelf. These soups are delicious diluted with equal parts of milk. In addition, a can of bouillon should be kept for quick aspics and for use in the place of stock.

Canned tomato juice and canned clam juice make good cocktails, the former makes a quick aspic and the latter a fine cream of clam soup.

Beef cubes are in general use, but Savita, a meatless Battle Creek product, is a better substitute. No substitute, however, can compare with good home-made stock.

Most recipes for soup stock begin with "Take 5 lbs. of lean beef, 2½ lbs. marrow bone, etc." — thereby putting this dish among the luxuries.

By following the French custom of the "pot au feu" good soup stock may be kept on hand by utilizing scraps. Keep bits of bone, cooked meat, chicken carcasses, roast trimmings, vegetable parings, the outer leaves of lettuce, unshapely tomatoes, celery tops, peapods, parsley, etc., for the soup pot.

Use lamb and mutton sparingly, they are frequently strong in flavor — and pork is too rich and sweet to make good soup.

If your scraps are insufficient, buy a soup bone, or an oxtail and a soup bunch.

The proportions of the "pot au feu" (anglicized — "ice box soup") vary greatly.

A good rule is to use twice as much water as meat, bone and fat, adding vegetables as desired. It is well to soak the meat for an hour in order to draw the juices into the water that is to be used in making the soup.

Use but little seasoning until the soup is to be served, as it is difficult to gauge the amount needed.

Vegetables should be added for the last hour of cooking only because they are apt to absorb the delicate flavor of the meat.

Soup made from cooked meat and left-overs requires less cooking than soup made from fresh ingredients. One to two hours' simmering is sufficient to extract the juices from cooked food, in which time the liquid will be reduced to about three-fourths of the original amount.

Soup made from fresh meat requires at least four hours' simmering, in which time it will be reduced to about one-half the original amount.

One measuring cup of soup is equal to two average servings.

Soup is best one day old, when its flavor is intensified and its seasoning is higher than on the day on which it is cooked.

SOUP STOCK I.

Made with raw meat. Cut the meat from the bones into one inch cubes. Reserve one-third of the meat. Put the remainder with the bones into cold water for one hour—use 2 cups of water for every pound of meat, bone and fat. Sear the reserved meat in hot marrow (or other fat) until it is dark brown (this will give flavor as well as color to the soup), and add it to the water. Bring the water slowly to the boiling point, reduce the heat, and simmer the soup for four hours, or more. Add seasoning and vegetables for the last hour of cooking —about 2 cups of diced vegetables to every pound of meat. Strain the soup, chill it, remove the grease, and reheat the soup. It may be served clear, or with marrow balls, farina balls, etc., and chopped parsley.

SOUP STOCK II.

Made with cooked meat. Cut the meat from the bones. To every pound of bones, meat and fat, use 2 or 2½ cups of water. Soak the meat and the bones in the water for one hour, bring it slowly to the boiling point—reduce the heat and simmer it for one hour. Add vegetables and a little seasoning and simmer it one hour longer. If a cereal is desired, add it with the vegetables. Vegetables may be varied in kind and quantity. Tomatoes, fresh or canned, lettuce, cabbage, onions, carrots, turnips, celery stalks with leaves, parsley, leeks, etc. make good soup. Salt, pepper corns, paprika, celery salt, bay leaves and mace are in general use for seasoning. Strain the soup, chill it, remove the grease and reheat the soup.

LEFT-OVER SOUP
6 Small Servings

2 cups meat and bone	1 cup tomatoes
5 cups water	2 teaspoons barley
Left-over gravy	½ teaspoon sugar
1 cup vegetables (carrots, turnips, celery)	Salt
	Paprika
1 onion	Celery salt

If clear soup is desired, omit the gravy and the barley. Follow the method for making Soup Stock II.

LEFT-OVER CHICKEN SOUP

1 chicken carcass	Lettuce leaves
1 cup celery with leaves	Parsley
1 large onion	4 cups water
1 cup carrots	2 tablespoons rice
½ cup turnips	Salt, paprika, celery salt
Left-over gravy	

If clear soup is desired, omit the rice. Follow the method for making Soup Stock II.

TURKEY SOUP

The following is a good "swan song" for a turkey dinner:

1 turkey carcass	½ cup onions
8 cups water	¼ cup parsley
1 cup carrots	1 cup tomatoes
1 cup celery with leaves	3 tablespoons barley
½ cup turnips	Seasoning

Soak the turkey carcass in the water for one hour. Simmer it for one hour, add the vegetables and the barley and simmer the soup until the cereal is tender. Strain, chill, skim and reheat it. Serve it with chopped parsley.

Vary this according to your fancy, or your materials on hand. It is sure to be good. Add the left over gravy, if you wish.

SPLIT PEA OR BEAN SOUP

Made with a Turkey's carcass or a ham bone.

1 turkey carcass or 1 ham bone	1 tablespoon flour
	1 stalk celery
1 cup split peas or beans	2 tablespoons butter or
1 onion	soup fat
8 cups water	Seasoning

Soak the peas in the water for 12 hours. Add the turkey carcass or ham bone and simmer the soup covered for four or five hours. Add the vegetables for the last hour of cooking. Strain the stock and chill it. Press the peas through colander or ricer and add the purée to the stock, from which the grease has been removed. As the ingredients will separate, they must be bound. Melt the butter or fat, add the flour and when they are bubbling, add the stock. Season the soup well and serve it with croutons.

SPLIT PEA OR BEAN SOUP WITH SALT PORK

1 cup dried split peas or
  beans
8 cups water
2 cups stock, or milk
½ onion — large
1 cup celery

½ cup carrots
2 tablespoons flour
1½ teaspoons salt
⅛ teaspoon pepper
2 inch cube of salt pork
  (optional)

The water in which a ham bone has been cooked may be used in place of other stock, or a ham bone may be added to the water, in either case, omit the salt pork. Soak the peas in water for 12 hours, or more. Drain them, add the 8 cups of water, the pork and the vegetables. Simmer the soup for 3 or 4 hours — until the peas are very soft. Drain the peas, reserving the liquor, and rub them through a colander. Combine the liquor, the strained peas and the stock (or milk). Melt the butter, add the flour and pour the soup on slowly. When thick and smooth add the seasoning and serve the soup.

CHICKEN GUMBO

1 stewing chicken
Flour
Bacon grease
4 cups boiling water
1 cup okra, sliced

2 cups tomatoes skinned
½ cup corn
1 cup potatoes, diced
1 small onion, diced
8 cups water

Cut the chicken in pieces and dredge it with flour. Brown it in bacon fat, pour the boiling water over it and simmer it covered until the meat falls from the bones. Drain the stock well and chop the meat. Place the remaining ingredients in a soup kettle and boil them until they are tender. Combine them with the chicken stock and meat. Thicken the gumbo with flour, or with boiled rice, season it well and serve it.

MEATLESS VEGETABLE SOUP I.
About 5 Servings

This is an acceptable, moderately thick vegetable soup. Vary the vegetables, if you like, keeping about the same proportion of liquid and solids.

¼ cup carrots
¼ cup turnips
¼ cup celery
½ cup potatoes
¼ cup onion
3 cups water

2 tablespoons butter
½ tablespoon flour
¾ teaspoon salt
½ teaspoon or more Savita
3 tablespoons parsley

Dice the vegetables. Melt 3 tablespoons of butter, add the

carrots, turnips and celery and cook them for 10 minutes. Add the potatoes and cook them for 2 minutes. Add the onion and the water and simmer the soup for 1 hour. Melt the butter, add the flour and a little of the soup. Return the soup to the kettle and cook it 1 hour longer. Add the Savita. Beat the soup with a wire whisk, or a fork, to break up the vegetables, add the parsley and serve it.

MEATLESS VEGETABLE SOUP WITH CEREAL II
About 6 Servings

This is a deliciously flavored thick vegetable soup. The proportions may be varied, or altered, but it is very good as it is.

5 cups water
1 cup potatoes — pared and diced
½ cup onions, finely sliced
½ cup carrots diced
1 cup chopped lettuce, or ½ cup chopped cabbage
½ cup canned tomatoes
1 cup celery — diced and some of the leaves, chopped
½ cup cooked rice
½ cup turnips (optional)
1 tablespoon butter
½ teaspoon sugar
Salt, paprika, celery salt

Prepare the vegetables, add them to the water and simmer them for one hour. Add the cooked rice and simmer the soup for ½ hour. Last add the butter and the seasoning.

VEGETABLE BISQUE
4 Servings

Utilizing the water in which vegetables have been cooked.

2 tablespoons butter
1½ tablespoon flour (scant)
1½ cups vegetable water, (asparagus, etc.)
½ cup cream
Salt, paprika, celery salt
½ cup cooked, diced or strained vegetables (optional)
Chopped parsley may be added to the soup

Melt the butter, add the flour and stir these ingredients until they are smooth. Add the vegetable water and the cream. When the soup is thick and smooth add the seasoning and the strained or diced vegetables, or omit the cream — use 2 cups of vegetable water and add 1 teaspoon of Savita.

CLEAR SOUP WITH VEGETABLES

Add dried vegetables to boiling soup stock and cook them until they are tender

EMERGENCY SOUPS

Here are two recipes for delicious soup, delicately flavored and quickly made. They are neither thick nor thin. Both call for stock. If this is not available, use Savita, or beef cubes, in this case an acceptable substitute. (½ teaspoon Savita, or 1 beef cube to 1 cup of boiling water).

TOMATO SOUP

1 No. 2 can of tomatoes
1 small onion
3 ribs of celery with leaves
2 tablespoons butter
2 tablespoons flour
2 cups stock or 2 cups
   water and

1 teaspoon Savita
½ teaspoon sugar
⅛ teaspoon paprika
Salt
3 tablespoons chopped
   parsley

Boil the tomatoes with the onion and the celery for ten minutes, then strain them. Melt the butter, add the flour and when smooth add the stock and the strained tomato. Boil these ingredients for one minute. Add the seasoning and the chopped parsley and serve the soup.

PEA SOUP
Canned Peas

1 No. 2 can of peas
2 cups of stock, or 2 cups
   water and 1 teaspoon
   Savita

Juice of 1 small lemon
Salt, paprika
1 tablespoon butter

Put the peas through a ricer. Add the liquor from the can, the stock, the lemon juice and the seasoning. Heat the soup to the boiling point, add the butter and serve the soup.

CREAM OF CLAM SOUP

This is also an emergency soup. It is more quickly made than the two preceding soups and is equally good.

1 cup clam juice (bottled or
   canned) or minced clams
1 cup cream

1 cup milk
1 teaspoon butter
Paprika

Heat the clam juice in one saucepan. Heat the milk, cream and butter in another saucepan. When they are very hot, but not boiling, combine them and season and serve the soup immediately. Each cup may be garnished with a tablespoon of whipped cream, sprinkled with paprika and decorated with a small sprig of parsley.

Canned Soup and Canned Milk Recipes

CANNED TOMATO SOUP

1 Can Campbell's Tomato Soup	(or ½ fresh and ½ canned milk)
An equal amount of milk,	½ teaspoon of salt

Heat the soup and add the hot milk slowly, stirring it constantly. Do not permit it to boil. Add the salt and serve it immediately. To reheat the soup, or to keep it hot, place the saucepan over hot water.

CANNED ASPARAGUS SOUP

1 can Campbell's Asparagus Soup	(or ½ fresh and ½ canned milk)
An equal amount of milk,	No seasoning is required

Heat the asparagus soup and add the hot milk slowly, stirring constantly. Heat the soup thoroughly, but do not boil it. Serve it at once. To reheat or to keep it hot, place the saucepan over hot water.

Cream Soups

The trouble with cream soups is that they are frequently served (with whipped cream) as the first course of a heavy meal.

The wonderful thing about cream soups is that they are nearly a meal by themselves. Balanced by a green salad, or a piece of fruit, they make a perfect luncheon for a non-reducing partake.

CREAM OF TOMATO SOUP
Without Soda

2 cups of tomatoes	2 large ribs of celery with leaves
2 teaspoons sugar	
½ onion (medium sized)	

Boil these ingredients for 15 minutes. Meanwhile prepare:

4 tablespoons flour	1 teaspoon salt
4 tablespoons butter	1/8 teaspoon paprika
4 cups milk or milk and	
cream scalded	

Melt the butter in the top of a double boiler over a low fire, add the flour and when these ingredients are well blended add the scalded milk. Stir this until it is thick and smooth. When the tomato mixture is ready, strain it into the milk mixture. Add the seasoning and place the top part of the double boiler on the bottom part, which has been filled with boiling water. Cover the soup with a lid and serve it in fifteen minutes.

NOTE: Recipes for Tomato Soup usually call for soda (1/4 teaspoon). I have experimented carefully and have made good soup without it by the above method, thereby retaining the delicate flavor of the soup.

CREAM OF CORN SOUP

1 No. 2 can of corn (2 cups corn)	2 sprigs of parsley
	2 tablespoons butter
2 cups boiling water	2 tablespoons flour
2 cups milk	1 teaspoon salt
1 slice of onion	1/8 teaspoon paprika
2 ribs of celery with leaves	

Pour the boiling water over the corn, add the celery and the parsley and simmer these ingredients for 20 minutes, then strain them well. Scald the milk with the onion, remove the onion and add the strained stock. Melt the butter, add the flour and when these ingredients are boiling add the strained stock and milk mixture. Season the soup. Permit it to reach the boiling point and serve it with chopped parsley (optional).

CREAM OF CELERY SOUP

1 tablespoon butter	1 large onion sliced
1 cup or more of chopped celery with leaves	(optional)

Melt the butter in a saucepan, add the vegetables and cook them for 2 minutes. Add 2 cups stock, or 2 cups water to which 1/2 teaspoon Savita, or one beef cube has been added. Simmer this for 30 minutes. Strain the stock and add 1 1/2 cups milk and bring these ingredients to the boiling point. Dissolve 1 1/2 tablespoons cornstarch in 1/2 cup milk, and add these ingredients to the boiling stock.

Season the soup with:

Salt   Nutmeg (optional)
Paprika   Celery salt

Add 2 scant tablespoons of butter and serve the soup with chopped parsley.

ONION SOUP

3 tablespoons butter   Chopped parsley
3 large onions, thinly sliced   Grated cheese (½ American
1 tablespoon flour   cheese and ½ Parmesan)
4 cups milk and stock (or   1 teaspoon Worcestershire
  milk or stock)   Sauce (optional)
Salt   ¼ teaspoon Tobasco Sauce
Paprika   (optional)
Nutmeg

Melt the butter, add the onions and cook them until they are a golden brown. Add the flour and stir it until it is smooth. Add the milk and simmer the soup until the onions are very tender, then strain and season it. Place 1 tablespoon of grated cheese in each cup and 1 teaspoon of chopped parsley and pour the soup over them. Serve it at once.

CREAM OF MUSHROOM SOUP

½ pound mushrooms   2 tablespoons butter
2 cups stock or water   2 tablespoons flour
1 small stalk celery   2 cups top milk or cream
2 carrots   1¼ teaspoon salt
½ onion   ⅛ teaspoon paprika
Several sprigs of parsley   ⅛ teaspoon nutmeg

Wash the mushrooms, trim the stems and cover the mushrooms with 2 cups of cold water. Add the celery and parsley, the peeled carrots and onion and simmer the soup until the mushrooms are tender (20 minutes). Drain the vegetables, reserving the stock, and put them through a food chopper using the finest knife. Melt the butter, add the flour and when they are well blended add the mushroom stock slowly and the hot milk or cream. Add the ground vegetables and the seasoning and serve the soup topped with whipped cream garnished with paprika and small sprigs of parsley.

CHICKEN BISQUE

2 tablespoons butter	Salt
2 tablespoons flour	Paprika
3 cups chicken stock	3 tablespoons cream
1 cup top milk	whipped
1 cup cooked ground chicken	

Melt the butter, add the flour and when these ingredients are smooth, add the chicken stock and the milk. When the soup is thick, add the chicken and the seasoning. Place the whipped cream in the bottom of a bowl and pour the hot soup over it.

Oyster Stews

Here are three good recipes for oyster soup, which are like the little bear, the big bear and the great big bear in nutritive value and effort.

The first calls for milk and is unthickened.
The second calls for milk and flour.
The third calls for milk, cream, flour and egg yolks.
The following recipe is used in the well-known Oyster Bar of New York:

OYSTER STEW
Unthickened—4 Servings

1 pint oysters — with liquor	1/2 teaspoon salt
1/4 cup butter	1/8 teaspoon pepper
1 1/2 cups milk	2 tablespoons chopped
1/2 cup cream	parsley

Use the top of a double boiler. Melt the butter, add the oysters, bring them to the boiling point, but do not permit them to boil. Pour the milk and cream over the hot oysters. Place the boiler over hot water. When the oysters come to the surface, add the chopped parsley and serve the soup.

OYSTER STEW
Thickened—6 Servings

4 cups milk	liquor
4 tablespoons butter (1/4 cup)	1 teaspoon salt
	1/8 teaspoon pepper
1 pint oysters and oyster	1 1/2 tablespoons flour

Scald 3 1/2 cups of the milk, add 1/2 of the butter and the seasoning. Place the remaining butter in a saucepan, add the oysters and their liquor and heat these ingredients thoroughly, but do not boil them. Combine the remaining milk with the flour. When these ingredients are well blended, add them to the scalded milk and boil the mixture until it thickens, then pour it over the oysters. Place the stew in a double boiler for 15 minutes before serving it.

OYSTER BISQUE

1 pint oysters	½ teaspoon paprika
1½ tablespoons butter	⅛ teaspoon nutmeg
1½ tablespoons flour	2 egg yolks
2½ cups milk	2 tablespoons cold water
½ cup cream	Chopped parsley
1 teaspoon salt	

Drain the oysters. Reserve the liquor, strain it and add it to the oysters. Heat the oysters thoroughly, but do not boil them. Drain them, (reserving the liquor,) and chop them until they are fine, or grind them. Melt the butter in a saucepan, add the flour, then the milk, the cream and the oyster liquor. When the sauce is smooth and boiling, add the chopped oysters. Beat the egg yolks with the cold water and add them slowly to the hot bisque. Reduce the heat and simmer it for 1 minute. Then serve it at once, or place it over hot water until ready to serve. Sprinkle it with chopped parsley immediately before serving.

JELLIED SOUP
(Aspic)

Stock made from a veal knuckle bone and a beef bone will jell readily. To jell other stock use gelatine. Flavor the soup with lemon, vinegar, or cooking Sherry. Season it well and serve it very cold. The proportion given on the gelatine packages is usually 1 tablespoon of gelatine to 4 cups of liquid. This is right for jellied soup, which should not be firm, but it is not enough for aspic jelly, for which at least 1 tablespoon of gelatine to 3 cups of liquid is required. See Aspic Salad—Page 13.

JELLIED BOUILLON

2 tablespoons gelatine	1 teaspoon Worcestershire
¼ cup cold water	Sauce
1 No. 2 can tomatoes	Salt
3 cans Beef Bouillon	Pepper

Soak the gelatine in the cold water for 5 minutes. Boil the tomatoes for five minutes, mash and strain them. Dissolve the soaked gelatine in the hot tomato juice. Add the remaining ingredients and chill the bouillon until it is set.

Garnishes for Soups

CUSTARD

½ cup milk or stock   Salt, paprika, nutmeg
1 egg

Scald the liquid, pour it over the beaten egg and add the seasoning. Cook the custard until it is firm in a double boiler or in a dish set in a pan of hot water in a slow oven. Drop bits of custard into simmering soup and serve it.

FARINA BALLS

Farina balls being heavier than soup custard are best served with a light meal. They are fine for invalids and for children.

2 cups milk   Salt, paprika, nutmeg
¾ cup farina   2 eggs
1 tablespoon butter

Boil the milk, add the butter and the seasoning. Add the farina and stir it constantly until it thickens. Remove it from the fire and beat in the eggs one at a time. Drop the batter from a teaspoon into simmering stock and cook the balls until they are done, for 2 minutes or more.

NOODLES

1 egg   ⅔ cup flour
¼ teaspoon salt   (approximately)

Beat the egg slightly—add the salt and enough flour to make a rather stiff dough. Knead it well and permit it to stand for ½ hour. Roll it until it is very thin and let it dry until it is no longer sticky. Before it becomes brittle, fold it over several times and cut it into narrow strips. Toss the noodles lightly with the fingers and spread them until they are dry, when they may be used at once, or kept in jars for future use. Drop the noodles into simmering stock or water and cook them for five minutes.

CROUTONS

Dice bread and sauté it in butter until it is an even brown, or butter slices of bread, cut them into dice and brown them in a moderate oven.

FORCE MEAT

Grind or chop chicken, veal, clams or oysters.

¾ cup ground meat
1 egg white
Cream

Seasoning
Chopped onion (optional)

Combine the meat with the egg white, season it and add enough cream to make the mixture the right consistency to roll into small balls. Drop them into simmering soup and cook them until they are done. See Liver Dumplings—Page 143.

CRACKER BALLS

1 egg
2 tablespoons butter
6 tablespoons cracker
  crumbs

1 tablespoon parsley
1 tablespoon milk
Salt, paprika, nutmeg

Combine the ingredients in the order given. Shape them into balls and cook them in simmering soup for ten minutes.

MARROW BALLS I

6 Servings

⅛ lb. marrow (fresh)
2 tablespoons butter
3 eggs

Salt, nutmeg
Chopped parsley
Cracker crumbs

Beat the marrow and the butter until they are creamy and add the remaining ingredients, using just enough cracker crumbs to make the mixture right consistency to roll into balls. Place the marrow balls in simmering soup for fifteen minutes.

MARROW BALLS II

2 one inch slices of stale
  white bread
1 egg separated
1 tablespoon marrow (fresh)

Salt, paprika, nutmeg
Chopped parsley (optional)
Flour

Soak the bread in water for five minutes, then press the water from it. Beat the egg yolk with the marrow and add the bread, the parsley and the seasoning. Fold in the stiffly beaten egg white and shape the mixture into balls. Roll them lightly in sifted flour and cook them for 15 minutes in simmering soup stock.

Eggs . . . Luncheon and Supper Dishes

The first thing to impress upon the novice is that eggs cook with a very low degree of heat.

"It was so hot that you could fry an egg upon the sidewalk" is to be taken literally. It can be done under favorable conditions. Eggs solidify so readily that it is well to remember when cooking egg dishes to place them over a low flame, or in a double boiler, to avoid the disaster of a curdled dish. Should a custard or sauce misbehave and curdle — owing to an excess of heat — remove it at once from the fire, dump it into a cold dish and beat it vigorously with a wire whisk. By this treatment it may sometimes be induced to behave.

LUNCHEON DISHES
Served in pastry, bread shells, etc.

Creamed dishes, eggs and left-overs may be attractively served in various ways:

1 In patty shells.
2 On rounds of bread lightly buttered and toasted.
3 On Holland Rusks lightly buttered and heated.
4 In bread shells prepared in the following way:
   Cut slices of bread 1¼ inches thick with a large biscuit cutter. Press a small biscuit cutter into these rounds, but not through them. Hollow the centers, leaving a shell and a bottom at least ¼ inch thick. Butter the insides lightly and place the shells in a slow oven until they are toasted.
5 In small rolls that have been hollowed, buttered lightly on the inside and toasted in a slow oven.

6 In a loaf of bread that has been hollowed, buttered lightly on the inside and toasted in a slow oven.
7 In one large, or in individual pie shells—See Page 209.
8 In one large, or individual noodle rings—See Page 42.
9 In one large or in individual rice rings—See page 45.
10 In a pastry roll—See Page 55.
11 On or between waffles.
12 In tomatoes, peppers, potatoes, cucumbers, apples, etc., as embodied in the recipes in the following chapter.

Before deciding upon your luncheon menu, read the chapter on Hors d' Oeuvre.

Eggs

BOILED EGGS

Place the eggs in boiling water, reduce the heat and keep the water under the boiling point—6 minutes for delicately coddled eggs; 8 minutes for firmly coddled eggs; 30 to 35 minutes for hard cooked eggs. Plunge the last, when done, into cold water to prevent discoloration of the yolks.

SAUTÉD EGGS
"Fried" Eggs

1 tablespoon butter	Salt
4 eggs	Paprika

Place the butter in a small skillet. When it is melted reduce the heat to a low flame, add the eggs and cook them gently until they are done. Slash across the egg whites several times to permit the heat to penetrate the lower crust. When the eggs are firm, season and serve them.

EGGS IN BLACK BUTTER—AU BEURRE NOIR

4 eggs	1 teaspoon vinegar or
2 tablespoons butter	lemon juice
	Salt, paprika

Melt 1 tablespoon butter in a small skillet. Place four eggs in it and cook them gently until they are firm. Remove the eggs to a hot platter add 1 tablespoon butter to the skillet, cook it until it is brown, add 1 teaspoon vinegar and pour this mixture over the eggs. Serve them garnished with parsley.

POACHED EGGS

Fill a small skillet two thirds full of water and bring it to the boiling point, add 1/2 teaspoon salt to 4 cups of water. Reduce the heat until the water is below the boiling point. Break an egg into a dish and slip it gently into the water. Repeat this. The water should cover the eggs. When there is a film over the tops of the eggs and the whites are firm, remove them with a buttered skimmer and serve them on rounds of toast. Eggs may be poached in a small amount of milk or stock.

EGGS POACHED IN TOMATO SOUP

The following recipe is a well-balanced meal, prepared in a few minutes. It is very good and most attractive looking.

1 can tomato soup	4 teaspoons chopped parsley
1/2 can water	4 Holland Rusks, or 4
1/4 teaspoon sugar	rounds of toast
4 eggs	

Combine the soup and the water in a small skillet — 8 inches in diameter — and bring them to the boiling point. Slip in the eggs one by one and cook them gently until they are firm. Remove them with a pancake turner and place each one on a round of toast, or on a rusk. Pour the soup over them and sprinkle them with parsley. Serve them at once.

SCRAMBLED EGGS, WITH OR WITHOUT ONIONS
2 Servings

1 tablespoon butter	3 eggs
1/2 tablespoon onions chopped fine (optional)	1/8 teaspoon salt
	1/8 teaspoon pepper

Melt the butter, add the onions and when they are heated add the eggs beaten with the seasoning. Reduce the heat to a low flame. When the eggs begin to thicken break them into long shreds with a fork. When they are done serve them on lightly buttered toast.

EGGS SCRAMBLED IN TOMATO SOUP
4 Servings

1 1/2 tablespoons butter	3/4 cup tomato soup
1 tablespoon onions chopped	4 eggs
1 tablespoon green pepper chopped	1/8 teaspoon salt
	Paprika

Melt the butter, add the onion and pepper and sauté them

slowly for 3 minutes. Beat the eggs with the soup, add the seasoning and pour them slowly over the vegetables. Stir these ingredients constantly over a slow fire. When they are thick and creamy, serve them at once on hot toast.

EGGS SCRAMBLED WITH TOMATOES

1 tablespoon butter	1/8 teaspoon pepper
1 teaspoon scraped onion	1 teaspoon or more brown
1 cup strained tomatoes—	sugar
canned or fresh	4 eggs
1/4 teaspoon salt	

Melt the butter, add the onion, the tomatoes and the seasoning. Cook these ingredients covered for 5 minutes, cool them slightly and add the lightly beaten eggs. Break them into large curds as they cook over a low flame. Serve them on toast.

EGGS AND RICE WITH TOMATO SAUCE

The following recipe is so simple that it makes a very good every day luncheon dish.

Eggs poached or sautéd	Parsley or celery chopped
Rice cooked and shaped in	(optional)
small mounds	Tomato sauce

Prepare the eggs and place them on the mounds of hot rice—see Page 43, to which the parsley or celery has been added. Serve them with tomato sauce—one can of tomato soup, undiluted, to which 1 tablespoon of butter has been added.

EGGS IN MUSTARD SAUCE

6 eggs	2 tablespoons bread crumbs
1 cup cream sauce	3 tablespoons grated
1 teaspoon French mustard	cheese (optional)
1/4 teaspoon salt	

Make the Cream Sauce—Page 154, add the salt, the mustard and the cheese. Break the eggs into a baking dish, cover them with the sauce, sprinkle them with bread crumbs and dot them with butter. Bake them in a moderate oven—350° for 12 minutes.

PLAIN OMELET

The following omelet is the survival of the fittest. It is even better, I think, than the famed omelets of France—which is saying a great deal for it:

4 eggs	1 tablespoon butter
4 tablespoons milk	1 tablespoon chopped
1 teaspoon baking powder	parsley (optional)
½ teaspoon salt	

Combine the milk, egg yolks and baking powder and beat them well. Place the egg whites in a separate bowl, add the salt, beat them to a stiff froth and fold in the yolk and milk mixture. Place a skillet on a slow fire, melt the butter, pour the omelet into the skillet and cover it with a lid. From time to time slash across the omelet with a knife—permitting the heat to penetrate the lower crust. When the omelet is done (after about 12 minutes) it may be placed on the center grate of a moderate oven until the top is set, or it may be folded over and served at once. (Make an incision with a knife on either side of the omelet where you want it to fold. Tip the pan and push the omelet gently with a spatula or a broad knife until it folds over).

Creamed dishes (celery, sweetbreads, spinach, mushrooms, oysters, etc.) are good served with omelet.

A well-balanced everyday combination is omelet with boiled macaroni and tomato sauce.

SWEET OMELET

Make a Plain Omelet adding 1 tablespoon of sugar. Before folding it over, spread it with jam or jelly. Sprinkle the top with powdered sugar. See the Chapter on Puddings for other sweet omelets.

TOMATO OMELET

Make a Plain Omelet and serve it with the following sauce:

2 tablespoons butter	½ green pepper chopped
1 tablespoon onion chopped	1 tablespoon capers
6 olives shredded	(optional)
1¾ cups tomatoes	¼ teaspoon salt
1 tablespoon parsley chopped (optional)	Cayenne
	1 teaspoon sugar

Heat the butter, add the onion and the olives, and cook them for 2 minutes. Add the green pepper and the tomatoes and cook the sauce until it is thick. Then add the remaining ingredients.

CREAMED EGGS ON TOAST

When carefully prepared, these creamed eggs are delicious.

6 eggs
2 tablespoons chopped
  parsley or celery
Salt, paprika
Nutmeg

1 cup cream sauce, or
  tomato sauce
6 rounds of lightly buttered
  toast, or 6 Holland Rusks
  buttered and heated

Grease individual molds with butter. Place a little chopped parsley and seasoning in each mold and cover them with a raw egg. Place the molds in a pan of hot water on the top of the stove and steam them gently until the eggs are firm. Turn the eggs on to rounds of toast and serve them with well seasoned Cream Sauce—Page 154, or with Tomato Sauce—Page 157.

EGGS AND CHEESE IN BREAD CASES

8 slices of stale bread 1¼
  inches thick
2 tablespoons melted butter
4 eggs
⅛ teaspoon mustard

½ teaspoon salt
Cayenne
¾ cup cream
1 cup grated cheese

Cut the bread in rounds with a large biscuit cutter. Cut into each round, but not through it, with a smaller biscuit cutter, and take out the center, leaving a bottom and rim ¼ inch thick. Place the cases in a moderate oven or under a low flame until they are lightly toasted. Brush the insides with melted butter and sprinkle them with grated cheese. Break the eggs into a bowl and add the seasoning and the cream. Beat these ingredients well and fill the cases with the mixture. Sprinkle the tops with grated cheese and bake the cases in a moderate oven 350° until the cheese is brown.

CREAMED EGGS AND ASPARAGUS

The following recipe always meets with favor. It is a fine Sunday night dish with a green salad:

5 hard cooked eggs, finely
  sliced
1 lb. can asparagus tips, the
  tips cut in two
2 cups cream sauce
4 tablespoons butter

4 tablespoons flour
2 cups asparagus water
  and cream or milk
Paprika, salt, nutmeg
½ cup bread crumbs
1 tablespoon butter

Cook the eggs—Page 34, chill and slice them. Make the Cream Sauce—Page 154, and while it is boiling add the asparagus and remove the mixture from the fire. Stir it as little as possible. Place a layer of eggs in the bottom of a baking dish, add a layer of creamed asparagus and repeat this process until the dish is filled. Cover the top with bread crumbs and dot it with butter. Heat the dish in a moderate oven, or under a broiler, but do not let it boil. To reheat it place it over hot water.

EGGS IN SPINACH WITH CHEESE

Half fill a buttered baking dish (or buttered individual molds) with Creamed Spinach—Page 107. Sprinkle the top with grated Parmesan cheese, and press hollows into it with a large spoon. Break an egg into each hollow. Sprinkle the eggs with salt, paprika and grated cheese. Cover them with Cream Sauce—Page 154 or with Bechamel Sauce—Page 157. Place the baking dish in a pan of hot water in a moderate oven 325° until the eggs are set (for about 12 minutes.)

For individual molds use about:

1 tablespoon spinach	1½ tablespoons grated
1 egg	cheese
1 tablespoon sauce	And the desired seasoning

EGGS IN A NEST
4 Servings

The following is a good sequel to a ham dinner:

2 cups mashed potatoes	3 tablespoons chopped
5 tablespoons milk	parsley
½ cup chopped ham or	Salt, paprika
fried minced bacon	4 eggs

Soften the mashed potatoes with the milk, add the ham, parsley and seasoning. Put this mixture in the bottom of a baking dish and make four large hollows in it with a tablespoon. Break an egg into each hollow. Sprinkle the top with bread crumbs and dot it with butter—(this is optional). Place the dish in a moderate oven—375°—and bake it until the eggs are firm, but not hard (about 25 minutes). If well seasoned, this dish needs no sauce. It is good, however, with tomato sauce.

CUSTARD RING OR TIMBAL
6 Servings

In France the salad is served with the meat course and the vegetable is served in solitary state. (It is usually worthy of this exalted position). Sometimes it is accompanied by a mound or ring of delicious custard.

2 cups milk	½ teaspoon grated nutmeg
4 eggs	(2 or 3 eggs may be used
1 teaspoon salt	instead of 4)
½ teaspoon paprika	

Combine the ingredients and whip them with a wire whisk. Place the mixture in a greased ring, or mold, and set in a pan of hot water. Bake the custard until it is firm (about 45 minutes) in a moderate oven 325°. It is done when a knife or spoon inserted and withdrawn remains uncoated. Invert the contents of the mold on a hot platter and fill the center with a cooked vegetable.

Rules for Boiling Spaghetti, Macaroni, Creamettes and Noodles

½ pound spaghetti, maca- roni, creamettes or noodles	2 quarts boiling water 2 teaspoons salt

Drop the spaghetti slowly into the boiling, salted water and cook it until it is tender, (about 20 minutes for spaghetti, macaroni and noodles, from 10 to 12 minutes for creamettes). Drain it well and rinse it with at least 1 quart of cold water. Spaghetti, macaroni and creamettes will double in bulk. I cup noodles will be 1¼ cup noodles when cooked.

SPAGHETTI I.

½ pound spaghetti — boiled	1½ green peppers, chopped
4 tablespoons butter	1 can tomato soup
½ onion, chopped	½ pound cheese, diced
4 tablespoons flour	1 pound lobster, crab or
2 cups stock or milk	shrimp, diced

Melt the butter, add the onion and cook it for 1 minute. Add the flour and the milk or stock. When the sauce is thick, add the hot tomato soup very slowly, stirring it constantly, and the diced cheese. Cook this mixture until the cheese is melted, then add the fish and cook it for 1 minute. Last add the boiled spaghetti. This dish may be prepared in advance and reheated over hot water. Veal, chicken or mushrooms may be substituted for the fish.

SPAGHETTI II.
Steamed or Baked

6 oz. Spaghetti — cooked until soft
3 slices of bacon minced
1 medium sized onion
1/2 lb. round steak ground
2 tablespoons olive oil
1 No. 2 can of tomatoes
2 green peppers chopped
1 No. 1 can mushrooms
chopped, (1/2 lb. to 1 lb. of sautéd fresh mushrooms sliced, may be substituted)
Mushroom liquor
Salt, cayenne, paprika
1/2 lb. grated cheese
1/2 cup stock or canned bouillon (optional)

Try out the bacon, add the onion, the olive oil and the ground meat. Cook these ingredients until the meat is nearly done, then add the tomatoes, the green peppers, the mushroom, the mushroom liquor and the seasoning. Add the cooked and drained spaghetti and the bouillon if the mixture seems dry.

To use the above for *Steamed Spaghetti* add the cheese and steam the spaghetti in a double boiler, or in a mold for one hour.

For *Baked Spaghetti* place the prepared spaghetti in a baking dish, cover it with the cheese and bake it for 15 or 20 minutes in a moderate oven 375°.

BOILED MACARONI WITH CHEESE

1 cup macaroni
2 quarts boiling water (8 cups)
2 teaspoons salt
1/2 cup cream or milk

Break the macaroni into pieces and drop it into the boiling salted water. Boil it until it is tender — about 25 minutes. Place it in a strainer, drain it well and pour 4 cups of cold water over it. Return it to the saucepan, add the milk, reheat it and sprinkle it with grated cheese. Serve it with Tomato Sauce — Page 157.

BAKED MACARONI

1 cup macaroni — boiled
2/3 cup milk
1 or 2 eggs
1 cup grated cheese
Salt, paprika
A few grains of cayenne
1/4 cup bread crumbs

Follow the rule for boiled macaroni. Butter a baking dish. Place alternate layers of macaroni and cheese in it, reserving 1/8 cup of cheese for the top. Beat the eggs, add the milk and the seasoning and pour this mixture over the macaroni. Sprinkle the top with the remaining cheese combined with the bread crumbs. Bake the macaroni in a quick oven 400° until it is well browned.

CREAMETTE LOAF OR MACARONI LOAF

This delectable dish is very attractive in appearance:

1½ cups creamettes	1 cup grated cheese
1 cup soft bread (without crusts)	3 pimentos, sliced
	½ green pepper (cut into small pieces)
1 cup of milk scalded	
3 eggs, beaten	Salt, paprika
½ cup butter, melted	A few grains of cayenne

Drop the creamettes into 9 cups of boiling water, to which 3 teaspoons of salt have been added. Boil them for 10 minutes, drain off the water and pour a quart or more of cold water over them. Beat the eggs and pour the milk over them, combine this with the other ingredients and place them in a buttered baking dish. Bake the creamettes for 1 hour in a moderate oven 350°—and serve them with Tomato Sauce—Page 157 or with Mushroom Sauce—Page 155.

Macaroni or spaghetti may be substituted for creamettes, but they require 20 minutes boiling.

BOILED NOODLES

2 cups of dry noodles

Boil the noodles—See Page 40. Reheat them in 1 table-spoon butter or in 1 tablespoon cream. Serve them plain, or garnished with ¼ cup bread crumbs sautéd in 2 tablespoons of butter. Boiled noodles may be arranged in a ring on a platter and the center filled with a creamed meat or vegetable. This is a nice simple way of serving hash.

BAKED NOODLE RINGS
4 Servings

1½ cups dry noodles— (about 2 cups boiled noodles)	¾ tablespoon butter, melted
	Salt, paprika
2 eggs	¼ teaspoon nutmeg (optional)
½ cup milk	

Cook the noodles—See Page 40. Beat the egg yolks, add the milk, the butter and the seasoning. Combine the mixture with the noodles. Beat the whites of the eggs to a stiff froth and fold them lightly into the noodles. Butter a ring mold, or individual ring molds. Fill them with the noodle mixture and bake them set in a pan of hot water in a moderate oven until done. (About 45 minutes for a large mold or 30 minutes for the small ones.) Invert the contents of the molds on hot plates and fill the centers with creamed spinach, peas, mushrooms, hash, stewed tomatoes, etc.

NOODLE RING WITH CHEESE
10 to 12 Servings

3 cups noodles	1 tablespoon catsup
1½ cups milk	Salt
4 egg yolks	Pepper
1 tablespoon Worcester- shire Sauce	1¼ cups grated cheese

Boil the noodles—Page 40, rinse and drain them. Beat the yolks with the milk and seasoning. Add the cheese and pour the custard over the noodles. Bake them in a baking dish or mold set in a pan of hot water in a moderate oven 350° for about 45 minutes.

HAM NOODLES

The following recipe is capable of a wide interpretation and its proportions may be varied:

1½ cups of dry noodles	½ cup shredded green pep-
¾ cup ground ham	pers and celery (optional)
½ cup grated cheese	1 or 2 eggs
(optional)	Salt, (if needed)
1½ cups milk	Paprika

Boil the noodles—Page 40. Place a layer of boiled noodles in a greased baker, cover it with the ham, cheese and vegetables and repeat this process until all of these ingredients have been used. Combine the milk, the egg and the seasoning, and pour them over the noodles. The top may be covered with bread crumbs. Bake the dish in a moderate oven—350°—for 1 hour.

Rice and Rice Dishes

BOILED RICE

(1 cup rice equals 3 or more cups of cooked rice.)

When rice is prepared by the first method in the following recipe, its entire nutritive value is retained; when rice is cooked by the second method, some of the nutritive value is lost, but many people prefer the drier, crisper grains.

2 quarts of water (8 cups)	1 cup rice
1 teaspoon salt	

Wash the rice and drain it. Boil the water, add the salt and stir the rice in very slowly so as not to disturb the boiling. Cook it without stirring until it is tender, (about 25 minutes.)

1ST METHOD

Cook the rice until the water is absorbed. Serve the rice with paprika and chopped parsley, or

2ND METHOD

Pour the rice into a strainer and let 2 cups of cold water run over it, return it to the pan and place it uncovered over boiling water, or put it in the oven to reheat and dry the kernels. Stir the rice with a fork. Serve it with 2 or 3 tablespoons of melted butter poured over it.

STEAMED RICE

The following rice is frequently served in place of a starchy vegetable, or it is served as a main dish with Tomato Sauce.

1 cup rice	2 tablespoons chopped
2 tablespoons butter	celery
3 cups boiling water	1 tablespoon chopped
1 teaspoon salt	parsley (optional)

Place the water in the top of a double boiler directly over a flame. Drop the rice slowly into the boiling water, stirring it with a fork. Cook it for five minutes, then remove the top container from the direct flame and put it in the bottom container of the double boiler which has been filled with boiling water and placed on the fire. Add the salt and celery and steam the rice until it is tender (about 45 minutes). Uncover, add the butter and steam the rice until it is dry. Serve it with the chopped parsley. If the rice is very moist, drain it before adding the butter.

MILK RICE

The following is a nice simple dessert:

1 cup rice	1 teaspoon salt
4 cups milk	

Place the ingredients in a double boiler and steam them until the rice is done (about 1 hour). Stir them from time to time with a fork. Serve the rice hot with cinnamon and sugar. (1 part cinnamon to 4 parts sugar,) or sweeten the rice lightly and serve it with Caramel Sauce Page 323.

CHEESE RICE
Boiled

The following is a good dish to serve with a cold supper:
Prepare boiled rice—Page 43, by the first method. When the water is nearly absorbed, add:

½ cup or more of grated cheese	¼ teaspoon paprika A few grains of cayenne

Stir the rice over a low flame until the cheese is melted.

CHEESE RICE
Baked

1 cup rice, boiled—Page 43	4 tablespoons bread crumbs
2 cups milk	1½ teaspoons salt
2 eggs	A few grains of cayenne
¾ cup grated cheese	¼ teaspoon paprika
2 tablespoons butter	

Drain the rice, rinse it with cold water and drain it again. Combine the eggs and the milk and add the seasoning. Place alternate layers of rice and cheese in a baking dish. Pour the egg mixture over this, cover the top with bread crumbs and dot it with butter. Bake the rice in a moderate oven—350°—until it is tender and crisp.

ITALIAN RICE
Risotto

Melt ¼ cup butter. Add 1 cup rice and sauté it for 1 minute. Add slowly 4 cups of hot soup stock and ½ cup grated cheese.

Season the rice with a few grains of cayenne, ¼ teaspoon paprika, and if desired, with ⅛ teaspoon saffron. Cook it in a double boiler for one hour, stirring it several times during the steaming. Do not add salt until the rice is cooked, as the bouillon may be sufficiently seasoned.

RICE RING WITH CREAMED CHICKEN

1 cup rice, boiled—Page 43	¼ cup butter—melted
½ teaspoon nutmeg	

Rinse the rice, season it, place it in a well greased ring mold and pour the butter over it. Set it in a pan of hot water and bake it for 20 minutes in a moderate oven—350°. Loosen the edges and invert the contents of the mold onto a platter. Fill the center with creamed chicken, creamed mushrooms, or with a creamed or buttered vegetable.

WILD RICE RING

1 cup wild rice	4 tablespoons butter—
2 teaspoons salt	melted
4 cups boiling water	

Wash the rice and place it in a double boiler. Pour the boiling water over it and permit it to steam until it is tender—about three quarters of an hour. Stir it several times while it is steaming. Add the butter and put the rice in a well greased ring mold. Set the mold in a pan of hot water and bake the rice in a moderate oven—350°—for 20 minutes. Loosen the edges with a knife, invert the contents onto a platter and fill the center with creamed meat or fish.

RICE LOAF

2 cups cooked rice (generous ½ cup uncooked rice)	1 tablespoon chopped onion
1 cup heavy cream sauce	½ cup chopped celery (optional)
1 egg yolk	Lemon or Worcestershire Sauce
1 cup salmon, boiled fish or meat, diced	Salt, paprika, nutmeg
¼ cup bread crumbs	
1 tablespoon chopped parsley	

Line a buttered loaf mold with cooked rice, reserving ¼ for the top. Prepare the cream sauce, lower the heat, add the egg yolk and permit it to thicken slightly, add the fish and the remaining ingredients. Fill the mold and place the reserved rice over the top. Cover this with a piece of buttered paper. Set the mold in a pan of hot water and bake or steam it until it is set (about 30 minutes.) Serve it with Tomato Sauce—Page 157.

TOMATO RICE WITH CHEESE AND MUSHROOMS

2 cups tomatoes skinned and chopped, or 2 cups canned tomatoes	2 cups boiled rice—Page 43 (½ cup rice uncooked)
1 teaspoon sugar	1 cup American cheese, diced
1 teaspoon salt	1 green pepper, chopped
⅛ teaspoon pepper	1 cup mushrooms, sautéd and diced
½ teaspoon or more onion juice	½ cup stale bread crumbs
	2 tablespoons butter

Combine the first nine ingredients, place them in a baking dish, cover them with bread crumbs and dot them with butter. Bake them in a moderate oven — 350° for 40 minutes.

SPANISH RICE

6 slices of bacon	1 can tomatoes (No. 2)
1 cup rice, washed and	2 tablespoons paprika
drained	1 tablespoon salt
1 cup thinly sliced onions	

Cut the bacon into strips and sauté it until it is brown, add the rice, cook it until it is brown and add the onions. When the onions are brown, add the tomatoes and the seasoning and cook the rice very slowly for one hour — adding water or additional tomato, if necessary. A clove of garlic may be cooked with the rice.

CURRIED RICE

The first time I ate the following dish, I could hardly wait to ask how it was made and what gave it its delicious flavor. As soon as decency permitted, I did so, and was told to my surprise that the seasoning was curry. On the Chinese theory of "He who burns his mouth with hot soup, eats cold soup ever after" — I had avoided curry since first tasting it. The success of this dish with non-likers of curry is undoubtedly due to the restraint with which the spice is used.

1 cup rice	fine
1 cup tomatoes	3 tablespoons butter
1½ teaspoons salt	1½ teaspoons curry powder
1 large onion — sliced fine	4 cups hot water
1 small green pepper — sliced	

Wash the rice, pour the hot water over it and place it where it will keep hot, but will not cook for 30 to 45 minutes. When the grains are swollen to twice their size, add the other ingredients, place the mixture in a baking dish and bake it in a moderate oven 350° (for 1½ hours or more) until done, stirring it from time to time. At first there will be a great preponderance of liquid, but gradually the rice will absorb it. Remove the dish from the oven while the rice is still moist.

RICE RAMEKINS

Combine equal parts of boiled rice and crabmeat, shrimp, or cooked fish. Add one-half as much cream sauce as there are solids and season the ingredients well with salt, paprika, Worcestershire sauce, Sherry or prepared mustard. Fill ramekins (or a baking dish), cover the tops with bread crumbs and dot them with butter, or sprinkle cheese over them. Heat them in a quick oven until the crumbs are brown.

Luncheon and Supper Dishes

CREAMED CRABMEAT, TUNA, SALMON OR SHRIMP

1 can of crabmeat (6 oz.)	4 tablespoons bread crumbs
¾ cup rich cream sauce	Butter, or grated cheese
½ teaspoon prepared mustard	1 tablespoon chopped parsley (optional)

Place the flaked crabmeat in the boiling cream sauce, to which the mustard has been added. Remove the crab from the fire and put it in a baking dish or in individual dishes. Cover the top with bread crumbs and dot it with butter. Brown the crumbs under a broiler, or bake the crabmeat, set in a pan of hot water in a moderate oven—375°—until the crumbs are brown.

DEVILED CRABMEAT

1 can of crabmeat (6 oz.)	1 teaspoon Worcestershire Sauce, or 1 tablespoon Sherry
2 hard cooked eggs, sliced	
1 cup rich cream sauce	Seasoning

Follow the rule for Creamed Crabmeat.

CRAB FLAKE NEWBURG
6 Servings

3 tablespoons butter	1 tablespoon cornstarch
2 cups crab flake	1 cup cream (hot)
1 teaspoon salt	2 egg yolks
⅓ teaspoon paprika	2 teaspoons Sherry
⅓ teaspoon nutmeg	

Melt the butter in a saucepan. Stir the crab flake in it and add the seasoning. Push the flake to one side and tip the saucepan. Add the cornstarch to the butter and cook it until it bubbles. Right the saucepan and add the hot cream. Stir the crab flake until the sauce is boiling, reduce the heat and add the egg yolks. Cook them for 1 or 2 minutes (until they thicken slightly), but do not let them boil. Add the Sherry and serve the crab flake at once on hot buttered toast.

FISH AND NUT TIMBALS

½ cup dry bread crumbs
1 cup milk
½ cup ground pecans, or
    almonds

1 cup cooked fish, ground
2 eggs
Salt, pepper
Pimento

Soak the bread crumbs in the milk for 10 minutes. Add the nuts, the fish and the eggs, lightly beaten. Season the mixture well. Garnish individual molds with pimento. Fill them with the mixture and steam them for 15 to 20 minutes. Serve them hot with Tartar Sauce.

LOBSTER NEWBURG

4 tablespoons butter
2 cups lobster meat, diced
Salt
Paprika

Nutmeg
3 egg yolks
1 cup cream
¼ cup salted cooking sherry

Melt the butter in a double boiler, add the lobster and cook it for 3 minutes, stirring it constantly. Add the seasoning and cook it for 1 minute longer. Beat the eggs with the cream, add them to the lobster and beat the sauce well. Permit the lobster to cook for 2 minutes, add the Sherry and serve it at once on hot buttered toast.

CODFISH BALLS

1 cup shredded codfish
6 medium sized potatoes,
    peeled

1 tablespoon butter
⅛ teaspoon pepper
1 beaten egg

Put the fish and the potatoes in boiling water and cook them until the potatoes are done. Drain these ingredients, separate them with a fork and permit the steam to evaporate. Add the seasoning, the butter and the egg, combine them lightly with a fork and shape the mixture into balls. Fry them in deep fat, or sauté them in butter.

SHRIMP WIGGLE

4 tablespoons butter
2 tablespoons flour
1¼ cups milk
1 cup shrimp
1 cup peas, drained

Salt, paprika, celery salt
1 egg yolk (optional)
1 teaspoon lemon juice, or
1 teaspoon cooking Sherry
(optional)

Make a cream sauce of the first three ingredients. When it is boiling, add the shrimp and the peas. Add the egg yolk, cook it for 1 minute over a low flame and then add the lemon juice, or sherry. Serve the Wiggle on rounds of buttered toast, or buttered heated rusks, or in hot patty shells. To reheat it, place it over hot water.

SANDWICH LOAF

Cut a loaf of bread, from which the crust has been trimmed, lengthwise in three equal parts. Butter the inner sides of the layers and spread the chicken, or shrimp salad between them, or vary the filling by using the salad on one layer and crushed, drained pineapple minced with cream cheese on the second. Other good combinations may be used. Wrap the loaf firmly in a moist towel and chill it well, then place it on a platter. Before serving it cover the loaf with softened cream cheese, or with mayonnaise, to which a little soaked and dissolved gelatine has been added—See General Rules, and which is ready to set. Garnish the loaf with pimento, nuts and parsley and serve it at the table by cutting it into slices.

CHICKEN POT PIE

The following is a fine dish for it dresses up a plain chicken stew in an imposing manner:

Follow the rule for Stewed Chicken and Stewed Chicken Gravy—Page 145. Drain the chicken and make the gravy—3 cupfuls if possible, as the crust is apt to soak up quite a bit of it. Add top milk, or cream to the pot liquor. Place the chicken in a baking dish and pour the gravy over it. Prepare the following:

BATTER

1 cup flour	1 tablespoon butter, melted
3/4 teaspoon salt	7 tablespoons milk
1 teaspoon baking powder	1 egg well beaten

Beat the batter well and pour it over the chicken. Bake the pie in a moderate oven 375° until it is a light brown.

CHICKEN À LA KING

1 cup cooked chicken, diced	1/4 cup canned pimento cut into strips
1/2 cup sautéd mushrooms, diced	1 1/2 cups cream sauce
	1 egg yolk
	Sherry (optional)

Prepare the first three ingredients, and make the cream sauce, using:

3 tablespoons chicken fat
  or other shortening
3 tablespoons flour

1½ cups liquid, (chicken
  stock and cream)

When the sauce is smooth and boiling, add the chicken, mushrooms and pimento. Reduce the heat and add the egg yolk. Permit this to thicken, stirring the mixture gently for 1 minute, then add the Sherry and serve the chicken at once. To reheat, place the chicken in a pan over hot water.

CHICKEN MOUSSE I.
Baked

This good chicken is similar to a soufflé, but calls for fewer eggs:

2 cups cooked chicken
  ground
1 cup thick cream sauce
½ cup dry bread crumbs
½ teaspoon salt
½ teaspoon pepper

1 tablespoon chopped
  parsley
2 egg yolks, beaten
  separately
2 egg whites

Combine the first seven ingredients and fold in the stiffly beaten egg whites. Pour the mixture into a mold lined with waxed paper. Set it in a pan of hot water and bake it for 1 hour in a moderate oven — 325°. Serve the chicken with Mushroom Sauce — Page 155.

CHICKEN MOUSSE II.
Jellied

1½ tablespoons gelatine
¼ cup cold water
½ cup hot stock
3 egg yolks

1½ cups milk
1 cup minced chicken
1 cup heavy cream, whipped
Salt, pepper, paprika

Soak the gelatine in the cold water for 5 minutes and dissolve it in the hot stock. Beat the yolks, add the milk and cook these ingredients in a double boiler until they are smooth and fairly thick. Add the dissolved gelatine, the seasoning and the chicken. Chill the jelly and when it is about to set fold in the whipped cream. Chill the mousse in a wet mold for several hours. Serve it with a fruit or a green salad.

See Index for other aspics.

JELLIED HAM MOUSSE

1 tablespoon gelatine	1/4 cup chopped celery
4 tablespoons cold water	1 tablespoon chopped onions
1 1/2 cups boiling water	1/2 cup salad dressing
1/2 teaspoon salt	1/4 cup chopped pickles
1/4 teaspoon pepper	(sour or sour sweet)
2 cups cooked chopped ham	

Soak the gelatine in the cold water, dissolve it in the boiling water. Chill it until the jelly is nearly set, then combine it with the remaining ingredients. Add lemon juice and seasoning if needed (dependent upon the salad dressing used). Hard cooked eggs may be molded into the mousse at this time. Chill the mousse and unmold it on lettuce leaves.

HAM CAKES WITH EGGS

1 cup ground or minced ham	1 tablespoon water
1 egg	Paprika, or pepper

Combine these ingredients. Press them into muffin tins, leaving a large hollow in each center. Drop an egg into each hollow and bake the cakes in a slow oven 325° until the eggs are firm. Garnish the cakes with parsley.

CHICKEN AND HAM CREAMED

Creamed dishes combine very well with hot waffles.

1 1/2 tablespoons butter	1 teaspoon parsley
1 1/2 tablespoons flour	1/4 cup celery minced
3/4 cup chicken stock	1 egg yolk
1/4 cup cream	Paprika
1/2 cup chicken diced	Salt
1/2 cup ham diced	

Make a sauce of the first four ingredients, and when it is boiling add the meat and the vegetables. Combine the egg with a little of the sauce, reduce the heat and add it to the rest of the sauce. Permit it to thicken slightly and season the dish. A tablespoon of Sherry may be added just before serving it.

CHICKEN OR VEAL CROQUETTES

3 tablespoons butter
¼ cup flour
1¼ cups cream
Pepper, salt
1 teaspoon lemon juice
¾ cup chicken — chopped
  or ground

1 large egg
1 teaspoon parsley chopped
1 teaspoon onion chopped
¼ cup nut meats chopped
  (optional)

Make a sauce of the butter, flour and cream. Reduce the heat, add the egg and thicken it slightly, stirring the sauce constantly. Season the sauce highly and add the remaining ingredients. When the mixture is cool, shape it into balls, roll them in seasoned bread crumbs, then in egg diluted with 1 tablespoon of water and again in crumbs. Cook the croquettes in deep fat until they are brown and serve them with mushroom sauce.

SAUCE FOR CROQUETTES

1 tablespoon butter
1 teaspoon chopped onion
2 tablespoons flour
1 cup cream or milk

2 eggs beaten
Salt
Paprika or pepper
Nutmeg

Melt the butter, add the onion and sauté it for 2 minutes. Add the flour, stir it until it is smooth and add the milk. When the sauce is thick, reduce the heat and add the eggs and the seasoning. Cook the sauce for 2 minutes longer, stirring it constantly.

CROQUETTES

Make the sauce for croquettes and combine it with 2 cups of fish or meat and vegetables. ½ cup of bread crumbs may be added. Shape the croquettes, dip them in bread crumbs, in egg that has been diluted with 1 tablespoon of water and again in bread crumbs. Fry the croquettes in hot fat 390° until they are a delicate brown — See page 200.

SWEETBREAD CROQUETTES

Sweetbreads are delicate and light and it is well to combine them with chicken or mushrooms to give them body. Follow the rule for Croquettes, substituting part boiled Sweetbreads —Page 141 and part Sautéd Mushrooms—Page 123.

SALMON CROQUETTES

Follow the rule for Croquettes.

CHEESE CROQUETTES

½ cup croquette sauce—
  Page 53. (one half the
  portion given)

1½ cups grated cheese
2 egg whites, stiffly beaten

Shape the croquettes lightly, dip them in bread crumbs and fry them in deep fat until they are light brown. These croquettes are not dipped in egg.

POTATO CHEESE PUFFS
6 Puffs

This is a very nice potato dish—and a very good looking one:

1⅓ cups mashed potatoes,
  hot or cold
3 tablespoons hot milk
⅓ cup grated cheese
2 egg yolks beaten
¾ teaspoon salt
¼ teaspoon paprika

¼ teaspoon celery salt
½ teaspoon onion finely
  chopped
1 teaspoon green pepper
  chopped (optional)
2 egg whites, beaten
1½ tablespoons soft butter

Beat the potato with the milk and add the cheese and the yolks. When these are fluffy, add all but the last two ingredients. Fold in the stiffly beaten whites and place the batter in mounds in a greased pan. Round off the tops and spread them with butter. Bake the potatoes in a moderate oven 350° for 20 minutes.

BAKED POTATOES AND ROQUEFORT CHEESE

6 large Idaho Potatoes
6 tablespoons butter
3 ounces Roquefort cheese

3 tablespoons hot cream
Salt, paprika

Bake the potatoes—Page 98. Cut them in two. Scoop out the pulp, combine it with the other ingredients, refill the shells and bake them in a quick oven until the tops are brown.

MASHED POTATO PIE

This is a very good way of using a small quantity of cold mashed potatoes and bits of meat and vegetables:

Left-over mashed potatoes
1 egg white
Cold meat

Cold vegetables
Gravy or cream sauce

Line individual molds with a wall of mashed potatoes — about ¼ inch thick. Brush the insides with the white of an egg. Fill the molds with the chopped meat and vegetables, combined with a little thick gravy, or with well seasoned cream sauce or tomato sauce. Cover them with a layer of mashed potatoes ¼ inch thick and place the molds in a pan of hot water in a quick oven, 400°, for 15 minutes, or until the potatoes are brown.

SHEPHERD'S PIE

Prepare Hash — Page 56, and place it in a baking dish. Spread the top with fresh hot mashed potatoes, whipped with a little hot milk. Cover the top with melted butter and bake the dish in a quick oven — 400° until the potatoes are browned.

BACON LEFT-OVERS

Cooked meat, ground
Cooked rice
Left-over gravy or cream

Salt, pepper
Onion juice, or minced onion
Strips of bacon

Measure the meat, add 1/5 as much rice, moisten it with a little gravy or cream and season the mixture well. Roll it into small balls, wrap a strip of bacon around each one and secure it with a toothpick. Place the meat in a greased pan, or baking dish, in a hot oven — 450° — until the bacon is crisp (about 15 minutes). This is good with Tomato Sauce — Page 157.

SCALLOPED MEAT WITH RICE AND TOMATOES

Cooked chopped meat
Cooked rice
Canned or raw tomatoes,
  skinned

Seasoning
Bread crumbs
Butter

Place alternate layers of meat, rice and tomatoes in a small baking dish. Season the layers with salt, paprika and a little brown sugar. Cover the top with bread crumbs and dot it with butter. Bake the dish for 30 minutes in a moderate oven — 375°.

MEAT LOAF IN PASTRY OR BISCUIT DOUGH

Prepare a beef loaf, following the rule for any one of the three given on Page 132, or make a meat loaf of cooked, ground meat. Bake the loaf until it is nearly done, basting it frequently. Make pie dough — Page 209, or biscuit dough — Page 187. Roll it until it is very thin and wrap the meat in it, covering it completely, moistening the edges lightly to hold them down. Bake the covered loaf in a quick oven — 450° — until it is done (about 15 minutes). Serve it with gravy made of the pan drippings — Page 153, or with Tomato Sauce — Page 157.

MEAT PIE ROLL

Here is an attractive way of serving a small amount of left-over meat:

Mince or grind cooked meat and moisten it slightly with left-over gravy, with Cream Sauce, or with thick Brown Sauce — Page 155. Season it well. Make Pie Dough — Page 209, and roll it until it is very thin. Cut it into an oblong shape and brush it well on both sides with the white of an egg — using a pastry brush. This will keep the crust from being soggy. Spread the oblong of dough with the prepared meat and roll it loosely like a jelly roll. Cut the roll into slices ¾ inch thick. Place the slices in a lightly greased pan and dot the tops with butter. This roll may be prepared in advance and placed in the refrigerator until ready for use. Bake the slices in a hot oven — 450° — until they are done. Serve them very hot with Brown Sauce or Tomato Sauce — Pages 155-157.

LEFT-OVER MEAT IN BISCUIT OR PIE DOUGH

Roll biscuit dough until it is ⅛ inch thick. Cut it into squares. Place minced, seasoned meat, moistened with gravy or cream in the center of each square. Brush the edges of the dough with cold water and fold it over. Place the triangles in a greased pan, brush them with butter and bake them in a quick oven — 450°.

HASH WITH CELERY

There is no set rule about making hash. In fact, it makes an immense appeal to the imagination. Cooks lacking that nerve-racking quality, will find the following recipe helpful:

1 cup cooked meat, diced
½ cup celery, cut in small
  pieces

¾ cup gravy or sauce
Seasoning

Drop the celery into ¾ cup of boiling water, add a slice of onion and cook it covered until the celery is tender (¼ cup of shredded green peppers may be boiled with the celery). Drain the celery saving the liquor and make the following:

Hash Gravy:

If there is left-over roast gravy available, use it. If there is not enough, thicken the celery water with 1 tablespoon flour and add it to the roast gravy. If there is no gravy, use celery water and enough boiling water to obtain the required amount. Add to this ½ teaspoon Savita, or 1 beef cube. Make the gravy with:

1½ tablespoons butter
 melted
1½ tablespoons flour
Celery water

Boiling water (¾ cup)
½ teaspoon Savita or 1
 beef cube

Color it with a few drops of Kitchen Bouquet. Taste this to see whether additional seasoning is required. A tablespoon of tomato pulp, or a teaspoon of catsup may be added. Heat the gravy to the boiling point, add the drained celery and boil it, add the meat and remove the hash from the fire as soon as the meat is heated. Do not let the gravy boil after adding the meat. Unnecessary boiling does not improve the flavor of beef and sometimes it causes it to become tough. To keep the hash hot, place the saucepan in hot water. Serve the hash on toast or in a hot pie shell.

RAGOUT FIN

16 Servings

1 square can asparagus
 tips, (15 ounces)
½ pound fresh mushrooms,
 sautéd
1 pair sweetbreads
3 cups cream sauce

2 egg yolks
Salt, paprika, nutmeg
2 tablespoons Sherry wine,
 or 1 tablespoon lemon
 juice

Boil and prepare the sweetbreads (See Page 141). Cut the asparagus in two. Make the Cream Sauce (See Page 154) with the asparagus water and cream or stock — (6 tablespoons butter, 6 tablespoons flour to 3 cups of liquid.) Add the asparagus, the sweetbreads and the mushrooms to the boiling sauce. Reduce the heat to a low flame, add the egg yolks and cook the ragout without boiling it for 1 minute. Remove it from the fire, season it well and add the Sherry or lemon juice. To keep the ragout hot, or to reheat it, place it in a double boiler. Serve it in hot patty shells, on toast, in bread cases, or in a baked noodle ring.

MUSHROOMS UNDER GLASS
3 Servings, Small

In former years the following dish was associated in my mind with extreme luxury. Today it is within the reach of anyone with a few cents and a glass bowl that will fit closely over a baker:

½ pound mushrooms	⅛ teaspoon paprika
2 tablespoons butter	1 or 2 one-half inch slices
1 teaspoon lemon juice	of bread
2 teaspoons chopped parsley	¼ cup cream
¼ teaspoon salt	1 tablespoon Sherry

Wipe the mushrooms and trim the stem ends. Cream the butter, add the lemon juice slowly, then the parsley and the seasoning. Cut the bread into rounds with a biscuit cutter and toast them. When cold, spread them lightly on both sides with some of the butter mixture and spread the rest of it on the mushrooms. Place the buttered toast in the bottom of a small baking dish, pile the mushrooms on top in cone shape and pour the cream over them. Cover them closely with a glass bowl. Bake them in a moderate oven — 375° — for 25 or 30 minutes, adding more cream if they threaten to become dry. Add the Sherry and serve the mushrooms at once garnished with parsley.

OYSTERS AND MUSHROOMS AU GRATIN
Ramekins

18 oysters	⅛ teaspoon paprika or
18 mushrooms	cayenne
2 tablespoons butter	1 cup cream sauce
½ teaspoon salt	Cracker crumbs
	Cheese or butter

Sauté the mushrooms in the butter — Page 123. Place three oysters in each ramekin, add three mushrooms. Season them and cover them with boiling cream sauce. Sprinkle the tops with bread crumbs and cheese (or dot the crumbs with butter) and place the ramekins in a quick oven until the tops are brown.

MUSHROOMS AND OYSTERS

12 large mushrooms	3 tablespoons butter
12 large oysters	Salt, paprika
	1 cup brown sauce

Remove the mushroom stems. Sauté the mushrooms in 2 tablespoons of melted butter for five minutes — See Page 123. Place a drained oyster in each mushroom cap, season them and dot them with the remaining butter. Place the pan in a moderate oven 350° until the oysters are plump. Serve them at once with Brown Sauce—Page 155.

WELSH RAREBIT

Good Welsh Rarebit can be bought canned and ready to be heated and served.

1 tablespoon butter
1½ cups cheese diced
⅛ teaspoon salt
¼ teaspoon dry mustard
A few grains of cayenne

1 teaspoon Worcestershire
  Sauce
1 cup cream or top milk
1 egg yolk

Melt the butter in a skillet, add the cheese and melt it over a slow fire. Add the seasoning and then the cream very slowly. Add the egg yolk and beat it in well. Serve the Rarebit at once over toasted crackers or bread.

WELSH RAREBIT OVER GRILLED TOMATOES, OR RAW TOMATOES

Prepare Grilled Tomatoes—Page 118. Prepare rounds of toast, place the tomatoes upon them and pour Welsh Rarebit over them. Serve them at once. Raw tomatoes may be substituted for grilled tomatoes.

TOMATO RAREBIT WITH HARD COOKED EGGS

4 hard cooked eggs—sliced
  or quartered
2 tablespoons butter
2 tablespoons onion, finely
  chopped
1 can tomato soup
1½ cups grated cheese

1 teaspoon Worcestershire
  Sauce
1 egg
Salt, paprika
A few grains of cayenne
4 rounds of toast, or 4 rusks

Cook the eggs, chill and slice them. Melt the butter and sauté the onion in it for 2 minutes. Add the tomato soup and when it is hot reduce the heat and add the cheese. Permit the cheese to melt, then pour part of the liquid over the egg which has been beaten. Return all the liquid to the pot and add the seasoning. Permit the egg to thicken slightly. Stir the rarebit constantly until it is done, then pour it over the eggs and toast and serve it at once.

CHEESE MONKEY

¾ cup milk	¾ cup grated cheese
¾ cup soft stale bread crumbs	1 egg slightly beaten
	½ teaspoon salt
1 tablespoon butter	A few grains of cayenne

Cook these ingredients over a slow fire. Heat the milk and add the crumbs and the butter. When they are well blended add the cheese. Stir until the cheese is melted, then add the egg and the seasoning. Permit the egg to thicken slightly, stirring constantly. Serve the Monkey while very hot over crackers or toast.

WOOD-CHUCK

1 quart can tomatoes	2 eggs, beaten
½ pound yellow cheese diced	Salt, cayenne, paprika

Cook the tomatoes until they are soft. Beat them with a wire whisk into a purée. When they are smooth reduce the heat and add the cheese. Continue to beat until the cheese melts, then add the lightly beaten eggs and stir the mixture until it thickens (about 2 minutes). Serve it hot over toast, crackers, or rusks.

CHEESE CUSTARD PIE
4 Servings

In Switzerland we had a vile tempered cook named Marguerite. Her one idea, after being generally disagreeable, was to earn enough to own a small chalet on some high peak where she could cater to mountain climbers. While she was certainly not born with a silver spoon in her mouth—although it was large enough to accommodate several—I am convinced she arrived with a cooking spoon in her hand. If she has attained her ideal, many a climber will feel it worth while to scale a perilous peak to reach her kitchen. The following Cheese Custard Pie was always served in solitary state. Its flavor varied with Marguerite's moods and her supply of cheese. It was never twice the same, as she had no written rule, but I have endeavored to make one like hers for it would be a pity to relegate so good a dish to inaccessible roosts:

Pie dough:
1 cup flour—pastry
2½ tablespoons lard
1½ tablespoons butter
¾ teaspoon baking powder

⅓ teaspoon salt
3 tablespoons ice water, or just enough to hold these ingredients together. Combine them as directed on Page 209

Roll the dough and fit it into a small pan or baking dish, about 8½ inches in diameter. Bake the crust for 20 minutes in a hot oven 450°. Remove it from the oven, cool it slightly and fill it with Cheese Custard.

¾ cup top milk	⅛ teaspoon of salt
1 cup grated cheese (or less)	A few grains of cayenne
2 eggs	Paprika

Scald the milk, remove it from the fire. Add the cheese and stir it until it melts. Add the seasoning and the beaten eggs and stir the mixture well with a wire whisk. Fill the pie crust and bake it in a slow oven 325° until set, about 45 minutes. Serve it while very hot. The size of the pan is not important, but the custard is best about 1½ inches deep.

BREAD, EGG AND CHEESE DISH

4 cups diced bread	Paprika
¼ pound cheese — grated (1 cup)	½ teaspoon mustard (optional)
1 cup milk	A few grains of cayenne
2 eggs	These proportions may be
1 teaspoon salt	varied

Butter ½ inch slices of bread lightly and cut them into cubes. Cut two slices of the buttered bread into triangular pieces. Place a layer of the diced bread in a greased baking dish and sprinkle it generously with cheese. Repeat this process. Combine the milk, eggs, salt, paprika and a few grains of cayenne and pour them over the bread and cheese. Place the triangles of bread upright around the edge of the baker as a garnish. Bake the cheese dish in a moderate oven 350° for 20 minutes, then serve it at once.

LUNCHETTES

Toast rounds of bread and butter them lightly. Place a thick slice of skinned tomato on each round and cover them closely with finely chopped green peppers and onions. Season them well with salt and pepper. Put a slice of American cheese on each round and top them with a strip of bacon. Place the lunchettes under a broiler until the bacon is crisp and serve them at once.

CHEESE FONDUE

This Swiss dish is unusually good: It is appropriate for after the theatre parties, or for cold suppers. It will serve about eight people, but it meets with such favor that it is better to count on only six portions if nothing else is being served:

2 pounds of brick cheese	2 eggs
3/4 cup of butter	1/2 teaspoon salt
3/4 cup milk, warm	

Cut the cheese into small pieces, combine it with the melted butter and stir it constantly over a very low fire until the cheese is melted. Add the warm milk and stir the mixture with a wire whisk until it is smooth. Remove the cheese mixture from the fire and beat in the eggs and the salt. Serve the fondue at once over toast.

PIMENTO CHEESE

This is a very good way of preparing luncheon cheese:

1 pound Ohio cheese	2 teaspoons salt
2 cups condensed milk	2 teaspoons dry mustard
1 small can pimentos fine-	2 eggs
ly chopped (3½ oz.)	

Dissolve the cheese slowly in the heated milk, add the next four ingredients and bring them slowly to the boiling point, stirring them constantly. Pour a little of this mixture over the beaten eggs, return it to the pot and let the eggs thicken slightly. Pour the cheese into a mold and chill it until it is firm.

CHEESE SPREAD

The following good sandwich spread will keep for a week or more:

1/2 cup milk	1/2 teaspoon salt
1 egg	3/4 pound American Cheese
1/4 teaspoon dry mustard	

Scald the milk, add the remaining ingredients and cook them in a double boiler, stirring them constantly, for 15 minutes. Cool the cheese, spread it on slices of bread and toast them in a moderate oven until the cheese melts.

For other toasted sandwiches see Index.

SWEET POTATOES, BACON AND PINEAPPLE SLICES
4 Servings

These are decorative and unusually good:

4 small, or two large fat	4 slices of canned pineapple
sweet potatoes	Brown sugar
5 strips of bacon	Pineapple juice

Boil the sweet potatoes in their jackets until they are tender, but no longer. Peel them and trim them so that they will cover a slice of pineapple. Surround each potato with a strip of bacon, securing it with a toothpick, taking care that the bacon does not overlap heavily. Cut the remaining piece of bacon into fourths and place a piece on top of each potato. Put the pineapple into a shallow pan. Cover each slice with as much brown sugar as can be pressed into it and place a potato on each slice. Bake the potatoes in a moderate oven 375° until the bacon is crisp. Baste them with hot pineapple juice.

TOMATO PUDDING, OR SCALLOPED TOMATOES

The following is a wonderful tomato dish:

10 ounce can of Tomato Purée	1/4 teaspoon salt
1/4 cup boiling water to rinse the can	1 cup fresh white bread crumbed
6 or 7 tablespoons brown sugar	1/4 cup melted butter

Heat the purée and the water to the boiling point, add the sugar and the salt. Place the bread crumbs in a casserole and pour the butter over them. Add the tomato mixture and cover the dish closely. Bake the pudding for 30 minutes in a moderate oven 375°. Do not remove the cover until ready to serve the tomatoes.

TOMATO PANCAKES

These seem "queerish." They have an attractive red brown color, a good flavor and are highly esteemed by cake fanciers:

2 cups stewed tomatoes, or canned tomatoes, strained	1/4 teaspoon pepper
2 tablespoons butter, melted	1/2 teaspoon sugar
1 teaspoon salt	1 1/2 cups flour
	1 teaspoon baking powder

Strain the tomatoes. Sift the dry ingredients and combine them with the tomatoes. Melt the shortening in a frying pan, add the tomato batter by the spoonful and sauté the cakes until they are a nice brown. Serve them with or without syrup.

YORKSHIRE PUDDING AND PORK SAUSAGES
6 Servings

1 pound link pork sausages	1 teaspoon baking powder
1 egg	1/2 teaspoon salt
1 cup flour	1/2 cup milk

Separate the sausages and prick them with a fork. Cover them with boiling water for 1 minute. Drain and place them in a 9x16 inch pan. Bake them in a hot oven—425°—for 10 minutes. Beat the egg and make a batter with the remaining ingredients. Remove the pan from the oven and pour off all but ½ inch of fat. Pour the batter over the sausages and the fat. Bake the pudding in a hot oven—475°—for 15 minutes. Reduce the heat to a moderate oven—350°—and bake it for 20 minutes. Cut it into squares and serve it at once.

VEGETABLE DISH WITH BACON

This dish, served with Spoon Bread, is a complete and delicious luncheon:

Green peppers, shredded
Onions, skinned and sliced
Tomatoes, skinned and
    sliced
Seasoning

Brown sugar
Stock (or dissolved Savita
    or bouillon cubes)
Bacon

Cut the tops from the peppers, remove the seeds and the veins and slice the peppers. Place alternate layers of peppers, onions and tomatoes in a greased baking dish, season each layer lightly and sprinkle a little brown sugar over the tomatoes. Cook the vegetables covered in a hot oven—400°—for 30 minutes. Remove the cover, drain the vegetables. To every cup of stock allow 1 tablespoon butter and 2 tablespoons flour. Melt the butter, add the flour and then the stock. Taste the sauce to see whether additional seasoning is needed and pour it over the vegetables. Place slices of bacon over the top, raise the heat to 500° and bake the dish until the bacon is crisp.

TOMATOES AND CORN

1 cup tomatoes
1 cup corn, canned or fresh
2 tablespoons chopped
    onions
1 tablespoon chopped
    green pepper
2 tablespoons chopped
    celery

¼ cup bread crumbs
2 eggs
½ teaspoon salt
⅛ teaspoon paprika
¾ teaspoon sugar

Combine the ingredients, place them in a buttered baking dish, set in a pan of hot water and bake them for 25 minutes in a moderate oven—350°.

CORN À LA KING

1 can corn (No. 2)
1 green pepper, shredded
1 pimento, chopped
1 egg, beaten

½ cup milk
1 tablespoon butter
½ teaspoon salt
⅛ teaspoon paprika

Place the corn in a double boiler, add the green pepper and the pimento and cook them for 20 minutes. Beat the egg with the milk, add the butter and the seasoning and combine these ingredients with the vegetables. Cook the corn until it is slightly thickened and serve it on toast.

BRAISED ENDIVE OR LETTUCE

2 slices bacon or 2 tablespoons butter
1 carrot sliced
3 tablespoons onion,
  chopped

2 sprigs of parsley
3 heads of endive, or 2
  heads of lettuce

Place these ingredients in a covered baking dish. Bake them for 10 minutes in a moderate oven, add 1 cup of well seasoned stock and bake them until they are done. Thicken the sauce with flour before serving the endive.

LEFT-OVER VEGETABLE DISH

Combine left-over vegetables. Raw celery, green pepper, etc. may be added to them. Moisten the vegetables with stock, milk or tomato juice and season them well. Sprinkle bread crumbs and grated cheese over them. Cook them in a moderate oven until they are thoroughly heated and the cheese is melted.

BACON CORNMEAL WAFFLES
6 Waffles

This dish is a "find" for the efficiency housekeeper. It is a complete meal and requires no scouring of pots or pans. (An electric waffle iron may be used. If there is an excess of grease, wipe off the iron with absorbent paper.)

2 eggs
1¾ cups milk
1 cup cake flour, or ⅞
  cup bread flour
4 teaspoons baking powder
1 tablespoon sugar

½ teaspoon salt
1 cup yellow cornmeal
1 tablespoon bacon fat (or
  other shortening)
6 to 12 slices of bacon

I. Beat the eggs slightly and add the milk.
II. Sift the flour, baking powder, sugar and salt and add the cornmeal.

Combine I and II and add the melted shortening. Cut the bacon into 4 or into 2 pieces. Heat the iron, place a piece of bacon on each section and pour the batter over them.

CORN OYSTERS
16 Oysters

These delicious corn cakes are quickly made and are a pleasant addition to any meal.

1 cup corn — fresh or canned	1/8 teaspoon salt
2 eggs	3/8 cup flour
1/2 teaspoon baking powder	1/4 teaspoon nutmeg

Use a good brand of corn, drain it and mash it with a potato masher. Beat the eggs until they are light, add the corn, flour, seasoning and baking powder. Melt two tablespoons of butter in a small skillet. When it is very hot add the batter by the tablespoonful. Permit the bottom of the oysters to brown, reverse them and brown the other side. Serve them at once. For best results prepare the batter immediately before using it.

GNOCCHI
4 Servings

Gnocchi is an Italian dish, which is frequently served as a separate course, or in place of potatoes. Properly prepared, it is delicate and delicious.

1/8 cup butter	1 cup milk scalded
1/8 cup flour	1 egg yolk
1/8 cup cornstarch	1/2 cup grated cheese
1/2 teaspoon salt	(optional)

Melt the butter, add the flour and the cornstarch and when these ingredients are smooth, add the milk gradually. Beat the batter with a wire whisk until it is smooth and thick. Reduce the heat, add the salt, the egg yolk and if desired 1/4 cup of cheese. Beat the batter until the cheese is melted — then pour it onto a platter, or shallow pan. When it is cool, cut it into strips two inches long. Place them in a greased pan. Pour melted butter over them, sprinkle them with cheese and bake them in a moderate oven until the cheese is browned. The cheese may be omitted both in the batter and later. This is the original recipe. I prefer poaching the strips in gently boiling water or stock, draining them and serving them with melted butter, to baking them. Cut into small shapes, this batter is good served in soup.

TOMATO CASES

Cut large hollows in unpeeled tomatoes. Salt them and invert them to drain for 15 minutes. Fill them with cooked eggs, fish, meat, rice, macaroni, or vegetables, and place the tomatoes in a pan with just enough water to keep them from scorching. Bake them in a moderate oven 350° for ten or fifteen minutes.

TOMATOES FILLED WITH ONIONS

6 tomatoes	½ teaspoon salt
4 tablespoons bacon drippings	1 tablespoon celery seed
	¾ cup bread crumbs
3 onions, finely chopped	1 tablespoon butter, or
½ tablespoon brown sugar	¼ cup grated cheese

Prepare six Tomato Cases—Page 66. Heat the drippings and sauté the onions until they are brown. Chop the pulp taken from the centers, combine it with the onions, sugar, celery seed and salt and cook these ingredients for 20 minutes. Fill the tomato cases, cover the tops with bread crumbs, dot them with butter, or sprinkle them with cheese. Cook the tomatoes as directed on Page 66.

TOMATOES FILLED WITH MASHED POTATOES

6 medium sized tomatoes	½ cup nut meats
1 cup mashed potatoes	

Prepare six Tomato Cases—Page 66. Place the tomatoes in a pan with enough water to keep them from scorching and bake them for 10 minutes in a moderate oven 350°. Prepare mashed potatoes—Page 96, add the broken nut meats and fill the tomatoes, or fill the tomatoes and use the whole nuts as a garnish for the tops. Return the tomatoes to the oven and bake them for 10 minutes, or until they are done.

TOMATOES FILLED WITH CREAMED FOOD

Prepare Tomato Cases—Page 66. Prepare meat or fish with celery, asparagus, etc. Combine them with heavy well seasoned cream sauce, putting the solids into boiling sauce to prevent it from becoming watery, and using ½ as much sauce as there are solids. Fill the tomatoes, cover the tops with bread crumbs and dot them with butter, or sprinkle them with grated cheese. Bake them as directed on Page 66.

TOMATOES FILLED WITH CORN

Prepare Tomato Cases—Page 66. Fill them with corn dressing for green peppers—Page 70. Bake them according to directions—Page 66.

TOMATOES FILLED WITH MACARONI

Prepare Tomato Cases—Page 66. Prepare the Macaroni Filling for green peppers—Page 71. Fill the tomato cases and bake them as directed on Page 66.

TOMATOES FILLED WITH STUFFED OLIVES

6 tomatoes
Salt
3 tablespoons brown sugar
1/2 cup stuffed olives
3/4 cup cracker or bread
    crumbs

2 tablespoons melted butter
1/4 teaspoon paprika
1/2 teaspoon salt
1 tablespoon butter

Prepare Tomato Cases—Page 66. Place 1 1/2 teaspoons brown sugar in the center of each one. Chop the removed tomato pulp and add to it the remaining ingredients, saving 1/4 cup bread crumbs for the tops. Fill the tomato cases, cover them with bread crumbs and dot them with butter. Place the tomatoes in a baking dish, adding 1 slice of onion and 1/2 cup water. Bake the tomatoes in a moderate oven 350° basting them frequently until they are done.

TOMATOES FILLED WITH EGGS
6 Servings

6 large tomatoes
6 eggs
6 rounds of buttered toast

2 cups of cream sauce
1 green pepper chopped

Prepare 6 Tomato Cases—Page 66. Drop an egg into each hollow and place the tomatoes in a pan with just enough water to keep them from scorching. Bake them for 20 minutes in a moderate oven until the eggs are firm, but not hard. This is the recipe as given to me. I have worked repeatedly to get the tomato soft and to keep the egg soft at the same time, and I find the following method an improvement:

Prepare the Tomato Cases—Page 66. Place them in a pan with a little water and bake them for 10 minutes in a moderate oven. Remove the pan from the oven and drop an egg into each tomato and return the pan to the oven and bake the tomatoes until the eggs are firm, but not hard. The eggs may be sprinkled with bread crumbs, seasoned and dotted with butter. Serve the tomatoes on rounds of buttered toast with the following:

Sauce:

2 cups cream sauce
  (4 tablespoons butter)
  (4 tablespoons flour)
  (2 cups milk)
1 tablespoon chopped onion

1 green pepper, chopped
Worcestershire Sauce
Salt, paprika
Celery salt

Chop the pulp removed from the tomatoes and add it to the boiling cream sauce. Add the remaining ingredients and season the sauce highly.

TOMATOES OR GREEN PEPPERS STUFFED WITH CREAMED MUSHROOMS

Prepare 4 Tomato or Pepper Cases — Page 66 to 69. Prepare Creamed Mushrooms — Page 123, using ½ lb. of mushrooms. Thicken them with ¼ cup of bread crumbs, season them well, fill the cases with the dressing and cover the tops with bread crumbs dotted with butter. Bake them as directed on Pages 66 and 69.

TOMATOES FILLED WITH RICE

Prepare Tomato Cases — Page 66. Chop the tomato pulp and combine it with cooked rice and chopped ham; seasoned with onion juice, sugar, salt and paprika, and moistened with a little melted butter. Fill the tomato cases. Follow the rule on Page 66 for baking them.

PEPPER CASES

Cut the stem ends from green peppers and remove the seeds. Drop the peppers into a small quantity of rapidly boiling salted water. Cook them gently for 15 minutes, or until they are nearly done. Drain them well. Fill them with rice, macaroni, creamed meat, or fish, creamed or buttered vegetables, etc., and place them in a pan with enough water to keep them from scorching. Bake them for 10 to 15 minutes in a moderate oven 350°.

PEPPERS OR TOMATOES STUFFED WITH CREAMED ASPARAGUS

5 small peppers
1 cup canned asparagus tips
½ cup cream sauce
¼ blanched and shred-

ded almonds, or pecans
Seasoning
Bread crumbs, butter

Prepare the Pepper Cases—Page 69. Cut the asparagus into 1 inch lengths. Make the cream sauce with:

1½ tablespoons butter   ¼ cup asparagus liquor
1¼ tablespoons flour   ¼ cup cream

When it is boiling add the drained asparagus, the nuts and the seasoning. Fill the pepper cases, cover the tops with bread crumbs, dot them with butter or sprinkle them with cheese and bake them as directed—Page 69.

PEPPERS FILLED WITH CORN

4 medium sized peppers   or cream
1 cup corn, drained   Salt, paprika
1 pimento, chopped   ½ teaspoon sugar, if corn
½ green pepper, chopped   is green
2 tablespoons celery,   Bacon cooked and minced
  chopped   Bread crumbs
½ cup bread crumbs   Butter, or cheese grated
2 tablespoons corn liquor

Prepare the Pepper Cases—Page 69. Combine the corn with all but the last two ingredients. Fill the peppers, sprinkle the tops with crumbs, dot them with butter (or cheese) and bake the peppers as directed on Page 69.

PEPPER CASES FILLED WITH CREAMED OYSTERS

4 green peppers   Chopped parsley
½ pint oysters   Bread crumbs and butter,
½ cup cream sauce   or cheese

Prepare the Pepper Cases—Page 69. Prepare Creamed Oysters—Page 76, using ½ the amount. Add the parsley to the sauce (optional). Fill the pepper cases, cover the tops with bread crumbs and butter (or cheese) and place the peppers in a moderate oven 350° for 10 minutes, as directed on Page 69.

GREEN PEPPERS FILLED WITH PEAS

Prepare the Pepper Cases—Page 69. Prepare and cook Green Peas—Page 111. Fill the peppers and bake them as directed on Page 69. Canned peas may be substituted. Boiled Carrots—Page 111, may be added to the peas.

GREEN PEPPERS FILLED WITH MACARONI

4 or 5 green peppers
½ cup creamettes or mac-
  aroni (1 cup when
  cooked)
¾ cup grated cheese
¾ cup thick cooked toma-
  toes, (tomato pulp, or

tomato soup)
½ cup bread crumbs
Salt
A few grains of cayenne
Sugar
1 teaspoon Worcestershire
  Sauce (optional)

Prepare the Pepper Cases—Page 69. Boil and drain the macaroni—Page 40. Combine the macaroni with the remaining ingredients and fill the pepper cases. Bake them as directed—Page 69. Serve them with Tomato Sauce—Page 157.

GREEN PEPPERS WITH RICE FILLING

5 green peppers
⅓ cup rice (or 1 cup
  cooked rice)
½ cup stock, cream or
  tomato pulp
Salt, paprika, a few grains
  of cayenne

½ teaspoon curry powder
  (optional)
½ cup or more grated
  cheese
Bread crumbs
Butter

Prepare the Pepper Cases—Page 69. Prepare the rice by the second method—Page 43. Drain it well and add the stock, seasoning and cheese. Fill the peppers, cover the tops with bread crumbs and dot them with butter. Bake them as directed on Page 69.

PEPPERS FILLED WITH MASHED POTATOES, ETC.

Prepare Pepper Cases—Page 69. Fill them with any palatable combination of left-over food, well seasoned, moistened with gravy, cream or stock. If there is insufficient meat, combine it with cooked potatoes or rice, noodles, etc. Bake them as directed on Page 69.

ZUCCHINI CASES
Vegetable Marrow

Zucchini is an Italian squash now frequently found in American markets. Choose short round zucchini, scrub but do not peel them. Zucchini cook quickly when young. Drop them into boiling salted water and cook them until they are partly done. Drain them. Cut off the long end and hollow the short end. Sauté chopped onion in butter for 1 minute, add the chopped zucchini pulp and cook these ingredients 1 minute longer. Combine them with bread crumbs and chopped cooked meat, or fish, moistened with butter, cream, stock or cream sauce, and fill the zucchini shells with the mixture. Place them in a pan with a very little water and bake them in a moderate oven until they are tender.

SCALLOPED CABBAGE

1 medium sized head of
   cabbage
1½ cups cream sauce
2 tablespoons chopped
   green peppers
2 tablespoons chopped

pimentos
1 cup or less grated cheese
1 cup bread crumbs
Bacon cooked and chopped,
   or butter

The cream sauce may be made with bacon drippings instead of butter. Boil the cabbage—Page 105. Drain it well. Place layers of cabbage in a greased baking dish. Cover each layer with boiling cream sauce, sprinkled with peppers and pimentos and with cheese. Cover the top with bread crumbs dotted with cooked minced bacon or with butter. Bake the cabbage in a moderate oven 375° for 10 minutes.

ONION CASES FILLED WITH MEAT OR FISH

Pour boiling water over Spanish, or other large onions and permit them to stand for 2 minutes. Drain them and peel them under cold water. Drop them into boiling water and cook them in an open kettle for 40 minutes. Drain them well, cut a slice from the top and remove the centers, leaving a shell ½ to ¾ inch thick, or cut the onions into lengthwise halves and remove the center. Chop the pulp taken from the centers and combine it with bread crumbs, or cooked rice, add minced cooked chicken or other meat, fish, nuts, or sautéd chopped mushrooms. Moisten these ingredients with a little cream, butter, gravy, cream sauce or stock, season them and fill the onion cases. Cover the tops with bread crumbs, dot them with butter, or sprinkle them with cheese. Place the onions in a pan with just enough water to keep them from scorching and bake them in a moderate oven 350° for 20 minutes, or until they are tender. Spanish onions require longer cooking. Allow at least 1 hour in all for small onions and longer for large ones. If raw food is used in the filling, shorten the time of boiling and prolong the time for baking the onions.

BAKED ONIONS AND CHEESE

12 medium sized onions
1 cup grated cheese
¼ cup butter

Pepper, salt
Stock or hot water

Prepare the onions as for onion cases. Boil them until they are partly tender and core them with an apple corer. Drain them and fill the centers with cheese. Season them and dot them with butter. Place the onions in a baking dish with just enough stock, or water, to keep them from scorching, cover them and bake them slowly, in a moderate oven 375° until they are nearly tender. Remove the cover and bake them 5 minutes longer. For other onion dishes see Index.

STUFFED CARROTS

2 bunches of carrots
1 egg, or 3 tablespoons
cream
1 small onion, minced
⅛ cup bread crumbs
½ cup cooked meat,
chopped

Salt
Paprika
Sage (optional)
Parsley, chopped
1 egg
Bread crumbs

Boil the carrots until they are nearly tender, peel them and scoop out the centers with an apple corer. Chop the pulp taken from the centers and combine it with the remaining ingredients. Stuff the carrots, roll them in bread crumbs, in 1 egg beaten and diluted with 1 tablespoon of water, and again in bread crumbs. Season them lightly. Fry the carrots in deep fat until they are brown, or sauté them in butter.

CUCUMBER CASES

Peel cucumbers and cut them lengthwise into halves. Remove the seeds and if the cucumbers are very thick, cut out some of the inner shell, leaving a case about ½ inch thick. Fill the cases and place them in a pan with a very little water, just enough to keep them from scorching. Bake them in a moderate oven — 350° — for 35 minutes. Serve them with or without cream sauce made with sour cream.

CUCUMBERS FILLED WITH CREAMED FOOD

Prepare Cucumber Cases — Page 73. Fill them with chopped cucumber and creamed fish, or meat. Cover the tops with bread crumbs, dot them with butter and bake them as directed — Page 73.

73

CUCUMBERS FILLED WITH BREAD DRESSING

3 medium sized cucumbers
2 tablespoons butter
1 tablespoon onion, chopped
¾ cup bread crumbs

¼ cup nut meats, chopped
  (optional)
Salt, paprika
Butter, or cheese

Prepare the Cucumber Cases—Page 73. Melt the butter, add the onions and cook them for 1 minute, add the chopped cucumber pulp and cook it for 1 minute. Combine these with the remaining ingredients, reserving some of the crumbs for the tops. Fill the cases and cover the tops with bread crumbs dotted with butter, or sprinkle them with cheese. Bake them as directed on Page 73.

PIMENTOES FILLED WITH FISH OR MEAT

Line individual molds with pimentos, either whole, or in strips. Fill them with fish or meat, creamed with a little heavy cream sauce, and place them covered in gently boiling water on the top of the stove. Steam them until they are well heated—about 10 minutes. Serve them hot with cream sauce, to which Worcestershire sauce, or Sherry and a little chopped parsley have been added, or chill them, unmold them on lettuce leaves and serve them with mayonnaise.

NOTE: For creamed crabmeat, shrimp, etc. See the Chapter on Fish. For eggs stuffed with crabmeat see the Chapter on Hors d' Oeuvre.

BAKED APPLES STUFFED WITH SAUSAGE MEAT

6 large tart apples

1 cup well seasoned sausage
  meat

Scoop out the core and some of the pulp of the apples, leaving a half inch shell. Cut the pulp from the cores and chop it. Mix the chopped pulp and the sausage meat. Fill the apples with a heaping filling and bake them in a hot oven 380° until they are tender. Serve them with potatoes, or rice, or surround a mound of boiled noodles with stuffed apples.

APPLES STUFFED WITH LINK SAUSAGES

Cut the core from each apple with an apple corer and insert a sausage. Sprinkle the apples with brown sugar, place them in a pan with a little lemon juice and water. Bake them until they are tender in a moderate oven 375°. Baste them frequently.

POTATOES STUFFED WITH LINK SAUSAGES

Wash as many potatoes as you wish to use and grease them with lard. Cut a hole in each one with an apple corer and insert a sausage. Bake the potatoes until they are done in a good oven 380° for about one hour.

BAKED STUFFED POTATOES

Bake large shapely potatoes — Page 98. Cut them in halves, scoop out the pulp, mash it, add butter and seasoning to it and line the shells with the mixture. Fill the hollows with creamed mushrooms, shrimp, tuna fish, salmon, or with minced ham or hash. Sprinkle the tops with bread crumbs dotted with butter and brown them in a good oven 380° or under a broiler.

See the Chapter on Vegetables for Sweet Potatoes and Apples.

BAKED POTATOES AND MINCED HAM

Bake 6 large potatoes — Page 98. Cut a slice from each potato, scoop out the pulp and mash it. To about:

3 cups mashed potatoes add	2 egg whites — beaten until
6 tablespoons ham minced	stiff
6 tablespoons parsley chopped	Salt, paprika

Fill the potato shells with the mixture, return them to the oven, or place them under a broiler until brown. See the Chapter on Vegetables for other baked potato dishes.

HAM AND POTATO CASSEROLE

Cut very thin slices of smoked ham into 2 inch pieces. Brown it slightly in a dry hot skillet. Grease a baking dish and fill it with layers of raw, very thinly sliced potatoes. Season each layer with a very little salt and pepper, dredge it with flour, dot it with butter and place slices of ham on it. Cover over the top with potatoes and fill the dish 3/4 full with milk. Cover and bake the potatoes in a moderate oven 350° for 1/2 hour. Uncover and bake the potatoes until they are tender.

Oysters

There are various ways of preparing bulk oysters for cooking. The favorite method seems to be to place the oysters with their liquor in a sauce pan and to stew them until their edges curl. The oysters must be closely watched, as a degree too much cooking makes them tough. I prefer either of the two following methods:

Drain the oysters, reserving the liquor, place them in a single layer in a large colander over boiling water and steam them until they are plump; or place the drained oysters in the bottom of a large saucepan and put the pan in boiling water until the oysters are plump.

In the case of creamed oysters, or other dishes where drained oysters are to be put directly into boiling cream sauce, it is not necessary to cook them beforehand.

The oyster liquid may be added to cream sauce, or used in some other way in preparing oyster dishes.

CREAMED OYSTERS I.

1 pint oysters
1 cup heavy cream sauce
Salt, celery salt, paprika

Lemon juice, Sherry or
Worcestershire Sauce

Drain the oysters, reserving the liquor. Make a cream sauce of:

2 tablespoons butter
2 tablespoons flour

1 cup liquid (oyster liquid
and cream)
Seasoning

Add the oysters when the sauce is smooth and boiling. Heat them to the boiling point only, season them with lemon juice or other flavoring and sprinkle them with chopped parsley. Serve the oysters at once in bread cases, patty shells, or on buttered toast.

Example:

CREAMED OYSTERS IN BREAD ROLLS OR BREAD CASES

4 small hard rolls
½ pint oysters (drained)
½ cup cream sauce
Parsley, chopped

Lemon, Sherry or Wor-
cestershire Sauce
Bread crumbs, butter or
grated cheese

Prepare the rolls or bread cases — Page 33. Make ½ the portion of cream sauce given on Page 154, using the oyster liquor and cream. Place the oysters in the boiling cream sauce, cook them until they are plump. Remove them from the fire and add the flavoring and the parsley, or reserve the parsley for the top. Fill the rolls, sprinkle them with parsley and serve them, or cover the tops with bread crumbs, dot them with butter, or sprinkle them lightly with cheese. Place the rolls under a broiler until the crumbs are light brown. Serve them at once.

See Pepper Cases Filled with Oysters — Page 70.

CREAMED OYSTERS II.
(For ramekins, bread cases, etc.)

This is a very good oyster filling—richer by the addition of egg yolks than Creamed Oysters I.

1 pint oysters
2 tablespoons butter
2 tablespoons flour
2 tablespoons cream
Salt, paprika
2 egg yolks

A few drops of lemon juice, Worcestershire Sauce, or Sherry (optional)
1 tablespoon chopped parsley

Heat the oysters in their liquor until their edges begin to curl. Drain them well, reserving the liquor and chop them coarsely. Melt the butter, add the flour and when these ingredients are boiling, add the cream and the oyster liquor. Stir the sauce until it is smooth and boiling, season it and add the oysters, but do not let them boil. When the oysters are hot, reduce the heat, add the egg yolks and permit them to thicken slightly by cooking them one minute longer, stirring the mixture gently. Add the chopped parsley and the flavoring. Fill ramekins or bread cases, cover the tops with bread crumbs, dot them with butter, or sprinkle them with grated cheese and place the ramekins under a broiler until the tops are brown. To keep the oysters hot, or to reheat them, place them in a pan over hot water.

CREAMED OYSTERS III.

1 pint oysters
2 tablespoons butter
2 tablespoons flour
1 cup cream
Salt

Paprika
Nutmeg
2 egg yolks
Toast

Scald the oysters in their liquor and drain them, reserving the liquor. Melt the butter, add the flour and when these ingredients are smooth, add the cream, the liquor and the seasoning. Cook the sauce, stirring it constantly until it is thick. Reduce the heat, add the egg yolks and cook the sauce, but do not boil it, until the eggs thicken slightly. Add the oysters and serve them at once in toast.

OYSTER LOAF

Prepare a loaf of bread by cutting off the top and taking out the center, leaving a shell ½ inch thick. Butter the shell lightly (using melted butter and a pastry brush) and toast it in a moderate oven 350°. Prepare double the quantity of creamed oysters — Page 76. Fill the shell, sprinkle the top with chopped parsley and serve it at once.

SCALLOPED OYSTERS

1 pint oysters drained	Salt, paprika
½ cup dry bread crumbs	2 tablespoons chopped
1 cup cracker crumbs	parsley (optional)
½ cup melted butter	½ cup chopped celery or
6 tablespoons cream and	green pepper
oyster liquor	

Combine the bread and cracker crumbs and pour the butter over them. Plan to use two layers of oysters (no more), and three layers of crumbs — placing the first crumbs on the bottom and the last on top. Season each layer of oysters and pour one-half of the liquid over it. If the vegetables are used, sprinkle them over the oysters. The last layer of crumbs should be dry. Bake the oysters for 20 minutes in a hot oven.

FRIED OR SAUTÉD OYSTERS

Drain 12 large oysters in a colander, pour 1 cup of water over them and dry them between towels. Beat 1 egg with 1 tablespoon of water. Dip the oysters (inserting a fork in the tough muscle of the oyster) in seasoned bread crumbs, in the egg and again in the crumbs. Permit the oysters to stand for ½ hour. Fry them in deep fat for 4 minutes at 375° or sauté them in butter.

BROILED OYSTERS

Place oysters in a pan and pour a mixture of melted butter, Worcestershire sauce, salt, pepper and paprika over them. Place them under a broiler until they are plump and serve them at once on hot toast.

BROILED OYSTERS
Breaded

1 pint oysters drained	¾ cup cracker crumbs
¼ cup melted butter	Salt, paprika, celery salt

Dry the oysters between towels, place the melted butter in a small cup. Take up each oyster by inserting a fork in the tough muscle. Dip the oysters in the butter and then in the cracker crumbs to which the seasoning has been added. Place the oysters on a buttered tin sheet and broil them, turning them once, until they are brown. Serve them on buttered toast, garnished with lemon and parsley or with lemon butter and chopped parsley.

BUTTERED OYSTERS
2 Servings

This is recommended as an excellent dish quickly prepared:

1 pint oysters	Worcestershire Sauce or
2 tablespoons butter	Sherry
1/2 teaspoon lemon juice,	Salt
	Paprika

Drain the oysters, place them in a strainer over boiling water and steam them until they are thoroughly heated. Put the butter in a hot bowl, pour the oysters into it and season them well. Serve them at once. With grapefruit halves, Holland Rusks and a beverage, this is an ideal quick luncheon.

OYSTER CELERY

1 1/2 tablespoons butter	1 1/2 tablespoons flour
1/2 cup celery, finely chopped	1 1/2 cups top milk and oyster liquor, hot
1/2 cup green peppers, chopped	1 pint oysters, drained
1/4 cup onion, chopped (optional)	Seasoning
	1 egg, beaten

Place the butter in a saucepan, when it is hot add the celery, the green peppers and the onions. Sauté them for 1 minute, then add the flour and the milk mixture. When the sauce is thick and boiling, add the seasoning and the oysters. When the oysters are plump, reduce the heat and add the egg. Cook them for a minute longer, stirring them gently, and serve them at once.

For additional Oyster dishes see Hors d' Oeuvre.

Soufflés

THE SOUFFLÉ

Cream sauce and eggs usually form the basis of the soufflé. To this basis, cheese, vegetables, meat, fish, nuts, etc. are added.

RULE FOR SOUFFLÉ

Make a thick cream sauce of 3 tablespoons of butter, 3 tablespoons of flour and 1 cup of liquid (milk, stock, vegetable water, or cream).

Add the solids, cheese, etc. while the cream sauce is boiling. Reduce the heat to a low flame and add the beaten egg yolks. Cook the sauce, for one or two minutes, stirring it constantly, until the yolks thicken slightly, but do not permit it to boil. Season the sauce and remove it from the fire. When it is cool, fold in the stiffly beaten whites of eggs and place the mixture in an ungreased baking dish. It will rise higher when the dish is not greased, as it will cling to the dry sides.

The soufflé may be baked with an increasing heat, beginning with a slow oven and increasing the heat slightly every ten minutes until the oven is moderately hot (325° to 350°) or by placing the baking dish in a slow oven (325°) and baking it until the soufflé is firm — from 25 to 45 minutes — dependent upon the size of the soufflé.

Do not place the dish in hot water unless the recipe calls for it. The water will keep the soufflé soft and in some cases it is preferable to have it crisp and crusty.

However, when making a soufflé in a ring mold, or in any other dish, with the intention of inverting the contents when done, grease the mold well, fill it and set it in a pan of hot water. This will facilitate removing the soufflé from the mold and will give it a uniform consistency.

Soufflé's may be prepared in advance, with the exception of the beating of the egg whites, which must be done immediately before the soufflé is put into the oven.

Please observe that the Tomato Soup Soufflé calls for a slightly different method, but it also may be prepared in advance.

Onions and garlic add greatly to the flavor of the soufflé. If you like them, place finely chopped onions in the butter and sauté them for a minute before making the cream sauce, or place a bit of garlic in the butter, sauté it for a minute and remove it before making the cream sauce.

Condensed milk makes a good soufflé. When using it take half milk or stock and half condensed milk and decrease the flour from 3 tablespoons to 2 tablespoons to one cup of liquid.

Carrots, onions and celery may be used raw if they are finely minced, or put through a food chopper.

CHEESE SOUFFLÉ

1 cup thick cream sauce
½ cup grated cheese
3 eggs, separated

Salt, paprika
A few grains of cayenne

Follow the Rule for Soufflé.

VEGETABLE SOUFFLÉ

1 cup thick cream sauce
1 cup boiled minced
  vegetables

3 eggs, separated
Salt, paprika, nutmeg

Use ⅓ cream and ⅔ vegetable stock in making the cream sauce, or 1 cup milk. Celery, onions and carrots finely minced may be used raw. Cooked oyster plant, eggplant, cauliflower, peas, onions, carrots, celery, canned or fresh asparagus, mushrooms, etc. may be used alone, or in any good combination. Small quantities of left over vegetables may be combined with raw carrots, celery and onions finely minced.

Follow the Rule for Soufflé.

SPINACH SOUFFLÉ

1 cup thick cream sauce
1 cup cooked, finely
  chopped spinach
2 teaspoons onions finely
  chopped (optional)

3 eggs, separated
Salt, paprika, nutmeg
1/8 cup grated cheese
  (optional)

Follow the Rule for Soufflé.

POTATO SOUFFLÉ

1 cup boiled riced potatoes
1 cup thick cream sauce
Follow the Rule for Soufflé.

2 eggs, separated
Seasoning

TOMATO SOUP SOUFFLÉ

1 cup thick cream sauce
1/4 cup grated cheese
  (optional)

3 eggs, separated
1 cup tomato soup
  (undiluted)

Make the cream sauce. When it is boiling, add the cheese and reduce the heat. When the cheese is melted, add the egg yolks and cook them for two minutes, stirring them constantly until they are slightly thickened. Cool the mixture and just before baking it add the tomato soup and the stiffly beaten egg whites. Follow the Rule for Soufflé.

TOMATO SOUFFLÉ

3½ cups skinned tomatoes,
  (a No. 2½ can)
3 ribs of celery, finely
  chopped

½ onion, finely chopped
¾ teaspoon salt
1 teaspoon sugar

Boil these ingredients for 20 minutes, strain and mash them. This soufflé may be made with the strained juice alone, or with the pulp added. There should be 1½ to 1¾ cups of pulp and juice. If there is not, substitute stock to obtain the required amount. Make the soufflé with:

3 tablespoons butter
3 tablespoons flour

Tomato juice and pulp
3 eggs, separated

Melt the butter, add the flour and gradually add the tomato juice and pulp. Follow the rule—Page 80—for adding the eggs and baking the soufflé.

ONION SOUFFLÉ

1 cup onions (boiled, drained and minced)
1 cup cream sauce
1½ tablespoons butter
1½ tablespoons flour

½ cup milk
½ cup condensed milk
3 eggs, separated
Seasoning

Cook the onions in a quantity of boiling salt water until they are barely tender. For a mild soufflé use the Spanish onion. For a sharp soufflé, use small white onions. Condensed milk is very good in soufflés. If sweet milk is used, take 3 tablespoons of flour and 3 tablespoons of butter and 1 cup of milk for the sauce. Nutmeg and celery salt are good for seasoning. Follow the Rule for Soufflé.

CORNMEAL SOUFFLÉ
4 Small Servings

This is a good luncheon dish combined with cold ham and a green salad:

2 cups milk
1 tablespoon butter
1 teaspoon salt
½ cup cornmeal
3 egg yolks

¼ teaspoon paprika
A few grains of cayenne
2 tablespoons or more of grated cheese
3 egg whites

Heat the milk to the boiling point, add the butter, seasoning and cornmeal and stir them well. Add the cheese and cook these ingredients to the consistency of mush. Add the egg yolks and cook and stir them for 1 minute. Remove the mush from the fire and when it is cool fold in the stiffly beaten egg whites. Bake the soufflé in a moderate oven until it is slightly crusty. In Italy, bits of ham and seafood are added to the batter, which is baked until it is very crisp.

EGGPLANT SOUFFLÉ
See page 121.

FISH OR MEAT SOUFFLÉ

1 cup fish flaked, or 1 cup meat finely chopped
¼ cup finely chopped raw carrots, celery and parsley
1 cup thick cream sauce

1 teaspoon lemon juice or Worcestershire Sauce
Salt, paprika, nutmeg
3 eggs, separated

Follow the Rule for Soufflé. See Page 91 for Steamed Fish Pudding.

HAM SOUFFLÉ

½ cup cooked minced
  vegetables
½ cup cooked minced ham
1 cup thick cream sauce

3 eggs, separated
Worcestershire Sauce
Mustard, salt (if needed)
  and paprika

Follow the Rule for Soufflé.

ECONOMY SOUFFLÉ

Cooked left-overs may be utilized to make a very good soufflé.

¼ cup mashed potatoes, or
  cold potatoes riced
¾ cup minced, cooked
  vegetables and meat
1 cup cream sauce
  (2½ tablespoons flour,
  2½ tablespoons butter,

1 cup liquid)
3 eggs, separated
1 tablespoon chopped
  parsley
1 tablespoon minced onion
Seasoning

Follow the Rule for Soufflé.

OYSTER SOUFFLÉ
4 Servings

Oyster Soufflé is both delicate and delicious.

½ pint oysters
1 cup heavy cream sauce

3 eggs, separated
Seasoning

Drain the oysters, keeping the liquor. Use the liquor with cream or milk in making the cream sauce. Remove the tough muscle and drop the oysters into the boiling cream sauce. Add the egg yolks and cook the mixture over reduced heat until it thickens slightly, then chill it well. Fold in the stiffly beaten egg whites and bake the soufflé in a moderate oven 325° until it is firm.

CRABMEAT SOUFFLÉ
6 Servings

3 tablespoons butter
3 tablespoons flour
1 cup milk
1 small can crabmeat
  (6½ ounces)
Salt

Pepper or paprika
3 eggs, separated
⅓ cup olives, shredded
1 teaspoon Worcestershire
  Sauce (optional)

Melt the butter, add the flour and when this bubbles, add the milk and stir the sauce until it is thick and smooth. Add the seasoning and when the sauce is boiling add the crabmeat and the olives. Reduce the heat to a low flame and add the yolks, stirring the sauce constantly. Cook it for one or two minutes, remove it from the fire and cool it. Whip the egg whites to a stiff froth and fold them into the cooled mixture. Place this in a baking dish set in a pan of hot water and bake it in a moderate oven 350° until it is firm (about 30 minutes). Serve the soufflé with Hollandaise sauce.

HALIBUT SOUFFLÉ WITH ALMOND SAUCE
4 Servings

½ pound raw halibut, finely chopped	½ cup cream
	Whites of 2 eggs
1 cup bread crumbs	¼ teaspoon salt

Make a paste of the cream and the bread crumbs and cook it. When it is hot add the chopped fish. Remove this mixture from the fire and when it is cool fold into it the whites of the eggs, which have been combined with the salt and whipped to a stiff froth. Place the soufflé in a buttered baking dish, set it in a pan of hot water and bake it in a moderate oven for 45 minutes.

Almond Sauce:

⅓ cup almonds	1 cup cream or top milk
1 tablespoon butter	¼ teaspoon salt
1 tablespoon flour	⅛ teaspoon paprika

Blanch and shred the almonds and brown them in the butter. Combine the flour and the cream and place them with the almonds and butter in a double boiler. Add the seasoning and cook the sauce until it thickens.

CHICKEN SOUFFLÉ
16 Servings

We use the following soufflé so frequently as a company dish that I am giving it as I first "composed" it. Since, it has gone through endless variations. In a modified form it is now our regular follow-up dish to any chicken dinner (provided the partakers thereof have not been too hungry):

3 cups heavy cream sauce	fowl)
(½ cup chicken fat	1 cup nut meats, chopped
½ cup flour	1 cup cooked vegetables,
3 cups chicken stock and cream or milk)	chopped
	9 eggs, separated
2½ cups boiled chicken minced (a 3½ pound	Salt, paprika, nutmeg

85

Follow the Rule for Soufflé. Serve the soufflé with cream sauce, to which chopped parsley and capers have been added, or with mushroom sauce. This recipe has more body than any of the others given. Its proportions may be varied.

FOLLOW-UP CHICKEN SOUFFLÉ
5 Servings

1 cup heavy cream sauce
(3 tablespoons chicken
fat or butter, 3 table-
spoons flour, 1 cup chicken
gravy, stock or milk)

1 cup solids—minced
chicken, nuts and cooked
or raw vegetables
Seasoning

Follow the Rule for Soufflé.

MUSHROOM SOUFFLÉ WITH SWEETBREADS OR CHICKEN
6 Servings

2 tablespoons butter
1 slice onion
1½ cups mushroom caps,
   finely chopped
1 pair sweet breads—par-
   boiled and finely chopped
   or 1 cup minced chicken

1 cup cream sauce
(2½ tablespoons butter
2½ tablespoons flour
1 cup liquid)
¼ cup stale bread crumbs
1 pimento, chopped
½ teaspoon salt
Yolks of 2 eggs
Whites of 2 eggs

Sauté the onion in the butter for 5 minutes, then remove it from the pan. Add the mushroom caps and the sweetbreads to the butter. Heat the cream sauce to the boiling point and combine it with the mushroom mixture. Add the bread crumbs, the pimento, the salt and the egg yolks. Cook these ingredients for one minute, stirring them constantly, then cool the mixture. Whip the egg whites to a stiff froth and fold them lightly into the combined ingredients. Place the soufflé in buttered timbal molds, (or in a buttered baking dish,) set them in a pan of hot water and bake them in a moderate oven 325° (covered with a piece of buttered paper) for 15 minutes. Invert the contents of the molds onto a platter and surround them with

Mushroom Sauce

5 large mushroom caps,
   sliced
3 tablespoons butter
2 tablespoons flour

1 cup chicken stock (or
   canned chicken soup)
⅓ cup cream

Slice the mushrooms and sauté them in the butter for 5 minutes. Dredge them with the flour, add the hot cream and the hot stock and cook them for 2 minutes. Season the sauce with salt and paprika.

VEAL SOUFFLÉ (STEAMED)
10 Servings

The following is an inexpensive, good soufflé:

1½ pounds ground veal	1 tablespoon butter
½ pound pork	1 tablespoon onion juice
1½ cups cracker crumbs, finely rolled	1¼ teaspoons salt
3 egg yolks	¼ teaspoon pepper
¾ cup milk	¼ cup chopped celery
¼ teaspoon nutmeg	⅛ cup chopped parsley

Combine these ingredients and fold in the whites of 3 eggs, stiffly beaten. Grease a pudding mold, fill it with the soufflé mixture, close it tightly and steam the soufflé for 2½ hours. See Rule Page 309. Serve it with mushroom sauce and capers, or with Allemande sauce. See Veal Loaf—Page 136.

RING MOLD SOUFFLÉS

The recipes given in the Chapter on Soufflés may all be used for ring molds (or for any other mold, with the intention of inverting the contents onto a platter) by greasing the mold and baking the soufflé with the mold set in a dish of hot water. When the soufflé is firm, run a knife around the edges and invert the mold. Fill the center of the soufflé with creamed meat, fish or vegetables.

SPINACH RING WITH MUSHROOMS, ETC.
5 Servings

1 cup of cooked spinach	½ cup cream or canned milk
1 tablespoon chopped onion	
3 tablespoons butter	3 eggs, separated
3 tablespoons flour	Paprika, nutmeg, salt
½ cup of milk or stock	Green coloring

Prepare and cook the spinach—Page 107. Chop it until it is very fine. Melt the butter, add the onion, cook it for 1 minute and add the flour and the milk. When these ingredients are smooth and boiling, add the spinach. Beat the egg yolks, reduce the heat and add them to the sauce. Cook this mixture for a minute or two to permit the yolks to thicken slightly. Season it well and cool it. Add a little green coloring to improve the looks of the soufflé. Beat the egg whites to a stiff froth and fold them into the spinach mixture. Bake the soufflé and serve it filled with creamed or sautéd mushrooms, with chicken à la King, or some other creamed dish.

CANNED SPINACH RING
5 Servings

This isn't one bit exciting, but as an emergency dish it is to be recommended.

1½ cups canned spinach
1⅓ slices bread 1 inch thick
  (about 2 cups of bread
  very loosely packed)

2 eggs, separated
Salt, paprika, nutmeg,
  green coloring

Soak the bread in water. Squeeze the water from it and break up the bread with a fork. Combine it with the chopped spinach, the yolks, the seasoning and a little green coloring to improve the looks of the soufflé. Beat the egg whites until they are stiff and fold them into the spinach mixture. Fill a well greased ring mold, set it in a pan of hot water and bake the soufflé in a moderate oven (325°) until it is firm.

CARROT SOUFFLÉ AND PEAS
5 Servings

½ cup cooked mashed
  carrots
½ cup finely chopped
  celery
1 cup heavy cream sauce

3 eggs, separated
Salt
Paprika
Celery salt or nutmeg

Follow the Rule for Soufflé. Fill the center of the soufflé with fresh or canned buttered peas, garnished with chopped parsley, to which sautéd mushrooms may be added.

Fish

BOILED FISH

Boil enough water to cover the fish. Add 1 tablespoon vinegar, 1 small onion, 2 ribs of celery with leaves, and 1 teaspoon salt. Immerse the fish and simmer it until it is tender (12 minutes to the pound.) Do not permit the fish to boil at any time, as that robs it of its delicate flavor. Drain it well and place it on a platter garnished with half slices of lemon that have been dipped in chopped parsley and with sprigs of parsley. Serve it with melted butter or with cream sauce and capers.

BAKED FISH

Cut gashes in the sides of a fish and put bacon in them. Rub the fish with salt and butter and dredge it with flour. Place it in a shallow pan with butter and bacon drippings. Baste it frequently with a mixture of butter and hot water. Bake the fish in a moderate oven 375° allowing 15 minutes to the pound. The fish may be stuffed with a dressing made of:

2 cups bread crumbs	2 tablespoons parsley
2 tablespoons onion, chopped	1 or 2 eggs beaten
	Melted butter or top milk
½ cup celery, chopped	Salt, paprika

Use enough milk or butter to make a loose dressing and season it well. Fill the fish and sew its sides together with a coarse needle and thread. Serve the fish on a platter garnished with slices of lemon and sprigs of parsley and surround it with Tomatoes Stuffed with Mashed Potatoes—Page 67. The drippings may be strained, thickened with flour and seasoned with Worcestershire sauce or lemon.

BAKED FISH WITH CHEESE

3 pounds of fish
1½ cups cracker or bread
crumbs
½ cup mushrooms (canned
or fresh, sautéd)
1 teaspoon chopped onion
¼ cup shredded green

pepper
1 egg
¼ cup melted butter
1 teaspoon salt
¼ teaspoon paprika
4 tablespoons grated cheese
Stock, or melted butter

Season the fish with salt and pepper. Make a dressing of the crumbs, mushrooms, onion, green pepper, egg, melted butter, salt and paprika. Stuff the fish and sew it up with a coarse needle and thread. Roll it in the grated cheese, or spread it with snappy cheese. Bake it in a pan lined with heavy waxed paper in a moderate oven 375° — allowing 15 minutes to the pound. Baste it, if necessary, with a little stock, or melted butter and hot water. Serve it with Hollandaise Sauce.

PLANKED FISH

Clean the fish and remove the entrails. Split the fish, place it on its back and remove the bones. This can be done by making incisions in the inside of the fish along the backbone and scraping the meat from the bones with the back of a knife. The backbone and the rib bones may then be removed in one piece. Go over the fish carefully and remove the smaller bones. Place the fish, skin side down on a plank of hickory, oak or ash. Sprinkle it lightly with salt and paprika and pour ½ cup of melted butter over it and 1 cup of corn flakes, rolled. Place the fish in a moderate oven 375°. Allow 15 minutes to the pound and brown it for about the last 5 minutes under a broiler.

BROILED FISH

Prepare a fish as for Planked Fish. Place a piece of heavy wax paper in a pan and put the fish flat upon it, skin side down. Season it with salt, dredge it with flour or with cracker crumbs. Dot it with butter and sprinkle it well with paprika. Cook it on the upper grate of a hot oven 425° from 20 minutes to ½ hour.

FRIED FISH
(Sautéd)

Dry the fish well and roll it in flour to which salt and paprika have been added. Melt butter or bacon drippings in a hot skillet. Turn the fish in this over a hot fire, reduce the heat slightly and cook it until it is tender (dependent upon the thickness of the fish) from three to five minutes. If the fish is large cut it into pieces.

SHAD ROE

Cover Shad Roe with boiling water, add ½ tablespoon of vinegar and simmer it for 15 minutes. Drain it, cover it with cold water and permit it to stand for 5 minutes. Drain it, place it in a buttered pan, cover it with ¾ cup of tomato sauce — Page 157 and bake it in a hot oven for 20 minutes, basting it every 5 minutes. Serve it with Tomato Sauce.

STEAMED FISH PUDDING
6 Servings

This is a delicious way of preparing a left-over fish. For three people reduce the amount by one-half, and boil the pudding in a large baking powder can:

2 cups flaked fish, or 1 pound canned salmon	¾ cup bread crumbs
	3 egg yolks
4 tablespoons melted butter, or 4 tablespoons cream	2 teaspoons lemon juice
	Seasoning

Combine these ingredients and fold in 3 stiffly beaten egg whites. Steam the pudding in a mold for one hour — Page 309, or bake it until it is firm in a slow oven, putting the baking dish in a pan of hot water. Serve it with cream sauce, to which Worcestershire sauce has been added, or with Mustard Sauce.

See Halibut Soufflé — Page 85.

BROILED OR BAKED LOBSTER

Clean and split a lobster and remove the intestines. It may be broiled, or baked, the result being much the same.

To broil: Glaze it with olive oil, broil it under a hot flame for 8 minutes on the flesh side, turn it and broil it for 6 minutes on the shell side. Season it with salt and cayenne and dot it generously with butter.

To bake: Place the lobster in a spider in a hot oven. Baste it frequently with butter and season it when it is done with salt and cayenne.

CANNED FISH

Salmon, crab and tuna fish make good aspics, salads, sandwich fillings and creamed dishes.

For "Mock Chicken" — place the contents of a can of tuna fish in a colander and pour two cups of boiling water over it.

There are creamed fish recipes to be found in the Chapter on Egg and Luncheon Dishes, and it is fun to concoct new ones. Put cooked or canned fish into boiling cream sauce and serve it at once. If you wish to keep creamed fish hot or to reheat it, put it in a saucepan set in boiling water. This will keep it from being unpleasantly "fishy." Worcestershire sauce, lemon, capers and pickles are good additions to fish dishes.

See Index for Creamed Crabmeat, Tuna, Salmon or Shrimp in Ramekins and other fish dishes.

Vegetables

There are as many opinions about the best way to cook vegetables as there are cooks, but, as in contract bridge, a few general rules have been evolved, which it seems safe to follow.

I. Wash vegetables, but do not soak them in water for any length of time. If they are wilted, place them in water for a few minutes. Have a large container with a lid on hand for the purpose of keeping vegetables fresh. Fit a rack into it and keep a half inch or more of water in the bottom. Place the vegetables on the rack, cover the container and put it in the refrigerator.

The exceptions to this rule are cauliflower, artichokes, Brussels sprouts and broccoli. These vegetables must be soaked in water for small insects and dust settle in them and they cannot well be cleaned otherwise.

II. Boil vegetables, closely covered, in as little water as possible, so that when they are tender they will have absorbed all the moisture in the pan. Add a small quantity of boiling water, if necessary, to keep them from scorching. This method will keep their mineral salts and vitamins from escaping.

The exceptions are: cabbage, cauliflower, kohlrabi, onions, Brussels sprouts. These vegetables are cooked uncovered in a quantity of boiling, salted water — 1½ teaspoons to the quart.

Broccoli is cooked uncovered in boiling, salted water that barely covers it.

Green Corn is cooked covered in a quantity of boiling, salted water.

NOTE: The strong odor of the first six vegetables may be lessened if a crust of bread is laid on top of them as soon as they are placed in the boiling water.

Drop the vegetables gradually into rapidly boiling salted water so that the boiling point is maintained. Rapid boiling will help to retain their color. The use of soda is to be avoided. It will help retain the color of vegetables, but it will destroy their vitamins.

III. Cook vegetables as short a time as possible. As soon as they are barely tender, drain them at once. If they are served with melted (drawn) butter, allow about 1 tablespoon of butter to a cup of vegetables. If they are served with cream sauce, allow ½ to 1 cup of cream sauce to 2 cups of vegetables.

A steamer is a closed kettle with a perforated tray and a water container. Vegetables cooked by this method are delicious and their full flavor and food value is retained.

There are heavy covered saucepans on the market, in which vegetables are cooked in a very little water—the so-called Waterless Cookers. Good results are obtained by this method.

Excellent results are obtained by cooking vegetables in parchment.

There are a number of papers on the market that are sold in large sheets with directions for use.

A sheet is spread on the table and sprinkled like laundry—prepared vegetables are placed upon it and salt, pepper or paprika, cream or butter are added. The edges of the paper are gathered up into a bag which is tied tightly and the corners are turned back to prevent steam or water from entering the bag. It is then placed in a pan of boiling water and when the vegetable is tender it is taken from the bag ready to be served. This process takes a little longer than when vegetables are cooked in an open or closed saucepan.

Stewed fruit may be cooked in the same way. The paper may be washed, dried and used repeatedly.

Several bags containing food may be placed in the same pan of water. Cooking in paper has the great advantage of doing away with the scouring of pots.

It is impossible to tell exactly how long a vegetable must be cooked in order to be palatable—the age and the size of the vegetable being determining factors.

The following chart, given me by a teacher of Domestic Science, is a good guide for cooking vegetables. You may differ about some of the amounts of water and the length of cooking—(I do) but that is the privilege of the experienced cook:

Table for boiling vegetables in portions which yield four servings — approximately two cups when cooked.

Vegetable	Measure of Water	Time to Cook
Asparagus	5 Cups	Tips 5 to 10 min. Butts 20 to 25 min.
Beans, green	4 Cups	30 to 35 min.
Beets, young	4 Cups	40 to 60 min.
Brussels sprouts	5 Cups	9 to 10 min.
Cabbage, green	8 Cups	6 to 8 min.
Cabbage, white	5 Cups	8 to 9 min.
Cabbage, red	4½ Cups	20 to 25 min.
Carrots, young	3 Cups	20 to 25 min.
Carrots, old	3 cups	30 to 40 min.
Cauliflower	6½ Cups	8 to 10 min.
Onions, white	9 Cups	25 to 35 min.
Onions, yellow	9 Cups	20 to 25 min.
Parsnips	3 Cups	25 to 30 min.
Peas, shelled	3 Cups	20 to 30 min.
Potatoes, Irish	4 Cups	25 to 30 min.
Potatoes, sweet	3 Cups	15 to 25 min.
Rutabagas	9 Cups	25 to 30 min.
Spinach, stems removed	5 Cups	4 to 5 min.
Squash	4 Cups	20 min.
Turnips, white	8 Cups	20 to 25 min.

When serving vegetables with melted butter, allow 1 tablespoon of butter to 1 cup of vegetables.

When serving vegetables with cream sauce, allow approximately one-half as much sauce as there are vegetables.

To butter crumbs, allow 1/3 cup of melted butter to 1 cup of crumbs.

Potatoes

In recent years the mania for girth control has played havoc with the fair name of the potato — bringing "insinuendoes" against it that are almost as damaging as the charges brought against the erstwhile virtue of bread.

Time was when this highly respectable vegetable was held in great repute. Those who have visited Hirschhorn in the sweetly romantic Neckar Valley and who have climbed the hill to the partly ruined castle that dominates the little village, will remember being confronted by a "Potato Monument" dedicated piously "To God and Francis Drake, who brought to

Europe for the everlasting benefit of the poor—the Potato".
Please don't say that Sir Walter Raleigh or Governor Lane imported the potato, for it really doesn't matter, does it?

BOILED POTATOES

Pare and soak potatoes in cold water for $1/2$ hour in the autumn and from 1 to 2 hours in the winter and spring. Drain them and cook them uncovered in boiling salted water to cover until they are soft (about 25 minutes.) Allow 1 teaspoon salt to 6 or 7 potatoes. When they are done, drain them well and keep them only partially covered (permitting the steam to escape) until ready to serve them or place the potatoes in a light saucepan and shake them gently over a good fire for a minute or two. This will dry them and make them mealy. Avoid putting them in a covered dish if you wish to keep the potatoes dry.

NEW POTATOES

Place new potatoes in their jackets in boiling water to cover, (or soak them for 30 minutes in cold water, scrape them and drop them in boiling water). Cook them uncovered until they are tender, remove the skins and serve the potatoes with chopped parsley or place the potatoes in a skillet with 2 or more tablespoons of melted butter and shake them gently over a low flame until they are well coated. Serve them sprinkled with chopped parsley.

RICED POTATOES

Put boiled potatoes through a ricer or strainer. Heap them on a dish and pour 2 tablespoons of melted butter over them (optional).

MASHED POTATOES

6 potatoes (medium sized)	1 teaspoon salt
3 tablespoons butter	$1/3$ cup hot milk or cream

Follow the rule for boiled potatoes—Page 96. Mash them with a fork, or put them through a ricer. Add the remaining ingredients and beat them with a fork until they are creamy. The Chapter on Eggs and Luncheon Dishes has a number of recipes that call for cold mashed potatoes.

BROWNED POTATOES

Prepare Boiled Potatoes — cooking them for 15 minutes only. Drain them well. Melt 2 tablespoons of butter and cook and turn the potatoes in it until they are light brown. Season them with salt and bake them in a hot oven 400° until they are crisp and brown. Add more butter if needed. Turn the potatoes to brown them evenly.

SCALLOPED POTATOES I.

Put layers of thinly sliced raw potatoes in a baking dish. Dredge each layer with flour and dot it with butter. Season hot milk and pour it over the potatoes until it can be seen through the top layer. Bake the potatoes in a moderate oven 350° until they are done — about 1¼ hours. The potatoes may be turned while cooking to insure even baking.

SCALLOPED POTATOES II.

4 cups raw thinly sliced potatoes	1½ cups milk
¼ pound cheese, grated	Salt
3 tablespoons flour	Dash of cayenne
3 tablespoons butter	¾ cup shredded green pepper and pimento

Make a cream sauce of the butter, flour, milk and seasoning add the cheese, pepper and pimento. Grease a baking dish and fill it with alternate layers of potatoes and cream sauce. The potatoes may be parboiled, this will shorten the time for baking. Bake the potatoes in a moderate oven 350° (turning the potatoes several times to insure even cooking) until they are done. If raw potatoes are used, it is well to allow two hours for baking.

CHANTILLY POTATOES

The following recipe is reminiscent of the old colored man, who said all he could find that college had done for his children was to put ma on 'lasses and pa on 'taters. Surely this is putting pa on 'taters.

3 cups mashed potatoes	½ cup cream, whipped
½ cup grated cheese	

Season the potatoes well and stack them on a pyrex dish. Cover them with the whipped cream that has been seasoned with salt, a dash of cayenne and combine with the cheese. Place the dish in a hot oven 380° until the cheese is melted and the top is slightly browned.

BAKED POTATOES

Wash the potatoes, dry them and rub the skins with lard. Bake them in a hot oven 380° for 40 minutes. Serve them at once, or puncture the skins so that the steam may escape and prevent the potatoes from becoming soggy.

POTATO BOATS

6 potatoes	Salt
3 tablespoons butter	2 egg whites
3 tablespoons hot milk, or	½ cup grated cheese
cream	Paprika

Follow the rule for Baked Potatoes. Cut them in halves and scoop out the centers. Add the butter and the cream to the hot potato pulp, season it well with salt and beat it with a fork. Whip the eggs to a stiff froth and fold them in. Fill the potato shells and sprinkle the cheese and paprika on top (or the cheese may be combined with the potato pulp before the eggs are folded in). Place the potatoes on the middle rack of a broiler and heat them until the cheese melts.

For other Baked Potato recipes see Index.

FRENCH FRIED POTATOES

Peel potatoes and cut them into long strips ¼ inch thick. Soak them in cold, salted water for 1 hour. Drain them and dry them well between cloths. Fry them in deep fat heated to 395° until they are a golden brown (about 4½ minutes.) Drain them on paper, sprinkle them with salt and serve them very hot.

FRIED POTATO PUFFS

2 cups hot mashed	1 teaspoon baking powder
potatoes	¼ teaspoon salt
2 eggs	Paprika

Combine the ingredients in the order given. Beat them well and drop them by the teaspoonful into hot fat. Cook the puffs until they are brown and place them on paper to drain. Serve them while they are hot, or reheat them in a hot oven.

See Index for Potato Cheese Puffs.

PEAR POTATOES

6 medium sized potatoes	1 egg yolk
¼ cup butter	6 whole cloves
¼ cup hot milk, or cream	Paprika
1 teaspoon salt	

Follow the rule for boiled potatoes—Page 96. Drain the potatoes, mash them, add the butter, hot milk and salt and beat them with a fork until they are smooth and fluffy. Divide them into 6 parts. Roll them into pear shape, brush them with the yolk of an egg and dust one cheek with paprika. Stick a clove in the blossom end and a bit of stem in the other. Place them in an oiled pan in a good oven 375° until they are hot. These potatoes may be prepared in advance.

SLICED POTATO PIE

6 medium sized potatoes	Paprika
2 tablespoons butter	Butter
Salt	

Peel the potatoes and cut them in very thin slices. Soak them in cold water for two hours, placing them in the refrigerator. Dry them well between towels. Heat a skillet, add 2 tablespoons butter and when it is hot add ½ of the potatoes. Dot them with butter and season them, then add the second half and repeat the process. Do not stir them at any time. Cook them over a high flame until the potatoes are brown on the bottom — about 10 minutes. Then cover them and cook them over a low flame until the potatoes are done—½ to ¾ hour. Dot the top with butter and brown the potatoes under a broiler for 15 minutes. Slice them like pie and serve them.

Uses for Cold Boiled Potatoes

CREAMED POTATOES

Cut cold boiled potatoes into dice. Prepare one-half as much cream sauce as there are potatoes and combine them. Place them in a double boiler for ½ hour, or put them in a baking dish, cover the top with bread crumbs, dot them with butter and bake them in a moderate oven until the crumbs are brown. Chopped parsley may be added to the cream sauce.

CREAMED POTATOES WITH CHEESE
Au Gratin

Follow the rule for creamed potatoes, adding paprika, or a dash of cayenne to the cream sauce and omitting the parsley

Place alternate layers of potatoes and cream sauce in a baking dish, sprinkling each layer with grated cheese. Cover the top with bread crumbs and cheese and bake the potatoes in a moderate oven until the cheese is melted.

LEFT-OVER POTATOES
O'Brien

6 boiled potatoes diced	(optional)
1 green pepper, chopped	Salt, paprika
1 onion, chopped	A dash of cayenne
1 tablespoon flour	Breadcrumbs
1 cup rich milk	Butter
¾ cup grated cheese	

Combine the first three ingredients, sprinkle them with salt, paprika and flour and add the cheese, if desired. Place them in a greased baking dish and pour the milk over them. Cover them with bread crumbs, dotted with butter, and bake them in a moderate oven 350° for 15 minutes.

SAUTÉD POTATOES

2 tablespoons (or more) of fat	Cold potatoes, sliced Seasoning

Heat the fat, add the potatoes and the seasoning and sauté them, turning them frequently until they are light brown.

HASHED BROWN POTATOES

¼ cup of fat (Salt pork, bacon grease, or other shortening)	2 cups boiled potatoes, finely chopped Salt, pepper

Melt the fat in a small skillet, add the potatoes and the seasoning and mix them well, stirring them for two or three minutes. Press them with a broad knife into a cake. Cook them until they are browned underneath, then loosen them from the bottom with a knife and invert them onto a plate or lid. Replace them in the skillet with the uncooked side down. Brown this side, turn the potatoes onto a platter and serve them at once.

POTATO CAKES

Shape cold mashed potatoes into little cakes. Roll them in flour (this is optional). Melt butter in a skillet. When it is hot put in the cakes, brown one side, reverse them and brown the other side. A little chopped celery or parsley may be added before shaping the potatoes.

BAKED MASHED POTATOES

1½ cups mashed potatoes   ¾ cup milk or cream
2 tablespoons butter   Salt, paprika
1 egg

Combine the ingredients in the order given, beat them well and place them in a greased baking dish. Bake them in a quick oven 380° until they are brown. If cold potatoes are used, heat the milk.

MASHED POTATO PUFFS

2 cups well seasoned   2 egg yolks
    mashed potatoes   2 egg whites

Combine the potatoes and the yolks and beat them well. Fold in the stiffly beaten egg whites and bake the puffs in lightly greased gem pans—or in a baking dish, in a moderate oven—350°—until the potatoes are brown.

BOILED SWEET POTATOES

Sweet potatoes may be boiled and served in their jackets, or they may be peeled and cooked in boiling water to cover until they are done. Add salt to the water, 1½ teaspoons to the quart.

BAKED SWEET POTATOES

Prepare and bake them like white potatoes, Page 98.

STUFFED SWEET POTATOES

6 sweet potatoes   (optional)
2 tablespoons butter   Bread crumbs and butter,
¼ cup hot cream or milk   or marshmallows
Salt   (optional)
1 tablespoon Sherry

Bake the potatoes, cut them lengthwise in halves and scoop out the pulp. Add the butter, cream, salt and Sherry, and beat these ingredients with a fork until they are fluffy. Fill the shells, cover the tops with crumbs dotted with butter, or with marshmallows. Bake the potatoes in a moderate oven 375° until they are brown, or reheat them under a broiler.

CANDIED SWEET POTATOES

6 sweet potatoes
¾ cup brown sugar
½ lemon, rind and juice

2 tablespoons butter
Salt, paprika

Cook the potatoes until they are nearly tender. Peel them and slice them in ½ inch lengthwise slices. Place them in a shallow greased pan, season them, sprinkle them with brown sugar, lemon rind and juice and dot them with butter. Bake them in a good oven 375° for 20 minutes.

MASHED SWEET POTATOES

Peel and boil 6 sweet potatoes. Put them through a ricer and add 1 tablespoon of butter to every cup of potatoes. Add ½ teaspoon of salt and moisten them with a little hot milk or cream. Beat them with a fork until they are light.

SWEET POTATO PUDDING, OR CARAMEL SWEET POTATOES
6 to 8 Servings

12 medium sized sweet potatoes
3 tablespoons butter
½ cup brown sugar

¼ cup black walnut or other nut meats (broken)
½ teaspoon salt

Peel the sweet potatoes, drop them into boiling salted water to cover, cook them until they are tender and put them through a ricer. Place the butter and the sugar in an iron skillet and when the sugar is dissolved add the nuts, the salt and the riced potatoes. Place these ingredients in a greased baking dish, cover the top with marshmallows (optional) and bake the pudding in a moderate oven — 375° — for about 15 minutes.

SWEET POTATO PUFFS
Baked in mounds or in ramekins.

This is a good way of utilizing left over sweet potatoes. Serve them to people who like pumpkin, for they are not unlike pumpkin pie filling.

4 medium sized sweet potatoes (about 2 cups)
1 large ripe banana
1½ teaspoons salt
1½ tablespoons butter

⅛ teaspoon nutmeg
⅓ teaspoon paprika
1 egg yolk
Hot milk or cream
1 egg white beaten

Boil the potatoes in their jackets. Peel and rice them. Rice the banana and combine all the ingredients except the egg white.

Beat them, using sufficient hot milk or cream to make the batter fluffy. Fold in the egg white. Place the mixture by the tablespoonful well apart in a greased pan. Bake the puffs in a hot oven 500° for 12 minutes.

See Index for Sweet Potatoes, Bacon and Pineapple.

SWEET POTATOES AND APPLES

The following is an exceptionally good dish, especially with pork roast, baked ham or a game course:

2 cups sweet potatoes— boiled until nearly done and cut into 1/4 inch slices	4 tablespoons butter
	Salt
	1/2 cup brown sugar (or more)
1 1/2 cups thinly sliced apples parboiled in a very little water	1/2 cup apple water, or water

Put the potatoes and the apples in layers in a baking dish. Sprinkle the layers with sugar, dot them with butter and pour the water over them. Bake them in a moderate oven for 1 hour. If the apples are not tart, sprinkle them with lemon juice.

SOUTHERN SWEET POTATO PUDDING

This unusual recipe is given in its original form. As the amount of sugar seems excessive, it may be cut to one half, or one-fourth of the measurement.

3 cups raw grated sweet potatoes	2 cups sugar (?)
	1 teaspoon allspice
1 egg beaten	

Combine these ingredients and place them in a well greased baking dish. Cook the pudding in a moderate oven 375°. When the top is browned, stir the pudding. Repeat this three or four times until the pudding is done (about 30 minutes), permitting the top to brown before serving it.

SWEET POTATO BALLS

Prepare mashed sweet potatoes—Page 102. Form potato balls around marshmallows, dip them in a beaten egg diluted with 1 tablespoon of water, then roll them in corn flakes. Fry them in deep fat—Page 200.

BOILED CAULIFLOWER

Cut off the stem, remove the leaves and soak the cauliflower in cold water, head down, for 30 minutes. Cook it, head up and uncovered in a quantity of boiling salted water (1½ tea-spoons to the quart) until it is tender. Drain it well. Pour 3 tablespoons of melted butter over it. (2 tablespoons of bread crumbs may be sautéd in the butter), or pour 1 cup of boiling cream sauce over it, to which ⅛ teaspoon of nutmeg has been added.

SCALLOPED CAULIFLOWER

Prepare boiled cauliflower. Drain it well. Separate the flowerets. Place them in a greased baking dish. Pour 1 cup of boiling cream sauce seasoned with nutmeg over them, cover the top with bread crumbs and dot them with butter. Brown the cauliflower in a hot oven 450° or place it under a broiler to brown.

CAULIFLOWER AND CHEESE

Place boiled cauliflower whole or separated in a greased baker —sprinkle it generously with grated cheese and place it in a moderate oven 450° until the cheese is melted. Pour 1 cup of boiling cream sauce around it and serve it at once.

The cream sauce may be made with stock instead of milk. It may be poured around the cauliflower before it is placed in the oven.

CAULIFLOWER AND EGG SAUCE

Prepare boiled cauliflower. Drain it well and separate the flowerets. Pour the following sauce over them:

2 egg yolks, beaten	⅛ teaspoon nutmeg
¼ cup cream	1 tablespoon lemon juice
½ teaspoon salt	2 tablespoons butter

Cook the first five ingredients in a double boiler. When they are thick, add the butter, a very little at a time. Pour the sauce over the cauliflower at once and serve it.

BROCCOLI

Soak Broccoli for 15 minutes in cold water. Drain it well, trim the stems and the large leaves, and tie it in bunches. Drop it in a pan of boiling salted water (1½ teaspoons to the quart) so that it is nearly immersed, and cook it uncovered until it is tender. Drain it and serve it with melted butter, or with lemon juice sprinkled over it.

BRUSSELS SPROUTS

Pull the outer leaves from the sprouts, if wilted, and cut off the stems. Soak the sprouts for 12 minutes in cold water to which a little salt has been added. Drain them and drop them into rapidly boiling salted water and cook them uncovered until they are barely tender. Drain them and serve them with melted butter or with cream sauce.

BOILED CABBAGE

The old way of cooking cabbage is to cut it in sections and boil it from 1/2 to 1 hour. The new way is to shred it finely and to barely cook it, allowing only 7 to 8 minutes boiling. Remove the outer leaves from a head of cabbage. Cut it into sections, remove the tough core and shred or chop the cabbage. Drop it into a quantity of rapidly boiling salted water (1½ teaspoons to the quart), cook and drain it. Pour melted butter over it, (about 1 tablespoon of butter to 1 cup of cabbage) and serve it. Bread crumbs may be added to the butter.

CREAMED CABBAGE

| 1 small cabbage | Grated cheese, or butter |
| 1½ cups cream sauce | Bread crumbs |

Prepare Boiled Cabbage — Page 105. Drain it well and combine it with the boiling cream sauce to which grated cheese may be added; or drain boiled cabbage well and place it in layers in a baking dish. Sprinkle the layers with grated cheese, season them with salt and pepper and pour the boiling cream sauce over them. Cover the top with bread crumbs, dot it with butter or sprinkle it with cheese. Bake the cabbage in a hot oven — 450° — until the crumbs are brown.

BAKED CABBAGE

Prepare finely shredded Boiled Cabbage — Page 105. Drain it well.

Combine:

| 2 eggs | ½ cup cream or milk |
| 1 tablespoon melted butter | Salt, paprika |

Pour this over the cabbage and bake it in a greased dish in a slow oven 325° until it is light brown. The top may be covered with bread crumbs, dotted with butter, or sprinkled with cheese.

RED CABBAGE

3 slices of bacon (or 2
  tablespoons other fat)
1 medium sized red
  cabbage
1/4 teaspoon salt, if bacon
  is used, or 1 teaspoon salt,
  if not

1 apple, thinly sliced
2 tablespoons flour
1/8 cup boiling water
3/4 cup vinegar
1 teaspoon sugar

Pull the outer leaves from the cabbage. Cut it into sections, remove the hard core and shred the cabbage. Cut the bacon into small pieces, put it into a stew pan and try it out over a low flame. When it is well melted, remove the hard scraps of bacon and put in the cabbage, which has been washed and is slightly moist. Cover it and let it simmer for 10 minutes, add the salt, the apple and a very little boiling water—just enough to keep the cabbage from scorching, cover it and let it simmer about 1½ hours. Ten minutes before it is done, add the flour dissolved in water and the vinegar and sugar. Simmer it for 10 minutes and serve it.

STUFFED CABBAGE
Gefuellter Krautskopf

1 medium sized head of
  cabbage
Meat dressing:
  1/2 lb. pork, ground
  1/2 lb. beef, ground
  1/2 lb. veal, ground

1 slice of bread 1 inch thick
3 eggs beaten
Salt, pepper

Soak the bread in water for 2 minutes, then press the water from it and combine it with the other ingredients. Season them highly. Separate the leaves of a head of cabbage and parboil them uncovered in a quantity of boiling salted water (1½ teaspoons of salt to the quart). Drain them well, keeping the liquor. Line a bowl with a large clean cloth and fill it with alternate layers of the leaves and the meat dressing. Cover the top with one or two large leaves, gather up the cloth and tie it with a string. Place the bag in boiling water to cover (the water in which the cabbage was boiled, and as much fresh boiling water as needed). Boil the cabbage gently for 2 hours. Drain it on a colander, untie the bag and place the cabbage in a hot serving dish. Serve it with:

Onion Sauce:

4 tablespoons butter	2 cups stock or cabbage
2 tablespoons flour	water
½ cup chopped onions, or	Seasoning
more	

Brown the butter, add the flour and brown it, add the seasoning, the onions and a little of the stock. Cook the onions in a covered double boiler until they are tender, adding the stock gradually. The gravy is best when it is thick with onions.

KOHLRABI

Wash the kohlrabi. Cut off the tops and pare the roots. Slice the roots, drop them into a quantity of rapidly boiling, salted water and cook them until they are barely tender, then drain them well. Boil the tops separately, in the same manner. Drain them well, chop them until they are very fine and combine them with the roots. Prepare a sauce with the following ingredients:

2 tablespoons butter	1 cup stock or kohlrabi
2 tablespoons flour	water

Cook this for 1 minute, add the kohlrabi and serve them.

CREAMED SPINACH

This delicious European way of preparing spinach is highly recommended.

½ peck of spinach (2 lbs.)	1 cup cream, milk or stock
after cooking 1⅓ to 1½	1 tablespoon chopped onion
cups	(optional)
3 tablespoons butter	Salt, paprika, nutmeg
2½ tablespoons flour	

The French recipes call for 1 teaspoon of powdered sugar and the grated rind of ½ a lemon. These ingredients and the onion are optional. The flour is sometimes browned before using it. Canned milk (undiluted) is delicious in spinach. Stock or milk may be substituted for cream, or they may be used in combination. Wash the spinach in several waters and cut off the roots. If spinach is old, use only the leaves. Boil old spinach in 1 quart of salted water for 20 minutes, or until it is tender. 1/3 teaspoon of soda may be added to improve its color. Place young spinach, wet, but without additional water, in a covered saucepan and cook it for six minutes, or until it is tender. Drain it well and put it through a ricer, or chop the spinach, old or young, until it is as fine as puree, using a board and a knife, or a chopping bowl and a knife. Put the butter in a skillet, add the onion and cook it for 1 minute, add the flour and the hot cream and cook these ingredients until they are smooth. Add the spinach and stir and cook it for three minutes, or until it is thoroughly blended with the sauce. If the spinach seems too thick, add additional cream or milk. Season it well with salt, paprika and nutmeg, and serve it garnished with slices of hard cooked egg.

See Spinach Ring — Page 87 and Spinach Soufflé Page 82.

SWISS CHARD

Follow the recipe for Creamed Spinach — Page 107.

ASPARAGUS

Wash the asparagus, dry it and cut off the hard part of the stems. Skin the lower ends of the stalks with downward strokes of a knife and tie the asparagus in bunches. Place them upright in a deep stew pan, the lower ends in boiling salted water, and cook them covered — the steam will cook the tips, (time for cooking about 15 minutes); or, place the asparagus in a small amount of boiling salted water, keeping the tips out for the first 10 minutes, immersing them for the last five. Drain the asparagus well and serve it with melted butter and bread crumbs, with cream sauce, or with Egg Sauce — Page 104. The ends, the scrapings and the asparagus water may be used for soup — Page 20 and Page 24.

BOILED CARROTS
Buttered

Carrots may be boiled peeled, or unpeeled. They may be cut into slices, into dice, or if small, they may be served whole. Wash and scrape carrots, or merely wash them. Place them in a small quantity of boiling, salted water and cook them covered until they are tender, permitting them to absorb the water in which they are cooked. If necessary add a small quantity of boiling water. Skin the carrots, if they have been cooked in their jackets. Serve the carrots with melted butter (1 tablespoon to 1 cup of carrots), or with cream sauce ($\frac{2}{3}$ cup sauce to 2 cups carrots.)

BOILED CARROTS
Slightly Thickened

cup boiled carrots	2 tablespoons hot stock, or
tablespoon butter	water
½ tablespoon flour	

Place the butter in a saucepan and melt it. Add the carrots, sprinkle the flour over them and add the stock. Simmer the carrots, stirring them gently for several minutes and serve them.

PARSLEY CARROTS

This is an unusually nice vegetable dish:

6 large carrots	½ teaspoon lemon juice
2 tablespoons butter	2 tablespoons chopped
1 tablespoon chopped onion	parsley
Salt, paprika	

Boil the carrots in their jackets until they are tender. Skin and cut them into very fine slices. Melt the butter, add the onion and sauté it for 1 minute, add the seasoning and the lemon juice. Cook the carrots quickly in the butter and when they are well heated, add the parsley and serve them at once.

CARROTS AND CANNED PEAS

Boiled carrots, sliced or diced, Page 108 may be combined with canned peas (the proportions are unimportant). Drain the vegetables well. Season them with salt and pepper and pour melted butter over them. Chopped parsley may be added just before serving them, or the peas and carrots may be heated in cream sauce and the chopped parsley may be added.

TURNIPS

Wash and peel turnips, cut them into slices or into dice. Drop them into a small quantity of boiling salted water and cook them covered until they are tender. Season them with paprika and serve them with melted butter, or mash them with a fork, season them, add a little melted butter and beat them until they are fluffy. Turnips may be served with cream sauce.

BEETS

Beet greens may be prepared like Spinach—Page 107. Beet roots are usually cooked in their jackets. Leave one inch of stem. Wash the beets and drop them into boiling salted water to cover. Cook them covered. Beets require long cooking, from 1 to 4 hours and must be watched, as it is frequently necessary to add more boiling water to keep them from scorching. When they are tender, skin them, cut them into quarters, season them with salt and pepper and pour melted butter over them.

See Pickled Beets—Page 169.

OYSTER PLANT

Dissolve 1 or 2 tablespoons of flour in water. Scrape and cut oyster plant in one-half inch slices and drop it at once into the water. This will prevent discoloration and the oyster plant may be washed subsequently and will remain white. Drain the oyster plant and cook it covered in a small quantity of boiling salted water until it is tender. Drain it and serve it in cream sauce. Oyster plant may be cooked whole, seasoned, dredged with flour or rolled in bread crumbs and sautéd in hot butter until it is browned.

BEETS À LA KING

5 medium sized beets, cooked—Page 110	1/8 teaspoon paprika
	1/8 teaspoon pepper
1 tablespoon butter	1/2 teaspoon sugar
1 tablespoon flour	3 tablespoons vinegar
1/2 teaspoon salt	3 tablespoons cream

Skin the beets and slice them. Melt the butter, add the flour, the seasoning and the vinegar and cream. When the sauce is thick and smooth pour it over the sliced beets.

GREEN PEAS I.

Peas cooked by this method are delicious.

1 lb. of peas is about 1 cup of peas hulled. Hull the peas and place them in the top of a double boiler. Cover them with large moist lettuce leaves and cook them stirring them once or twice until they are tender. This is a slow process—dependent upon the age of the peas—(about 3/4 hour). Remove the lettuce leaves and add salt, paprika, a bit of cayenne, butter or cream. Sprinkle the peas with chopped parsley before serving them.

GREEN PEAS II. AND CARROTS

Wash and hull the peas and cook them covered in a very small quantity of boiling water. Lettuce leaves may be placed over them. When tender, drain them (if there is any water left) and season them with salt, paprika and sugar, moisten them with butter or cream and combine them with Boiled Carrots, sliced or diced — Page 108. When cooking peas in water a few pods may be added for flavor.

FRESH PEAS AND ONIONS

2 lbs. of fresh peas
Tiny onions, or green onions
  cut in small pieces
2 tablespoons butter, or 4
  tablespoons thick cream

Sugar
Salt
Chopped parsley (optional)

Cook the peas — Page 111 — and the onions — Page 115 — separately and drain them well. There should be 2 cups of vegetables. Melt the butter, pour it over the vegetables and add sugar and salt as desired.

FRESH OR CANNED PEAS AND MUSHROOMS

See Page 124.

CREAMED GREEN PEAS

1½ cups shelled peas (about
  1½ lbs. unhulled)
1 tablespoon butter
1 small onion
1 heart of lettuce

5 or 6 sprigs of parsley
½ teaspoon salt
¼ cup cream
⅛ cup stock from the
  vegetables

Melt the butter, add the vegetables and the salt, and pour enough boiling water over them to cover the bottom of the pan. Cook them over a high flame for 10 minutes. Reduce the heat, cover the pan closely and simmer the vegetables until the peas are tender. Remove the lettuce and the parsley. Drain the peas. Heat the cream and the vegetable stock and pour them over the peas. Serve them at once.

CREAMED GREEN PEAS AND MINT SAUCE

2 cups cooked peas (about
  2 lbs.)

½ cup cream sauce
¼ cup chopped mint

Cook green peas — Page 111. Drain them and serve them with cream sauce to which chopped mint has been added.

STRING BEANS I.

String straight young beans and tie them loosely into small bunches. Cook them (uncovered, if you wish to preserve the color, covered, if you wish to preserve the vitamins) in a small amount of boiling salted water, or cook them in a paper bag — Page 94. When they are tender, drain and untie the beans, placing them crosswise on a platter or dish. Make a broad path down the center of the stack with the following sauce (or serve them with melted butter).

1 tablespoon flour	2 egg yolks
1½ tablespoons butter	1 tablespoon lemon juice
1 cup stock, or milk	Salt, paprika

Melt the butter, add the flour and stir it until it is smooth, add the liquid, and when the sauce is thick and boiling remove it from the fire and beat in the egg yolks. Reduce the heat and return the sauce to the fire for 1 minute. Add the seasoning and the lemon juice. To keep the sauce hot, place it over hot water. Pour the sauce over the beans and serve them at once.

STRING BEANS II.

String the beans and shred them lengthwise. Drop them into a small quantity of boiling salted water. Cook them until they are tender, no longer (about 20 minutes). The addition of an onion gives the beans a fine flavor. Drain the beans and serve them with melted butter, or in cream sauce. Stock may be added to the batter, or to the cream sauce.

LIMA BEANS

Cover lima beans with boiling, lightly salted water. Bring them quickly to the boiling point, then simmer them slowly until they are tender. Drain them and serve them with melted butter.

BAKED BEANS

1½ cup dried beans	2 tablespoons dark molas-
¼ pound salt pork diced	ses, scant
½ onion, minced	2 or 3 tablespoons catsup
Salt, paprika	1 tablespoon dry mustard

Cover the beans well with water and bring them slowly to the boiling point. Drain them, cover them with water and simmer them long and slowly, adding the onion and salt pork. If the beans are very hard, a pinch of soda may be added. When they are tender, drain the beans and combine them with the remaining ingredients. Place them in a greased baker, decorate them with salt pork and bake them covered in a very slow oven for 6 hours. If they become dry, add a little well seasoned stock. Uncover the beans for the last hour of cooking.

STEWED CELERY

Wash the celery, remove the strings from the outer ribs, and cut the stalk into small pieces. Drop the celery gradually into a small quantity of boiling, lightly salted water and cook it covered until it is tender, allowing it, if possible, to absorb the water. If the water is not absorbed, drain the celery. Serve it with melted butter, or drop it into boiling cream sauce for 1 minute. If there is celery water left, it may be used in making the cream sauce, (2 parts celery water and 1 part cream), or it may be used for soup — Page 24.

CELERY AU GRATIN

Prepare Creamed Celery. Place it in a greased baking dish, cover the top with bread crumbs, dotted with butter, or sprinkled with grated cheese and bake it in a good oven 400° until the cheese is melted.

CREAMED CELERY AND GREEN PEPPERS

Prepare stewed celery and drain it. Wash green peppers, cut off the tops and remove the seeds and the veins. Cut the peppers into small pieces and drop them into a small quantity of boiling salted water. Boil them for 15 minutes, or until they are tender, then drain them. Drop the celery and the peppers into seasoned boiling cream sauce. The proportions of the celery, peppers and cream sauce are unimportant. A good combination is 2 cups stewed celery, 1/2 cup stewed peppers, 3/4 cup cream sauce.

BRAISED CELERY

Clean dwarf celery and cut off part of the leaves. Place the stalks in a small quantity of boiling stock, cover them, and simmer them until they are tender. Large stalks may be used, but their leaves must be cut off and the stalks must be quartered. Serve the celery hot on toast with a little of the stock, thickened with flour, serve it with melted butter, or chill the celery and serve it as a salad with French dressing. Canned Bouillon, Savita, or beef cubes may be substituted for stock.

BRAISED LETTUCE

This is a very good "quick" hot vegetable. It is frequently served in France with unthickened meat gravy.

Remove the outer leaves from a head of lettuce, cut the head into quarters and place them in a very small quantity of boiling stock. Cook the lettuce covered for about 8 minutes, in which time most of the liquor should be absorbed. Seasoning and a little melted butter may be added before serving the lettuce. Canned Bouillon, Savita, or beef cubes may be substituted for stock.

BRAISED ENDIVE OR LETTUCE

2 slices bacon or 2 tablespoons butter	3 tablespoons onion, chopped
1 carrot sliced	2 sprigs of parsley
	3 heads of Endive

Place these ingredients in a covered baking dish. Bake them for 10 minutes, add 1 cup of well seasoned stock and bake them until they are done. Thicken the sauce with flour before serving the endive.

ONIONS

To prepare onions: Pour boiling water over onions and permit them to stand for 2 minutes. Drain them and peel them under cold water.

To boil onions: Drop prepared, sliced onions into a quantity of rapidly boiling salted water and cook them uncovered until they are tender. Drain them, season them and serve them with melted butter.

SCALLOPED ONIONS

If onions were costly, surely they would be considered a great delicacy. The following is as good a vegetable dish as I know, (but then, I like onions).

1½ cups diced onions	Bread crumbs
¾ cup cream sauce	Butter or cheese

Prepare boiled onions. Drain them well and place them in the boiling, well seasoned cream sauce. Cook them for 1 minute, then place them in a baking dish (or in ramekins), sprinkle the top with bread crumbs, dot it with butter and place the dish under the broiler to brown. Serve it at once. If prepared in advance, reheat the onions over hot water before placing them in the baker, or ramekins. Grated cheese may be substituted for butter.

SMALL ONIONS BRAISED

Prepare small onions (pickling onions) — Page 114. Pour boiling stock over them to the depth of ½ inch. Cook them covered over a slow fire, permitting them to absorb the liquid. When they are tender, season and serve them. Additional stock may be added as required.

YOUNG GREEN ONIONS

Green onions are best cooked in a very small quantity of boiling, salted water. Boil them covered until they are barely tender. Drain them and pour melted butter over them. Serve them in rows on very thin slices of toast, or cut them into small pieces and serve them combined with other vegetables — peas, beans, new potatoes, etc.

BAKED ONIONS
4 Servings

12 onions	2 tablespoons butter
1 teaspoon salt	Parsley
⅛ teaspoon paprika	Toast
2 teaspoons brown sugar	

Peel the onions and cut them in crosswise halves. Season them and dot them with butter. Place them in a buttered baking dish in a slow oven — 325° — until they are done (about 1 hour). Serve them on thin buttered toast with parsley dipped in lemon juice.

SPANISH ONIONS ROASTED

Prepare Spanish Onions — Page 114 and cut them in three crosswise slices. Place them in a pan, season them with salt and pepper and dot them generously with butter. Add boiling soup stock to the depth of ¼ inch and bake the onions in a moderate oven 350°, basting them frequently until they have absorbed the stock and are tender and brown. Add boiling stock as needed.

GLAZED ONIONS

8 small onions   2 tablespoons sugar
3 tablespoons butter

Prepare small onions—Page 114.   Drain them well.   Prick
them through the center and place them in a small quantity
of boiling, salted water.   Cook them covered until they are
nearly tender, permitting them to absorb the water.   Drain and
dry them on a cloth.   Melt the butter, add the sugar and cook
this syrup for 1 minute.   Add the onions and move them about
until they are well coated.   Cook them for about 15 minutes,
using an asbestos plate toward the end.   Serve the onions with
pork roast.

ONIONS FRENCH FRIED

Prepare onions—Page 114.   Cut them in 1/4 inch slices, soak
them for 1/2 hour in 1/2 cup milk, combined with 1/2 cup water.
Drain the onions, spread them on brown paper and dredge them
with flour.   Season them and fry them until they are light brown
in deep fat heated to 360 to 370 degrees.

ONION RINGS IN BATTER

Prepare large onions—Page 114.   Cut them crosswise in slices.
Break the slices into rings.   Prepare a thin batter:

2 egg yolks   3/4 cup cake flour
1/2 cup milk   1/2 teaspoon salt

Drop the onion rings separately into the batter and fry them
in a kettle of deep fat heated to 395°.   Drain the onions on
brown paper, keeping them hot until ready to serve them.

See Index for other onion dishes.

STEWED TOMATOES

Wash tomatoes and cover them for 1 minute with boiling
water.   Skin them, cut them into quarters and place them in a
stew pan over a slow fire for 20 minutes.   Stir them occasional-
ly to keep them from scorching.   Season them with salt and
paprika, add a little white or brown sugar, if desired, and butter.
Tomatoes may be thickened with bread crumbs.

CANNED TOMATOES STEWED

Follow the rule for Stewed Tomatoes.

See Index for Tomato Pudding and other Tomato Dishes.

TOMATOES CREOLE

These are unusually good:

2 tablespoons butter
4 large tomatoes, skinned
   and sliced
1 green pepper, shredded
1 large onion, chopped

¾ teaspoon salt
Paprika
2½ teaspoons brown sugar
1½ tablespoons flour
Cream

Melt the butter in a saucepan. Add the vegetables, season them and cook them until they are tender (about 12 minutes). Strain the juice, add enough cream to make 1½ cups of liquid. Thicken it with 1½ tablespoons flour. Cook the sauce, combine it with the vegetables and serve them hot on toast.

BROILED TOMATOES I. WITH BREAD CRUMBS

Cut tomatoes crosswise into halves and slice a small piece off the tops and the bottoms. Sprinkle the halves with salt and pepper, dip them in bread crumbs, then in egg (diluted with 1 tablespoon of water) and again in bread crumbs. Place them in a greased pan in a moderate oven until they are nearly soft, then broil them under a broiler, turning them once, until they are brown.

BROILED TOMATOES II. WITH CHEESE

4 firm tomatoes
Sugar
Salt
Pepper
Celery salt

1 cup bread crumbs
¼ cup grated cheese
2 teaspoons butter
1 tablespoon chopped onions
   or more (optional)

Wash the tomatoes, but do not peel them. Cut them crosswise in ½ inch slices. Season them well, cover them closely with crumbs and place them in a shallow greased pan. Sprinkle the tops with cheese and onions and dot them with butter. Broil them for 10 minutes under a moderate flame or bake them for 15 minutes in a moderate oven 375°.

BROILED TOMATOES III. WITH BROWN SUGAR

Cut tomatoes into halves. Season them with salt and pepper, cover them with brown sugar and dot them generously with butter. Place them in a pan and broil them under a slow flame, or place the pan in a moderate oven. When the tomatoes are done, pour off the juice, add a little cream and thicken the sauce with flour. Cook it until it is smooth and thick. Prepare rounds of buttered toast, place the tomatoes on them and pour the sauce over them.

SAUTÉD TOMATOES

This recipe is much like Broiled Tomatoes III, but it may be useful when broiling is out of the question.

4 medium sized tomatoes sliced in ¾ inch slices	Brown sugar (optional)
	2 tablespoons butter
1 teaspoon salt	¾ tablespoon flour
¼ teaspoon pepper	1 cup milk

Season the tomatoes. Melt the butter and add the tomato slices, and sauté them on both sides. Remove the tomatoes to a hot platter. Add the flour to the butter and when this is smooth add the milk. Stir the sauce well, boil it and pour it over the tomatoes.

SAUTÉD CORNMEAL TOMATOES

Select tomatoes that are not quite ripe. Wash them and cut them into ½ inch slices. Season them and dip them in corn-meal. Place them in ¼ inch of hot fat and cook them, turning them once, until they are a golden brown.

GRILLED TOMATOES AND ONIONS

Prepare onions—Page 114, and cut them crosswise in ⅓ inch slices. Drop them into boiling water and cook them for 5 minutes, then drain them. Wash tomatoes and cut them crosswise in ½ inch slices. Season the onions and the toma-toes, dot them with butter and bake them in a pan in a moder-ate oven. When they are nearly tender, broil them on both sides under a good flame. Serve them in stacks of alternate layers. Brown sugar may be added to the tomatoes.

OKRA AND TOMATOES

2 tablespoons butter	tomatoes, skinned
1 onion chopped fine	Salt
1 lb. okra sliced	Paprika
1 can tomatoes—No. 2 or 2½ cups of fresh	Sugar

Melt the butter and sauté the onion in it. When it is brown add the okra and cook it for 5 minutes. Add the tomatoes and seasoning and simmer these ingredients until the okra is ten-der. Green peppers chopped, and garlic, may be added, if de-sired.

ARTICHOKES

Soak the artichokes in cold water for 30 minutes. Cut off the stems, the tough bottom leaves and ¼ off the top leaves, and plunge the artichokes into boiling water to cover, to which salt, a sliced onion, two or more ribs of celery, with leaves, and the juice of half a lemon have been added. Boil them for 45 minutes, drain them well and serve them.

I. Hot, with melted butter.

II. Cold, with mayonnaise, Hollandaise, or Béchamel sauce.

Very good results are obtained by dropping soaked and drained artichokes into boiling soup and cooking them covered until they are tender. Unless completely immersed, they will discolor slightly, but both the soup and the vegetable will gain in flavor. Pour boiling water over the artichokes to free them from grease.

CORED ARTICHOKES

Soak artichokes for 30 minutes in cold water. Drain them well, remove the outer leaves, trim the upper fourth of the top leaves, cut the stem off close to the blossom, dig down into the centers with a knife, or spoon, and remove the chokes. Tie up the artichokes with a string, and boil them as directed on Page 119. Drain them well, untie them and serve them either hot or cold, the center filled with Hollandaise sauce, or serve them cold, the centers filled with marinated shrimp and mayonnaise.

STUFFED ARTICHOKES BAKED

The following excellent recipe is the contribution of my interested Italian friends and vegetable vendors:

Make a dressing of bread crumbs, garlic or onion minced, chopped celery, and anchovy (or anchovy paste.) Season it well. Prepare the artichokes by soaking and trimming them — Page 119, drain them and push a little of the dressing down between the leaves. Pour a little olive oil over the artichokes. Place them in a baking dish and cover the bottom of the dish with ¼ inch of boiling water or stock. Bake them covered in a moderate oven until they are done — about 1 hour. Baste them frequently with olive oil or stock.

CORN ON THE COB

Prepare the ears by removing the husks and the silk. Boil a large quantity of salted water (1½ teaspoons of salt to a quart of water) and drop the corn into this piece by piece, so as not to disturb the boiling point. Cover the kettle and boil the corn from 8 to 10 minutes. Remove it at once from the water and serve it.

FRESH CORN CUT FROM THE COB

Cut corn from the cob, or grate it. Cook it for several minutes until it is tender in its own juice and a little butter. Season it with salt and pepper and add milk or cream.

COOKED CORN CUT FROM THE COB

Cut or grate cooked corn from the cob. Add seasoning, butter, or cream, and heat it.

MULLED CUCUMBERS

The cucumber is banned from many tables as indigestible, or even poisonous. Digestion, alas! is an individual matter. Since it is said that good judgment is the result of experience and that experience is the result of bad judgment; why not give the cucumber the benefit of the doubt — at least once — to see whether it has really been maligned? These are most innocuous and very good:

Pare and seed cucumbers and cut them into strips. Drop them into a small amount of boiling water and cook them until they are barely tender. Drain them well. For 1 cup of cucumbers prepare ½ cup of rich cream sauce. Use sour cream, sweet cream, or milk. Season the sauce with salt, paprika, a dash of nutmeg and, if made with sweet cream or milk, add 1 teaspoon or more of lemon juice. When the sauce is boiling, add the drained cucumbers. Remove them to the top of a double boiler and steam them for a few minutes before serving them.

See Index for Baked Cucumbers.

ZUCCHINI
Italian Squash, or Vegetable Marrow

Zucchini are a delectable addition to the vegetable list. They are procurable throughout the summer.

Scrub, but do not pare, young Zucchini. Cut them crosswise in one inch slices and drop them into a small amount of boiling, salted water. Cook them until they are tender (from 10 to 20 minutes, according to the size and age of the vegetable). Drain them well, add a little melted butter and serve them, or drain them, place them in a little hot olive oil, drain them and serve them. Zucchini may be boiled and creamed, or served with tomato sauce. In Italy they are usually sautéd in oil.

See Index for Zucchini Salad.

SUMMER SQUASH

To be good, squash must be young and tender. Wash it, peel it and cut it into small pieces. Cook it in a small amount of boiling, salted water until it is tender (about 20 minutes). Drain it well, mash it with a fork, add cream, butter and pepper and beat it until it is fluffy.

BAKED SQUASH

Cut squash into pieces, remove the seeds and strings. Place the pieces in a dripping pan in a moderate oven for 1 hour. Cover the pieces generously with butter and sprinkle them with brown sugar. Cook them for 1 hour longer, basting them frequently, adding butter, if necessary.

BAKED OR BROILED EGGPLANT

I once heard an artist say: "If only the eggplant were as good as it looks, what a gastronomic treat it would be."

There are now several ways of preparing this vegetable that make it taste almost as luscious as it looks. The old-fashioned way of dipping it in batter and frying it in deep fat has given way to newer ones, of which the Baked Eggplant recipe which follows is a good example. Besides being digestible, non-fattening and exceedingly good, it is very quickly prepared.

Pare an eggplant and cut it crosswise into slices ½ inch thick. Spread the slices on both sides with soft butter and season them with salt and paprika. Place them on a baking sheet and bake them in a quick oven 400° until they are tender, turning them once — (approximate time 12 minutes). Or place them under a broiler and broil them until they are tender, under a moderate flame. Serve the eggplant while it is very hot with Lemon Butter — Page 156, or with sliced lemon.

EGGPLANT SOUFFLÉ—NO. I WITH CREAM SAUCE

In the following recipes the pulp is scooped out of the center of the eggplant, is combined with various ingredients and is replaced in the eggplant shells, in which it is then baked and from which it is served:

Cut an eggplant in lengthwise or crosswise halves. Scoop out the center, leaving a shell ¼ inch thick. Cook the pulp in boiling, salted water, to which ½ tablespoon vinegar, or lemon juice, has been added. Drain it and mash it with a fork.

1 cup cooked eggplant pulp
1 cup cream sauce, (2½ tablespoons flour, 3 tablespoons butter, 1 cup milk)

3 eggs (separated)
½ cup or less nut meats, chopped
Salt, paprika, nutmeg

Make the cream sauce. When it is boiling add the pulp and cook it for 1 minute. Reduce the heat, add the egg yolks, the seasoning and the nuts. Cook them, stirring them constantly for 1 minute. Cool the mixture, beat the whites of the eggs until stiff, and fold them into it. Fill the shells and bake them in a moderate oven until the soufflé is set—about 30 minutes. A little water may be placed in the pan to keep the shells from scorching.

EGGPLANT SOUFFLÉ—NO. II WITH BREAD CRUMBS

Prepare an eggplant as for Soufflé No. 1. Combine the cooked eggplant pulp, mashed, with:

½ cup nuts chopped
¾ cup bread crumbs
2 egg yolks

1 tablespoon melted butter
Salt, paprika, nutmeg

If the filling seems stiff, add a tablespoon or more of milk. Last fold in the stiffly beaten whites of 2 eggs. Fill the shells, cover the tops with bread crumbs dotted with butter, place them in a pan with a little water and brown them under a flame, or in a moderate oven for about 10 minutes.

BAKED EGGPLANT WITH CHEESE

1 small eggplant
3 tablespoons bread crumbs
2 tablespoons or more of sharp cheese, grated

Salt
1 tablespoon butter
A few grains of cayenne

Prepare the eggplant shells and boil the pulp—Page 121. Combine the drained and mashed pulp with 1 tablespoon of bread crumbs and the cheese. Season it well. Fill the shell with this mixture and cover the top with bread crumbs dotted with butter. Place the eggplant in a pan and bake it in a moderate oven—325°—for 30 minutes. A little water may be placed in the pan to keep the shell from scorching.

MUSHROOMS

Mushrooms are now found in the market throughout the winter at a low cost. They form an acceptable addition to the everyday menu, frequently taking the place of meat. To prepare mushrooms, brush them with a brush, or wipe them with a cloth and separate the caps from the stems. When young and fresh, they need not be skinned. When old, pull off the cap skins with the fingers, or with a knife, and pare the stems with a knife. To mince, break the caps into pieces and slice the stems with a knife. If the stems are tough, use them for stock, and save all the skins and parings for this purpose.

MUSHROOM STOCK

Place mushroom scraps in water to cover, add a slice of onion, some celery leaves and ribs, a carrot and a bit of parsley. Boil them gently for ½ hour, then strain the stock. Season it when ready to use it.

SAUTÉD MUSHROOMS

1 cup mushrooms Salt, paprika
2 tablespoons butter

Prepare the mushrooms—Page 123. Melt the butter in a skillet over a quick fire. (The skillet may be rubbed with a clove of garlic). When hot, add the mushrooms and cook them quickly, shaking the skillet until they are coated with butter. A few minutes cooking will suffice. Season and serve them on toast or on a mound of rice.

CREAMED MUSHROOMS

½ lb. of mushrooms broken ½ cup of cream sauce made
into pieces and sautéd with stock and cream

Sauté the mushrooms for 2 minutes. Place them in the boiling cream sauce, cover and simmer them for 5 minutes.

Use the stems and peelings for Stock—Page 123.

STEWED MUSHROOMS

½ lb. mushrooms Flour
3 tablespoons butter ½ cup hot milk or stock
Salt, paprika

Prepare the mushrooms—Page 123. Melt the butter, add the mushrooms and cook them for 2 minutes over a quick fire. Sprinkle them with salt and pepper and dredge them with flour.

Add the hot milk and simmer the mushrooms, covered, over a slow fire for 5 minutes.

BROILED MUSHROOMS

Prepare the mushrooms — Page 123, keeping the caps whole. Place them, cap side down on a hot greased broiler and broil them
for 5 minutes, turning them once. Put a small lump of butter in each cap, season the mushrooms with salt and paprika, sprinkle them with chopped parsley and serve them at once on toast. After adding the butter, keep the cap side up to preserve the juices.

PEAS AND MUSHROOMS

The following is very good made either with fresh, or with canned peas and mushrooms:

1 lb. mushrooms or more
3 tablespoons butter
1/4 teaspoon salt
1 can peas — No. 2, or 2 lbs.
    fresh peas cooked

1/4 cup liquor from the can
    or the pot
2 teaspoons chopped parsley

Prepare the mushrooms and sauté them in the butter — Page 123. (The skillet may be rubbed with a clove of garlic.) Drain them, keeping the juice. Add 1/2 tablespoon flour to the hot juice and cook it until it bubbles, then add 1/4 cup of the liquor and cook it until it is smooth. Place the peas and the mushrooms in a double boiler and pour the sauce over them. Heat them thoroughly. Chopped parsley may be added before serving the vegetables. The proportions of peas and mushrooms may be varied.

CHESTNUTS—HOW TO PREPARE THEM

Make two cross cut gashes on the flat side of each chestnut with a sharp pointed knife. Sometimes the shell will come off while doing this, but the inner skin will protect the kernel. Place the nuts in a pan over a quick fire, dropping oil or butter over them — 1 teaspoonful to 1 pound of nuts. Shake them until they are coated, then place them in a moderate oven until the skins can be easily removed.

STEAMED CHESTNUTS

2 cups prepared chestnuts
1 cup chicken stock
2 tablespoons butter

1 tablespoon flour
Brown sugar (optional)

Place the chestnuts in a covered baking dish and pour the

stock over them. Season them with salt and paprika and add brown sugar (optional). Cover them and cook them in a slow oven 325° for three hours. Pour off the stock, melt the butter, add the flour and the stock. When the sauce is smooth and thick, pour it over the chestnuts and serve them.

Meat

Time Chart for Cooking Meat

BROILING

Beef steak, 1 inch thick — 6 to 10 minutes.
Beef steak, 1½ inches thick — 8 to 15 minutes.
Lamb chops, ¾ inch thick — 10 to 15 minutes.
Spring chicken, 1 lb. — 20 minutes.

ROASTING

It requires about 15 minutes to heat a medium sized roast or fowl. Make this allowance, then add the time which is given per pound.

Beef	from 15 to 25 minutes
Veal	30 minutes
Lamb	20 minutes
Pork	30 minutes
Turkey	20 minutes
Chicken	20 minutes
Goose	15 minutes
Duck (Domestic)	from 40 to 60 minutes

See — A General Rule for Roasting Meat — Page 127.

BOILING

Meat should be placed in boiling water for 5 minutes, after which it is gently simmered until done. The time allowed is per pound.

Beef	from 40 to 60 minutes
Mutton	20 minutes
Ham	20 minutes
Chicken	20 minutes

Meat should be kept cold and at an even temperature. Unwrap it as soon as it is brought into the house and place it in a covered dish in the electric refrigerator (or on a plate in the icebox). Clean it by wringing a cloth out of cold water and wiping the meat thoroughly. Dry it with a cloth, trim off the hard edges and the surplus fat and it is ready to be cooked.

There are two main objects when cooking meat. To keep it juicy and to keep or make it tender.

The first is accomplished by intense heat, either by searing, or by immersion in boiling water. This seals the outer pores and encloses the juices. The second by slow heat, as slow cooking breaks down the fibre of meat.

So all well cooked meats, with few exceptions, are first exposed to extreme heat, which is followed by cooking over a low flame, by slow oven heat, or by gentle simmering.

The terms "roasting," "boiling" and "broiling" are well known and need not be explained, but there is one that is so frequently misused that it calls for explanation — "frying."

Frying is immersion in deep fat.

Sautéing is cooking in a small amount of fat on top of the stove.

Larding is drawing narrow strips of salt pork, or bacon, through meat. A needle is made for this purpose, but it can be done with a small sharp knife.

SEASONING MEAT

There is a diversity of opinion about this. Salt toughens meat, but it helps bring out the flavor. On the whole the tendency is to season meat before cooking it, or after searing it.

Certain meats and fowl are rubbed with butter. This results in a glazed surface.

When rubbed with butter and flour combined, a crackling crust is obtained.

A still heavier crust may be had by using the latter method and dredging the roast with flour when it is half done.

A GENERAL RULE FOR ROASTING MEAT

Prepare the meat as directed in the foregoing pages. Place it on a dripping rack in a very hot oven 480 to 500 degrees until it is browned. Reduce the heat to a slow oven 350°, pour a cup of stock over the roast and cover the pan. Cook the roast until it is done, basting it frequently. It may be uncovered for the last half hour.

Exceptions to this rule:

Roast Beef and Filet of Beef.

Some cooks prefer cooking roasts uncovered. Some prefer cooking them (with the exception of veal) without the addition of stock, placing an onion in the pan. These matters are optional.

If stock is not available for basting meat, follow the rule on Page 154 for Vegetable Stock. The paragraph on Gravy may prove helpful to the inexperienced cook.

A GENERAL RULE FOR STEWING MEAT

Sear meat in hot fat. Pour boiling stock over it (covering the bottom of the pan to the depth of ½ inch). See Vegetable Stock Page 154. Cover the meat closely and simmer it until it is done (from 1 to 2 hours); or, drop meat into boiling water which has been lightly seasoned and to which vegetables have been added, and simmer it covered until it is tender (1 to 2 hours). Remove the meat at once from the pot and follow the rule for Roast Gravy — Page 153.

Beef

ROAST BEEF
3 Rib Roast

Heat a roasting pan on top of the stove. When it is very hot, place the roast in it and sear it on all surfaces. Raise the roast in the pan and slip a dripping rack under it. Place it skin side up in a very hot oven 480° and cook it uncovered for ½ hour. Pour off part of the fat and pour 1 cup or more of boiling stock over the roast. Reduce the heat to a slow oven 250° or 275°, cover the roast and cook it, basting it every 10 minutes until it is done — 1 hour or more — adding more stock, if necessary.

For stock see Page 153.

Tomato used with discrimination is a good flavor for beef gravy.

When the roast is done, remove it at once from the pan, place it on a platter and keep it warm. Make the gravy — Page 154 and serve the roast garnished with parsley and surrounded with browned potatoes, or with squares of Yorkshire Pudding.

FILET OF BEEF

A filet of beef, being deliciously tender of its own accord, calls for a slightly different method of cooking than other meat.

Remove the surplus fat and skin. Lard the filet with narrow strips of salt pork or bacon — Page 127. Fold over the thin ends of the filet and secure them with string or skewers. If the filet is not larded, spread it generously with butter, or place strips of bacon over it. Season it with salt and pepper, dredge it with flour and place it on a rack in a roasting pan in a very hot oven 500°. Place a piece of salt pork or bacon in the bottom of the pan. Bake the filet from 20 to 30 minutes only (according to its size). Make the gravy of the fat and juices and add sautéd mushrooms, or serve the meat with broiled mushrooms and gravy. See Page 153 for gravy.

POT ROAST

Beef shoulder, chuck and rump make good Pot Roast. The meat is improved by larding — See Page 127. Season it and dredge it with flour. Heat an iron pot over a very hot fire. Melt 1 tablespoon of fat and sear the meat in it on all sides. Add two cups of boiling stock or vegetable stock — Page 154. Reduce the heat and cover the pot closely. Do not boil the meat at any time. Simmer it slowly until it is done. Use additional stock if the roast becomes dry. Make gravy of the stock as directed on Page 154. Serve the roast with mashed potatoes, or noodles.

GERMAN BEEF À LA MODE
SAUERBRATEN

Frequently, when I have seen Beef à la Mode on a menu, I have ordered it only to say later in disappointed tones "Why it isn't anything like Sauerbraten." You may not like Sauerbraten at all, but if you do, you are apt to like it very well indeed.

Lard a 5 lb. cut of beef shoulder, or choose a piece of meat with fat. Rub it with salt and pepper, put it in a crock or bowl and pour the following mixture over it. Vinegar diluted with water (in equal parts if vinegar is very strong) to which 1 onion, sliced, 2 bay leaves, salt, 1 teaspoon pepper corns and 4 tablespoons sugar have been added. Pour this while hot over the beef, so that it is more than half covered. Place a lid over the crock and put it in the refrigerator. Leave the meat there for a week or ten days, turning it once a day. Drain it, saving the vinegar and cook the meat like pot roast, using the vinegar mixture in place of stock. When it is tender, remove it from the fire and make the gravy — Page 153, adding 1 cup of sweet, or sour cream. I like the gravy "straight." Some cooks add raisins, catsup and gingersnaps, but I have never had the courage to do so. Serve the roast with Potato Dumplings — Page 151.

BROILED STEAK

Grease a hot broiler with a bit of suet, and place a 1½ inch steak on it, as near the flame as possible. Sear the steak on one side, turn it and sear it on the other side, letting each side brown for 2 minutes. Lower the broiling pan, but not the heat, and allow the steak to cook for about 12 minutes, turning it from time to time. When the steak is half done, season it with salt and pepper. When it is done, spread it with butter. Serve it garnished with Sautéed Mushrooms.

PAN BROILED STEAK

Heat a frying pan until it is smoking hot. Rub it with a tiny bit of suet. Put the steak in the pan and sear it for 1 minute, turn it and sear the other side. Season the steak with salt and paprika. Reduce the heat to a low flame and continue cooking the steak until it is done, about 10 minutes for a 1½ inch steak. Pour off the fat in the pan. If it is allowed to accumulate, the steak will be sautéed and not broiled. If at all doubtful of the tenderness of the steak, cover it with a lid when the flame is reduced. This gives it more of a steamed than a broiled quality, but it does help to soften it.

FILET OF BEEF STEAKS

Upon request, a butcher will usually cut filet steaks, shape them and surround them with a strip of bacon, secured by a bit of wood. If not, it must be done at home. The thickness of the steaks varies from ¾ of an inch to an inch or more. Prepare the steaks, grease a hot broiler and place the steaks upon it close to the flame, turning them until they are well browned, from 10 to 12 minutes. Season the steaks, and spread them while hot with butter, or with Hollandaise Sauce — Page 158. Serve them on a hot platter garnished with lemon, parsley and broiled mushrooms (optional).

BEEF ROLLS

Cut round steak that is ⅓ inch thick into 2x4 strips. (The same rule applies to veal). Season the strips and place on each one a thick slice of carrot, a piece of celery rib and a small piece of salt pork, or a slice of bacon. Roll the strips and tie them with thread. Brown them in salt pork or bacon trimmings. Cover them with ¼ inch of boiling vegetable stock — Page 154, and simmer them closely covered for 2 hours. Do not let the stock boil at any time. Remove the rolls and cut the threads. Make the gravy — Page 154 and pour it over the meat. Serve the rolls with mashed potatoes, or noodles.

SWISS STEAK
6 Servings

A 2 pound round steak, 2 inches thick
½ cup flour combined with 1 teaspoon salt and a dash of pepper

¼ cup bacon or ham drippings
2 cups strained tomato juice

Pound the flour into both sides of the steak, using the edge of a heavy plate. Heat the fat in a large casserole, or skillet, and sear the steak in it. Add the boiling tomatoes, cover the casserole closely and place it in a slow oven 275° for 2 hours. 1 cup of carrots, onions and green peppers may be put into 2 cups of boiling water and substituted for the tomato juice, or the vegetables may be added to the tomato juice. Make gravy of the drippings — Page 154, and pour it over the steak. The drained vegetables may be returned to the gravy after it has been thickened.

BEEF BALLS—HAMBURGER STEAK I.

1 pound round steak
¼ pound salt pork
4 tablespoons milk
¼ teaspoon salt

¼ teaspoon celery salt
1 tablespoon chopped onion
1 tablespoon chopped parsley

Mix these ingredients thoroughly, shape them into balls and flatten them into cakes. Place 2 tablespoons of butter in a pan. When it is hot add the cakes and brown them on both sides. Add ¾ cup hot stock, cover the pan and cook the steaks until they are done — about five minutes. Make gravy with the drippings — See Page 153.

BEEF BALLS—HAMBURGER STEAK II.

Round steak ground
Seasoning

Butter or drippings
Minced onion (optional)

Season the meat and add the onion. Shape the meat into balls and flatten them into cakes. Place 2 or more tablespoons of fat in a pan and when it is hot add the meat balls and sear them well on both sides. Reduce the heat and cook the meat slowly until it is done. The onion may be added to the butter.

SCRAPED BEEF

The following is a good way of preparing meat for a convalescent, or a child:

Scrape round steak with a spoon or a dull knife. Season the fine scrapings, roll them into a ball, flatten it slightly and pan broil it in a hot skillet that has been rubbed with a very little butter or suet. Sear the meat on both sides over a good flame — reduce the heat, turn the meat several times dotting the upper side with a very little butter each time.

IRISH STEW

1½ pounds beef	Salt, pepper
⅓ cup turnips, diced	1½ cups potatoes, diced
¼ cup carrots, diced	2 tablespoons flour
¼ cup onions, diced	½ cup stock

The vegetables may be varied in kind and proportions. Cut the meat into pieces and brown them in hot fat. Cover them with boiling water and reduce the heat. Cover the pot closely and simmer the meat for one hour. Add the turnips, carrots, onions and seasoning and simmer the stew for one hour longer. Add the potatoes for the last 25 minutes of cooking. Dissolve the flour in ½ cup of cold stock, or water and add it to the gravy. Serve the stew with dumplings or biscuits.

BEEF LOAF I.
4 to 6 Servings

Here are three good recipes for Beef Loaf, the first calls for an egg yolk and bread crumbs, the second for ground vegetables, and the third for vegetables and a can of tomatoes.

1 pound of beef ground, (¼ of this may be pork)	1 tablespoon bread crumbs (optional)
1 egg yolk	1 teaspoon lemon juice
2 tablespoons chopped parsley	1 teaspoon salt
1 tablespoon butter	¼ teaspoon pepper
	½ teaspoon onion juice

Combine the ingredients and roll them into a loaf. Wrap it in wax paper and place it in a pan. Bake it in a moderate oven

350° for one hour, basting it every 5 minutes with ¼ cup butter and 1 cup of boiling water, with stock, or with Vegetable Stock —Page 154. Make the gravy with the drippings—Page 154.

BEEF LOAF II.
4 to 6 Servings

1 pound beef ground (¼
   of this may be pork)
3 carrots
1 stalk dwarf celery
2 small potatoes

½ onion
1 tablespoon chopped
   parsley
Salt, paprika

Put the vegetables through a food chopper, combine them with the remaining ingredients and shape them into a loaf. Bake the loaf for one hour in a moderate oven 350°. Baste the loaf frequently with stock, or tomato juice. Make the gravy with the drippings—Page 154.

BEEF LOAF III.
8 to 10 Servings

1 pound beef ground
1 pound pork ground
1 large can of tomatoes
   (2½) drained

3 large green peppers
   ground
1 large onion ground
1 cup of crackers ground
Salt, pepper

Combine the ingredients and shape them into a loaf. Dredge it with flour and place 5 or 6 strips of bacon over the top. Bake the loaf for 1 hour in a moderate oven 350°. Baste it frequently with tomato juice. Make the gravy—Page 154 of the drippings and tomato juice. If the tomato juice is insufficient, add Vegetable Stock—Page 154.

See Index for Left Over Meat in Biscuit Dough and Hash.

CORNED BEEF

Place corned beef—tied to keep it in shape—in cold water to cover. Bring it to the boiling point, remove the scum, reduce the heat and simmer the meat until it is tender. Leave it in the water in which it was cooked until it is lukewarm. Remove it and press it with a weight, or serve it warm and unpressed with boiled vegetables and horseradish sauce.

CORNED BEEF HASH

Cut cold, pressed, corned beef into dice. Prepare one-half as much cream sauce as there is meat, using milk or stock. Add the meat when the cream sauce is boiling and serve it on toast or with boiled vegetables.

Veal

VEAL ROAST, STUFFED BREAST OR SHOULDER

Have the butcher cut a pocket in the meat. Fill the pocket with dressing—Page 152 and sew it up with a coarse needle and thread. Season the meat and if it is not fat, rub it with butter and dredge it with flour. Place it on a dripping rack in a roasting pan in a very hot oven 480° until it is well browned. Reduce the heat to a slow oven 300°, pour 2 cups of stock, or of Vegetable Stock—Page 154 over the roast and bake it covered until it is done, basting it every 10 minutes. (Tomato does not improve the flavor of veal). Add more stock if necessary. Make the gravy of the drippings—Page 154.

VEAL ROAST, KIDNEY, LOIN, ETC.

Follow the Rule for Breast or Shoulder. This roast is good served with Dumplings or "Spatzen"—a fine German dish—Page 151.

BREADED VEAL SLICES

The following Veal Slices are so delicate that they may be served as a company dish in preference to some more costly meat course:

1 slice of round, ¾ inch thick	Seasoning
1 egg	Butter
Bread crumbs	Cream

Pound the meat well with the edge of a plate and cut its surface lightly with criss-cross gashes. Cut the meat into pieces the size of a large oyster. Season them well, dip them in bread crumbs, in egg to which 1 tablespoon of water may be added, and again in crumbs. Sauté them in butter until they are brown, then half cover them with cream, and cook them covered for one hour over a very, very low flame. Serve them with mushroom sauce, or gravy made with drippings—Page 153.

VEAL CUTLETS

Dip the cutlets in seasoned bread or cracker crumbs, then in egg, which may be diluted with 1 tablespoon of water, and again in the crumbs. Brown the cutlets in hot butter, or drippings, over a quick flame, then cook them slowly until they are tender (about ½ hour) over a low flame, or in a moderate oven 350°. Serve them with gravy—Page 153, and slices of lemon and parsley.

VEAL STEAK—WIENER SCHNITZEL

Pieces of veal from the round ½ inch thick prepared, cooked and served like veal cutlets.

VEAL STEW

Cut veal into pieces about 1½ inches square and sear them in hot butter, or drippings, in a heavy pot, or saucepan. Add enough Vegetable Stock—Page 154 to cover the bottom of the pot to the depth of ½ inch. Cover the pot closely and simmer the veal until it is tender—about 2 hours. Remove the meat from the pot, make the gravy—Page 154, return the meat to the pot, heat and serve it. Veal stew is very good with a baked top crust. Use the recipe for Chicken Pot Pie Crust—Page 50.

VEAL BIRDS

Thin slices of veal from the round	Pepper
	Paprika
Salt pork	Lemon juice
Bread or cracker crumbs	Stock
Minced onion	Flour
Minced celery	Butter
Salt	Cream

Pound the meat with the edge of a plate and cut it into pieces of about 2x4 inches. Chop the trimmings and combine them with an equal amount of chopped salt pork. Make a dressing with bread or cracker crumbs, (adding one half the amount of the chopped meat), onion, celery and seasoning, and enough stock or cream to hold it together. Spread the meat lightly with the dressing and roll it, securing it with skewers or thread. Sprinkle the birds with salt and paprika and roll them in flour. Sauté them in butter over a quick fire until they are brown. Reduce the heat, add boiling cream or milk until the birds are half covered, cover the pot closely and cook them until they are tender—about 20 minutes. Make the gravy—Page 154 and pour it over the meat.

See Beef Rolls for a more simple way of making Veal Birds.

VEAL LOAF
8 to 10 Servings

1½ pounds veal ground twice
¼ pound salt pork, ground
6 tablespoons rolled crackers
1 small green pepper, ground
2 tablespoons cream, or stock

1 tablespoon lemon juice
1½ teaspoons salt
¾ teaspoon pepper
1 large onion, chopped and browned in 2 tablespoons of butter

Combine the ingredients and place them in a small loaf pan. Brush the top of the loaf with the white of an egg and bake it in a slow oven 300° for 2 hours, or more, pricking the loaf frequently. Baste it with ½ cup of stock—Page 154, or ¼ cup pork fat. Make gravy with the drippings—Page 154.

Cooked ground veal may be made into a loaf by the same rule. Bake it only until it is brown and firm.

See Veal Soufflé—Page 87.

Lamb

LAMB ROAST

Season the meat and dredge it with flour. Place it on a dripping rack in a roasting pan and put it into a very hot oven 480° for ½ hour. Dredge the meat again with flour. Reduce the heat to a slow oven 300°, baste the roast with 1 cup of stock— Page 154, cover it and baste it every ten minutes until it is done. Uncover it for the last half hour of roasting, if desired. Prepare the gravy—Page 154, adding sour milk or cream to it. Serve Roast Lamb with gravy and with mint sauce.

CROWN ROAST OF LAMB

Protect the ends of the bones by putting heavy wax paper or cubes of salt pork on them. Season the roast and dredge it with flour. Place it in a hot oven 480° and follow the rule for Lamb Roast. Uncover the roast for the last half hour of cooking. When the roast is done remove the paper and place a paper chop frill on each bone. Make the gravy—Page 154. Fill the hollow of the roast with buttered peas, or with prepared chestnuts, and garnish it with parsley. Serve it with the gravy and with mint sauce.

MOCK VENISON

This is both delicate and delicious:

Cover a leg of lamb or mutton with sour milk. Soak it for 24 hours or more. Drain it, lard it and dot it with butter. Season it well and dredge it with flour. Roast it in a hot oven for 15 minutes 480° add ½ cup of hot vegetable stock—Page 154, reduce the heat to 300° and cover the roast closely. Baste it frequently. When it is nearly done, remove the cover, pour 1 cup of sour cream over the roast and permit it to brown for 10 minutes. Make the gravy with the drippings—Page 154 and serve the roast surrounded by browned potatoes, garnished with parsley.

LAMB CHOPS—BROILED

Follow directions for Broiled Steak, allowing a shorter time for cooking, (according to the thickness of the chops).

LAMB CHOPS—PAN BROILED

Season lamb chops and sear them in a hot frying pan (without fat) for 1 minute, then reduce the heat and cook them slowly until they are done. Place a mound of mashed potatoes in the center of a platter. Make a slight depression in the top and pour the hot drippings into it. Surround the potatoes with broiled chops, and garnish them with parsley. Place a sprig of parsley in the center of the potato mound. Serve the dish while the chops are very hot.

LAMB STEW

Follow the rule for veal stew, but do not sear the meat unless it is very lean. Drop it into a small quantity of boiling Vegetable Stock—Page 154, cover it and simmer it until it is tender. If a top crust is desired, make the batter given for Chicken Pot Pie and follow the rule for baking it. Capers, or chopped pickles may be added to the gravy.

Pork

PORK ROAST

Follow the rule for Lamb Roast, placing ½ cup of water in the pan to keep the roast from sticking. Serve Pork Roast with Apple Sauce—Page 162, or with Sweet Potatoes and Apples—Page 103.

CROWN ROAST OF PORK

Prepare the roast like crown Roast of Lamb, fill the hollow with 2½ lbs. of pork sausage, combined with ½ cup bread crumbs, seasoned with chopped onion and celery, or fill it with bread dressing. Follow the Rule for Pork Roast. Serve the roast garnished with glazed onions and baked apples.

PORK TENDERLOIN

Split a pork tenderloin lengthwise. Flatten it out, spread it with bread or apple dressing and sew or tie it up, or cut small lengthwise pieces of tenderloin, spread them with dressing and roll them up. Season the meat and dredge it with flour. Sear it in a hot pan with very little fat. Place it in a slow oven 300° in a covered pan for about 30 minutes, basting it frequently with hot stock, sour cream or milk.

PORK TENDERLOIN FRENCHED

Cut the meat into crosswise slices, flatten them slightly, season them and cook them like Pork Chops.

PORK CHOPS

Sear pork chops in a hot pan, using as little grease as possible. Reduce the heat, season the chops and cook them slowly, covered or uncovered, until they are done. If they are very fat, pour off the excess grease, while cooking them. Make gravy with the drippings — Page 153.

BREADED PORK CHOPS

Prepare the chops like Veal Cutlets. Cook them in a minimum of grease in a hot pan. Reduce the heat, pouring off the excess grease, and cook them until they are done. Make gravy with the drippings — Page 153.

PORK CHOPS AND APPLES

Thick pork chops, (¾ inch or more)	Brown sugar
	Seasoning
Apples	Cream

Sear the pork chops in a hot spider, season them and place them in a hot pan. Cut the apples crosswise, core them and place them on the pork chops cut side up. Cover them with brown sugar. Add enough hot cream to the pan, sweet or sour, to cover the bottom well, cover the pan and place it in a moderate oven 350° from 30 to 40 minutes. Baste the chops frequently and when they are done, make the gravy with the drippings — Page 153.

STUFFED PORK CHOPS
Glorified Pork Chops

These are so good that if I were writing a Baedaker I'd give them a triple star * * *:

Rib pork chops ¾ inch thick, or more. Cut the bone from the meat. Trim off the excess fat and cut a large gash or pocket into the side of each chop. Make a dressing of bread crumbs, ½ as much finely chopped celery and onions as there is bread, chopped parsley and seasoning. Moisten the dressing with milk. Fill the pockets with it and sew them up with a coarse needle and thread. Sear the chops in a hot spider and place them in a pan with a little milk or cream. Cover the pan and bake the chops in a moderate oven 350° until they are done (¾ to 1 hour). Make the gravy with drippings — Page 153.

SPARE-RIBS AND SAUERKRAUT I.

Sear spare-ribs in pork fat and season them with salt and pepper. Place them in a casserole between two layers of raw sauerkraut and cover these ingredients with boiling water. Cover them closely and bake them in a slow oven 325° for two hours. Frankfurter sausage may be substituted for spare-ribs. Serve the spare-ribs with mashed potatoes.

SPARE-RIBS AND SAUERKRAUT

Place spare-ribs in boiling water, to which seasoning, onion and other vegetables have been added. Simmer them until they are tender, drain them and serve them around a mound of mashed potatoes with canned sauerkraut.

Ham

BAKED HAM

Soak the ham in cold water to cover for 12 hours. Allow 4½ hours' cooking in all for a 12 pound ham. Place it in a kettle of fresh cold water, bring the water to the boiling point, reduce the heat and simmer the ham for 3½ hours. Drain it and strip off the skin. Cover the top of the ham with brown sugar (to which a little dry mustard may be added) and stud it with whole cloves. Place a cup of cider, pineapple juice, or orange juice in the pan and bake the ham in a hot oven 425° for 20 minutes, basting it frequently. Dredge it again with sugar, lower the heat to 350° and cook it without further basting for a half hour or more. Serve it garnished with pineapple slices (that have been put in the pan for the last 15 minutes of the baking) Maraschino cherries and parsley.

"LEFT-OVER" HAM

Use bits of ham ground, combined with chopped onion, or celery, moistened with cream or dressing as a sandwich spread. Use the ham bone for Split Pea Soup. Grind the dry ends of the ham and use it for Ham Noodles, or Ham Soufflé.

See Index for other Ham dishes.

Here are three recipes for preparing a slice of smoked ham. The first calls for brown sugar, mustard and milk; the second for brown sugar and pineapple; and the third for brown sugar and condensed milk. In each case, if desired, the ham may be soaked in warm water for one hour before it is cooked.

HAM BAKED IN MILK

A small round of ham, 1¼ or more inches thick
2 teaspoons prepared mustard
2 tablespoons brown sugar
Milk

Spread the ham on both sides with the mustard and the brown sugar. Place it in a small skillet, cover it with milk and bake it in a moderate oven — 375° — for about 45 minutes. Baste it frequently as the milk evaporates.

HAM BAKED WITH PINEAPPLE

A 2 pound slice of ham
6 slices of pineapple
½ cup brown sugar
⅔ cup pineapple juice

Sear the ham on both sides in a hot skillet. Place it in a baking dish. Brown the drained pineapple slices in the skillet and place them on top of the ham. Place the sugar and the pineapple juice in the skillet and simmer them for 3 minutes, then pour the syrup over the ham and pineapple. Cover the baking dish and bake the ham in a moderate oven 350° for about 30 minutes.

SLICE OF HAM BAKED
6 Servings

1 slice of ham — 2 inches
  thick
2 tablespoons brown sugar

1 tablespoon flour
¾ cup water
¾ cup condensed milk

Trim the fat from the ham, cut the fat into small pieces and combine it with the sugar. Rub the flour into the ham and put it in a baking dish. Sprinkle the combined sugar and fat over it and pour the water around it. Place it in a hot oven, 425° for 15 minutes. Reduce the temperature to a slow oven, 275°. Bake the ham for about 2 hours. Add the milk the last 15 minutes of baking. Thicken the drippings for gravy.

BROILED HAM

Cover a 2 inch slice of ham with cold water. Let it cook slowly 20 minutes to the pound (until nearly tender.) Drain it, cover it with brown sugar and stick it with cloves. Broil it until done, or pan broil it.

BROILED HAM II.

Soak slices of ham ⅓ inch thick one hour in luke warm water. Drain them, wipe them and broil them for 3 minutes under a quick flame.

"FRIED" HAM

Cover a slice of ham with tepid water and place it on the back of the range for 30 minutes. Drain and dry it. Heat a pan and brown the ham quickly on one side, reverse it and brown it on the other. Serve it with eggs fried gently in tried out ham fat.

BACON

Place strips of bacon on a fine wire broiler in a dripping pan. Bake them in a hot oven until the bacon is crisp and brown — or place the bacon in a cold skillet and cook it slowly until it is done. Pour off some of the drippings while cooking the bacon to insure crispness.

Sweetbreads, Brains, Kidneys, Liver, Tongue.

SWEETBREADS BOILED AND CREAMED

Soak a pair of sweetbreads in cold water for 20 minutes. Drain them, plunge them into rapidly boiling water to cover, to which the juice of 1/2 lemon, 2 ribs of celery with leaves, or 1/2 onion, 1/2 teaspoon of salt and a few pepper corns have been added. Reduce the heat and simmer the sweetbreads for 20 minutes. Place them in cold water to harden for 15 minutes. Drain them and remove the skin and membrane. Break them into pieces and drop them into 1 cup of rich, hot cream sauce. Heat them, add 1 or more teaspoons of Sherry to the sauce and serve them at once. To reheat sweetbreads place them in a double boiler.

SWEETBREADS BROILED

Parboil Sweetbreads — Page 141. Chill them and remove the skin and membrane. Split them crosswise, season them with salt and paprika and broil them for 5 minutes under a good flame. Serve them with Maitre d' Hotel butter.

SWEETBREADS IN BLANKETS

Parboil Sweetbreads — Page 141. Chill them, skin them and break them into large pieces. Surround each piece with a strip of bacon, secure it with a toothpick and broil the sweetbreads in a hot skillet until the bacon is crisp.

See Index for other Sweetbread Recipes.

CALVES' BRAINS

Calves' brains are generally in bad repute. They are charged with being too soft, but properly treated they become palatable and there are several good ways of preparing them. They combine well with other food — eggs, salads, soufflés, ragout, etc., and need only a little pep in flavor, sherry, Worcestershire Sauce, etc. to make them very good.

Soak calves brains in cold water for 1 hour. Remove the membrane and cook the brains like Sweetbreads — Page 141. Drain and put them into cold water to harden for 10 minutes.

See Index for other Brain recipes.

STEWED KIDNEYS

2 beef kidneys	Black pepper
6 onions, minced	Butter
Salt	Flour
Red pepper	

Remove the gristle from the kidneys and cut them into 1/2 inch squares, add the onions and cover them with boiling water. Stew them gently for 3 hours, permit them to cool, add the seasoning and cook them one hour longer. Make gravy with the stock allowing 3 tablespoons butter and 2 tablespoons flour to a cup of liquid.

LIVER

Remove the skin and veins from the liver and cut it into 1/2 inch slices. Season the slices with salt and pepper and dredge them with flour. Sauté them in hot bacon drippings until they are done. Serve them with crisp bacon.

LIVER DUMPLINGS—LEBERKLOESSE

Being the child of a South German, I cannot well compile a cook book without including a dish that is typical of that neck of the woods — (not exactly a handsome one, but it has qualities. Besides, liver is now "de rigueur"):

1/2 pound calves liver, or chicken livers
1 slice of white bread (1/2 cup)
1 egg yolk
2 tablespoons soft butter
1 teaspoon chopped onion

1 tablespoon chopped parsley
1 teaspoon salt
1/2 teaspoon pepper
1 tablespoon flour
1 egg white, stiffly beaten

Skin the liver, remove the fibre and chop or grind the liver until it is very fine. Soak the bread in water for three minutes, then wring the water from it. Beat the egg yolk with the butter and add the remaining ingredients, folding in the stiffly beaten egg white last. Shape this mixture into small balls and drop them into boiling soup. Cook them for five or six minutes. These dumplings may be cooked in boiling water, drained and served with chopped onions sautéd in butter.

A good follow-up dish is Liver Dumplings sautéd in onion butter.

BEEF TONGUE
Fresh

Place a beef tongue in boiling water and simmer it for one hour. Skin it, remove the roots and place it on a dripping rack in a roasting pan. Dice 2 cups of vegetables, carrots, turnips, onion, celery, etc., add 4 cups of the water, heated, in which the tongue was boiled and pour this around the tongue. Cover the pan closely and bake the tongue in a slow oven 275° until it is tender (about 2 hours for a large tongue). Remove the tongue.

Strain the vegetables and place them about it, or serve the tongue with creamed spinach. Make the gravy — Page 154 with the stock.

BOILED SMOKED TONGUE

See Page 14 for Tongue in Aspic and follow the rule for boiling it.

CALVES' TONGUES

Place calves' tongues in boiling water to cover, to which an onion, several ribs of celery with leaves, a carrot, a bay leaf and pepper corns have been added. Simmer them until they are tender. Remove the skin and split the tongues lengthwise. Serve them with gravy made with the stock — Page 154 to which prepared horseradish or capers and lemon juice may be added. Chopped pickles may be substituted for capers.

Fowl and Game

If you are a new cook and are called upon to dress a chicken, remember, please, that among other things it has a crop that must be removed—(I am speaking from experience). The following is the best way to prepare a large chicken of doubtful age.

STEWED CHICKEN

Clean a chicken and cut it into pieces. Drop the pieces into boiling water, to which an onion, a carrot, a rib or two of celery with leaves and seasoning have been added. As the liquid will increase in volume, the chicken need only be covered to the depth of ⅓ inch. Cover the pot closely and simmer the chicken until it is tender (2 hours or more), but do not boil it at any time. Remove the chicken from the pot and make the gravy—Page 154, adding milk or cream to it. When it is boiling add the chicken and serve it at once, preferably with dumplings, or rice.

ROAST CHICKEN

Stuff a large chicken—about 3½ pounds—with Boiled Rice, Bread or Potato dressing—Page 152. Rub it well with salt and with 3 tablespoons butter, creamed with 2 tablespoons flour. Truss the chicken and place it uncovered in a roasting pan in a hot oven 475°. When it is well browned (about 25 minutes) baste the chicken with ½ cup of seasoned stock, cover it and reduce the heat to 325°. Baste it with the drippings in the pan every ten minutes, adding a little additional stock, if the pan threatens to become dry. Turn the chicken so that it may brown evenly. A thicker crust may be had by dredging the chicken with flour while it is cooking. If a glazed skin is preferred, omit the flour. Time for cooking, about 1½ hours.

CHICKEN STOCK

Boil 3 cups of water, 3 ribs of celery with leaves, ½ onion, a carrot and 3 sprigs of parsley. Add the chicken giblets, neck and wing tips. Simmer this until the giblets are tender. Remove the giblets and the neck and strain the stock.

Chicken Gravy:

Strain the drippings, pour off the fat.

To 6 tablespoons of fat add   2 cups of stock
    4 tablespoons of flour and

The giblets may be chopped and added to the gravy — Page 154.

YOUNG CHICKENS BAKED

Cut the chickens into quarters. Season them with salt and pepper and brown them well in butter in a hot skillet. Place them in a covered pan in a slow oven 325° for 1 hour or more. Add ½ cup of hot stock, or water, and baste them frequently. Make gravy with the drippings, adding cream to the stock, if desired.

BROILED SPRING CHICKEN

Select chickens weighing about 1 pound. Rub them with butter on both sides and sprinkle them with a very little salt (if the butter is unsalted.) Place them in a pan, skin side down. The skin side will brown quicker than the under side. Broil them until they are brown, under a good flame, turning them frequently, after 15 minutes add butter, if needed, and put ½ cup of stock in the bottom of the pan. Cover the pan and bake the chickens in a slow oven 275° basting them every 10 minutes. This will require about 30 minutes. Very small chickens may be broiled for 20 minutes and require no baking. See the rule for Stock — Page 146. See the rule for Chicken Gravy — Page 146.

SAUTÉD CHICKEN
In ordinary parlance—Fried Chicken

Do not attempt to sauté chicken in this way unless it is young and tender.

Season chicken that has been cut into small pieces and dredge it with flour. Place butter, or bacon drippings in a skillet and when it is hot, add the chicken, turning it in the hot fat until it is brown. Reduce the heat, cover the skillet and continue cooking the chicken until it is done, (from 20 to 30 minutes, according to size). Remove the chicken from the pan and make the gravy—Page 153. Serve the chicken garnished with parsley.

SAUTÉD CHICKEN (FRIED) SOUTHERN STYLE

Cut a young chicken into small pieces. Sprinkle it lightly with flour, pepper and salt. Beat an egg with 1/4 cup of milk. Dip the chicken in this and then in fine bread or cracker crumbs. Brown the chicken in hot butter or lard. Place 1/4 cup of boiling stock or water in the bottom of the pan, cover the skillet and bake the chicken in a slow oven—325°. A two and a half pound chicken calls for about one hour's cooking in all—30 minutes on top of the stove and 30 minutes in the oven.

SMOTHERED CHICKEN

A good way of preparing middle-aged chicken.

Cut a chicken into quarters or small pieces, roll them in flour and season them well. Brown them in fat which has been heated in a pot and to which several slices of onion have been added. Combine stock, cream and a sprig of parsley. Heat this to the boiling point and pour it over the browned chicken until the bottom of the pot is well covered. (Boiling water may be used in place of stock and cream). Cover the pot and simmer the chicken until it is tender. Make gravy with the drippings—Page 153, adding stock or cream and a few drops of Kitchen Bouquet. Pour it over the chicken before serving it.

FROG LEGS

Season frog legs—roll them in flour and sauté them in hot butter—onion may be added to the butter, or the skillet may be rubbed with garlic. When they are brown, reduce the heat, pour 1/2 cup of boiling stock over them and cook them closely covered for about 10 minutes. They may then be rolled in sautéd bread crumbs to which a little lemon juice and chopped parsley have been added, or they may be covered with rich boiling cream sauce flavored with Sherry and served garnished with parsley.

BROILED SQUAB

Split the birds down the back and flatten the breasts. Follow the rule for Broiled Chicken—Page 146. Allow 25 to 40 minutes for cooking squab.

BAKED SQUAB

Rub squab with salt, both inside and out. Stuff them with wild rice, or with bread dressing. Brush them with melted butter and sprinkle them with flour and place them in a closely covered pan. Bake them in a hot oven 450° for 45 minutes, reduce the heat to 400° and bake them for about 45 minutes longer. Baste them frequently with melted butter.

TO CLEAN DUCKS:

Clip the wing tips and remove the coarse guard feathers, leaving the ducks covered with down. Melt a cake of parafine and paint the ducks, using a brush and covering the entire surface of the birds with the hot wax. Allow the parafine to harden and pull it off. It will carry the feathers with it.

WILD DUCKS

Stuff ducks with apples and raisins, or with sweet potatoes and apples. — See Index for dressings. Place the ducks on a rack in a roasting pan. Sprinkle them with salt and pepper and cover the breasts with thin slices of salt pork or bacon. Place them in a hot oven for ½ hour — 460°. Reduce the heat to a moderate oven 325° and pour ½ cup of boiling stock over the birds. Cook them uncovered and baste them frequently (1¼ hours are usually required for roasting). Make the gravy, — Page 154, adding sour milk or cream. Serve the ducks with currant jelly or cranberries.

ROAST GOOSE

Stuff a goose with raw, quartered and cored apples, with bread or chestnut dressing. Truss it and sprinkle it with salt and pepper. Put 6 thin slices of salt pork over the breast and place the goose in a rack in a dripping pan in a hot oven 500° for ½ hour. Reduce the heat to 300° cover the pan and roast the goose, basting it frequently until it is done. Uncover the pan and remove the pork for the last ½ hour of roasting. If the fowl is young and fat it will require no stock or water for basting. If it is not, add the stock before covering the pan. A goose will require from 1 to 4 hours' roasting.

ROAST TURKEY

Clean a turkey and fill it with bread or chestnut dressing. Spread the entire surface of the fowl with salt and follow this with a coat of ⅓ cup of butter creamed with ¼ cup of flour. If the fowl is lean, a piece of salt pork may be put across the breast. Place the turkey on a dripping rack in a roasting pan in a hot oven 500°. If the turkey browns too fast, cover it with a piece of buttered paper. When it is well browned (15 minutes) reduce the heat to a slow oven 275°, pour 1 cup of stock—Page 154 over it, cover it and roast it until it is done, basting it every 15 minutes. Remove the pork and cook it uncovered for the last half hour (optional). Turn the turkey so that it may brown evenly. Add additional stock, if necessary. The time for cooking a 12 lb. turkey by this method is approximately 3 hours.

RABBIT STEW

Cut a rabbit into pieces. Season and dredge them with flour. Sear them in hot drippings, or butter, on top of the stove until they are well browned. Cover them to the depth of ¼ inch with boiling stock, or Vegetable stock—Page 154 and place a lid over them. Simmer them until they are done, but do not boil them at any time. Remove the rabbit from the pot and make gravy with the drippings—Page 154, adding sour milk or cream and a few drops of Kitchen Bouquet.

RABBIT SAUTÉD

If rabbit is young, follow the rule for Sautéd chicken, adding sour cream to the gravy.

SMOTHERED RABBIT AND ONIONS

1 rabbit cut in pieces	Butter or bacon drippings
Salt	Sliced onions
Pepper	1 cup thick sour cream
Flour	

Sprinkle the rabbit with salt, pepper and flour; brown it in butter or bacon drippings. Cover it with a thick layer of onions, sprinkle the onions with salt and pour the cream over them. Cover the pot closely and simmer the rabbit for one hour, or place the pot in a slow oven—325°—and bake the rabbit until it is tender (about 1 hour).

RABBIT À LA MODE
Haasenpfeffer

Cut a rabbit into pieces and place them in a crock or jar. Cover them with equal parts of vinegar and water, add a sliced onion, salt, pepper corns and a bay leaf. Soak the rabbit for 2 days, then remove the meat, keeping the liquor. Follow the rule for Rabbit Stew, using the vinegar water in the place of stock and adding sour or sweet cream to the gravy.

Dressings for Meat
Dumplings—Croutons

Yorkshire Pudding was originally made in England under the roast rack. The batter was poured into the pan and the roast drippings fell upon it, enriching it and also making it incredibly soggy. A Michigan cook taught me to appreciate this dish by cooking it separately. The finished dish, soft and fluffy to the center, crisp and crusty to the sides and bottom, forms an ideal accompaniment to roast beef. This is the recipe in its original form. If the amount of butter seems excessive a smaller amount may be used.

YORKSHIRE PUDDING

2 cups of bread flour	2 eggs beaten
(measured before sifting)	1 teaspoon salt
2 cups hot milk	¾ cup butter (melted)

Reserve ⅓ of the butter for the pan. Combine the hot milk and ½ the flour, add the salt and the eggs. Beat this well and add the remaining flour. Add the butter last. Pour the reserved butter into a shallow pan. Add the batter and bake the pudding in a quick oven 425° for ½ hour. Serve it cut in squares. It should be about ¾ inch thick.

DUMPLINGS

These dumplings are worth a trial as the experiment is apt to be repeated:

1 cup cake flour	1 egg
4 teaspoons baking	Milk
powder	2 or 3 cups Stock
½ teaspoon salt	

I. Sift the dry ingredients 3 times.

II. Break an egg into a measuring cup and fill it half full of milk. Beat this well and add it slowly to No. I, adding more milk if necessary, but keeping the batter as stiff as possible. Thicken the stock with flour until it has the consistency of gravy. Dip a spoon in the hot gravy, then place a spoonful of batter in it and continue doing this until the dumplings are just touching. Then cover them and simmer them for 2 minutes, turn them, cook them 2 minutes longer and serve them at once.

CROUTONS

Cut bread into ½ inch cubes. Sauté them in hot butter, stirring them gently, or shaking the skillet until they are toasted. Serve them over noodles, Spaetzle or Potato Dumplings, or in soup.

POTATO DUMPLINGS
Kartoffel Kloesse

6 medium sized potatoes   1½ teaspoons salt
2 eggs   ½ cup flour

Boil the potatoes uncovered in their jackets and chill them thoroughly for 12 hours or more. Peel them and grate or rice them. Add the remaining ingredients and beat the batter with a fork until it is fluffy. Roll it into balls 1 inch in diameter and drop them into gently boiling salted water for 10 minutes. Drain them well. Melt ½ cup of butter or drippings, add ¼ cup of dry bread crumbs, or ½ cup of croutons and pour them over the dumplings.

SPATZEN OR SPAETZLE
German Egg Dumplings

Spatzen are good at any time, but they are particularly good served with Roast Veal.

1½ cups flour   1½ cups water
2 eggs (beaten)   ½ teaspoon Salt

Make a batter of these ingredients and beat it well. Drop small bits from a spoon into simmering salted water, or place the batter on a plate and cut shreds with a knife from the side of the plate into the water. Spatzen should be very light and delicate. Try out a sample and if they are too heavy, add water to the batter. Simmer them until they are done, drain them, place them in a dish and cover them with bread crumbs, or croutons sautéd in butter.

BREAD DRESSING WITH MUSHROOMS, OYSTERS, GIBLETS, ETC.

2 cups or more of bread or bread crumbs. (Cornbread crumbs may be used)
2 eggs (optional)
½ cup milk
2 tablespoons butter, melted

1 tablespoon minced onion browned in the butter
2 tablespoons chopped parsley
2 tablespoons to ½ cup chopped celery
Salt, paprika, nutmeg

There is no set rule for the proportions or ingredients for bread dressing. It should be palatable, light and moist, but not "runny", well flavored, but bland. Chopped green peppers, sautéd mushrooms and drained or lightly sautéd oysters may be added to it. Fowl giblets may be sautéd in the onion butter, chopped and added. Stock or oyster liquor may be substituted for milk.

WILD RICE DRESSING FOR GAME

Chopped giblets
1 cup wild rice
4 cups boiling water
1 teaspoon salt

3 tablespoons butter
2 tablespoons onion
1 tablespoon chopped pepper

Cook the giblets for 15 minutes in the boiling water. Remove them from the water and drop the rice into it. Cook it until it is nearly tender. Melt the butter in a skillet, add the onion and the pepper and cook them for three minutes. Add the hot rice and the chopped giblets.

POTATO DRESSING

I. Peel potatoes and cut them into thin slices. Sprinkle them with flour, season them, dot them with butter and moisten them with stock or milk.

II. Dice cold potatoes (cooked in their jackets). Brown them in butter to which chopped onion has been added, season them and add sage or chopped parsley.

APPLE AND SWEET POTATO DRESSING

See Sweet Potatoes and Apples—Page 103.

2 cups apples
1½ cups sweet potatoes
½ cup brown sugar

¼ teaspoon salt
Apple water

Boil the apples and sweet potatoes separately until they are

152

nearly tender. Drain them, combine and mash them and add the remaining ingredients, using just enough apple water (about ½ cup) to soften and hold them together.

CHESTNUT DRESSING

3 cups chestnuts
½ cup butter
1 teaspoon salt
⅛ teaspoon pepper

¼ cup cream
1 cup bread or cracker crumbs

Prepare the chestnuts — Page 124. Drop them into boiling salt water and cook them until they are soft. Put them through a potato ricer and combine them with the remaining ingredients.

Sauces and Gravies

My favorite cooking utensil looks like this and costs five cents. It is not an imposing implement, but armed with it you may scoff at lumps and curdles. It is a tremendous time saver. Vigorously wielded it will insure the smoothest of gravies and sauces. I use it in preference to a rotary beater because its action requires only one hand instead of two, and because it will do anything a rotary beater can do and more. It is called a spiral wire whisk and sometimes a spiral egg beater.

Please, new cooks, read the following instructions for making gravy:

RULE FOR MAKING GRAVY WITH PAN DRIPPINGS, IN WHICH MEAT HAS BEEN SAUTÉD

Remove the meat from the pan. Add 1 tablespoon of flour and stir it until it is smooth, add ¾ cup of boiling water, milk, or stock and cook the gravy until it is smooth and thick, stirring it with a wire whisk. Season the gravy and color it with a few drops of Kitchen Bouquet, strain and serve it. These proportions may be varied.

RULE FOR MAKING GRAVY FOR STEWS AND ROASTS:

Use soup stock if it is available, if it is not, prepare the following:

Vegetable Stock:

2 cups of water
1 onion sliced
Asparagus scrapings, or
vegetables that are used
in soups

2 or 3 celery ribs and leaves
chopped
1 carrot sliced
Parsley
Scant seasoning

If the stock is to be used for pot roast or stew, bring these ingredients to the boiling point and pour them over the seared meat. If the stock is to be used for roast, boil these ingredients gently for 30 minutes. Use 3 cups of water for a large roast. Follow the Rule for Roasting Meat — Page 127. After the meat is seared, pour part of the boiling stock over it and reserve the remainder for frequent basting. When the roast is done, remove it at once from the pan and place it where it will keep hot while the gravy is being made.

Gravy:

Strain the stock into a saucepan and place the pan in cold water. This will cause the fat to rise. Skim it carefully and use it as a basis for the gravy in about the following proportions:

3 tablespoons fat
2 tablespoons flour

1 cup strained stock
Seasoning

Heat the fat, add the flour and when this bubbles, add the stock. Stir the gravy until it is thick and smooth. When making gravy from fat meats, it will sometimes separate. This looks calamitous, but it is easily remedied. Add a little cream very slowly, stirring all the time, and the gravy will become smooth and thick. Taste the gravy and if it is not good, make it so. Add paprika, celery salt, catsup, (sparingly) beef cubes, or Savita, give it character. Having made it good, a great deal has been accomplished, but not enough, it must also look good. Keep a bottle of Kitchen Bouquet on hand. Add enough of this to make the gravy a fine color and it is ready to serve. Never over-season or add unnecessarily to good gravy. Doctor only the indifferent ones and color them to make them attractive. If you have no Kitchen Bouquet, a little burnt sugar will serve the purpose. There is no excuse, except inefficiency, for a whitish, lumpy, tasteless gravy, but one encounters them, alas! in endless varieties. Therefore these instructions.

WHITE SAUCE, OR CREAM SAUCE

2 tablespoons butter
1½ tablespoons flour
¼ teaspoon salt

⅛ teaspoon paprika
1 cup of hot milk

Melt the butter and add the flour. Stir these ingredients until they are smooth, then add the seasoning and gradually the hot milk. Use a wire whisk to stir the sauce and boil it for two minutes. This will make a thin sauce. For a heavier sauce, increase the flour to 2 or 3 tablespoonfuls and use an equal amount of butter. Cream may be substituted for milk. Nutmeg and lemon juice may be added for flavor.

VELOUTÉ SAUCE

Follow the rule for White Sauce, substituting stock for milk.

ALLEMANDE SAUCE

Make white sauce with stock, instead of milk. (Vegetable water may be used). Just before removing it from the fire, reduce the heat, beat in the yolk of 1 egg and add 1 teaspoon of lemon juice. This is very nice with asparagus and beans.

BROWN SAUCE

2 tablespoons butter	Salt
1/2 slice onion	1/8 teaspoon paprika or
2 tablespoons flour	pepper
1 cup brown stock	

One cup boiling water and 1/2 teaspoon Savita or 1 beef cube may be substituted for the stock. Melt the butter and sauté the onion in it until it is light brown. Remove the onion and stir the butter until it is brown. Add the flour and the seasoning and permit them to brown. Add the stock gradually, bring the sauce to the boiling point and boil it for 2 minutes. This sauce is good for left over meat dishes.

MUSHROOM SAUCE

Add 1/4 pound of Sautéd Mushrooms, sliced—Page 123 to Brown Sauce—Page 155. Mushroom stock—Page 123 may be substituted for brown stock. See Mushroom Sauce—Page 86.

MAITRE D' HOTEL BUTTER

1/4 cup butter	1/2 tablespoon chopped
1/2 teaspoon salt	parsley
1/8 teaspoon pepper	3/4 tablespoon lemon juice

Cream the butter. Add the salt, pepper and parsley. Add the lemon very slowly, stirring the sauce constantly.

LEMON BUTTER

¼ cup butter   1 tablespoon lemon juice

Cream the butter, add the lemon juice slowly and add salt if the butter is unsalted.

DRAWN BUTTER

Melt 2 tablespoons of butter for 1 cup of food. Add from 1 to 2 tablespoons of bread crumbs and sauté them for one minute, or add croutons (diced bread, sautéd in a very little butter until it is brown and crisp), and pour the crumbs or the croutons over vegetables or starchy food (macaroni, rice, etc.)

DRAWN BUTTER SAUCE
With parsley or lemon juice

This Sauce is good on broiled meat or fish.

Melt butter in the quantity desired. Season it and just before serving it add finely chopped parsley and lemon juice (optional).

SAUCE FOR BAKED FISH

Thicken the drippings by stirring in 1 tablespoon of flour and add enough vegetable stock or hot water to make the sauce the right consistency. Season it with salt, paprika, mustard and lemon juice and add chopped parsley, or chopped pickles.

MINT SAUCE

3 tablespoons water
1½ tablespoons powdered
  sugar

⅓ cup finely chopped mint
  leaves
½ cup strong vinegar

Heat the water, dissolve the sugar, cool the syrup and combine it with the remaining ingredients. This is best made a half hour before serving it.

CAPER SAUCE FOR BOILED MEATS, MUTTON, TONGUE, ETC.

Follow the rule for White Sauce, using the water in which the meat was boiled instead of milk, or part stock and part milk. Add 2 tablespoons of capers just before removing it from the fire.

QUICK TOMATO SAUCE

1 can of tomato soup	2 tablespoons butter

Heat the sauce and serve it with chopped parsley. The sauce may be thinned with boiling stock or water.

TOMATO SAUCE

2 cups or more of canned tomatoes, or fresh tomatoes stewed	1 carrot (optional)
	1/2 green pepper (optional)
1 slice of onion	3 tablespoons butter
2 ribs of celery with leaves (optional)	3 tablespoons flour
	1/4 teaspoon salt
Parsley (optional)	1/8 teaspoon pepper
	1/4 teaspoon sugar

Cook the vegetables for 15 minutes. Strain and season them. Melt the butter, add the flour and when this is smooth, add the strained stock gradually. Stir the sauce until it is smooth and thick. If the vegetables other than the tomatoes are cut in small pieces, tied in a bag and cooked with the tomatoes, they may be taken from the bag and replaced in the sauce just before it is removed from the fire.

MUSTARD SAUCE

This sauce is good served with corned beef, fish, etc.

Add 1 teaspoon of prepared mustard to 1 cup of Cream Sauce, or make a sauce of the following ingredients:

3 tablespoons melted butter	1 teaspoon boiling water
1 1/2 tablespoons flour	1/4 teaspoon salt
1 teaspoon prepared mustard	

BÉCHAMEL SAUCE

1 cup well flavored light meat and vegetable stock	4 tablespoons flour
	Salt
1 cup hot milk	1/8 teaspoon paprika
4 tablespoons butter	

Proceed as for White Sauce.

BÉCHAMEL SAUCE WITH EGG

Prepare Béchamel Sauce, reduce the heat and beat a little of the sauce with the yolks of 3 eggs. Return this part of the sauce to the pan, beat it all vigorously over a low flame for 1 minute and serve it.

HOLLANDAISE SAUCE
With or without boiling water

½ cup butter
2 egg yolks
1 tablespoon lemon juice

¼ teaspoon salt
⅓ cup boiling water
(optional)

Beat the yolks in a small saucepan, using a wire whisk. Add one-half the butter and all the lemon juice. Place the saucepan over (not in) boiling water. Stir the sauce until it thickens, then add the rest of the butter, bit by bit, add the water slowly, and should the sauce separate, add to it very slowly 2 tablespoons of heavy cream. Serve the sauce at once.

SAUCE BÉARNAISE

Add finely chopped parsley, taragon and shallot or onion to Hollandaise Sauce.

"EASY" HOLLANDAISE SAUCE

1 tablespoon butter
3 egg yolks
1 teaspoon cornstarch

½ teaspoon lemon juice
1 cup boiling water
Salt

Soften the butter, add the egg yolks and beat this well. Add the cornstarch and lemon juice. Just before serving the sauce add 1 cup of boiling water very, very slowly. Hold the pan over hot water, or high over a low flame and stir the sauce until it thickens. Add the salt and serve the sauce at once.

CHEESE SAUCE

3 tablespoons butter
3 tablespoons flour
1½ cups milk
1 cup (or less) mild cheese

cut into small pieces
Salt
Paprika
A few grains of cayenne

Follow the rule for Cream Sauce. When the sauce is done, lower the heat and add the cheese. Stir it until it is melted and season the sauce well.

CURRANT JELLY SAUCE

1 cup Brown Sauce
¼ glass currant jelly

1 tablespoon Sherry

Dissolve the jelly in the hot Brown Sauce or in one cup of lamb gravy and add the Sherry.

CUCUMBER SAUCE I.

¾ cup cream
⅓ teaspoon salt
2 tablespoons vinegar, or
  lemon juice

1 large cucumber, pared,
  very finely cut and
  drained

Beat the cream until it is stiff, add the vinegar slowly. Season the sauce and add the cucumbers.

CUCUMBER SAUCE II.

Cucumbers pared, seeded
  and grated
Salt

Paprika
Vinegar

TARTAR SAUCE

1 teaspoon mustard
⅛ teaspoon pepper
1 teaspoon powdered sugar
¼ teaspoon salt
Onion juice
Yolks of 2 eggs
½ cup oil

3 tablespoons vinegar
1 tablespoon chopped olives
1 tablespoon capers
1 tablespoon chopped
  cucumber pickles
1 tablespoon chopped
  parsley

Combine the ingredients in the order given, adding the oil slowly, alternately with the vinegar, as in Mayonnaise Dressing—Page 183. This sauce, with the parsley omitted, will keep for weeks.

SOUR CREAM AND HORSERADISH SAUCE

Sour cream
Grated horseradish, fresh
  or prepared

Vinegar or lemon
Salt
Sugar

Beat the cream well and season it as desired with the remaining ingredients. This is a good sauce to serve with cold meat.

Fruits
Fresh and Dried
Stewed and Baked

CRANBERRIES

4 cups cranberries
  (1 quart)

2 cups boiling water
2 cups sugar

Add the water to the berries and boil them for 20 minutes. Put them through a strainer, add the sugar and boil them for

5 minutes. Place the jelly in a mold and chill it well. Invert the contents of the mold onto a dish when ready to serve the jelly.

SYRUP FOR STEWING FRESH FRUIT

2 cups water
1 cup sugar

$\frac{1}{8}$ teaspoon of salt

Boil the syrup for 3 minutes.

PEACHES

Peel the peaches (and remove the stones, if desired). Drop them into the boiling syrup. Simmer them until they are tender, chill and serve them.

PEARS
of any kind

Even those uncompromising forget-me-nots the Kiefer Pears have been known to respond readily to this treatment:

Peel, quarter and core the pears. Add 2 sticks of cinnamon and $\frac{1}{2}$ a lemon sliced to the syrup. Drop the pears into the boiling syrup, simmer them until they are tender, chill and serve them.

APPLES

Follow the rule for pears.

PLUMS

Cut the plums into halves and remove the seeds, or keep the plums whole. Drop them into boiling syrup and simmer them until they are tender. A stick of cinnamon may be added to the syrup.

STEAMED RHUBARB

Wash rhubarb and cut it without peeling it into blocks of 1 inch. There should be about 1 quart. Place it in the upper part of a double boiler over boiling water. Cover it closely. Steam it for 20 or 30 minutes. Do not stir it at any time. When it is nearly tender, dissolve $\frac{1}{2}$ to $\frac{3}{4}$ cup of sugar and $\frac{1}{4}$ teaspoon soda in $\frac{1}{2}$ cup of hot water. Pour this over the rhubarb and steam it for 2 minutes longer. This is a good and a nice looking dish.

STEWED RHUBARB

Peel the rhubarb and cut it into small pieces. Place it in an earthen or enameled dish. Sprinkle it generously with sugar and permit it to stand for 12 hours, or more. Put it in a saucepan and cook it without the addition of water, simmering it gently until it is tender, or bake it covered in a slow oven.

BAKED PEACHES

Use firm juicy peaches. Peel them, cut them in halves and remove the stones. Place the peaches in a baking dish and fill each hollow with 1/2 teaspoon butter, 1 teaspoon sugar, a sprinkling of lemon juice and nutmeg or cinnamon. Place 2 tablespoons of water in the bottom of the dish. Bake the peaches for 20 minutes in a moderate oven 350°.

BAKED PEARS

Peel pears, cut them in halves, or quarters and remove the cores. Place the pears in a baker, sprinkle them with sugar and a little cinnamon, and add 1 tablespoon of water for every pear. Cover them closely and cook them from 2 to 3 hours in a very slow oven—300°. Seckel and other small pears are good baked whole.

BAKED APPLES

Wash the apples and core them. Peel the upper fourth of each apple. Place them in a casserole, or baking dish. Fill the centers with sugar, either white or brown and with a teaspoon or more of butter. Blanched shredded almonds, or other nuts may be added. Allow 1 tablespoon of water for every apple and pour it in the bottom of the dish. Cook the apples, covered, or uncovered, in a hot oven until they are tender, but do not permit them to lose their shape—20 to 30 minutes are usually sufficient. Serve them with, or without cream.

BAKED APPLES AND RED HOTS

Core and peel Roman Beauty apples. Make a syrup of 1 1/2 cups of sugar, 2 cups of water and 1/4 pound of cinnamon drops (red hots).

Cook it until the red hots are dissolved. When it is boiling, add a few apples at a time. Cook them gently until they are tender, then remove them from the syrup. Fill the hollows with blanched almonds. Dissolve 1 tablespoon of gelatine that has been soaked in a little cold water, in the hot syrup and pour it around the apples. Chill and serve them.

BAKED APPLES AND MINCE MEAT

Hollow apples, leaving a shell 1/3 inch thick. Chop the pulp and combine it with mince meat. Put 1 tablespoon of brown sugar in each apple and fill it with mince meat. Put the apples in a baking dish, and place 1 tablespoon of water for each apple in the bottom of the dish. Sprinkle them with brown sugar and bake them in a moderate oven 350° until they are done. Serve them with or without hard sauce flavored with Sherry or Brandy.

PEACHES AND MINCE MEAT

Fill well drained canned peach halves with mince meat. Place them in a shallow pan with enough peach juice to keep them from scorching and bake them in a slow oven for 25 or 30 minutes. Serve them with roast fowl or ham.

APPLE SAUCE

Wash the apples and cut them into quarters. Place them in a saucepan and nearly cover them with water. Old apples require more water than new ones. Add sliced lemon to tasteless apples. Stew the apples until they are tender and put them through a purée strainer, or ricer. Return the strained apples to the saucepan, add enough sugar to make them palatable and boil them for 3 minutes. Sprinkle the apple sauce with cinnamon, if desired.

SAUTÉD APPLES
"Fried Apples"

The following is good only when made with tart, well flavored apples, then it is delicious:

Butter or bacon drippings	A pinch of salt (if the
Tart apples	butter is sweet)

Pare, core and slice the apples. Melt the butter in a spider over a quick fire. When it is hot, add the apples. Reduce the heat when the apples are well coated. Sprinkle them lightly with salt and cook them covered over a gentle fire until they are nearly tender. If the apples are dry a little hot water may be added. Uncover them and cook them until they are tender. Add additional butter as needed. Serve them with a meat course.

BAKED BANANAS

Butter, sugar, lemon juice and salt are called for in most recipes for baked bananas. I have tried out a great many of them, but have discarded them all for: Bananas, peeled and placed in a greased baking dish, baked in a moderate oven 350° until they are very tender (30 to 45 minutes) seasoned with salt, and if desired, with lemon juice, after baking.

SAUTÉD BANANAS
Fried

Cut bananas in lengthwise slices, dredge them with flour and sauté them in butter. Serve them very hot sprinkled with powdered sugar.

SAUTÉD PINEAPPLE

Drain and dry large slices of canned pineapple, cut them in two, dip them in flour and sauté them in butter until they are light brown. Use them with parsley to garnish a meat platter.

BAKED ORANGES I.

Select medium sized oranges. Wash them, cut off the tops and take out the cores. Fill each center with sugar and a teaspoon of butter. Place the oranges in a baking pan half full of water, cover them and bake them slowly until they are done — about one hour. Remove the cover and brown them slightly. They may be topped with a marshmallow and the marshmallow may be roasted.

BAKED ORANGES II.

Wash thin skinned oranges of even size. Cut a slice from the top of each orange and remove the pulp. Remove the fiber and the seeds from the pulp and chop it. Add an equal measure of crushed pineapple drained, sweeten it with sugar and fill the shells with the mixture. Put a tablespoon of butter on each orange and place them in a baking dish. Cover them closely and bake them in a slow oven 325° until the skins are tender — about three hours. Refill the shells as the filling cooks down and baste the oranges frequently with pineapple juice.

STEWED DRIED FRUIT

The California Dried Fruit Association has supplied the following method for cooking dried fruit:

APRICOTS

1 lb. dried apricots	4 cups water
2 cups sugar	

Wash the apricots. Cover them with water and boil them gently for 35 minutes. Add the sugar and boil them for 5 minutes longer.

PRUNES
Quick Method

Cover prunes well with hot water and permit them to soak for 1 hour. Bring them to the boiling point in the water in which they were soaked and cook them gently until they are tender — from 30 to 40 minutes. Add sugar for the last 10 minutes of cooking, 2 tablespoons to 1 cup of prunes, measured before soaking, or cooking.

PRUNES
Slow Method

Cover prunes with water and soak them for 12 hours, cover them with additional water and bring them to the boiling point. Cook them very, very slowly for about two hours. Sugar is not needed when prunes are cooked in this way. A stick of cinnamon and a slice of lemon peel may be added while the prunes are cooking.

SPICED PRUNES

These prunes are deliciously spiced and their piquant quality makes them a good addition to a meat course:

Prepare prunes by the quick, or the slow method. Cook them until they are nearly tender, and drain them. Prepare the following:

Syrup:

1 cup brown sugar	1 teaspoon cinnamon, nut-
½ cup vinegar	meg, allspice and cloves,
1 lemon sliced	(combined)
A few grains of salt	

Boil the syrup for 5 minutes, add the prunes and cook them gently for three minutes. Placed in a jar and covered, these prunes will keep for a long time.

Salads

LETTUCE

Lettuce, endive and watercress should be served crisp and cold. They should be dressed immediately before being served (except in the case of wilted lettuce).

Soak the heads of lettuce in cold water for 1 hour. Separate the leaves, wash them well, drain or shake the water from them and place them in a bag on ice. See Page 93, for keeping vegetables fresh in mechanical refrigerators. When ready to serve the lettuce, add the dressing, or prepare the dressing at the table, and add it to the lettuce.

Watercress calls for the same treatment. The stalks are cut off and the coarse leaves are sometimes removed.

Heads of Iceberg lettuce are not separated. They are cut into wedge shaped pieces, or into crosswise slices.

WILTED LETTUCE

Sauté bacon and remove it from the pan. Cut it into small pieces. Dilute the drippings with mild vinegar, heat them and add the minced bacon. Pour the dressing while hot over lettuce and serve it at once with sliced hard-cooked eggs.

COLE SLAW

Remove the outer leaves and the core from a head of cabbage. Shred or chop the remainder, cutting only as much as is needed for immediate use. A deep bowl and the sharp edge of a baking powder can are fine for this purpose. Soak the chopped cabbage in ice water for 1 hour. Drain it well and chill it. Immediately before serving it, marinate the cabbage with French dressing, or with Boiled dressing, thinned with sour cream. Combine the cabbage, if desired, with chopped green peppers, apples and celery.

CABBAGE, APPLES AND NUTS
6 Servings

1 cup cabbage shredded
1 cup apples peeled and
   diced

½ cup walnuts or pecans
¾ cup mayonnaise or
   boiled dressing

WALDORF SALAD
6 Servings

1 cup celery diced
1 cup apples peeled and
   diced

½ cup walnuts or pecans
¾ cup mayonnaise

SEEDLESS GRAPES

Seedless grapes are good served on lettuce leaves with French Dressing, in Lemon Jelly and as an addition to all fruit and to many vegetable salads.

MALAGA AND TOKAY GRAPES

Skin and seed grapes and serve them in Lemon Jelly, or as an addition to Fruit Salad.

GRAPES AND COTTAGE CHEESE WITH FRENCH DRESSING

Place cottage cheese in a ring mold, or in individual molds. Chill it, invert it onto lettuce leaves and serve it dusted with paprika, with seedless grapes and French dressing.

JAPANESE PERSIMMONS

This is an attractive looking salad:

Serve ripe persimmons chilled and halved on lettuce leaves with French Dressing. They may be garnished with chopped green peppers.

MELONS

I.   Cut ripe, chilled melons into lengthwise slices, remove the rind and serve the slices whole, or in pieces on lettuce leaves. Sprinkle the melon slices with lemon, or lime juice, or serve them with French dressing.

II. Cut melon meat into balls with a potato cutter. Serve them in cocktail glasses, or on lettuce leaves. Use pink and green melons for a decorative effect.

MELONS AND COTTAGE CHEESE

Serve Melons I. and II. with cottage cheese, or cut chilled melons in half, remove the seeds and serve the halves filled with cottage cheese. The cheese may be sprinkled with paprika or chopped chives.

GRAPEFRUIT SALAD

Skin grapefruit. Separate it into sections and remove the thin skin carefully, keeping the sections whole, if possible. Place the fruit in a strainer and chill it well. Serve it with French dressing, using grapefruit juice in place of vinegar, and add a little powdered sugar.

BLACK-EYED SUSAN

Skin unbroken whole or half sections of orange or grapefruit and arrange them around a center of chopped dates and nuts. French dressing and cheese straws are good with this salad.

ORANGE AND GRAPEFRUIT SALAD

Skin unbroken sections of oranges and grapefruit. Place them on lettuce leaves and sprinkle them with chopped chives, or with parsley. Serve them with French dressing.

CHERRY AND HAZELNUT SALAD

Pit canned cherries and insert a hazelnut into each cherry. Serve them very cold with cottage cheese and mayonnaise.

PRUNE SALAD

Stew large prunes, drain them and remove the seeds. Fill the prunes with cream cheese, to which nuts and mayonnaise have been added, and serve them on lettuce leaves.

PEACH SALAD I.

I. Chill fresh peaches and peel them just before serving them, or prepare them in advance, wrap them in wax paper and place them on ice. Serve them on lettuce leaves with French dressing. Canned peaches may be substituted. The hollows may be filled with cream cheese and chopped nuts.

PEAR SALAD

Chill and peel fresh pears, leaving them whole and follow the rule for Peach Salad I. Brush one side of each pear with a dash of red coloring, or with paprika. Place a clove in the blossom end and a bit of water cress in the stem end. Serve the pears with French dressing and walnut creams, or use canned pears and fill the center with cream or cottage cheese.

PINEAPPLE SALAD I.

Serve slices of canned pineapple, drained, on lettuce leaves with mayonnaise, French or fruit dressing. Put cream cheese through a ricer and garnish the slices with it.

PINEAPPLE SALAD II.

Serve fresh pineapple, peeled and shredded, with French dressing, to which a little powdered sugar has been added.

AVOCADO PEAR, ORANGE AND GRAPEFRUIT SALAD
Alligator Pears

Peel avocado pears, slice them lengthwise and arrange them with skinned orange and grapefruit sections in wheel shape on lettuce leaves. Serve the salad with French dressing made with lime juice.

AVOCADO PEAR SALAD

Peel avocado pears and cut them into lengthwise slices. Serve them on lettuce leaves with French dressing, alone, or combined with pineapple and grapefruit slices, or serve half pears, unpeeled, on lettuce leaves with French dressing.

ZUCCHINI

Zucchini served in the following manner is similar to an Avocado pear:

Follow the rule for boiling Zucchini — Page 120. Drain and chill them. Serve them on lettuce leaves with French dressing.

CARROT SALAD

Raw carrots are served peeled and cut in lengthwise strips, or they are ground in a food chopper (the finest knife being used) and combined with shredded peppers and celery. They are served with mayonnaise, or French dressing. Riced or ground carrots are good in gelatine salads, alone, combined with other vegetables, or with fruits.

BEET SALAD

Prepare boiled beets — Page 110. Skin them and cut them in crosswise slices, or into quarters. While they are hot, pour over them a hot dressing of equal parts of vinegar and water, well seasoned with salt, pepper corns, paprika and bay leaves. Chill the beets well before serving them.

CUCUMBER SALAD

Chill cucumbers, peel them and cut them in crosswise slices. Marinate them with French dressing, or with sour cream dressing and serve them at once.

POTATO SALAD WITH MAYONNAISE

Boil potatoes in their jackets in a covered saucepan until they are tender. Chill them for several hours, peel and slice them. Marinate them well with French dressing and soup stock. Add hard-cooked eggs chopped or diced, onions, olives, capers, pickles, celery and cucumbers. Season the salad well. After 1 hour or more, add mayonnaise, or boiled dressing thinned with cream, or sour cream. Make the salad very moist, as it will absorb a great deal of liquid. This may be made in advance, in fact, it seems to be best the second day.

HOT POTATO SALAD WITH BACON DRIPPINGS
6 to 8 Servings

3 cups sliced potatoes	1/4 cup water
4 strips of bacon diced or	1/2 teaspoon sugar
2 tablespoons bacon drippings	Salt, paprika
	1/2 teaspoon mustard
1 small onion chopped	(optional)
1/2 cup vinegar	

Cook the potatoes in their jackets in a covered saucepan. Peel and slice them while they are hot. Place the bacon in a skillet and when it is hot, add the onions and sauté them until they are brown. Heat the water, vinegar and spices to the boiling point and pour them into the skillet. Pour this dressing, while hot, over the hot potatoes and serve them at once.

SWISS SALAD

The basis of Swiss Salad is potatoes and horseradish. After that its flourishes are many. It is best when prepared with hot potatoes, but cold mashed potatoes may be utilized, if a little hot stock, or cream, is added to soften them. Serve Swiss salad in small mounds or stuff tomatoes with it. It has a nice piquant quality. Garnish it with sprigs of parsley and paprika.

1 cup hot riced potatoes
1 tablespoon horseradish
  (fresh or prepared)
1 tablespoon chopped celery
1 tablespoon chopped
  parsley

1 tablespoon chopped
  pickles
1/3 cup French dressing or
  mayonnaise
Seasoning

Combine the ingredients and place the salad in molds. Chill and unmold them on lettuce leaves. The minor ingredients may be varied and olives, chives, or onions may be added, or substituted.

GUMBO (OKRA) FRENCH DRESSING

Cut the stems and a thin slice from the top of the okra. Drop the pods into boiling, salted water and cook them gently until they are tender (about 8 minutes). Drain the okra and rinse the pods with two cups of hot water. Drain them again, place them on a platter, cover them with well seasoned French dressing and chill them. Serve them very cold on lettuce leaves. (The rinsing of the okra is optional).

STRING BEAN SALAD

Cook String Beans—Page 112 until they are tender. Drain them and while hot, marinate them with French dressing, to which either chopped chives or chopped onions have been added. The dressing may be thinned with a little meat or vegetable stock. Chill the beans thoroughly and serve them on lettuce leaves.

CELERY SALAD

Wash and chill the amount of celery desired. Cut it into small crosswise pieces and serve it moistened with French dressing, with mayonnaise, or with boiled salad dressing thinned with sour cream.

CELERY, CABBAGE AND GREEN PEPPERS

See Cole Slaw—Page 165, combine it with shredded peppers, celery and mayonnaise.

CELERIAC OR CELERY ROOT SALAD
8 to 10 Servings

This is very nice with cold meat or sausage:

3 or 4 celery roots	Pepper
1 sliced onion	Vinegar and water, or
Salt	celery water

Peel the roots, drop them into boiling, salted water and cook them until they are tender (about 2 hours). Drain the celery and slice it. Heat an equal amount of water and vinegar, season it with salt and pepper and pour it over the celery. Serve the celery hot or cold, or slice the celery, chill it and serve it with mayonnaise.

SHRIMP SALAD
4 to 6 Servings

1 cup of shrimp, fresh or dry packed	1 teaspoon lemon juice
1 cup celery diced	1/2 cup mayonnaise
	Salt, pepper, celery salt

If canned shrimp are used, soak them in ice water for 1 hour, then drain them. Add the lemon juice to the shrimp and combine them with the other ingredients. Garnish the salad with hard cooked eggs.

TOMATOES AND ONIONS

Peel and chill medium sized tomatoes. Cut five or six crosswise gashes in the tomato equal distances apart. Place a thin slice of Bermuda onion in each gash. Serve the tomatoes on lettuce with French dressing.

HERRING SALAD
About 20 Servings

One of the recollections of my childhood is Herring Salad. Served at Christmas time, its rich color (thanks to the red of the beets) and elaborate garnishing made this dish an imposing sight:

6 milter herring	1 cup almonds
1/2 pound cold veal roast	4 hard cooked eggs
2 cups apples	2 tablespoons horseradish
1 1/2 cups pickled beets	2 tablespoons chopped
1/2 cup onions	parsley
1/2 cup pickles	1 cup vinegar
2 stalks celery	1 cup sugar
1/2 cup cold boiled potatoes	

Soak the herring in water over night, skin them and remove the bones. Rub the milt through a colander with some of the vinegar. Cut the veal, apples, beets, onions, potatoes, pickles and celery into dice the size of a large pea. Shred the almonds. Combine the vinegar, milt and sugar with the remaining ingredients. Garnish the salad with pickles, sardelles, hard cooked eggs, olives and parsley.

FRESH TOMATO RELISH

2 cups tomatoes, skinned and diced	¼ cup chopped onion
1 tablespoon lemon juice	1 teaspoon salt
	1 teaspoon sugar

Combine the ingredients and chill them for 2 hours before serving them.

TOMATOES

A bit of tomato skin was once as out of place at a dinner table as a bowie knife. The discovery that tomato skins contain highly valued vitamins makes them "Salonfaehig," so whether to serve tomatoes skinned or unskinned rests with the hostess' sense of delicacy or her desire for health. After all, tomato skins are rather uninviting.

TO PREPARE AND SKIN TOMATOES

Wash all tomatoes, as they are frequently sprayed with chemicals.

I. Peel very ripe tomatoes by pulling off the skin with a knife.

II. Immerse tomatoes in boiling water for 1 minute. Drain, skin and chill them.

III. Place a tomato on a fork and hold it over heat for a few seconds. The loosened skin is easily removed. Chill the tomatoes and serve them, whole or sliced on lettuce with French dressing or mayonnaise.

STUFFED TOMATOES

Skin tomatoes, hollow them and invert them to drain for 20 minutes. Chill them and fill the hollows with:

Cole slaw	Chopped onions
Celery	Stuffed olives
Asparagus, cooked and chilled	Cucumbers
	Nut meats
Green peppers	Fresh pineapple

172

alone, or in some good combination, moistened with French dressing or mayonnaise. In addition to the ingredients suggested, tomatoes may be stuffed with the following:

Cottage cheese, garnished with chives or nut meats and mayonnaise, fish salad, chicken salad, Swiss salad, minced onions combined with thick sour cream, etc.

TOMATOES FILLED WITH PINEAPPLE AND CELERY

Prepare Tomato Cases — Page 66. Fill them with:

1 part celery	1 part pineapple, fresh or
1 part walnuts	canned

Moisten these ingredients with mayonnaise.

TOMATOES FILLED WITH EGGS AND ANCHOVIES

Prepare Tomato Cases — Page 66. Fill them with a mixture of hard cooked eggs, chopped, anchovies, chopped, or anchovy paste, onion juice, paprika and salt. Cover the tops with mayonnaise and place an anchovy in the center of each top. Anchovy may be added to cottage cheese and used as a filling.

TOMATOES FILLED WITH STUFFED EGGS

This is an easily handled picnic salad: Prepare Tomato Cases. Place half an egg, stuffed — See Page 15, in each hollow and serve the tomatoes on lettuce leaves.

TOMATO ASPIC
8 Servings

1 can tomatoes (No. 2½)	1 teaspoon salt
1 small onion minced	½ teaspoon paprika
1 bay leaf	1 teaspoon sugar
4 ribs of celery with	2 tablespoons mild vinegar
leaves	or lemon juice (optional)

Boil these ingredients for 20 minutes. Strain them. Soak 2 tablespoons of gelatine in ½ cup cold water for 5 minutes. Dissolve it in the hot tomato juice. Add water to make 4 cups of liquid. Chill the aspic until it is set. Olives diced, celery, green peppers, carrots minced, ground meat, or fish may be added to the aspic when it is about to set.

TOMATO ASPIC RING

Prepare Tomato Aspic. Pour it into a wet ring mold. Chill it until it is firm, unmold it onto lettuce leaves and fill the center with cottage cheese, with sliced cucumbers, or with fish or chicken salad.

QUICK TOMATO ASPIC

1 quart of canned, or bottled Tomato Cocktail, 2 tablespoons gelatine (1 pk.) Soak the gelatine in ½ cup cold cocktail for 5 minutes, dissolve it in hot cocktail. Mold and chill the aspic until it is firm.

The following Salads will be found in other parts of this book. Consult the Index for: Tongue in Aspic; Emergency Aspic; Deviled Eggs in Aspic; Tomatoes and Cottage Cheese; Molded Fish Salad; Aspic Salad; Chicken or Fish Salad in Aspic. Artichokes with Shrimp or Crabmeat.

FROZEN ASPIC
12 to 15 Cubes

This is fine for plate luncheons, frozen in refrigerator trays and served in cubes topped with a dab of mayonnaise:

2 teaspoons gelatine	½ bay leaf (optional)
½ cup cold water	1½ teaspoons salt
3 cups tomatoes	1 teaspoon sugar
2 slices of onion	½ teaspoon Worcestershire
3 ribs of celery with leaves	Sauce

Soak the gelatine in the cold water for 5 minutes. Boil the tomatoes with the next three ingredients for 20 minutes. Strain them and add the soaked gelatine. Season the aspic, cool it and freeze it in cubes.

GRAPEFRUIT ASPIC
12 to 14 Servings

Sometimes with the luck of a Madame Galvani — (only with less far reaching results) a hostess will hit upon an unusual combination. This is one.

2 tablespoons gelatine	Juice of 1 to 2 lemons
½ cup cold stock	Salt, paprika
3½ cups boiling stock	Sugar (optional)
Lemon rind	

Soak the gelatine for 5 minutes in the cold stock, dissolve it in the boiling stock. Add the lemon rind and as much juice as you think palatable. Season the aspic highly, as it is to go with unseasoned food. Chill it, and when it is about to set, combine it lightly with the following ingredients:

Skinned sections of 2 grapefruit	1 pair of sweetbreads, boiled and diced
1 large stalk of celery diced	

Mold and chill the salad and serve it with mayonnaise.

FOUNDATION RECIPE FOR JELLY I., FOR FRUIT SALADS
6 to 8 Servings

1 tablespoon gelatine
1/2 cup cold water
1 cup boiling water or
fruit juice
4 to 6 tablespoons sugar

1/8 teaspoon salt
1/4 cup lemon juice
1 1/2 cups fruit, diced or
sliced

Soak the gelatine for 5 minutes in the cold water, dissolve it in the boiling water. Add the sugar, the salt and the lemon juice. If sweetened fruit juice is used, take less sugar. Chill the aspic and when it is about to set combine it with the prepared fruit. Place it in a wet mold and chill it until it is firm. Serve it with cream mayonnaise.

FOUNDATION RECIPE FOR JELLY II., FOR VEGETABLE SALADS
6 to 8 Servings

1 tablespoon gelatine
1/2 cup cold water
1 cup boiling water, or light
colored stock
4 tablespoons sugar

1/2 teaspoon salt
1/4 cup mild vinegar, or
lemon juice
1 1/2 cups diced raw or
cooked vegetables

Combine these ingredients, following the rule for Foundation Jelly I.

FOUNDATION RECIPE FOR MAYONNAISE JELLY

This aspic has a rich, creamy consistency but is not at all rich. It is a desirable summer dish which combines well with meat, fish, vegetables or fruit.

1 tablespoon gelatine
1/4 cup cold water
1 1/2 cups boiling water

1/2 cup mayonnaise or salad
dressing
Salt, paprika

Soak the gelatine in the cold water for 5 minutes, dissolve it in the boiling water and add the remaining ingredients. Chill the jelly and when it is about to set add 2 cups of solid ingredients. The solid ingredients may be omitted and the jelly may be served on lettuce leaves.

MINT JELLY

Prepare Foundation Jelly I. pouring 1 cup of the boiling water over 1/4 cup crushed mint leaves and allowing them to steep for 5 minutes. Strain this infusion, add a few drops of green coloring and combine it with the other ingredients.

CELERY ASPIC IN RING MOLDS ON TOMATO SLICES
8 to 9 Servings

Prepare Foundation Jelly II. and when it is about to set add 1½ cups minced celery. Fill individual ring molds and chill the jelly until it is firm. Invert the contents of the molds onto large thick slices of cold skinned tomato. Place three stuffed olives in the center and serve the aspic with mayonnaise.

SEEDLESS GRAPE AND CELERY RING

Prepare Lemon Jelly—Page 312. When it is about to set, add to it 3 cups of seedless grapes and diced celery combined in any proportion. Place the jelly in a wet ring mold and chill it. Unmold it on lettuce leaves and fill the center with cream mayonnaise.

JELLIED SALMON OR TUNA FISH AND CUCUMBER SALAD

Use foundation Recipe for Jelly II.—Page 175. Pour it over 1½ cups of fresh, peeled and sliced cucumbers and flaked salmon combined. Lemon flavored gelatine powder may be used for the aspic by adding vinegar, salt, pepper and onion juice.

MOLDED VEGETABLE SALAD
12 to 15 Servings

2 tablespoons gelatine
(1 envelope)
½ cup cold water
2 cups boiling water
½ cup sugar
½ cup vinegar
1 teaspoon salt
½ cup shredded cabbage

2 cups diced celery
½ cup shredded green
pepper
½ cup shredded pimento
(optional)
¼ cup mint leaves chopped
(optional)

Soak the gelatine for 5 minutes in the cold water, dissolve it in the boiling water and add the sugar, salt and vinegar. Chill this and when it is about to set combine it with the remaining ingredients. Place the salad in a wet mold, chill it, unmold it on lettuce leaves and serve it with mayonnaise.

GOLDEN GLOW SALAD
8 to 10 Servings

This is good in flavor and lovely in color:

2 cups raw carrots grated
  or ground
1 cup crushed pineapple
  drained

⅞ cup water
⅞ cup pineapple juice
½ teaspoon salt
1 package lemon jello

Heat the liquids to the boiling point and dissolve the powder in them. Add the salt. Chill the jelly and when it is about to set, combine it with the remaining ingredients, 2 cups of carrots and 1 cup of crushed pineapple may be combined with Foundation Recipe for Jelly I., if the lemon jello is not available.

PINEAPPLE AND CUCUMBER SALAD
6 Servings

This is an attractive looking, very refreshing salad:

1 envelope gelatine
  (2 tablespoons)
½ cup cold water
1 cucumber pared and
  seeded
3 or 4 slices of pineapple

Juice from a No. 2 can
  pineapple (1 cup)
⅓ cup sugar
Juice of 3 lemons (about
  ½ cup)
Green coloring

Soak the gelatine in the cold water for 5 minutes. Put the cucumber and the pineapple through a grinder, saving the juices. Add the juices to the pineapple juice and enough water to make 1½ cups of liquid. Add the sugar and the salt. Bring this to the boiling point and dissolve the gelatine in it. Add a few drops of green coloring and chill the liquid slightly. Combine it with the ground cucumber and pineapple and place it on ice until it is firm. Unmold it and serve it with cream mayonnaise.

GINGER ALE SALAD
14 to 16 Servings

This, and the Pineapple Salad are the nicest molded fruit salads given:

2 tablespoons gelatine
2 tablespoons cold water
¼ cup boiling water or
  fruit juice

½ cup sugar
⅛ teaspoon salt
1 pint gingerale
Juice of 1 lemon

Soak the gelatine in the cold water and dissolve it in the boiling water. Add the remaining ingredients and chill the jelly until it is nearly set. Combine it with:

½ pound Malaga grapes
skinned and seeded
1 orange skinned and sliced
1 grapefruit in skinned
sections

12 Maraschino cherries,
cut in half
6 pineapple slices cut in
pieces
¼ pound canton ginger,
chopped

Place the salad in a wet mold. Chill it and unmold it on lettuce leaves. Serve it with cream mayonnaise.

MOLDED CRANBERRY, CELERY AND NUT SALAD
6 to 8 Servings

2 tablespoons gelatine
½ cup cold water
1 pint cranberries
1 cup boiling water

¾ to 1 cup sugar
¼ teaspoon salt
⅔ cup diced celery
½ cup nutmeats, chopped

Cook the cranberries covered for 20 minutes. They may be used strained, or unstrained. If the former, strain them at this time. Add the sugar and the salt and cook them for 5 minutes longer. Add the soaked gelatine. Chill the jelly and when it is about to set fold in the remaining ingredients. Place them in a wet mold until they are firm. Unmold them and serve them with mayonnaise.

24 HOUR FRUIT SALAD WITH CREAM
12 to 14 Servings

2 egg yolks
¼ cup sugar
¼ cup cream

Juice of 2 lemons
⅛ teaspoon salt

Cook these ingredients in a double boiler, stirring constantly, until they are thick. Chill them and add:

1 cup heavy cream whipped
6 slices of pineapple diced
2 cups Queen Anne cherries
½ pound grapes peeled and

seeded (optional)
1 cup almonds blanched
½ pound marshmallows
cut in pieces

Chill the salad for 24 hours. Serve it on lettuce leaves with mayonnaise, or as a dessert with whipped cream.

FROZEN FRUIT SALAD
10 to 12 Servings

1 tablespoon butter
1 tablespoon flour
Juice of 1 can of pineapple
(No. 2)
1 tablespoon sugar
1 egg

1 cup double cream,
whipped
1 can white cherries (No.
2½) pitted
1 can pineapple (No. 2)
1 can apricots (No. 2½)

Melt the butter, add the flour, the pineapple juice, lemon, sugar and the egg and cook these ingredients over hot water until they are thick and smooth. Then cool them and add the whipped cream and the drained fruit. Freeze the salad in a refrigerator, or in a mold packed in ice and salt—See Page 183. Unmold it and serve it with cream mayonnaise—Page 183.

GREEN PEPPER OR PIMENTO SLICES I.
8 to 10 Slices

These slices are highly decorative:

2 green or red peppers or
1 can American Lady
   pimento
2 packages of cream cheese

Cream or mayonnaise to
   moisten the cheese
   slightly

Combine the cheese and the cream or mayonnaise. Use paprika, if it does not interfere with your color scheme. Cut a piece from the stem end of the peppers and remove the seeds and the veins. Stuff peppers or pimentoes with the cheese mixture and chill them for 12 hours. Slice them with a sharp, hot knife and replace them on ice. Serve the pepper slices on lettuce leaves, or sliced tomatoes, or with any suitable salad dressed with French dressing or mayonnaise.

GREEN PEPPER SLICES II.

2 packages of cream cheese
1/2 cup crushed pineapple,
   drained
1 pimento, chopped
2 tablespoons pecans,

chopped
1 teaspoon gelatine, soaked
   for 5 minutes in 2 teaspoons pineapple juice,
   dissolved over hot water

Combine the ingredients and fill pepper shells, following the rule for Green Pepper Slices I.

MOLDED COTTAGE CHEESE
6 to 8 Servings

1 tablespoon gelatine
1/4 cup cold water
2 cups cottage cheese

3/4 teaspoons salt
1/8 teaspoon paprika
1/2 cup cream or milk

Soak the gelatine in the cold water for 5 minutes. Dissolve it by placing it over heat. Cool this. Beat the cheese until it is smooth, add the seasoning, the cream and the gelatine. Pour the cheese mixture into a small wet border mold and chill it until it is set. Unmold it on lettuce leaves and fill the center with fruit moistened with cream mayonnaise, or fill it with a vegetable salad.

MOLDED PINEAPPLE CHEESE SALAD
4 Servings

1½ teaspoons gelatine
⅓ cup cold water
⅓ cup boiling pineapple
  juice
2 tablespoons lemon juice

2 tablespoons sugar
⅛ teaspoon salt
⅔ cup diced or crushed
  pineapple, drained
⅔ cup cottage cheese

Soak the gelatine in the cold water for 5 minutes, dissolve it in the boiling pineapple juice, add the lemon juice, sugar and salt. Chill this but do not permit it to set. Combine the jelly with the cheese and beat it until it is smooth, add the pineapple and place it in a wet mold on ice. Unmold it on lettuce leaves.

MOLDED CHEESE MAYONNAISE
12 Servings

The following is placed in one large, or in individual molds — chilled, unmolded on lettuce leaves and served with fruit salad moistened with lemon juice.

1 tablespoon gelatine
¼ cup cold water
¼ cup boiling water
4 egg yolks
Olive oil
Salt

Paprika
1 teaspoon vinegar
Juice of ½ lemon
3 packages of cream cheese
  (9 ounces)
1 cup whipping cream

Soak the gelatine in the cold water, dissolve it in the boiling water and chill it until it is nearly set. Beat the yolks and add the vinegar, seasoning, lemon and oil as for mayonnaise. When it is as thick as butter, beat in the cheese and add the gelatine. Last fold in the stiffly whipped cream.

MOLDED CHEESE AND TOMATO SALAD
10 to 12 Servings

1 tablespoon gelatine
¼ cup cold water
3 packages Philadelphia
  Cream Cheese (9 ozs.) or
1 cup cottage cheese
1 can Campbell's Tomato
  Soup

½ cup oil mayonnaise
½ cup cream, whipped
Salt
⅓ cup each of small onions,
  green peppers and celery,
  diced
1 small cucumber, diced

Soak the gelatine in the water for 5 minutes. Dissolve the cheese in the warm soup, stirring it constantly, add the soaked gelatine and dissolve it. Cool this mixture and fold in the combined cream and mayonnaise and the salt. Add the vegetables and chill the salad in a ring mold, or in individual molds. Serve it with mayonnaise.

MOLDED TUNA FISH SALAD

2 teaspoons gelatine	Vinegar
½ cup cold water	1 cup tuna fish flaked
¾ cup mayonnaise	1 cup chopped celery
Salt	½ cup chopped olives
Paprika	3 tablespoons chopped pimento (optional)

Soak the gelatine in the cold water for 5 minutes, dissolve it over hot water. Cool it and combine it with the mayonnaise. Add salt, pepper and vinegar as the jelly is to go over unseasoned food. Chill the jelly until it is about to set, then combine it with the remaining ingredients. Place it in a wet mold until it is firm. Unmold it on lettuce leaves.

Garnishes for Salads

To garnish salads use the following:

Parsley or watercress in bunches or chopped; lettuce leaves, whole or shredded; heads of lettuce cut into slices or wedges; lemon slices (the edges Vandyked) dipped in chopped parsley; olives shredded or stuffed olives sliced; cooked beets cut into shapes; carrots; pickles; capers; cucumbers; green and red peppers shredded; mayonnaise forced through a tube (the mayonnaise may be colored); aspic jellies in small molds or chopped aspic and eggs hard cooked, sliced, riced or stuffed.

WALNUT CREAMS

Roll cream cheese into small balls. Press them between two walnut halves.

CRAB-APPLE GARNISH

Roll coarsely grated yellow cheese into small balls. Place the blossom end of a clove into one side and the stem of a clove into the other. Sprinkle one cheek with paprika.

EGG APPLES

Cook eggs until they are hard. While they are warm peel them and press them gently between the palms of the hands until they are round. Color them with beet juice, or red coloring. Place cloves in two sides to represent the blossom ends and the stems, or shape the eggs, add the cloves and paint the cheeks of the egg with a dash of red and a dash of green color.

CHEESE CARROTS

Grate yellow cheese and moisten it with cream, or with salad dressing, until it is the right consistency to handle. Shape it into small carrots and place a small piece of parsley in the blunt end.

Dressings for Salads

FRENCH DRESSING

There are many variations of French Dressing, but the basis is usually:

¾ part oil   Salt, pepper or paprika
¼ part vinegar, or lemon
   juice

These proportions and the seasonings may be varied. To keep French dressing, place it in a tightly closed jar and shake the jar well before using the dressing. Onion and garlic add flavor to French dressing. A clove of garlic may be placed in a quart of vinegar for 6 or 7 days. The clove is then removed and the delicately flavored vinegar is used for dressings, or the bowl in which a dressing is to be made may be rubbed with garlic. Very finely minced or grated onion, or onion juice may be substituted for garlic, or the dressing may be made without either. The use of tarragon vinegar is recommended.

FRENCH DRESSING
Yield ⅓ cup

4 tablespoons olive oil   ½ teaspoon powdered sugar
1 to 2 tablespoons vinegar   ¼ teaspoon mustard
   or lemon juice   (optional)
½ teaspoon salt   Garlic or onion juice
¼ teaspoon paprika   (optional)

Add the seasoning to 1 tablespoon of oil. Add one half the vinegar slowly. Beat this, with a fork or a wire whisk and add the remaining oil and vinegar alternately. The additions to French dressings are: Chopped parsley, hard cooked eggs, chives, green peppers and pimentos, minced sardines, grated horse-radish, anchovy paste, grated cheese, sweet or sour cream, pearl onions, etc.

FRENCH FRUIT SALAD DRESSING
Yield ⅔ cup

6 tablespoons oil
3 tablespoons grapefruit
  or lemon juice

⅔ teaspoon powdered sugar
⅔ teaspoon salt

Follow the rule for making French dressing.

MAYONNAISE DRESSING
Yield 1¼ cups

2 egg yolks
¼ to ½ teaspoon mustard
½ teaspoon powdered sugar
½ teaspoon salt

A few grains of cayenne
1 tablespoon vinegar
1 cup oil (well chilled)
1 tablespoon lemon juice

Add the dry ingredients to the yolks. Use a wire whisk or a fork, and stir the dressing constantly. Add a few drops of the vinegar. Add the oil slowly, one-half teaspoon at a time, beating constantly, until ½ cupful has been used, then add the oil one teaspoonful at a time, alternating it with the lemon juice and vinegar. If the ingredients are cold this will make a good thick dressing. In summer place the bowl in which the dressing is made over cracked ice. Should the dressing separate, place 1 egg yolk in a bowl and stirring it constantly, add the dressing to it very, very slowly at first, and slowly as the dressing thickens.

CREAM MAYONNAISE DRESSING

Add ½ to 1 cup of heavy cream whipped to mayonnaise dressing just before serving it.

RUSSIAN DRESSING

Season mayonnaise with chili sauce or Indian Relish.

THOUSAND ISLAND DRESSING

Mayonnaise dressing, Page 183.

¼ cup cream whipped or
  plain
2 tablespoons chili sauce
2 tablespoons stuffed olives,
  minced

1 tablespoon chopped green
  peppers
1 tablespoon minced onion,
  or chives

ROQUEFORT CHEESE DRESSING

1 cup Roquefort cheese
  broken into tiny pieces

½ teaspoon Worcestershire
  Sauce

Add these ingredients to Mayonnaise Dressing—Page 183.

SWEET OR SOUR CREAM DRESSING, FOR VEGETABLE SALAD

½ cup thick cream
1 tablespoon chopped taragon or parsley
3 tablespoons vinegar or

lemon juice
¼ teaspoon salt
⅛ teaspoon paprika

Beat the cream and add the other ingredients slowly. This dressing is equally good made with thin cream, or with sour cream. Taragon is a marvelously aromatic herb grown in foreign gardens, but frequently obtainable in this country. Serve the dressing over home grown lettuce, or cold asparagus.

CREAM HORSERADISH DRESSING

This dressing is good with cold meat:

½ cup cream
3 tablespoons lemon juice
  or vinegar
¼ teaspoon salt

⅛ teaspoon paprika
A few grains of cayenne
2 tablespoons grated
  horseradish

Beat the cream until it is stiff, add the lemon juice slowly, the seasoning and the horseradish.

QUICK UNCOOKED SALAD DRESSING, WITH CONDENSED MILK

1 egg yolk
¼ cup oil
¼ cup lemon juice or
  vinegar
⅔ cup condensed milk

½ to 1 teaspoon mustard
1 teaspoon baking powder
½ teaspoon salt
½ teaspoon sugar
A few grains of cayenne

Combine the ingredients and beat them well with a wire whisk.

Boiled Salad Dressings

Three recipes for boiled salad dressings are given. The first is a very economical, acceptable boiled dressing, it may be thinned with cream, but is good as it is over vegetable and potato salad. The second is made with condensed milk, is a little richer than No. I and is good over slaw, tomatoes, etc. The third is a delicious dressing that combines well with fruit.

BOILED SALAD DRESSING I.
Yield 1/4 cups

1/2 to 1 teaspoon mustard	1/2 cup cold water
1 to 2 tablespoons sugar	1 egg (whole) or 2 yolks
1/2 teaspoon salt	1/4 cup vinegar (mild)
2 tablespoons flour	2 tablespoons butter
1/4 teaspoon paprika	

I. Dissolve the first 5 ingredients in the cold water. II. Beat the egg with the vinegar and combine I. and II. Cook the dressing in a double boiler, stirring it constantly until it is thick and smooth. Add the butter last. This dressing may be thinned with sweet or sour cream.

BOILED SALAD DRESSING II, WITH CONDENSED MILK
Yield 1 1/3 cups

1 1/4 tablespoons sugar	2 1/2 tablespoons butter
1/2 teaspoon paprika or	3/4 cup condensed milk
pepper	1/2 cup vinegar (mild)
3/4 teaspoon salt	(2 tablespoons flour may
1/4 to 1/2 teaspoon mustard	be substituted for 2 egg
3 or 4 egg yolks	yolks)

Combine the dry ingredients, add the milk, the beaten yolks, the melted butter and the vinegar. Cook the dressing in a double boiler, stirring it constantly until it is thick and smooth. Strain, chill and serve it. This dressing may be thinned with lemon juice, or cream.

BOILED SALAD DRESSING III.
Yield 1 1/4 cups

1 teaspoon salt	3 tablespoons melted butter
1/3 teaspoon paprika	6 tablespoons cream
1/2 to 1 teaspoon mustard	3 eggs
(optional)	6 tablespoons lemon juice
1/4 to 1/2 cup sugar	or vinegar

Combine the first 6 ingredients, add the eggs and beat them well. Add the lemon juice slowly. Cook the dressing in a double boiler, stirring it constantly until it is thick and smooth. Fruit juice may be substituted for cream and the dressing may be thinned with fruit juice or cream.

CREAM FRUIT SALAD DRESSING

2 eggs
½ cup sugar
1 tablespoon butter

3 tablespoons lemon juice
A few grains of salt
1 cup cream, whipped

Beat the eggs until they are light, add the sugar and continue beating. Cook these ingredients over hot water, adding the butter, the salt and the lemon juice. When they are the consistency of custard, remove them from the fire, cool them and fold in the stiffly beaten cream.

ALMOND AND CUCUMBER DRESSING

This is good Fruit Salad Dressing:

Add ½ cup diced cucumbers (peeled and seeded) and ¼ cup almonds (blanched and shredded) to Boiled Salad Dressing.

NUT DRESSING

1 tablespoon pecan meats
1 tablespoon blanched
    almonds
2 tablespoons lemon juice

2 tablespoons olive oil
½ teaspoon salt
½ teaspoon paprika

Pound the nuts to a paste and beat in the remaining ingredients.

Breads

Biscuit

RULE FOR BAKING POWDER BISCUIT

Combine and sift the dry ingredients. Cut in the shortening with a knife until it is the size of a small pea. Add the milk slowly and handle the dough lightly. Put it on a board barely dusted with flour and roll it lightly until it is about 1/2 inch thick. Cut it with a floured biscuit cutter and bake the biscuit in a greased pan in a hot oven 450° for about 12 to 15 minutes.

BISCUIT

2 cups flour	3/4 tablespoon lard
4 teaspoons baking powder	1 tablespoon butter
1 teaspoon salt	3/4 cup milk, water or both

Follow the rule for Baking Powder Biscuit.

DROP BISCUIT

Use the ingredients for Biscuit, adding enough milk to make a dough soft enough to drop by the spoonful onto a greased tin, or into greased muffin tins. To bake, follow the rule for Baking Powder Biscuit.

WHOLE WHEAT BISCUIT

Follow the rule for Biscuit, substituting whole wheat flour for white flour and using 5 tablespoons of shortening.

FLUFFY BISCUIT

2 cups flour	2 tablespoons butter
4 teaspoons baking powder	1 tablespoon sugar
1½ teaspoons salt	¾ cup rich milk or cream

Follow the rule for Baking Powder Biscuit.

MOCK ROLLS

Make Fluffy Biscuit dough, using only ½ teaspoon of sugar. Roll the dough to the thickness of ⅓ inch and cut it with a biscuit cutter. Butter the tops, using a pastry brush and melted butter, and fold the biscuit over like pocketbook rolls. Spread the tops with melted butter and let the biscuit rise for 20 or 30 minutes. Bake them like Biscuit.

SOUR MILK BISCUIT

2 cups flour	3 tablespoons lard
1 teaspoon salt	¾ cup sour milk or butter
1 teaspoon baking powder	milk
½ teaspoon soda	

Follow the rule for Baking Powder Biscuit.

CHEESE BISCUIT

1 cup flour	1 tablespoon butter
2½ teaspoons baking powder	½ cup grated cheese
	⅜ cup milk and water
½ teaspoon salt	equal parts

Follow the rule for Baking Powder Biscuit, cutting in the cheese with the butter.

BLUEBERRY BISCUIT

Roll biscuit dough to the thickness of ¼ inch. Line greased muffin tins half way up with the dough. Fill the shells with sugared blueberries and cover them with a round of dough, moistening the edges of the shells and the rounds and pressing them lightly together, or cut the dough into squares, fit them into greased muffin tins, fill them with sugared berries and pinch the corners of the dough together. Bake the biscuit in a quick oven 450° from 12 to 15 minutes.

BROWN SUGAR ROLL

Follow the rule for Plain or Fluffy Biscuit dough. Roll it to the thickness of ½ inch. Spread the surface with 4 tablespoons of soft butter and ¾ cup of brown sugar. Roll the dough like a jelly roll, and cut it into 1 inch slices. Bake them in a greased pan set well apart, in a quick oven 425° for 15 to 20 minutes. Raisins and nuts may be added to the filling.

Muffins

RULE FOR MUFFINS

Measure and sift the dry ingredients. Add the milk, the melted shortening and the beaten eggs. Stir the liquid quickly into the dry ingredients, taking only 18 to 20 seconds in which to do it. Make no attempt to stir or beat out the lumps. Ignore them. Unnecessary handling of the batter results in tough muffins. Pour the batter at once into greased tins or paper baking cups, filling them about 1/3 full. Bake the muffins for 25 minutes in a hot oven 425°.

MUFFINS
10 to 20 Small Muffins

1¾ cups flour
¾ teaspoon salt
¼ cup sugar
3 teaspoons baking powder

¾ cup milk
2 tablespoons butter melted
2 eggs

Follow the Rule for Muffins.

BLUEBERRY MUFFINS

1¾ cups flour
¾ teaspoon salt
⅓ cup sugar
3 teaspoons baking powder
¾ cup milk

4 tablespoons butter melted
2 eggs
1 cup blueberries lightly
   floured

Canned blueberries, well drained, may be used. Follow the Rule for Muffins.

NUT OR DATE MUFFINS

Add ⅓ cup of chopped nuts or dates to the muffin batter. Follow the Rule for Muffins.

BACON MUFFINS

These muffins are good at any time, but especially for breakfast on a cold morning:

4 to 8 slices of bacon
1¼ cups flour
1 tablespoon sugar
1 teaspoon salt

2½ teaspoons baking
   powder
¾ cup milk
1 tablespoon bacon fat
1 egg beaten

Cook the bacon in a skillet until it is crisp. Remove it, let it cool and chop it into small pieces. Follow the Rule for Muffins in combining the other ingredients, last fold in the chopped bacon.

RICE MUFFINS

A good way of utilizing left over rice:

1 cup of boiled rice	1 tablespoon sugar
1¼ cups milk	½ teaspoon salt
2 egg yolks beaten	2 teaspoons baking powder
2 tablespoons melted butter	2 egg whites beaten until
1½ cups flour	stiff

Combine the rice and the milk, add the yolks, the melted butter, and the sifted dry ingredients. Follow the Rule for Muffins. Last fold in the whites of the eggs. Pour the batter into hot, greased pans and bake the muffins in a hot oven 425° for 25 or 30 minutes.

WHOLE WHEAT MUFFINS

2 cups whole wheat flour	2 teaspoons butter melted
2 teaspoons sugar	2 eggs
1 teaspoon salt	¼ cup chopped dates or
2 teaspoons baking powder	raisins (optional)
1¼ cups milk	

Follow the Rule for Muffins.

BRAN MUFFINS I.

A crisp bran muffin — good for general use:

2 cups white flour	1½ teaspoons soda
2 cups bran	½ cup boiling water
2 teaspoons salt	2 tablespoons butter melted
⅓ cup sugar	1 egg
1 teaspoon baking powder	½ cup raisins (optional)
2 cups sour milk	

Dissolve the soda in the boiling water and add it to the milk. Add the raisins last. Follow the Rule for Muffins.

BRAN MUFFINS NO. II.

These muffins are heavier and sweeter than No. I. Served with cheese they are an excellent picnic substitute for sandwiches:

2 cups graham flour
1½ cups bran
2 tablespoons sugar
¼ teaspoon salt
2 cups sour milk combined
   with 1¼ teaspoons soda

½ cup molasses
2 tablespoons butter melted
1 egg
1 cup nuts or nuts and
   raisins combined
   (optional)

Follow the Rule for Muffins.

Popovers

RULE FOR POPOVERS

The rise or fall of the popover depends upon:

I. The proper preparation and heating of the pans (preferably iron pans.)

II. The proper mixing of the ingredients.

III. The right heat with which to bake them.

Oil the pans and heat them for 10 minutes in a hot oven — 450°. Sift the flour and the salt. Beat the eggs until they are frothy, add the milk and then very slowly stir in the flour, and last add the melted butter. Beat the ingredients until they are well blended, but no longer, then pour the batter into the oiled and heated pans, filling them only ⅔ full. Bake the popovers in a hot oven 450° for 20 minutes, then reduce the heat and dry them in a moderate oven 350° for 15 minutes.

POPOVERS I.
8 large ones

1 cup flour
¼ teaspoon salt
⅞ cup milk

2 eggs
1 tablespoon melted butter

POPOVERS II.

1 cup flour
¼ teaspoon milk

1 cup milk
1 egg

CHEESE POPOVERS

1 cup flour
⅜ teaspoon salt
1 cup milk
1 egg

1 cup grated cheese com-
   bined with ⅛ teaspoon
   paprika, or a few grains
   of cayenne

Follow the Rule for Popovers for combining the first 4 ingredients, and preparing the pans. When the batter and the pans are ready, pour two scant teaspoonfuls in each cup, cover it with a teaspoonful of cheese and a teaspoonful of batter. Follow the rule for baking popovers.

GRAHAM POPOVERS

⅔ cup whole wheat flour
⅓ cup flour
¼ teaspoon salt

⅞ cup milk
1 egg
½ teaspoon melted butter

Follow the Rule for Popovers.

Corn Bread, Scones, Cheese Straws

CORN BREAD

1 cup yellow cornmeal
2 tablespoons flour
1 tablespoon sugar
1 tablespoon lard or butter

2 teaspoons baking powder
¼ teaspoon salt
1 egg
½ cup milk

Melt the shortening in the pan in which the bread is to be baked, then pour it into a mixing bowl. Add the other ingredients, mix them well and pour them into the greased pan. Bake the bread in a moderate oven 375° for 20 minutes.

CORN BREAD MUFFINS

Heat muffin pans for 10 minutes in a hot oven, grease them and fill them with Corn Bread batter. Bake the muffins in a quick oven 400° for 20 minutes.

CORN BREAD STICKS

Heat a bread stick pan, grease it and fill it with Corn Bread batter. Bake it in a quick oven 400° until the sticks are crisp and brown.

SCONES
Baking Powder

2 cups flour
4 teaspoons baking powder
2 teaspoons sugar
½ teaspoon salt

4 tablespoons butter
2 eggs
⅓ cup liquid (half cream
   and milk or water)

Combine and sift the dry ingredients. Cut the shortening into them, using a knife, until it is the size of a small pea. Beat the eggs and reserve about 2 tablespoonfuls of beaten egg. Beat the remainder with the liquid and add this to the dry ingredients. Handle the dough as little as possible. Place it on a floured board. Pat it until it is ¾ inch thick. Cut it into diamond shapes, brush them with the reserved egg, sprinkle them with salt or with sugar and bake them in a hot oven 450° for 15 minutes.

CHEESE STRAWS I.

4 tablespoons butter	⅛ teaspoon nutmeg
3 tablespoons grated cheese	(optional)
1 teaspoon sugar	2 tablespoons cream
½ teaspoon salt	1 egg
⅛ teaspoon paprika	Flour

Combine the ingredients, using just enough flour to roll the dough. Cut the dough into strips and bake them in a moderate oven 400° until they are a delicate brown.

CHEESE STRAWS II.

Roll pie dough until it is very thin, cut it into long strips, sprinkle it with grated cheese and paprika and bake it in a hot oven, or add grated cheese to the dough, roll and cut it and bake it in a hot oven.

Rolls and Buns

BRIOCHES

This French recipe makes 32 large, delicious brioches:

1 cup milk, scalded	½ to ⅔ cup butter or lard
1½ teaspoons salt	½ cup sugar

Combine these ingredients and when they are cool, add:

3 eggs, beaten	¼ cup luke warm water
2 cakes yeast dissolved in	4¾ cups flour

Beat the dough well, cover it with a cloth and permit it to rise in a warm place for 6 hours. Grease muffin tins, fill them ⅓ full with dough and permit the brioches to rise uncovered for 30 minutes. Bake them in a hot oven 425° from 15 to 20 minutes.

FOUR HOUR BREAD ROLLS
20 Small Rolls

1 tablespoon lard
1 tablespoon butter
1½ tablespoons sugar
1 egg or 1 egg white
   (optional)

1 cup warm milk
1 cake yeast
¼ cup lukewarm water
3 cups flour
1¼ teaspoons salt

Cream the shortening with the sugar. Add the egg and the warm milk and beat the batter well. Dissolve the yeast in the warm water and add it to the first mixture. Add 1½ cups of flour, stir the batter until it is smooth and permit it to rise for 1½ hours. Add the remaining flour and the salt by tossing the dough on a board and working it in very lightly. Place the dough in a bowl, cover it with a cloth and permit it to rise for 1½ hours. Pinch off bits of dough with buttered hands, shape them into small balls and place them in greased muffin tins. (The tins should be about ⅓ full). Or place three very small balls in greased muffin tins to make clover leaf rolls. Brush the tops with butter and permit the rolls to rise for 45 minutes. Bake them in a hot oven for about 20 minutes. Do not knead the dough at any time.

BREAD ROLLS—(Never fail.)
18 Small Rolls

These rolls, incredibly light in texture, are not unlike a brioche. They require no kneading:

I. Dissolve 1 cake yeast in
   ¼ cup lukewarm water
II. Dissolve
   ¼ cup lard
   1¼ teaspoon salt

2 tablespoons sugar, by
   pouring
1 cup boiling water over
   them

When II. is lukewarm combine it with I. Use a wire whisk to beat in 1 egg and about 2¾ cups flour, (enough flour to make a soft dough). Place the dough in a large bowl, cover it with a plate and set it in the icebox—(the dough will treble in bulk). Chill it from 2 to 12 hours. Pinch off small pieces of dough with buttered hands and place them in greased muffin tins, filling the tins about one-third full. Cover the tops with melted butter and permit the rolls to rise for about 2 hours. Bake them in a hot oven 450° until they are crisp and brown.

ICE BOX ROLLS
36 rolls baked in 2¹/₂ inch muffin tins.

8¹/₄ cups flour   ¹/₂ cup warm water
1 yeast cake

Sift the flour, and measure it lightly, heaping it with a spoon
into a measuring cup, (do not shake the cup). Dissolve the
yeast in the warm water, add ¹/₄ cup of the flour and let it
rise for ¹/₂ hour or until it reaches the top of the cup.

2 whole eggs, if large, if   1 cup warm water
   small, 3 eggs   ¹/₂ cup water
⅞ cup lard   1 tablespoon salt

Beat the eggs, add the water, flour, yeast mixture, lard, salt
and sugar. Work the dough with the hands until it is smooth.
Cover it and place it in the refrigerator for at least 24 hours.
Take out the quantity needed with buttered hands four hours
before baking it. Roll it lightly into small balls and place them
in greased muffin pans, filling the pans one-third full. Butter
the tops of the rolls and permit them to rise in a warm place.
Bake them in a quick oven 425° for about 12 minutes.

PARKER HOUSE ROLLS
Reduce these proportions by ¹/₂ for 6 to 8 servings

2 cups scalded milk   4 tablespoons butter
2 tablespoons sugar   1¹/₄ teaspoons salt

Combine these ingredients. When they are dissolved and
cooled to a lukewarm temperature, add:

1 cake of yeast (1 ounce)   lukewarm water and
   dissolved in ¹/₄ cup of   5¹/₂ cups flour

Stir in part of the flour, knead in the rest. Use only enough
flour to form a dough that can be handled easily. Place the
dough in a bowl, cover it and let it rise in a warm place until
it doubles in bulk. Toss it lightly onto a floured board, handling it as little as possible. Pat or roll it lightly to the thickness of one-third inch. Brush the surface with melted butter
and cut the dough into rounds with a floured biscuit cutter.
Dip the handle of a knife in flour and use it to make a deep
crease across the middle of each biscuit. Fold the biscuits over
and press the edges together lightly. Place the biscuits in
rows in a greased pan. Permit them to rise lightly, then bake
them in a hot oven 450° from 12 to 15 minutes.

CLOVER LEAF ROLLS

Shape bread dough into small balls and brush them with butter. Grease muffin tins and drop 3 balls in each tin, filling them less than half full. Permit the rolls to rise slightly and bake them like Parker House Rolls.

CINNAMON BUNS

Follow the rule for Parker House Rolls. Prepare the dough and let it rise until it has doubled in bulk. Roll it to the thickness of one-fourth inch. Spread it generously with melted butter, brown sugar, cinnamon and raisins. Roll it as for jelly roll, cut it in 3/4 inch slices and place them in a greased pan. Let them rise slightly and bake them in a quick oven 450° for 12 to 15 minutes.

CARAMEL BUNS

Prepare Cinnamon buns, cutting the slices 1½ inches thick. Cream 6 tablespoons of shortening with 6 tablespoons of brown sugar. Spread this mixture on the bottom and sides of an iron skillet. Place the slices in the skillet and permit them to rise for 15 minutes. Bake them in a hot oven 450° for 25 minutes. Serve them up side down.

Bread

WHITE BREAD

1 cup milk	2 teaspoons salt
1 cup hot water	1 yeast cake
1 tablespoon lard	1/4 cup warm water
1 tablespoon butter	6 to 6½ cups flour
2 tablespoons sugar	

Scald the milk and add the hot water. Pour this over the lard, butter, sugar and salt. Dissolve the yeast in 1/4 cup of warm water. When the first mixture is lukewarm, combine it with the dissolved yeast. Add 3 cups of flour slowly and beat the batter well. Add the remaining flour and toss the dough on a floured board. Knead it well, folding the edges of the dough toward the center and pressing it down, repeating this action until it no longer adheres to the board and is smooth, elastic and full of bubbles. Place the dough in a bowl, cover it with a cloth and let it rise in a warm place until it has doubled in bulk. Cut it down by kneading it to its original bulk, and let it rise again until doubled in bulk (for about 1 hour). Shape the dough lightly into loaves, place them in tins, filling the tins only half full—and let the dough rise again until doubled in bulk. Bake the loaves in a hot oven 450° for 15 minutes. Reduce the heat to 350° until it is done, when it will shrink from the sides of the pan. It requires about 1 hour of baking. Remove it at once from the pans and place it on a wire cake cooler, or in some way that it will have air from all sides.

NUT BREAD I.

2½ cups flour
3 teaspoons baking powder
½ teaspoon salt
½ cup sugar

1 egg
1 cup milk
¾ cup nut meats

Combine and sift the dry ingredients. Beat the egg with the milk and combine them. Add the nuts and place the dough in a greased pan. Let it rise for 20 minutes and bake the bread in a moderate oven 350° about ½ hour.

NUT BREAD II.

1½ cups graham flour
¾ cup flour
½ teaspoon salt
1½ teaspoons soda

1½ cups sour milk
⅓ cup dark molasses
½ cup nut meats, chopped

Sift the dry ingredients, add the milk to the molasses and combine the two mixtures. Add the nut meats and place the dough in a greased pan. Bake it in a moderate oven 350° for about ¾ hour.

ORANGE BREAD WITH NUTS

¾ to 1 cup sugar
1 egg beaten
3 cups flour
3 teaspoons baking powder
½ teaspoon salt

1 cup milk
1 cup chopped candied
   orange peel
1 cup nuts

Combine the ingredients in the order given, sifting the flour, salt and baking powder. Permit the bread to rise for 30 minutes and bake it in a moderate oven 350° for about ½ hour.

BRAN BREAD de LUXE

This recipe is worthy of three stars. It makes a wonderful tea sandwich with butter or cream cheese.

2 cups chopped dates
1 teaspoon soda
2 cups boiling water
2 eggs
¾ cup brown sugar

2 cups whole wheat flour
2 cups bran
2 teaspoons baking powder
1 teaspoon vanilla
1 cup (or less) nutmeats

Sprinkle the soda over the chopped dates and pour the boiling water over them. Permit this to stand while preparing the other ingredients. Beat the eggs and add the brown sugar gradually, beating constantly. Add part of the flour combined with the baking powder, part of the date mixture and then the remaining ingredients. Bake them in a greased pan in a moderate oven 350° for about 1 hour.

BRAN BREAD

Good, but not notable:

2½ cups sour milk	1 teaspoon salt
2 teaspoons soda	2 cups graham flour
½ cup molasses	2 cups bran
½ cup brown sugar	

Combine the sour milk and the soda, and add it to the rest of the ingredients. Bake the bread in a loaf in a fairly hot oven 400°—reducing the heat for the last hour (325°). It requires two hours of baking.

SPOON BREAD I. WITH SWEET MILK

These good Southern Spoon Bread dishes, served from a baking dish with a spoon, are used as a Northern hostess might see fit to serve macaroni:

2 cups white cornmeal	½ teaspoon salt
2 cups boiling water	2 cups milk
3 eggs	2 teaspoons baking powder

Scald the cornmeal with the boiling water, beat it well and let it cool. Beat in the eggs, one at a time, until they are very light and add the remaining ingredients. Pour the batter into a hot, greased baking dish and bake it in a moderate oven 350° until it is done, from 30 to 40 minutes.

SPOON BREAD II. WITH SOUR OR BUTTERMILK

1 cup white cornmeal	1 cup buttermilk
1½ cups boiling water	1 teaspoon soda
1 egg	¾ teaspoon salt
1 teaspoon cold lard	

Follow the Rule for Spoon Bread I.

GINGERBREAD

½ cup shortening
1 cup sugar
2 eggs
2 cups flour
A pinch of salt

1 teaspoon nutmeg
2 teaspoons soda
1½ teaspoons ginger
½ cup boiling water
½ cup molasses

I. Cream the shortening and the sugar and add the eggs.

II. Sift the dry ingredients.

III. Add the boiling water to the molasses.

Add II. and III. alternately to I. Beat the batter well and bake it in a greased pan in a moderate oven 325°.

Fritters, Doughnuts, Pancakes, Waffles

CHART FOR DEEP FAT FRYING

Food	Temperature	Time
Doughnuts and other raw dough mixtures	360° to 370°	Until brown.
Croquettes and other cooked foods	390°	Until brown.
French Fried Potatoes	395°	4½ minutes.
Fish, Meat, Oysters, Scallops	390° 360°	

Successful deep fat frying calls for a kettle three-fourths full of fat or oil, heated to the right temperature for the food that is to be cooked in it.

Food may be placed directly in the hot fat, or it may be placed in a wire basket (frying basket) and the basket may be lowered into the hot fat.

As soon as the food is well browned, remove it from the fat and drain it on absorbent paper — (paper towels, napkins or unglazed paper).

After frying the food, cool the fat, strain it through cheese cloth, or a fine sieve, and replace it on ice. The same fat may be used repeatedly. It if becomes dark, it may be clarified by adding a raw potato, peeled and sliced. Heat the fat slowly until the potato browns, then strain the fat.

BREADED FOOD

Prepare croquettes, etc., and roll them in bread crumbs, in an egg, to which 1 tablespoon of water has been added, and again in bread crumbs.

TO TEST THE HEAT OF FAT WITHOUT A THERMOMETER

Heat the fat until blue smoke begins to appear. Drop a one inch cube of bread into it. If the bread browns in 40 seconds, the fat is ready for frying uncooked food. If the bread browns in one minute, the fat is ready for frying cooked food.

Fritters

RULE FOR FRYING FRITTERS

Heat a kettle of fat from 360 to 390 degrees. Dip fruit in the batter and fry the fritters until they are a delicate brown. Drain them on paper and serve them with lemon juice and powdered sugar, or serve them with fruit sauce—Page 325.

FRITTER BATTER

These fritters may be fried in deep fat, or they may be sautéed in butter:

2 egg yolks	1 tablespoon lemon juice
½ cup water	or wine
1 cup flour	2 egg whites
1 tablespoon melted butter	¼ teaspoon salt
or oil	

Beat the yolks, add the water and pour this slowly into the flour. Combine the butter and the lemon juice and add them to the batter. Add the salt to the egg whites, beat them until they are stiff and fold them into the batter.

APPLE FRITTERS

Peel and core apples. Slice them or leave them in halves. They may be soaked for 2 hours in wine and powdered sugar. Drain them, dip them in batter and fry them.

PINEAPPLE FRITTERS

Drain canned pineapple slices. Follow the Rule for Apple Fritters.

BANANA FRITTERS

Peel bananas, cut them into halves lengthwise, and cut the pieces in two. Dip them in batter and fry or sauté them. Serve them with powdered sugar and lemon juice.

APRICOT FRITTERS

Use drained, canned apricots, or dried, stewed apricots drained. Dip them in batter and fry them in deep fat. Serve them sprinkled with powdered sugar.

ORANGE FRITTERS

Peel oranges, cut them in slices, remove the seeds. Sprinkle the slices with powdered sugar, dip them in batter and fry them.

CRULLERS

½ cup butter	¾ teaspoon grated lemon
1 cup sugar	rind
3 whole eggs	1½ teaspoons baking powder
1 cup milk	Flour

Cream the butter and the sugar, and combine the other ingredients in the order given. Use enough flour to make a dough that will roll. Cut the dough into strips with a pie jagger and cook the crullers in deep fat.

Doughnuts

DOUGHNUTS I.
Sweet Milk

5 tablespoons melted butter	¼ teaspoon nutmeg
1 cup sugar	(optional)
2 eggs	½ teaspoon salt
3 cups bread flour	¼ teaspoon cinnamon
4 teaspoons baking powder	(optional)
	1 cup milk

Cream the shortening with the sugar and add the well beaten eggs. Combine and sift the dry ingredients and add them to the first mixture alternately with the milk. Beat the batter well and add enough additional flour to make a very soft dough. Roll the dough to the thickness of ¼ inch and cut it into shapes. Fry the doughnuts in deep fat. See Page 200. Drain the doughnuts and sprinkle them with powdered sugar.

DOUGHNUTS II.
Sour Milk

1½ tablespoons butter	¼ teaspoon cinnamon
1¼ cups sugar	½ teaspoon nutmeg
3 eggs	1½ teaspoons salt
1 teaspoon soda	2 cups baking powder
3 cups flour	1 cup sour milk
2 teaspoons baking powder	

Follow the rule for Doughnuts I.

CHOCOLATE DOUGHNUTS

Add 1½ oz. grated chocolate to Doughnuts I. or II. using 3 tablespoons less flour.

ROSETTES

Rosettes are shaped with a small iron made for the purpose.

2 eggs slightly beaten	1 cup milk
1 teaspoon sugar	1 cup flour or more
¼ teaspoon salt	

(Note: If the rosettes are to be used as patties omit the sugar.)

Beat the eggs, until they are blended only, and add the remaining ingredients, alternating the milk and the flour, and beat the batter well. Rosettes are fried in deep fat heated to 360 to 370 degrees. Heat the iron by immersing it in the fat until it is entirely covered, dip it in the batter, but do not let the batter run over the top of the iron. Return the iron to the fat, immersing it completely from 20 to 35 seconds. Remove the rosette from the iron with a fork, heat the iron in the lard and repeat the process. Drain the rosettes on absorbent paper and serve them sprinkled with powdered sugar.

GRIDDLE CAKES AND PANCAKES

To cook griddle cakes successfully, use an iron griddle. Heat it, grease it and pour batter upon it from a spoon. When the cakes are brown underneath, turn them with a cake turner and brown the other side.

GRIDDLE CAKES, OR BATTER CAKES
Sweet Milk

1½ cups flour	2 eggs
2 teaspoons baking powder	1¼ cups milk
1 teaspoon salt	1 tablespoon melted butter

Combine and sift the dry ingredients. Combine and beat the liquids. Pour them slowly into the dry ingredients and beat the batter until it is smooth. The eggs may be separated and the stiffly beaten egg whites may be added last or the eggs may be omitted.

GRIDDLE CAKES

Sour Milk

1 cup cake flour or ⅞ cup
    bread flour
½ teaspoon soda
½ teaspoon salt

1 egg, beaten
1 cup sour milk
1 teaspoon melted butter

Sift the dry ingredients. Combine the liquid ingredients and stir them slowly into the dry ingredients. Beat the batter until it is smooth. Follow the rule for cooking griddle cakes, Page 203.

PICNIC BATTER CAKES

This recipe is planned to satisfy the appetites of from ten to twelve picnickers.

3 egg yolks, well beaten
2 tablespoons melted butter
¼ cup sugar
3 cups flour
2 cups cornstarch

2 teaspoons salt
4 teaspoons baking powder
4 cups milk
3 egg whites stiffly beaten

Combine the ingredients. Place the batter in glass jars. Beat it with a whisk or fork just before using it. Bake the cakes and wrap them around small broiled sausages or bacon.

PANCAKES

2 eggs
¾ cup flour
½ teaspoon salt
1 teaspoon baking powder

2 tablespoons sugar
    (optional)
⅔ cup milk
⅓ cup water

Beat the eggs and add the ingredients in the order given. Heat a skillet, melt 2 tablespoons of butter and when it is hot, pour the batter into the skillet. Cook it over a slow fire until it is brown underneath, turn it and brown the other side: heat a skillet and grease it with 1 teaspoon of oil, add a small quantity of batter and let it spread over the bottom of the pan. When it is brown underneath, reverse it and brown the other side. Spread the pancake with jelly, roll it and sprinkle it with powdered sugar. Use a teaspoon of oil for each pancake.

SOUR MILK PANCAKES

1 egg
1/2 teaspoon salt
1 teaspoon baking powder
1 cup sour milk

1/2 teaspoon soda, dis-
solved in 1 teaspoon
boiling water
7/8 cup of flour

Beat the egg and add the ingredients in the order given. Follow the rule for cooking pancakes. See Index for Tomato Pancakes.

BUCKWHEAT CAKES

1/2 cake yeast dissolved in
1/2 cup lukewarm water
2 cups buckwheat flour

1 cup bread flour
1 teaspoon salt

Combine these ingredients and permit them to rise over night. Add 1 tablespoon dark molasses and enough milk to thin the batter as desired. Cook the cakes on a greased griddle.

GERMAN POTATO PANCAKES

6 large raw potatoes
3 eggs beaten
1 teaspoon sugar
1/8 teaspoon baking powder

1 teaspoon salt
2 tablespoons flour
2 tablespoons milk
(optional)

Peel the potatoes and soak them for several hours in cold water. Grate them, put the potato pulp in a piece of cheese cloth and press out the excess water. Place the pulp in a mixing bowl and add the other ingredients. Sauté the batter in hot fat, turn the cakes when they are browned underneath to brown the other side. Serve them hot with apple sauce.

APPLE PANCAKES

Follow the recipe for Pancakes—Page 204. Use part butter and part lard for cooking them. Pour batter into the pan and sprinkle it generously with peeled, cored and thinly sliced apples. Pour additional batter over the apples, and turn the cake when it is browned underneath. Brown the other side and serve the cake while it is hot with powdered sugar.

BLUEBERRY PANCAKES

Follow the recipe for Pancakes—Page 204, adding the baking powder and 1 cup of blueberries to the batter just before cooking the cakes.

Waffles

WAFFLES
6 Waffles

1¾ cup cake flour
3 teaspoons baking powder
½ teaspoon salt
1½ cups milk

2 tablespoons or more
melted butter
3 eggs separated

Combine and sift the dry ingredients, add the milk gradually, then the well beaten yolks, the melted butter and last the stiffly beaten egg whites.

PECAN WAFFLES

Follow the Rule for Waffles, adding:
1 tablespoon sugar
1 teaspoon vanilla

¾ cup pecan meats, broken.

SOUR CREAM WAFFLES

These waffles are superlative:

2 cups thick sour cream
3 egg yolks
1 cup cake flour
2 teaspoons baking powder

1 teaspoon soda dissolved
in
1 tablespoon boiling water
3 egg whites

Combine these ingredients and fold in the stiffly beaten egg whites.

BACON AND CORNMEAL WAFFLES
See Page 65.

CORNMEAL WAFFLES

Follow the rule for Bacon Cornmeal Waffles—Page 65, omitting the bacon fat and substituting 2 tablespoons or more of melted butter.

GINGERBREAD WAFFLES
6 Small Waffles

2 cups cake flour
1 teaspoon ginger
½ teaspoon cloves
½ teaspoon cinnamon
⅔ teaspoon salt
2 tablespoons sugar

½ cup butter
½ cup molasses
1½ teaspoons soda
½ cup sour milk
2 eggs

Combine and sift the dry ingredients (except the soda). Heat the butter and the molasses to the boiling point and beat in the soda. Add the milk to the dry ingredients. Add the molasses mixture and beat in the eggs one at a time. Beat the batter well. Serve the waffles with ice cream, or whipped cream, or with cinnamon and sugar.

PINEAPPLE WAFFLES

These waffles are a delightful change:

1 cup flour	3/4 cup crushed pineapple,
1/3 teaspoon salt	drained
2 teaspoons baking powder	2 egg yolks
2 tablespoons sugar	1/4 cup melted butter
	2 egg whites

Combine and sift the dry ingredients, add the pineapple, the beaten yolks and the melted butter. Fold in the stiffly beaten whites. Serve the waffles with:

Pineapple Cream Sauce:

1/2 cup pineapple juice	1 1/2 tablespoons sugar

Cook these ingredients for 3 minutes, cool the syrup and add:

1/2 cup cream	1/8 teaspoon salt

ORANGE WAFFLES
6 Waffles

1 1/2 cups cake flour	1/2 cup orange juice
1 1/2 teaspoons baking	1/2 cup milk
powder	2 yolks
1/3 teaspoon salt	3 tablespoons melted butter
1 tablespoon sugar	2 egg whites, stiffly beaten
1 tablespoon grated orange	
rind	

Sift the dry ingredients, and add the remaining ingredients in the order given. Serve the waffles with orange marmalade or butter.

CHOCOLATE WAFFLES
6 Waffles

This is a delectable waffle with ice cream:

I. 1/4 cup butter (4 table-	II. 1 2/3 cups cake flour
spoons)	1 1/2 teaspoons baking powder
1 cup sugar	1/4 teaspoon salt
2 eggs (whole)	6 tablespoons cocoa
1 teaspoon vanilla	III. 1 1/4 cups milk

I.   Cream the butter and the sugar, beat in the eggs and add the vanilla.

II.   Sift the dry ingredients.

III.   Add the dry ingredients, alternately with the milk, to No. I.

Serve the waffles with chocolate sauce and vanilla ice cream, or whipped cream. The ice cream may be made with condensed milk.

Pies

CHART FOR BAKING PIES

Double crust fruit pies; Hot oven 450° for 30 minutes. Slow oven 325° for an additional 10 minutes.

Mince Pie, or any other double crust pie with a previously cooked filling; Hot oven 450° for 30 minutes.

Open Fruit Pies; Hot oven 450° for 20 minutes.

Custard Pie, Pumpkin Pie and other open pies, Hot oven 450° for 15 minutes, Slow oven 325° for an additional 30 minutes.

Deep Fruit Pies; 450° for 30 minutes, 325° for an additional 10 minutes.

Pie shells without filling; Very hot oven 500° for 12 minutes.

Dumplings or Turnovers; 450° for 15 minutes.

Meringue; 300° for 12 minutes.

PIE CRUST

1¾ cups cake flour	4 tablespoons lard
1 teaspoon baking powder	2 tablespoons butter
½ teaspoon salt	¼ cup ice water

RULE FOR MAKING PIE CRUST

All the materials should be as cold as possible. Sift the dry ingredients and cut in the shortening with a knife, or work it with a fork until it is the size of a pea. The less it is handled, the better. Do not work it until it is fine, or the crust will not be flaky. Add the ice water very slowly, using less than the amount given, if the dough will hold together. A good rule for making pastry is: "Keep the moisture out and the air in."

As soon as the dough will hold together, stop handling it. Divide it into two parts, one slightly larger than the other. Keep the smaller part for the top crust. If the room is hot, place this part on ice. Roll out the larger part for the bottom crust, to the thickness of ⅛ inch, using as little flour as possible on the board and on the roller. Do not stretch the dough. Cut it one inch larger than the pan to allow for shrinkage and full it around the edge.

Prick the under crust with a fork in several places and fit it into the pie pan. Do not grease the pan—good pastry makes this unnecessary.

If the pie is to be filled with a juicy filling, brush the bottom crust with the white of an egg to keep it from being soggy. Fill the pie and moisten the edges with a little water.

Roll the dough for the top crust, cut it one inch larger than the pan, and prick it with a fork in several places to allow the steam to escape. Place the top crust on the pie. Full in the surplus dough and press it down around the edges with a fork, or tuck it under the lower crust and press it around the edge with a fork.

If the pie is filled with juicy fruit, or custard, wring a strip of cotton one inch wide out of cold water and fasten it around the edge. This will keep the juices from boiling out.

If a lattice of pastry is desired, cut long narrow strips of dough with a knife, or a pie jagger (the latter makes a pinked edge). Place the strips across the top of the pie and moisten them slightly with water where they meet the edge of the pie.

If a shell or a pie crust is desired, bake it on the bottom of a pie pan, that is, invert the pan and fit the dough over the bottom. Prick it with a fork and press it down lightly around the edge. Cut a round for the top crust, prick it and bake it on a baking sheet. When making individual pies, use an inverted muffin tin. Cut rounds of dough 4½ or 5½ inches in diameter and fit them over the cups. Prick them before baking them for 12 minutes in a very hot oven—500°.

Pie dough made a day in advance and kept covered in a cool place will roll more readily than fresh dough.

A famous pie cook told me that she combined her dry ingredients with part lard and part cotta suet (made of cotton seed oil) crumbed it, and kept it for days in the icebox, taking out a part of it when needed and combining it with water.

HOT WATER PIE CRUST
One 2 crust pie

This recipe is an amazingly quick way of making pie crust— almost like magic: The process is so simple that it is absolutely fool-proof. While the result is not quite as good as the dough made with chilled ingredients, it is better than the average pie one encounters. The dough will keep for a week in a cold place.

¼ cup boiling water	½ teaspoon baking powder
½ cup lard	1½ cups flour
½ teaspoon salt	

I.   Pour the boiling water over the lard.

II.   Combine the dry ingredients.

When the lard is melted combine I. and II. Stir until they form a smooth ball. Chill the dough thoroughly before baking it. Use as little flour as possible in rolling it.

ZWIEBACK CRUST

This delicious crust may be used in the place of pie crust. It is much improved by being thoroughly chilled before it is baked.

4½ ounces Zwieback rolled	¾ teaspoon cinnamon
(1½ cups)	6 tablespoons melted butter
¾ cup sugar	

Combine the ingredients in the order given and work them lightly with the finger tips until they are well blended. Use a nine inch Pyrex baking dish. Press the crumb mixture on the bottom and against the sides of the dish to form a crust ¼ inch thick. Fill it with any desired cooked fruit, or custard filling.

Pies baked with fillings

APPLE PIE
9 Inch Pie

A friend of mine is so fond of Apple Pie that he says his coat of arms bears an apple pie rampant. Every attempt has been made to make this one couchant.

4 or 5 tart apples	1/2 teaspoon cinnamon
1/2 to 2/3 cup sugar	1 tablespoon butter (or
1 teaspoon lemon juice	more)
1 teaspoon grated lemon	Flour, if desired
rind	1/8 teaspoon salt

Peel and core the apples and cut them into thin slices. Fill a pie pan with pie dough and cover the bottom closely with the apples. Combine the dry ingredients and sprinkle them over the apples, add the lemon juice and a light dredging of flour, if desired. Dot the apples with butter and cover the pie with an upper crust—See Page 210. See Chart for Baking Pies.

PEACH PIE

Follow the Rule for Apple Pie, using a smaller quantity of sugar.

BERRY PIES

Strawberry	Gooseberry	Currant
Blackberry		Raspberry

2 cups berries
1/2 cup sugar—scant or generous according to the acidity of the fruit
1 1/2 to 2 1/2 tablespoons flour according to the juiciness of the fruit
1/8 teaspoon salt
1 tablespoon butter

Combine the sugar, flour and salt, and stir them into the fruit, which has been prepared and is ready for use. Pour the fruit into an uncooked pie shell and dot the top with the butter. Cover the pie with a punctured upper crust—or with strips of pastry—See Rule Page 210. This filling is for 2 nine inch pies. When using canned fruit, take about 2 cups of berries and 1 cup of juice. She Chart for Baking Pies.

BLUEBERRY PIE

Follow the rule for Berry Pies, adding 1 1/4 tablespoons lemon juice.

CHERRY PIE

Follow the Rule for Berry Pies.

RHUBARB PIE

Follow the Rule for Berry Pies.

CHERRY OR RHUBARB CREAM PIE

2 cups pitted cherries, or
  2 cups diced pink rhubarb
2/3 cup sugar
2 tablespoons flour

2 egg yolks
2 teaspoons lemon juice or
  water
1/8 teaspoon salt

Place the fruit in the bottom of an unbaked pie shell. Combine the remaining ingredients and spread them over the fruit. Bake the pie in a hot oven 400° for 20 minutes. Reduce the heat and bake it in a moderate oven 350° for 20 minutes.

CARAMEL NUT PIE

This is a rich, sweet pie:

1/2 cup dark brown sugar
1/2 cup maple flavored corn
  syrup
1/2 teaspoon flour

1/2 teaspoon vinegar
Pinch of salt
2 whole eggs (unbeaten)
1/4 cup pecans

Combine these ingredients and stir them well. Prepare a nine inch unbaked pie shell. Put the pecans in the bottom, dot them with a tablespoon of butter and pour the combined ingredients over them. Bake the pie for 10 minutes in a hot oven 450°, then for 30 minutes in a slow oven 300°.

PUMPKIN PIE
2 Nine Inch Pies

1½ cups pumpkin fresh or
  canned
2 egg yolks
2/3 cup brown sugar
1/2 teaspoon ginger
1/2 teaspoon cinnamon
1½ cups milk

1/2 cup cream
1 teaspoon vanilla
1 lemon, rind and juice
  (optional)
1/2 teaspoon salt
2 egg whites

Cook and strain the pumpkin. Combine it with the next eight ingredients, add the salt to the egg whites, whip them until they are stiff and fold them in last. Line pans with pie dough and pour in the filling. See Chart for baking pies. Serve the pie cold with cream, or whipped cream.

HOW TO COOK PUMPKIN

Wash the pumpkin and cut it in half crosswise. Remove the seeds and the strings. Place the pumpkin in a pan, shell side up and bake it in a moderate oven until it is tender and begins to fall apart. Scrape the pulp from the shell and strain it.

213

MINCE MEAT

4 pounds lean beef, chopped
2 pounds beef suet, chopped
1 peck Baldwin Apples,
  peeled, cored and sliced
3 pounds sugar
2 quarts cider
4 pounds seeded raisins
3 pounds currants
1½ pounds citron
½ pound dried orange peel
½ pound dried lemon peel

Juice and rind of 1 lemon
1 tablespoon cinnamon
1 tablespoon mace
1 tablespoon cloves
1 teaspoon pepper
1 teaspoon salt
2 whole nutmegs grated
1 gallon sour cherries with
  juice
2 pounds nut meats
  (optional)

Cook the ingredients slowly for two hours. Seal them in jars. Place the mince meat, adding brandy as desired, in a two crust pie. See Chart for Baking Pies.

MOCK MINCE MEAT
Yield about 12 qts.

1 peck green tomatoes,
  chopped
1 peck tart apples, pared
  and chopped
5 pounds brown sugar (13½
  cups)
1 pound seeded raisins (½
  of these chopped)

1 pound currants
½ pound of suet, finely
  chopped
3 tablespoons salt
2 tablespoons ground cloves
4 tablespoons cinnamon
3 tablespoons nutmeg
2 cups vinegar

Scald the tomatoes twice by pouring 2 quarts of boiling water over them. Drain them well. Combine them with the other ingredients and boil them for 20 minutes. If the apples are sweet instead of tart, do not add the full amount of sugar at first, taste the mixture to see how much is needed. Pack the mince meat into sterilized jars and seal them. Place the mince meat, adding brandy as desired, between two pie crusts. See Chart for Baking Pies.

DEEP FRUIT PIES

Peaches and apples are usually used for deep pies, but other fruits are equally good. Place prepared fruit in a baking dish, or in individual dishes. Sweeten it with white or brown sugar, (about ⅓ cup of sugar to 1 cup of fruit). Season it with lemon juice and grated lemon rind, or cinnamon. If the fruit is very juicy, add 2 tablespoonsful of flour to each cup of sugar, and if it is dry, add a small quantity of water. Juicy, or dry, it may be dotted with butter. Cover the fruit with pie dough rolled 1/4 inch thick, prick the pastry top and full it around the edge of the dish. These pies are frequently made in individual baking cups. She Chart for Baking Pies.

FRUIT DUMPLINGS OR TURNOVERS, APPLE, PEACH, ETC.

Peel and core medium sized apples. Fill the centers with brown sugar, allow 2 teaspoons of butter to each apple, a little grated lemon rind, cinnamon and a few grains of salt. Prepare rich pastry dough. Roll it and enclose each apple entirely in a piece of dough. Place the dumplings in a baking dish. Brush them over with melted butter. See Chart for Baking Pies. Serve them with Hard or Foamy Sauce.

APPLE SAUCE TURNOVERS

Roll pie dough 1/8 inch thick. Cut it in 2 1/2 inch squares. Place a teaspoon or two of apple sauce in the center, fold over the dough into a triangle and pinch the edges together. See Chart for Baking Pies.

Meringue Pies and Fillings for Baked Pie Shells

These fillings are for a nine inch pie shell unless directed otherwise.

RULE FOR MERINGUE
MERINGUE

2 egg whites
1/8 teaspoon salt

4 tablespoons sugar, granulated or powdered
1/2 teaspoon vanilla

Add the salt to the egg whites and beat them on a platter, using a flat wire whisk, until they stand up in peaks and are stiff, but not dry. Add the sugar very slowly, 1/2 teaspoon at a time, beating constantly. Beat in the vanilla and bake the meringue in a slow oven—300°—for about 12 minutes.

Note: The success of the meringue will depend upon the proper beating of the egg whites, the slow addition of the sugar and the slow oven.

APPLE PIE II.

Peel, core and slice 4 or 5 apples. Cook them in just enough water to keep them from scorching. Sweeten them with white or brown sugar and season them with lemon juice and cinnamon. A tablespoonful, or more, of butter may be added. Cool the apples and put them into a baked pie shell just before serving the pie, or cover them with meringue and bake the pie in a slow oven 300° for 15 minutes.

PEACH PIE II.

Follow the rule for Apple Pie.

BERRY PIES II.

Stew 2 cups of berries with ½ cup or more of sugar over a low fire, crushing some of the berries at the bottom to prevent them from burning. When they are soft, pour off a little of the juice and cool it. Add from 2 to 3 tablespoons of flour or cornstarch to it and return it to the pan. Permit the berries to boil and thicken and add 2 tablespoons of butter to them. Cool the fruit and pour it into a baked pie shell just before serving the pie.

PINEAPPLE MERINGUE PIE

2 cups crushed pineapple	1 tablespoon butter
1 tablespoon cornstarch	2 egg yolks
¾ cup sugar	2 egg whites

Cook the pineapple and cornstarch for 15 minutes in a double boiler. Add the butter and the sugar. Pour the hot mixture over the egg yolks and return it to the double boiler for 1 minute. Have a baked pie shell ready. Fill it with the pineapple mixture and cover it with a meringue made with the egg whites. See Page 215.

LEMON PIE I. (Economy)
1 Nine Inch Pie

1¼ cups sugar	½ teaspoon grated lemon
4 tablespoons cornstarch	rind
⅛ teaspoon salt	1½ tablespoons butter
1½ cups boiling water	2 or 3 egg yolks
¼ cup lemon juice	2 or 3 egg whites

Combine the first three ingredients and pour the water over them. Add the lemon juice and rind and the butter and cook the mixture over a very low flame, stirring it constantly until it is thick and smooth. Beat the yolks and pour a little of the mixture over them, then return it to the pan and permit the eggs to thicken slightly, stirring the custard constantly. Cool it and pour it into a baked pie shell. Cover it with a Meringue made with the egg whites. See Page 215.

LEMON PIE II.

4 egg yolks	3 tablespoons water
1 lemon, juice and rind	⅛ teaspoon salt
½ cup sugar	2 egg whites
2 tablespoons flour	2 egg whites

Cook the first five ingredients over hot water until they are thick and smooth, then cool them. Add the salt to the whites of 2 eggs, beat them until they are stiff and fold them into the custard. Fill a baked pie shell with the custard, and cover it with a Meringue made with two egg whites—See Page 215.

FAIRY LEMON TART
1 Large or 2 Small Pies

I. Soak 2 teaspoons of gelatine in ⅓ cup of cold water.

II. Place 4 egg yolks, slightly beaten, in a double boiler, add the rind and juice of 1 large lemon and 1⅛ cups of sugar. Cook these ingredients over hot water, stirring them constantly until they are smooth and thick. Add the dissolved gelatine and cool the mixture.

III. Beat the whites of 4 eggs until they are stiff, and fold them into I. and II. Have a baked pie shell in readiness and fill it with the lemon mixture. Chill the tart for several hours. Before serving it cover it with 1 cup of cream whipped, to which 1 teaspoon of vanilla and (if desired) 3 tablespoonsful of sugar have been added. This tart may be made a day in advance.

CUSTARD PIE

3 egg yolks	1 teaspoon vanilla
6 tablespoons sugar	¼ teaspoon grated nutmeg
2 tablespoons cornstarch	(optional)
¼ teaspoon salt	3 egg whites
2 cups milk scalded	

Beat the yolks, add the sugar gradually, the salt and the cornstarch. Pour the hot milk over this and place it in a double boiler. Cook the custard, stirring it constantly until it thickens. Cool it, add the vanilla and pour it into a baked pie shell. Cover it with a meringue made with the egg whites—See Page 215.

ZWIEBACK CUSTARD PIE

Follow the rule for Zwieback Crust. Follow the rule for Custard Pie filling. Fill the crust with the custard, pile a meringue —Page 215 on the custard, cover the top with rolled Zwieback crumbs and bake the pie in a moderate oven 300° for 12 minutes.

COCOANUT PIE

2 tablespoons cornstarch
6 tablespoons sugar
1/4 teaspoon salt
2 cups milk
2 egg yolks

1/2 to 1 cup grated
  cocoanut
1 teaspoon vanilla
3 egg whites

Combine the first three ingredients. Scald the milk and pour it slowly over them. Cook them over a very low flame, or in a double boiler, stirring them constantly until they are thick and smooth. Pour a small amount of this over the beaten egg yolks, beat them well and add them to the rest of the milk mixture. Permit the eggs to thicken slightly, stirring them constantly. Cool the custard and add the cocoanut and the vanilla. Fill a baked pie shell with the custard and cover it with a meringue made with the egg whites — See Page 215.

CHOCOLATE PIE

1 cup milk
2 tablespoons grated
  chocolate
1/2 cup sugar
1 1/2 teaspoons butter
1/8 teaspoon salt

3 1/2 teaspoons cornstarch
1/8 cup milk
2 egg yolks, lightly beaten
1/2 teaspoon vanilla
2 egg whites

Scald the milk with the chocolate, sugar, butter and salt. Dissolve the cornstarch in 1/8 cup of milk and add it to the first mixture. Stir and cook it over a low fire until it is thick and smooth. Pour part of it over the yolks, beat them well and return them to the pan. Let the yolks thicken slightly, stirring the custard constantly. Cool it and add the vanilla. Fill a baked pie shell with the custard and cover it with a meringue made with the egg whites — See Page 215.

BUTTERSCOTCH PIE

3/4 cup brown sugar
2 tablespoons flour
2 tablespoons butter
1/4 teaspoon salt

1 cup milk
2 egg yolks
1/2 teaspoon vanilla
2 egg whites

Combine the first four ingredients and cook them in a double boiler. Stir them constantly until they are well blended. Add the milk and stir the mixture until it is thick and smooth. Pour a little of this over the beaten yolks, return it to the pan and permit the yolks to thicken slightly, stirring them constantly. Cool the custard, flavor it with vanilla and pour it into a baked pie shell. Cover it with a meringue made with the egg whites — See Page 215.

BUTTERSCOTCH SPONGE PIE

2 egg yolks
1 cup brown sugar
1 tablespoon butter
1 tablespoon flour

1 cup milk (part cream)
½ teaspoon salt
2 egg whites

Combine the yolks and the sugar and cream them well, add the butter and the flour. Add the salt to the egg whites and whip them until they are stiff. Fold them into the egg mixture. Have a baked pie shell ready. Fill it with the custard and bake the pie in a moderate oven 375° until the top is brown.

CHIFFON LEMON PIE

½ cup sugar
2 tablespoons water
3 egg yolks
3 tablespoons lemon juice

Grated rind of 1 lemon
½ teaspoon salt
2 egg whites

Reserve 3 tablespoons of the sugar. Combine the remaining sugar, the water, egg yolks, lemon juice and rind and cook them over hot water, or over very low heat, stirring them constantly until they are thick. Add the salt to the egg whites, beat them until they are stiff and fold in the reserved sugar and the yolk mixture. Pour the custard into a baked pie shell. Brown the filling in a hot oven — 400° — for 10 minutes.

CHIFFON STRAWBERRY PIE

3 eggs
½ cup sugar
½ teaspoon salt

1 cup berries cut in pieces
1 baked pie shell, 1 inch
  deep, 6½ inches wide

Place the yolks in the top of a double boiler. Beat them until they are light, add the sugar and cook the mixture over hot water until it thickens. Add the salt to the egg whites, beat them until they are stiff and pour the hot custard over them. Return the custard to the double boiler, beating it constantly until it is thick and stands up well. Add the strawberries, fill the pie shell and bake the pie in a hot oven 400° for 10 minutes.

CHIFFON ORANGE PIE

¼ cup sugar
3 tablespoons flour
3 egg yolks
2 tablespoons lemon juice
¾ cup orange juice

½ teaspoon grated orange
  rind
2 tablespoons water
⅛ teaspoon salt
3 egg whites

Place the first seven ingredients in a double boiler. Cook and stir them until they are thick and smooth. If the orange juice is very acid, more sugar may be required. Add the salt to the egg whites, whip them to a stiff froth and fold them into the custard. Have a baked pie shell ready, fill it with the custard and brown the pie in a hot oven — 400° — for 10 minutes.

BLUEBERRY CUSTARD PIE WITH MERINGUE

If canned blueberries are used, be sure to have good ones, as they are frequently flat and tasteless.

2 cups blueberries, fresh or
   canned
2 egg yolks
¾ cup sugar
3 tablespoons flour

⅛ teaspoon salt
2 teaspoons lemon juice
2 tablespoons orange juice
2 egg whites

Cream the yolks with the sugar, add the flour and salt. Heat the berries, combine them with the yolk mixture and cook them over hot water, or over a low flame until they are thick, stirring them constantly. Have a baked pie crust ready, fill it with the blueberry custard and cover it with the meringue made with the egg whites. — See Page 215.

CHEESE PIE OR CAKE

This cheese pie, or cake, should be about 1½ inches in depth. Bake it in a pan with a removable rim, or in a pyrex baking dish 10 inches wide.

2 cups rolled Zwieback
½ cup melted butter
½ cup sugar

⅛ teaspoon salt
1 teaspoon cinnamon

Combine these ingredients and reserve ½ for the top of the cake. Line a deep baking dish and press the crust lightly on the bottom and against the sides. Fill it with the following:

Cheese Filling:

½ cup cream
1 cup sugar
2 pounds cottage cheese
4 egg yolks
3 tablespoons flour

1 teaspoon vanilla or ½
   lemon (rind and juice)
⅛ teaspoon salt
3 egg whites

Dissolve the sugar in the cream. Add the next four ingredients in the order given. Add the salt to the egg whites, beat them until they are stiff and fold them into the custard. Bake the cake in a moderate oven 350° for 1 hour. See Index for German Cherry Cake made with Zwieback crust.

Cakes

Cakes are divided into two classes:

I. Sponge Cakes.

II. Butter Cakes.

Sponge cakes are made without butter. Butter cakes call for butter, or other shortening.

The following general rules apply to both types of cake, special rules being given later.

The ingredients used in cakes must be measured accurately. The majority of recipes are very carefully balanced, and this balance must not be disturbed by careless measurements. All the measurements given in this book are level, unless otherwise stated.

Flour and sugar should be sifted before they are measured — and after being measured the flour should be sifted three times. The sugar need not be sifted again unless the recipe calls for it. These ingredients should be handled separately.

It is a help to use two squares of stiff paper in sifting the sugar and flour. Bend the paper when you wish to transfer these ingredients.

Use a tablespoon, or a small scoop to handle the sugar and flour when measuring them. Heap the flour lightly into a cup. Do not shake the cup. Fill it to overflowing, then level off the top with a knife.

Cake flour makes a light and delicious cake. Use it whenever it is available, but if bread flour is substituted, use ⅞ of a cup instead of 1 cup of flour. If cake flour is substituted for bread flour, use 1⅛ cups instead of 1 cup.

If flour has been exposed to moisture, it will make a "streaky" cake. Be sure to spread flour in shallow pans and dry it well in a slow oven before using it, if there is any doubt about its being dry, or sift it four or five times before the open door of a hot oven.

SPONGE CAKES

Beat the egg yolks until they are light and lemon colored. Add the remaining ingredients as directed in the recipes, using sifted sugar and sifted flour.

Do not beat a sponge cake batter unless the recipe calls for it. Fold in the ingredients lightly until they are blended only— enclosing as much air as possible.

Either the flour or the beaten egg whites may be folded in last Do not beat the egg whites until you are ready to use them.

Add a few grains of salt to the egg whites, and beat them on a large platter, using a flat wire egg beater. Beat them until they are stiff, stand up well in peaks and keep their shape, but not until they are dry.

Fold the stiffly beaten egg whites into the cake batter, that is, heap them onto the batter and with a downward motion of the spoon take up some of the batter and fold it lightly over the egg whites. Enclose all the air, do not stir or beat it out. Repeat this downward cut and upward folding motion until the ingredients are blended.

Have a cake pan ready, and pour the batter into it. The dough will cling to the sides of the ungreased pan and will rise higher than if it were greased.

Bake a sponge cake in a moderate oven—325°, or place it in a somewhat slower oven—300° and bake it with a slightly creasing heat.

Test the cake by inserting a wire cake tester, or a straw. If the tester emerges perfectly clean, the cake is done. The cake should be lightly browned and should be beginning to shrink from the sides of the pan. If pressed with a finger, it should at once come back into shape.

Remove the cake from the oven and invert the pan until the cake is entirely cold. Then run a knife around the sides and across the bottom and remove the cake from the pan. Trim off the hard edges, if there are any, (there really should not be), sprinkle the cake with powdered sugar, or cover it with icing.

BUTTER CAKES

Place the butter called for in the recipe in a warm place. Permit it to become soft, but do not permit it to melt, unless the recipe calls for melted butter. When the butter has softened somewhat, beat it with a wooden cake spoon, or work it with the hand until it is creamy. Add the sugar slowly and beat or work it into the butter until it is entirely dissolved.

This first step in the making of a butter cake is a very important one—do not hasten it. Cream the butter and the sugar until they are fluffy and foamy.

Next beat in the egg yolks, one by one, add a small amount of flour, which has been sifted with the baking powder, then a small amount of milk, or whatever liquid is called for—then alternate the flour and the milk until all of it has been used. Beat the batter well after each addition of flour, or liquid, as this will give the cake a fine grain. If beaten too long, the cake will be close.

Place the egg whites on a large platter, add a few grains of salt, and whip them with a flat wire egg beater until they are stiff, stand in peaks and hold their shape, but not until they are dry. Do not beat the egg whites until you are ready to use them.

Fold in the beaten egg whites, that is, heap them upon the cake batter and with a downward motion of the spoon take up some of the batter and fold it lightly over the egg whites. Enclose all the air, do not stir or beat it out. Repeat this downward cut and upward folding motion until the ingredients are blended.

Have a greased cake pan ready. Pour the dough into it and bake the cake in a moderate oven—350°—or place it in a somewhat slower oven—325°—and bake it with a slightly increasing heat.

Test the cake by inserting a wire cake tester, or a straw. If the tester emerges perfectly clean, the cake is done. The cake should be lightly browned and should be beginning to shrink from the sides of the pan. If pressed with a finger, it should at once come back into shape.

Invert the cake pan for five minutes. Then loosen the cake from the sides and the bottom of the pan, invert it onto a plate and turn it right side up on a cake cooler, or on a rack, so that the air may circulate from the bottom. This will keep the crust dry and prevent it from becoming soggy. Sprinkle the cake with powdered sugar, or cover it with icing.

Loaf and Layer Cakes
Sponge Cakes

The three following sponge cakes call for water and are exceptions to the rule that sponge cake batter must not be beaten:

SPONGE CAKES I. AND II.

These cakes call for the same ingredients, but the manner of combining them differs. Good results are obtained by either method.

No. I. has a little more body and is more quickly prepared.

SPONGE CAKE I.

3 egg yolks
1 cup sugar
3 tablespoons lemon juice
  or 1 teaspoon vanilla
1 teaspoon grated lemon
  rind

$\frac{1}{2}$ cup boiling water
$1\frac{1}{8}$ cups cake flour
2 teaspoons baking powder
$\frac{1}{8}$ teaspoon salt
3 egg whites

Beat the yolks and add the sugar gradually. Add the lemon juice and rind, the boiling water and the flour, which has been sifted with the baking powder. Beat the batter well. Add the salt to the egg whites, beat them to a stiff froth and fold them into the batter. 1 teaspoonful of vanilla may be substituted for the lemon rind and juice. Add it before folding in the egg whites. Bake the cake in an ungreased pan in a slow oven 325° for about $\frac{1}{2}$ hour.

SPONGE CAKE II.

3 egg yolks
$\frac{1}{2}$ cup cold water
1 cup sugar
3 tablespoons lemon juice
  or 1 teaspoon vanilla

1 teaspoon grated lemon
  rind
$1\frac{1}{8}$ cups cake flour
2 teaspoons baking powder
$\frac{1}{8}$ teaspoon salt
3 egg whites

Whip the yolks with the cold water until the liquid more than doubles in bulk. Add the sugar slowly. Beat this for two minutes, add the flavoring and fold in the flour which has been sifted with the baking powder, 1 tablespoonful at a time. Add the salt to the egg whites, beat them until they are stiff and fold them into the batter. Bake the cake in an ungreased cake pan in a slow oven 325° for about $\frac{1}{2}$ hour.

SPONGE CAKE MADE WITH YOLKS

This is a very good, quick little cake. It may be used for strawberry shortcake, layer, or loaf cake:

3 egg yolks	¾ cup cake flour, sifted
⅛ teaspoon salt	twice
⅓ cup sugar, sifted twice	2 teaspoons baking powder
¼ cup boiling water	1 teaspoon vanilla

Add the salt to the yolks and beat them until they are light. Add the sugar slowly, continuing to beat. Add the vanilla and the hot water. Combine the flour and the baking powder, sift them into the batter and mix the ingredients well. Bake the cake in one large, or two small layer pans for 30 minutes in a slow oven 350°. Spread the layers with jelly, with stewed fruit, or with a cake filling.

QUEEN MARY'S SPONGE CAKE

When King George was sick, his wife, who is reputed to have that inborn thing, "a light hand with pastry," bought him a volume of Marie Corelli's and baked a sponge cake for him. Who says that the lives of Queens are complicated?

This cake contains neither baking powder, nor cream of tartar, but depends for its lightness upon the air that is first beaten and then folded into it. This recipe makes a large, delicate, fine grained cake, which, if somewhat uninteresting, makes up for that by being highly digestible.

6 eggs	Rind of 1 lemon
1 cup sugar	Juice of ½ lemon
1 cup cake flour	¼ teaspoon salt

1 teaspoonful of vanilla and 1 teaspoonful of water may be substituted for the lemon juice. Separate the eggs and beat the yolks until they are light. Grate the lemon rind over the sugar, and add the sugar slowly to the egg yolks, stirring them briskly with a wire whisk. Add the lemon juice and when these ingredients are creamed, begin to fold in the egg whites, which have been whipped with the salt to a stiff froth. When the egg whites are partly folded in, being adding the flour—one tablespoonful at a time. Cut and fold lightly until the flour is blended, then pour the batter into an ungreased angel food pan and bake it in a slow oven 325° for one hour.

SUNSHINE CAKE

1¼ cups sugar
⅓ cup water
¼ teaspoon salt
5 egg whites

5 egg yolks
1 teaspoon vanilla
⅞ cup cake flour
½ teaspoon cream of tartar

Boil the sugar and the water to the soft ball stage, 238°. Add the salt to the egg whites and whip them until they are stiff. Pour the syrup over them in a fine stream, beating them constantly until the mixture cools. Add the flavoring and fold in the egg yolks. Then fold in the flour that has been sifted with the cream of tartar—one tablespoonful at a time. Bake the cake in an ungreased tube pan in a slow oven 350° for 40 minutes. Reduce the heat to 325° and bake it 30 minutes longer.

Angel Food Cakes

Every novice has a desire to make a perfect angel cake, and fortunately, the accomplishment of this dream is entirely within reach. It is a little disturbing to find that this goal may be attained by various means and ways. Every cook book I know advises a slow oven, but the best angel cake I have ever eaten is baked at first in a very hot oven and then with diminishing heat. Every cook book I know counsels great care in combining the ingredients, but I have a friend whose angel cake is superlative, who slaps it together without the usual careful sifting and folding. The beginner, however, had better follow the established rule. Beating the eggs on a platter and having absolutely fresh cream of tartar are helpful hints to success. The three following recipes differ considerably, both in proportions and in the manner of combining the ingredients. The first is light, the second lighter and the third is so light and moist that it seems to melt away.

ANGEL FOOD CAKE I.
Swansdown Recipe

1 cup cake flour sifted 5 times, once before measuring
½ teaspoon salt
1 cup egg whites—8 to 10 eggs

1 teaspoon cream of tartar
1¼ cups sugar, sifted once
½ teaspoon vanilla
¾ teaspoon almond extract

Add the salt to the egg whites and beat them until they are foamy, add the cream of tartar and beat them until they are stiff, but not dry. Fold in the sugar, one tablespoonful at a time.

Fold in the flavoring. Sift a small amount of the flour over the mixture and fold it in lightly. Continue to do this until the flour is used. Pour the dough into an ungreased tube cake pan and bake it in a slow oven 250° for 30 minutes, increase the heat to 325° and bake it 20 minutes longer.

ANGEL FOOD CAKE II.
Gold Medal Recipe

1¼ cups egg whites (10 eggs)
1 teaspoon cream of tartar
1½ cups granulated sugar
¼ teaspoon salt

1 teaspoon flavoring — vanilla or almond
1 cup cake flour

Sift the sugar twice. Sift the flour once before measuring it. Sift it three times with ½ cup of sugar and the salt. Beat the egg whites with a flat whip. Add the cream of tartar when the whites are frothy. Continue beating until the egg whites will stand up in peaks. Gradually beat in 1 cup of sugar. Fold in the flavoring and the flour mixture. Pour the dough into an ungreased tube pan and bake it in a very slow oven gradually increasing the heat — 250° to 350°. Bake the cake for 1 hour.

ANGEL FOOD CAKE III.
With Black Walnuts

1 cup cake flour
1 cup sugar
½ cup powdered sugar
¼ teaspoon salt
1½ cups egg whites
1 teaspoon cream of tartar

2 tablespoons lemon juice
1 teaspoon vanilla
2 teaspoons almond extract
1 cup black walnuts or other nut meats, finely chopped

Sift the flour, measure it and combine it with the sugars. Sift these ingredients five times. Add the salt to the egg whites and beat them until they are foamy, add the cream of tartar and beat them until they are stiff, but not dry. Fold in the flour mixture a little at a time. Fold in the flavoring, add the nuts and pour the dough into an ungreased tube pan. Bake the cake in a slow oven 275° for 1¼ hours.

White Cakes

The two recipes following are for white cake. The ingredients used are the same, but the proportions differ. The second is the better of the two cakes — (it is the best white cake recipe I know), but the first, an excellent cake, is more economical.

It is especially good baked in a shallow pan with a caramel or chocolate icing, garnished with nuts and cut into squares before serving.

WHITE CAKE I.

1/2 cup butter	3/4 cup milk
1 1/4 cups sugar	1 teaspoon vanilla
1 tablespoon boiling water	1/8 teaspoon salt
2 cups cake flour	3 egg whites
3 teaspoons baking powder	

Cream the butter and the sugar and add the hot water. Sift the flour with the baking powder and add this alternately with the milk. Add the vanilla and beat the batter well. Add the salt to the egg whites, beat them until they are stiff and fold them lightly into the batter. Bake the cake in a greased pan in a moderate oven 350° with slightly increasing heat.

WHITE CAKE II.

No. II. is usually made in layers and iced with a nut, raisin or other icing. It is the basis for the famous Lady Baltimore Cake:

1 cup butter	1 cup milk
2 cups sugar	1 teaspoon vanilla
3 1/2 cups cake flour	1/8 teaspoon salt
2 teaspoons baking powder	Whites of 7 or 8 eggs

Cream the butter and the sugar. Sift the flour once before measuring it, add the baking powder and sift it three times. Add the flour alternately with the milk to the butter mixture, add the vanilla, and beat the batter well. Fold in the stiffly beaten egg whites, to which the salt has been added. Bake the cake in a greased pan, or in greased layer pans, in a moderate oven — 350°.

LADY CAKE

The following recipe is a good tube pan cake, or loaf cake. It tastes and looks like a traditional wedding cake (that is, traditional since fruit cake fell from grace.)

3/4 cup butter	1 teaspoon almond extract
1 cup sugar	Grated rind of 1 lemon
1 3/4 cups cake flour	1/8 teaspoon salt
2 teaspoons baking powder	3 egg whites
1/2 cup milk	

Cream the butter and the sugar and add to them alternately

the flour (which has been sifted with the baking powder) and the milk. Add the flavoring and beat the batter well. Add the salt to the egg whites, whip them to a stiff froth and fold them lightly into the batter. Place the dough in a greased cake tin and bake it in a moderate oven 350° for about 45 minutes. Sprinkle the cake with powdered sugar, or ice it with White Icing.

MARBLE CAKE

This old-fashioned cake is still a favorite when served, but one seldom encounters it:

Prepare the ingredients for Lady cake. Cream the butter and the sugar, add the flavoring to the milk and combine the flour and the baking powder. Add the milk and the flour alternately to the butter mixture. Divide the batter into two parts. To one part add:

1½ squares chocolate, melted   2 tablespoons hot water

Beat the whites of the eggs until they are stiff and fold one half of them into each half of the batter. Grease a tube pan and place large spoonfuls of batter in it, alternating the light and the dark dough. Bake the cake for about 45 minutes in a moderate oven 350°. Sprinkle it with powdered sugar, or ice it with Chocolate Icing — Page 288.

POUND CAKE

I have tried any number of pound cakes (most of them very old recipes) and they have all had an objectionable solidity. If I have failed through ignorance, I shall be grateful to someone for enlightenment. The following recipe calls for milk, so perhaps it is not the "genuine article," but it is a mighty fine cake:

1 cup butter
2 cups sugar
3½ cups cake flour
3½ teaspoons baking
  powder
1 cup milk
1 teaspoon vanilla
1 teaspoon lemon juice
½ teaspoon almond extract

6 drops rose water
  (optional)
1 cup walnut meats
  (optional)
⅛ teaspoon salt
6 egg whites
1 tablespoon or more
  whiskey may be substi-
  tuted for the flavoring

Cream the butter and the sugar. Add a little of the flour that has been sifted with the baking powder, then alternate the milk and the flour until all has been used, beating the batter well after each addition, then add the flavoring and the nuts. Add the salt to the egg whites, beat them until they are stiff and fold them lightly into the cake batter. Pour the batter into a greased tube pan and bake the cake in a moderate oven — 350° — for about 1 hour. Ice the cake with white or with caramel icing. 4 eggs, separated, may be used instead of 6 egg whites. Add the yolks to the creamed butter and sugar.

CAKE FOR LAMB MOLD

Iron molds are made in two parts, in which a cake is baked in the shape of a lamb. This lamb is covered with white icing and sprinkled generously with grated cocoanut. A blue ribbon with a little bell, or a garland of decorative icing roses is placed around the lamb's neck, a red hot forms it lips and raisins are used for its eyes. Children love this cake:

½ cup butter	1 cup milk
1½ cups sugar	1 teaspoon vanilla
2½ cups cake flour	⅛ teaspoon milk
4 teaspoons baking powder	4 egg whites, stiffly beaten

Combine these ingredients in the order given, adding the baking powder to the flour and the salt to the egg whites before beating them. Bake the cake in the well greased lamb mold in a moderate oven 350°. Do not be at all alarmed if in taking the cake from the mold the lamp promptly loses its head. It probably will, but by lifting off the top mold and letting the cake cool first, this danger may be averted. If, however, it is not, stick the head on with some icing, using a few toothpicks as armatures.

Icing:

2 egg whites	1 teaspoon vanilla
4 cups sugar	¼ to ½ pound grated
1 cup water	cocoanut

Follow the rule for White Icing — Page 285. This makes a light coat. Increase the proportions by one-half for a heavier coating of wool. Press the cocoanut lightly onto the icing. If the tail is lost to sight, make a new one with additional icing. Bed the lamb on ferns, or shredded green paper and place a few small flowers about it.

Yellow Cakes

LOAF CAKE

1 egg

1 cup sugar
¼ cup butter
1 egg yolk
1¾ cups cake flour
3 teaspoons baking powder
¾ cup milk

1 teaspoon vanilla
⅓ teaspoon almond extract
(optional)
¼ cup nut meats (optional)
1 egg white

Cream the butter and the sugar. Add the egg yolk and beat the batter well. Add the flour, sifted with the baking powder, alternately with the milk. Add the flavoring and last fold in the stiffly beaten egg white. Bake the cake in a small greased pan in a moderate oven 350°.

NUT LOAF CAKE

1 cup butter
2 cups sugar
1 cup milk
4 egg yolks
3 cups cake flour
3 teaspoons baking powder

1 cup chopped nuts
1 teaspoon vanilla
½ teaspoon almond extract
(optional)
⅛ teaspoon salt
4 egg whites

Cream the butter and the sugar. Add the yolks, slightly beaten, and the vanilla. Sift the flour with the baking powder and add it alternately with the milk. Add the nuts and last fold in the stiffly beaten egg whites, to which the salt has been added. Bake the cake in a greased tin in a moderate oven 350°. Sprinkle it with powdered sugar, or ice it with Caramel Icing — Page 287.

YELLOW LOAF, OR LAYER CAKE

The following recipe calls for 8 egg yolks and is a fine way of utilizing them.

1¼ cups sugar
¾ cup butter
8 egg yolks
¾ cup milk

2½ cups cake flour
4 teaspoons baking powder
¼ teaspoon almond extract
½ teaspoon vanilla

Sift the flour once before measuring it. Add the baking powder and sift it 3 times. Sift the sugar once. Cream the butter and the sugar. Beat the yolks until they are light and lemon colored and add them to the butter mixture. Add the flavoring and, alternately, the sifted flour and baking powder and the milk. Beat the batter well. Bake the cake in a greased tube pan in a moderate oven 350°. Ice it with uncooked Orange Icing—Page 290.

SOUR CREAM CAKE

While this recipe calls for rich sour cream, it may be made with sour top milk. If the milk is used the cake will be good, but it will not keep as well as when the cream is used.

2 eggs	(scant)
1 cups rich sour cream	1/4 teaspoon soda
1 3/4 cups cake flour	1/8 teaspoon salt
1 cup sugar	1 teaspoon vanilla, or 1/2
2 teaspoons baking powder	teaspoon nutmeg

Beat the eggs with the sour cream. Combine and sift the dry ingredients. Add them to the egg mixture and beat the batter well. Add the vanilla and pour the batter into a greased cake tin. Bake the cake in a moderate oven 350°. Ice it with French Coffee Icing.

SOUR CREAM CHOCOLATE CAKE

Follow the rule for Sour Cream Cake using 1 1/2 cups flour and 1/4 cup cocoa.

HOT MILK CAKE
2 Large or 3 Small Layers

A light, fine-grained layer cake—easily made:

3 eggs	1/2 teaspoon salt
1 1/2 cups sugar	3/4 cup milk
1 1/2 cups cake flour	1/8 to 1/3 cup shortening
1 1/2 teaspoons baking powder	1 teaspoon vanilla

Beat the eggs until they are very light. Add the sugar slowly and continue beating. Sift the dry ingredients and add them to the egg mixture. Heat the milk with the shortening, to the boiling point and add it to the batter. Beat it well, add the vanilla, and pour the batter into greased layer pans. Bake the cake in a moderate oven 375° for about 1/2 hour. 1 teaspoon of lemon juice may be substituted for the vanilla.

COFFEE FLAVORED LAYER CAKE

Follow the rule for Hot Milk Cake, substituting 1/4 cup or more of very strong coffee for the same amount of milk.

HURRY UP CAKE

The name of this cake speaks for itself. It is surprisingly good. It can be used best as a flat cake that is iced and cut in cubes, or as a layer cake. It must be lightly iced.

1/2 cup soft butter	1/2 teaspoon salt
1 cup sugar	2 1/2 teaspoons baking
2 eggs	powder
1/2 cup milk	1 teaspoon vanilla
1 3/4 cups cake flour	

Place the ingredients in a bowl and beat them vigorously for 2 or 3 minutes with a wire whisk, or with a rotary beater. Pour the dough into a greased pan and bake the cake in a moderate oven 350° if baked in a loaf, 375° if baked in layers. Ice it with uncooked Chocolate Icing or some other light icing.

CARAMEL CAKES

The two following cakes call for brown sugar. I prefer them to caramel cakes calling for syrup because they hold up better (if they are not consumed too quickly).

The first is very fine grained and delicate, the second is somewhat heftier and somewhat cheaper, but they seem to be equally good and are highly recommended. They are both fine baked in a large flat pan, iced and cut into squares.

CARAMEL LAYER CAKE I.
2 Large or 3 Small Layers

1/2 cup butter	1/2 teaspoon salt
2 cups brown sugar	2 teaspoons vanilla
4 eggs separated	1 cup nuts, chopped
1 1/2 cups cake flour	(optional)
1 teaspoon baking powder	

Cream the butter and the sugar, add the yolks and beat the batter well. Add the sifted dry ingredients and the vanilla. Last fold in the stiffly beaten egg whites. Bake the cake in layers in a moderate oven 375° for 20 minutes. Ice the cake with White Icing, or with Caramel Icing, adding nuts, if desired. See Caramel Banana Cake—Page 252.

233

CARAMEL LAYER CAKE II.
2 Layers

½ cup butter
1½ cups brown sugar
2 eggs
1 teaspoon vanilla
2 cups cake flour

2 teaspoons baking powder
½ teaspoon salt
½ cup milk
⅔ cup nuts (optional)
⅔ cup dates (optional)

Melt the butter over a very slow fire. Add the sugar, stir it until it is dissolved and cool the mixture. Add the eggs one at a time and beat them well. Add the vanilla. Sift the flour with the baking powder and the salt and add these ingredients to the butter mixture, alternately with the milk. Add the nuts and dates last. Bake the cake in greased layer pans in a moderate oven 350°, and ice it with Caramel Icing — Page 287. Decorate it with pecan or walnut meats.

BURNT SUGAR CAKE

½ cup butter
1½ cups sugar
2 egg yolks
1 cup water
2 cups cake flour
3 tablespoons burnt sugar

1 teaspoon vanilla
½ cup flour
2 teaspoons baking powder
⅛ teaspoon salt
2 egg whites

Melt ½ cup of sugar in a skillet and permit it to burn. When the sugar is burnt black and while it is hot add ½ cup of boiling water and stir the syrup rapidly. Boil it until it is the consistency of molasses, and cool it. Cream the butter with the 1½ cups of sugar and when these ingredients are well blended, beat in the egg yolks and add the 2 cups of flour alternately with the water. Beat the batter for five minutes, then add the burnt sugar, the vanilla and the ½ cup of flour sifted with the baking powder. Add the salt to the egg whites, beat them until they are stiff and fold them lightly into the batter. Bake the cake in greased layer pans in a moderate oven — 375°. Ice the cake with White Icing, allowing 2 teaspoons of burnt sugar for every egg white in addition to the vanilla.

Chocolate Cakes

CHOCOLATE ANGEL FOOD

1¼ cups egg whites (10 to 12 eggs)
¼ teaspoon salt
1 teaspoon cream of tartar
1¼ cups sugar, sifted
1 teaspoon vanilla

½ teaspoon lemon extract
¾ cup cake flour — sifted before measuring
¼ cup cocoa — sifted 5 times with the flour

Add the salt to the egg whites and beat them until they are foamy, add the cream of tartar and beat them until they are stiff. Fold in the sugar, 1 tablespoonful at a time, and add the flavoring. Sift a small amount of the combined cocoa and flour over the egg mixture and fold it in. Repeat this until all the flour is used. Pour the dough into an ungreased tube pan and bake the cake in a slow oven 275° for 30 minutes. Increase the heat to a moderate oven 325° and bake it 30 minutes longer. When it is cool, cover the cake with White Icing and a coating of bitter chocolate.

CHOCOLATE SPONGE CAKE

The following recipe makes an unusually nice light chocolate cake. As it requires no butter, it is not rich and is therefore a good cake to bake for children. It gives a very generous return for the little it calls for:

3½ oz. (squares) chocolate	1¼ cups cake flour
1 cup hot milk	1 tablespoon baking powder
1 cup sugar	½ teaspoon vanilla
4 egg yolks	4 egg whites
1 cup sugar	

Melt the chocolate over hot water, add the milk and 1 cup of sugar and stir the mixture until it is smooth. Cream the yolks with one cup of sugar and add the hot chocolate mixture. Combine the flour and baking powder, sift them into the batter and beat it well. Add the vanilla and fold in the stiffly beaten egg whites. Bake the cake in an ungreased tube pan, or in layer pans in a slow oven — 325°. Ice it with White Icing and a coating of bitter chocolate — See Page 285.

CHOCOLATE CAKE

This cake is known as "Rombauer Special." It is a delicious chocolate cake and is always in demand:

2 scant ounces bitter chocolate	1¾ cups cake flour
5 tablespoons boiling water	4 teaspoons baking powder
½ cup butter	½ cup milk
1½ cups sugar	1 teaspoon vanilla
4 egg yolks	4 egg whites

Cut the chocolate into small pieces, melt it over a very low flame, add the hot water and cool the mixture. Cream the butter and the sugar slowly and add the egg yolks and the chocolate mixture. Add the flour, sifted with the baking powder, alternately with the milk and beat the batter well. Add the vanilla and fold in the stiffly beaten egg whites. Bake the cake in a shallow, greased pan (10x13 inches) in a moderate oven — 350°. Ice the top with thick White Icing and a coating of bitter chocolate — See Page 285. Cut the cake into squares.

BLACK WALNUT CHOCOLATE CAKE

Follow the rule for Chocolate Cake, adding 1 cup of black walnuts, coarsely chopped, or any other kind of nut.

CHOCOLATE FUDGE CAKE

This is a flat, rich, soggy cake, popular with young digestions:

¾ cup to 1 cup butter
2 cups sugar
4 eggs
4 ounces chocolate grated

1 cup to 1½ cups flour
¾ teaspoon baking powder
2 teaspoons vanilla
1 cup nut meats, chopped

Cream the butter and the sugar, beat in the eggs and the chocolate. Sift the flour with the baking powder, add it to the first mixture and beat the batter well. Add the vanilla and the nut meats. Bake the cake in a shallow pan lined with waxed paper in a slow oven — 350°.

CHOCOLATE POTATO CAKE

This chocolate cake has an excellent quality:

1 cup butter
2 cups sugar
4 egg yolks
1 cup unblanched almonds,
  ground, or 1 cup black
  walnuts, chopped
1 cup grated chocolate
1 cup cold boiled potatoes,
  grated

½ teaspoon cinnamon
2 teaspoons baking powder
1½ cups flour
½ cup cream or milk
4 egg whites
The use of the nuts is
  optional

Cream the butter and the sugar, add the egg yolks, almonds, chocolate and potatoes. Sift the cinnamon, baking powder and flour, and add them alternately with the milk. Last fold in the stiffly beaten egg whites. Bake the cake in a greased tube pan in a moderate oven 350° for 1 hour.

CHOCOLATE CUSTARD CAKE—DEVILS' FOOD

This is a smooth, fine grained chocolate cake. When the larger amount of chocolate is used, it is a black, rich Devil's Food:

2 to 4 ounces bitter
  chocolate
½ cup sweet milk

1 cup granulated sugar
1 egg yolk

Cook these ingredients in a saucepan over a very low flame. When they are thick and smooth, set them aside to cool.

Custard:

½ cup butter
1 cup light brown sugar
2 egg yolks

2 cups flour
½ cup sweet milk
1 teaspoon vanilla

Cream the butter and the sugar and add the other ingredients, alternating the flour with the milk. Add the custard and 1 teaspoon soda, dissolved in ¼ cup boiling water. Fold in the 2 egg whites, stiffly beaten. Bake the cake in two greased layer pans in a moderate oven 375°. Ice it with White Icing, or Boiled Chocolate Icing.

HALF HOUR CHOCOLATE CAKE
Economy Cake

It is claimed that the following cake can be mixed, baked and iced in one half hour and the claim is justified:

¾ cup sugar
2 tablespoons soft butter
1 egg
1 teaspoon vanilla

1 cup cake flour
1 teaspoon baking powder
¾ cup milk
2 ounces chocolate, melted

Melt the chocolate and cool it. Cream the butter with the sugar, the egg and the vanilla. Beat these ingredients well with a wire whisk. Sift the flour with the baking powder and add it to the butter mixture alternately with the milk. Add the chocolate and beat the batter well. Pour it into a greased pan and bake the cake in a moderate oven 350°. Cover it while it is hot with the following icing:

Icing:

1 heaping cup confectioner's
  sugar
2 tablespoons cocoa
1 tablespoon butter (scant)

¾ teaspoon vanilla
2 tablespoons coffee or
  cream

This cake is fine baked in a ring mold and served, uniced, the center filled with 1 cup of cream whipped and flavored. If it is to be an economy dessert, fill the center with 3 Minute Icing—Page 247, flavored to taste, or if it is to be eaten at once, with condensed milk Ice Cream—Page 342, and with hot Chocolate Sauce—Page 324.

Spice Cakes

The following recipes are various forms of spice cake:

CRACKER CAKE
A Small Cake

⅞ cup rolled and sifted
   soda crackers
5 eggs
¾ cup sugar

1 teaspoon cinnamon
¼ teaspoon cloves
¼ teaspoon almond extract

Cream the yolks and the sugar, and add the cracker crumbs and spices. Last fold in the stiffly beaten egg whies. Bake the cake in an ungreased tube pan in a slow oven 320°. Ice the cake with unboiled Chocolate Icing.

APPLE SAUCE CAKE

½ cup butter
1 cup sugar
1 egg beaten until light
1 cup raisins
1 cup currants or nuts
1¾ cups cake flour

¼ teaspoon salt
1 teaspoon soda
1 teaspoon cinnamon
½ teaspoon cloves
1 cup thick sweet apple
   sauce

Flour the nuts and raisins with part of the flour. Cream the butter and the sugar, add the egg and the nuts and raisins. Sift the flour with the soda and spices and add them to the first mixture. Last add the apple sauce, which has been heated. Bake the cake in a tube pan lined with paper in a moderate oven 350° for about 1 hour.

VELVET SPICE CAKE

This cake is well named, as it has a very delicate consistency. Its flavor is unequalled in spice cakes:

I. 1½ cups sugar and
   ¾ cup butter (scant)
     creamed with
  1 teaspoon baking powder
II. 2 cups cake flour — sifted
   3 times with

1 teaspoon soda (scant)
1 teaspoon nutmeg
1 teaspoon cinnamon
½ teaspoon cloves
½ teaspoon salt

Combine I. and II. and add 1 cup sour milk, or buttermilk. Beat the whites of 3 eggs until they are stiff. Beat the yolks of 3 eggs until they are light and lemon colored and fold them into the beaten whites. Fold the eggs lightly into the cake batter. Bake the cake in a greased tube pan in a moderate oven 350°. Ice the cake with Chocolate Fudge, or White Icing.

QUICK CINNAMON TEA CAKE

¼ cup butter
½ cup sugar
1 egg yolk
⅞ cup cake flour

1 teaspoon baking powder
¾ teaspoon cinnamon
¼ cup milk
1 egg white

Cream the butter and the sugar, beat in the egg yolk and add the flour (which has been sifted with the baking powder and cinnamon), alternately with the milk. Last fold in the stiffly beaten egg white. Spread the batter to the thickness of ¾ inch in a greased, shallow pan. Bake the cake in a moderate oven 375°. Sprinkle it with powdered sugar and cut it into squares.

ECONOMY SPICE CAKE

This cake is easily and inexpensively made and keeps well:

1 cup water
1½ cups raisins
1 cup brown sugar
⅓ cup shortening

½ teaspoon cinnamon
½ teaspoon allspice
½ teaspoon salt
⅛ teaspoon nutmeg

Boil these ingredients for 3 minutes — cool them and add:

1 teaspoon soda, dissolved in
1 tablespoon boiling water

2 cups flour, sifted well
½ teaspoon baking powder

Bake the cake in a greased tube pan in a slow oven 300° to 325° for an hour or more.

BLITZKUCHEN—Lightening Cake
8 Servings

A delicious tea cake and a good accompaniment to a heavy dessert:

½ cup butter
1 cup powdered sugar
4 egg yolks
1⅛ cups cake flour

1 teaspoon baking powder
A pinch of salt
½ teaspoon vanilla
4 egg whites

Combine and sift the dry ingredients. Cream the butter and the sugar, add the vanilla and the lightly beaten egg yolks. Add the dry ingredients and beat the batter well. Last fold in the stiffly beaten egg whites. Spread the batter in a shallow pan to the thickness of ¼ inch.

Sprinkle the top with:
  ¾ cup sugar
  3 tablespoons cinnamon

½ cup blanched shredded
  almonds or other chopped
  nuts

Bake the cake in a moderate oven 375°. When cold cut it into diamond shaped pieces. (It may be served hot.)

Prune Cake

This recipe makes a moist, rich cake, which keeps fresh for a week or more. It is good as a loaf or layer cake with any kind of icing, but is best baked in one large layer, iced with unboiled white icing flavored with rum, decorated with nuts and cut into small shapes:

1 cup sugar	1½ cups cake flour
1 cup shortening	1½ teaspoons soda
1 cup cooked prune pulp	1 teaspoon cinnamon
(½ pound prunes)	¾ teaspoon cloves
2 eggs	½ cup nuts
½ cup sour milk	

Cream the shortening and the sugar. Add the prune pulp, the beaten eggs, and the flour, which has been sifted with the soda, alternately with the milk. Last add the spices and the nuts. This makes three layers, or a large tube pan cake. Bake the layers for 25 minutes in a moderate oven 375°. Bake a loaf cake in a somewhat slower oven 350° with slightly increasing heat, for one hour.

CRUMB SPICE CAKE

This really deserves mention of some kind, but I have run out of adjectives:

2 cups bread flour	½ teaspoon cinnamon
2 cups brown sugar	2 teaspoons baking powder
½ cup butter, generous	1 cup sour milk
½ teaspoon salt	½ teaspoon soda
¼ teaspoon nutmeg	2 eggs

Combine the flour and the butter until they are crumby. Reserve ½ cup of these crumbs. To the remainder add the spices and baking powder. Beat the sour milk with the soda and combine it with the eggs. Stir this into the butter and spice mixture. Spread the batter to the thickness of ¾ inch in a shallow pan and sprinkle the top with the reserved crumbs, to which ½ teaspoon cinnamon and ¼ cup blanched shredded almonds have been added. Bake the cake in a moderate oven 375° until it is done.

BANANA LOAF CAKE

Follow the rule for Banana Cake—Page 252. Bake it in a greased loaf pan and sprinkle it with powdered sugar, or ice it with White Icing.

Coffee Cakes

Is there anything better than good coffee cake? I am told that the King of Spain "dunks". Perhaps that affords him some comfort.

YEAST COFFEE CAKE

½ cake yeast
1 cup luke warm milk

1 teaspoon sugar
1 cup flour

Dissolve the yeast in the milk and add the other ingredients. Beat the sponge well and permit it to rise for an hour or more in a warm place.

Add:

1 cup warm milk
1 teaspoon salt
¼ cup sugar

2 whole eggs
½ cup butter, melted
4 to 5 cups of flour

Place the dough in a deep bowl, cover it with a cloth and permit it to rise in a warm place until it doubles in bulk. Toss the dough on a floured board, knead it lightly and spread it to the depth of ½ inch in greased pans. Permit it to rise for an hour. Melt 3 tablespoons of butter and spread it over the top of the cakes. Sprinkle them with cinnamon, sugar and chopped nuts. Bake them in a moderate oven 350° for 20 minutes

YEAST COFFEE CAKE WITH CRUMBS—Streusel

Just before baking coffee cake dough brush it with melted butter and sprinkle the following combined ingredients over the top:

2 tablespoons flour
2 tablespoons butter

5 tablespoons sugar
½ teaspoon cinnamon

Rub the butter and the flour until it is crumby—add the cinnamon and sugar.

YEAST COFFEE CAKE WITH APPLES, PEACHES OR PLUMS

Spread Coffee Cake dough ¼ inch thick in greased pans. Cover the entire surface of the dough with rows of fruit, placed closely together. Sprinkle the tops with cinnamon and sugar and dot them with butter or in place of the butter, combine the yolk of an egg and 4 tablespoonsful of cream and pour them around the fruit. Bake the cake in a hot oven 400° until it is done and the fruit is soft.

BAKING POWDER COFFEE CAKE

1/2 cup butter
1/2 cup sugar
2 eggs
2 1/4 cups bread flour
2 teaspoons baking powder

1/2 cup milk
3/4 teaspoon grated lemon
rind or 1/2 teaspoon
vanilla

Cream the butter and the sugar, add the eggs and the flour (that has been sifted with the baking powder), alternately with the milk. Add the flavoring and spread the dough in a shallow greased pan. Cover the top with cinnamon and sugar and dot it with butter. Bake the cake in a moderate oven 375°.

SOUR CREAM COFFEE CAKE

This cake may be made with sour top milk. It is both light and good.

1 1/2 cups flour
1 cup sugar
2 teaspoons baking
powder
1/8 teaspoon salt

sifted together
1 cup sour cream
1/2 teaspoon soda
1 or 2 eggs

Add the soda to the cream. Add the egg and beat it well. Add the sifted ingredients and spread the dough in a shallow lightly greased pan. Bake the cake in a moderate oven 350°. While it is hot, spread the top with powdered sugar and chopped nuts, or with butter, cinnamon and powdered sugar.

CRUMB COFFEE CAKE—Baking Powder

3/4 cup sugar
1/2 cup butter
3 cups bread flour
2 teaspoons baking powder

1 cup milk
2 eggs
1/8 teaspoon salt
Rind of 1 lemon

Combine the flour, sugar and butter, rubbing them lightly with the finger tips until they are crumby. Reserve 1 cup of this. To the remainder add the baking powder. Combine the milk with the beaten eggs, and add them to the crumb mixture. Spread the batter to the thickness of 3/4 of an inch in a shallow greased pan. Sprinkle the reserved crumbs over the top, to which 1/2 cup blanched shredded almonds may be added. Bake the cake in a moderate oven 375°.

HIGH COFFEE CAKE—Yeast—Bund Kuchen or Kugelhopf

3 cakes yeast
1 cup luke warm milk
1 cup soft butter
¾ cup sugar
5 whole eggs

4 cups flour
1 teaspoon grated lemon
  rind
1 cup seedless raisins
⅓ cup sliced almonds

Dissolve the yeast in the lukewarm milk, add 1 cup of flour and set the sponge to rise in a warm place. Cream the butter and the sugar, beat in the eggs one at a time and add the remaining flour and the other ingredients. Place the almonds in the bottom of a well-greased tube pan. Pour the dough on top of them and permit it to rise until it is very light. Bake the cake in a moderate oven 350° from 45 to 60 minutes. When it is cold, sprinkle the top with powdered sugar.

HIGH COFFEE CAKE—Baking Powder—Kugelhopf

1 cup shortening (½
  butter, ½ lard)
1 cup sugar
5 eggs
4 cups flour
4 teaspoons baking powder

1 cup milk
1 cup raisins
½ cup citron chopped or
  ground
1 teaspoon grated lemon
  rind

Cream the butter and the sugar. Beat in the eggs well, one at a time, then add the flour, (which has been sifted with the baking powder), alternately with the milk. Beat the batter well. Add the remaining ingredients and bake the dough in a greased tube pan in a moderate oven 350°. When the cake is cold sprinkle it with powdered sugar.

STOLLEN—Yeast Raisin Cake

This cake is made in German homes at Christmas time:

1½ cakes yeast
1½ cups lukewarm milk
6 cups flour
1½ cups butter
¾ cup sugar
3 eggs

¾ teaspoon salt
1 teaspoon grated lemon
  rind
½ pound raisins
½ pound chopped almonds

Dissolve the yeast in ½ cup of warm milk and add 1 cup of flour and the remaining milk. Permit this to rise in a warm place for several hours. Flour the raisins and nuts lightly with part of the flour. Cream the butter and the sugar and beat in the eggs one at a time. Add the salt, the lemon rind, the yeast mixture and the remaining flour. Knead the dough until it is smooth and elastic. Add the raisins and nuts. Permit the dough to rise until it doubles in bulk. Toss it onto a floured board. Divide it into three or more parts. Shape the parts into loaves. Brush the tops with melted butter, let the loaves rise until they double in bulk and bake them in a moderate oven 350° for almost 45 minutes. When they are cool, brush them with icing.

Icing:

1 cup powdered sugar
2 tablespoons boiling water
 or milk

¼ teaspoon vanilla or 1
 teaspoon lemon juice

Fruit Cakes

Here are three recipes for very good fruit cake. Basically, they call for nearly the same ingredients, but they differ in flavor.

No. I. calls for spices and wine.
No. II. for grape juice and grape jelly.
No. III. for molasses and sour milk. This is the darkest and the heaviest of the three.

FRUIT CAKE I.
About 14 pounds

1 pound butter (2 cups)
1 pound brown sugar
 2⅔ cups)
15 eggs
1 pound flour (4 cups)
1 tablespoon cinnamon
½ tablespoon mace
1 tablespoon cloves
1 tablespoon allspice
1 tablespoon grated nutmeg

1½ teaspoons salt (if butter
 is unsalted)
¼ cup wine
¼ cup whiskey, or in place
 of wine and whiskey ½ cup
 thick fruit juice
2½ pounds raisins
2½ pounds currants washed
 and dried
1 pound citron, finely cut
1 pound pecans, broken

Cream the butter with the sugar, sift the dry ingredients and flour the fruit and the nuts lightly in additional flour. The ingredients may be combined in the order given—the eggs being added alternately with the flour—each egg being beaten in well, or the eggs may be separated, the yolks added alternately with the flour and the whites stiffly beaten and folded in before the fruit and nuts are added. Place the dough in loaf pans lined with a layer of heavy wax paper, or with 4 layers of thin wax paper. Cover the bottom of the oven with pans filled with 1 inch of hot water and bake the loaves in a very slow oven 300° from two to three hours. Permit the loaves to cool and remove them from the pans. Remove the wax paper, wrap the loaves in fresh wax paper and store the cake in tightly covered tin boxes. Should the cake become dry, place it in a closed container over hot water until it is hot. Heat wine or grape juice (but do not let it boil), and pour it from a small pitcher, very slowly, drop by drop, onto the hot cake. Use as much as the cake will absorb.

FRUIT CAKE II.

1 pound butter
2 cups sugar
½ cup grape jelly
½ cup grape juice
½ cup brandy or wine
12 egg yolks slightly beaten
4 cups flour
1 teaspoon cinnamon
½ teaspoon cloves
½ teaspoon nutmeg

2 pounds raisins (seedless)
1 pound citron
¼ pound diced orange and
  lemon peel
2 pounds whole pecan
  meats
1 pound figs, chopped
12 candied cherries
  (optional)
12 egg whites

Cream the butter and the sugar. Combine the flour and the spices, and dredge the fruit lightly with the flour. Combine the ingredients in the order given, adding the stiffly beaten egg whites last. Follow the rule for baking Fruit Cake I.

FRUIT CAKE III.
About 9 pounds

½ pound butter (1 cup)
½ pound brown sugar
  (1⅓ cups)
6 eggs
½ pound flour (2 cups)
1 teaspoon cinnamon
1 teaspoon allspice
1 teaspoon cloves
1 teaspoon nutmeg
1 teaspoon salt, if butter
  is unsalted
¼ cup wine, whiskey or
  fruit juice

½ cup molasses
½ cup sour milk
1 teaspoon soda
1 pound raisins (seeded)
1 pound currants (washed
  and dried)
½ pound citron, cut fine
1 pound almonds, (blanched
  and shredded) or pecans
  broken
½ cup maraschino cherries

Cream the butter with the sugar, sift the dry ingredients and flour the fruit and the nuts lightly in additional flour. Add the soda to the milk. Combine the ingredients like Fruit Cake I., alternating the eggs and the liquids with the flour. Bake the cake like Fruit Cake I.

SCOTCH CAKE

1 cup butter
1 cup white sugar
1⅓ cups brown sugar
6 egg yolks
4 cups cake flour
5 teaspoons baking powder
½ nutmeg grated

6 egg whites, beaten
½ cup whiskey
½ New Orleans molasses
1 pound shelled pecans, broken
2 pounds seeded raisins

Flour the raisins and the nuts with part of the flour. Sift the remainder of the flour with the baking powder and the nutmeg. Cream the butter with the sugars, beat in the egg yolks and add the flour, alternately with the egg whites. Combine the whiskey and the molasses and add them to the batter. Add the nuts and the raisins and bake the cake in a slow oven 300° for the first 45 minutes, then increase the heat to 350°.

Cakes with Fruit, Creams and Fillings, that Serve as a Complete Dessert Course

WHIPPED CREAM

1 cup heavy cream
1 teaspoon vanilla, coffee, etc.

2 tablespoons or more powdered sugar (optional)

Whip the cream with a wire whisk, add the sugar slowly and the vanilla or other flavoring.

CONDENSED MILK WHIPPED

The following is the new rule given by the Condensed Milk Companies, which is considered an improvement over all others.

1¼ cups canned milk
½ teaspoon gelatine

2 teaspoons cold water

Soak the gelatine in the cold water for 5 minutes. Place the milk in the top of a double boiler. When it is scalded add the soaked gelatine. Stir it until the gelatine is dissolved. Chill the milk until it is icy cold, then whip it like cream. Condensed milk whipped retains a slight caramel flavor. A small amount of vanilla, caramel, coffee, etc. may be added to it.

MERINGUE

See Rule Page 215.

THREE MINUTE ICING

2 egg whites, unbeaten
½ cup sugar
⅛ teaspoon salt

2 tablespoons cold water (or
caramel, coffee, etc.)

Place these ingredients in a double boiler over boiling water and beat them for 3 minutes, or until stiff with a rotary beater.

Flavor the icing as desired and use it as a substitute for baked meringue, or whipped cream.

QUICK SPONGE LAYER CAKE

To be served with fresh or canned fruit and cream, or with cream only.

1 cup flour
1 teaspoon baking powder
⅞ cup sugar

3 eggs
1½ tablespoons water
1 teaspoon vanilla

Sift the flour and the baking powder into a bowl. Add the sugar and stir it into the flour. Make a hole in the center of these ingredients and break the eggs into it. Add the water and beat the batter well. Pour it into an ungreased pan and bake it in a moderate oven 350° for about 20 minutes.

SPONGE CAKE WITH FRUIT

Follow the rule for Sponge Cake I or II, make ½ the amount and bake the cake in a large flat pan. Place the cake on a platter and cover it with stewed or sugared fruit.

WASHINGTON PIE OR CREAM PIE

⅓ cup butter	3 teaspoons baking powder
¾ cup sugar	¼ teaspoon salt
2 eggs, beaten	½ cup milk
1½ cups cake flour	1 teaspoon vanilla

Cream the butter and the sugar and beat in the eggs. Combine and sift the flour, baking powder and salt and add them, alternately with the milk, to the butter mixture. Beat the batter well, add the vanilla and bake the cake in greased pans in two layers in a moderate oven 375° for 20 or 25 minutes. Place a filling between the layers and sprinkle the top with powdered sugar. Spread whipped cream, a cooked cream filling, (adding cocoanut to it, or other nuts), jam, jelly, or fruit between the layers. See Page 292 for Fillings.

APPLE, PLUM OR PEACH CAKE
Kuchen

1 cup bread flour	1½ tablespoons butter
2 teaspoons baking powder	1 egg
⅛ teaspoon salt	Milk
2 tablespoons sugar	

Sift the dry ingredients, add the butter and work the dough lightly (like pastry). Add the egg and a very little milk, just enough to make a soft dough. Spread it to the thickness of ½ inch in a shallow pan, or pyrex dish, and cover the top very closely with fruit. Sprinkle it with sugar and cinnamon and bake the cake in a moderate oven 375°. This dough may be used as an "up side down cake" over berries, or other fruit.

FRENCH APPLE CAKE
or Peach Cake

Grease a deep pie pan and cover it well with sliced apples, sprinkle them with sugar, cinnamon, nutmeg and the rind and juice of 1 lemon. Dredge the fruit with 1 tablespoon flour and dot it with 2 tablespoons butter. Pour over it the following batter:

2 egg yolks	1 cup bread flour
½ cup sugar	1 teaspoon baking powder
1 tablespoon butter	¼ cup milk

Bake the cake in a moderate oven 375°. Reverse it on a platter, cover it with meringue and bake it in a slow oven 300° until the meringue is set. For Fruit Cake made with yeast dough—See Page 241.

APPLE STRUDEL

Strudel is to the Hungarian what pie and biscuit are to the American. Flour, egg and water are combined with a little salt and are kneaded until they become so elastic that the dough can be stretched until it is as thin as paper. This is done on a large table covered with a cloth. The dough is then sprinkled with fruit, or vegetables, cream and nuts, rolled like a huge jelly roll, twisted into a pan and baked in a moderate oven. The result is superlative.

1½ cups flour	⅓ cup warm water or milk
¼ teaspoon salt	1 egg, slightly beaten

Place the dry ingredients in a large bowl. Add the warm liquid slowly and mix these ingredients with a knife. When they are blended, put the dough on a floured board and knead it until it is elastic and no longer sticks to the board. Place it on a floured board and cover it with a warm bowl for 30 minutes or more. Strudel is stretched to tremendous width and breadth (2x2 yards, or more). Work the dough with 2 tablespoons of melted butter and place it in the center of a large table covered with a floured cloth. Gently pull and stretch the dough, placing both hands under it, palms down, until it is as thin as paper. Spread the dough with:

4 pounds tart apples, finely sliced	¼ pound almonds, blanched and shredded
1 cup seeded raisins	1 cup sugar
½ cup currants	6 tablespoons melted butter
1 teaspoon cinnamon	

Fold the dough over one side, hold up the table cloth and let the strudel roll itself into a huge roll. Twist the roll into a large, greased pan, or cut it into pieces, trim the edges and bake the strudel for ½ hour in a hot oven 400°, reduce the heat to 350° and bake it until it is crisp and brown. Serve it before it is cold.

FRUIT ROLL

8 Servings

2 cups flour
4 teaspoons baking powder
½ teaspoon salt

¼ cup butter or lard
¾ to 1 cup milk

Sift the dry ingredients, cut in the butter and add the milk. Handle the dough as little as possible. Roll it on a floured board to the thickness of ⅓ inch. Brush it with the white of an egg, this will keep it from being soggy. Place a filling upon the dough and roll it like a jelly roll. Cut the roll, if desired, into 1 inch slices, or leave it whole. Bake the roll in a greased pan in a moderate oven 375° for about 30 minutes. Serve it hot with Fruit Sauce, Hard Sauce, or cream.

Fillings for Fruit Roll

Raisin and Nut Filling:

⅓ cup raisins
⅓ cup nuts
⅓ teaspoon cinnamon

¼ cup sugar, brown or
  white
⅓ cup butter

Spread the raisins and nuts on the dough. Sprinkle them with the sugar and dot them with butter and proceed as directed.

Apple Filling:

3 pounds apples—pared,
  cored and sliced (7
  large apples)

1 cup water
¾ cup sugar

Boil the water and the sugar. Add the apples and cook them until they are tender. Drain and cool them. Spread them on the dough, sprinkle them with:

¼ cup of brown sugar, ⅓ teaspoon of cinnamon, dot them with ⅓ cup of butter and proceed as directed.

Apricot Filling:

Stew ¾ pound of apricots—Page 163. Drain them. Reserve ⅓ of the apricots, spread the rest on the dough and dot them with butter. Bake the roll and serve it hot with

Apricot Sauce:

4 tablespoons butter
1 cup powdered sugar
1 egg yolk

½ cup strained apricot
pulp

Cream the butter and the sugar, beat in the yolk and add the fruit. Chill the sauce.

Fruit Fillings:

Cover the dough with any other stewed fruit—peaches, cherries, berries—and proceed as directed.

PINEAPPLE SKILLET CAKE—Up Side Down

8 Servings

¼ to ½ cup butter
1 cup brown sugar
1 cup pecan meats

(optional)
8 slices canned pineapple
drained, (1 No. 2½ can)

Melt the butter in a nine or ten inch iron skillet. Add the sugar and stir it until it is dissolved. Scatter the nuts over the bottom of the pan and place the pineapple slices side by side on top of them. Cover them with the following:

Cake Batter:

1 cup cake flour
1 teaspoon baking powder
4 egg yolks
1 tablespoon melted butter

1 teaspoon vanilla
4 egg whites
1 cup sugar

Combine and sift the flour and the baking powder. Beat the egg yolks, add the butter and the vanilla. Beat the egg whites until they are stiff, but not dry, and fold in the sugar 1 tablespoon at a time. Fold in the yolk mixture, then fold in the sifted flour—¼ cup at a time. Bake the cake in a moderate oven 325° for about 1 hour. Serve it up side down.

INDIVIDUAL FRUIT SHORTCAKE

Make Fluffy Biscuit Dough—Page 188 and cut it with a biscuit cutter. Bake the biscuits, split them while they are hot and spread them with butter. Place sugared, or cooked fruit between the biscuit halves and pour fruit over them.

BANANA CAKE

½ cup butter
2 cups sugar
1 cup mashed banana
2 eggs
¼ cup sour milk or cream
1 teaspoon soda

1 cup white flour
1 cup whole wheat flour
1 cup nut meats, finely
  chopped, (optional)
Salt
Vanilla

Cream the butter and the sugar, mash the bananas with a fork, and add them to the butter mixture. Add the eggs and then the sour cream, in which the soda has been dissolved. Add the sifted white flour, the whole wheat flour, and the nuts. Bake the cake in two greased layer pans in a moderate oven 375°. Place sliced bananas between the layers, sprinkle the top with powdered sugar, or cover it with icing. Serve the cake with plain or whipped cream.

CARAMEL BANANA CAKE WITH WHITE OR CARAMEL ICING

This is a good combination:

Bake Caramel Cake I. or II. in layers—Page 233. Cover the bottom and middle layers closely with thin slices of banana topped with White or Caramel Icing and ice the top and the sides of the cake. Decorate the cakes with walnut halves, (optional).

LADY BALTIMORE CAKE

Bake White Cake II.—Page 228 in 3 layers. Place the following filling between the layers:

Lady Baltimore Filling:

1 cup sugar
½ cup water
1/16 teaspoon cream of
  tartar
2 egg whites

1 cup seeded raisins, cut
  fine
1 cup chopped nuts
1 teaspoon vanilla

Cook the sugar, water and cream of tartar until the syrup spins a thread—Page 284 and pour it slowly onto the partially beaten egg whites. Beat until the icing will hold a point then add the raisins and nuts. Spread it between the layers, and ice the top of the cake with White Icing—Page 285.

CHOCOLATE CAKE WITH FRUIT FILLING

Prepare Chocolate Custard Cake—Page 236, using 2½ ounces of chocolate, and bake it in two layers. Place the following filling between the layers:

Fruit Filling:

¾ cup condensed milk	¼ cup figs, chopped
¼ cup water	¼ cup raisins, chopped
¾ cup sugar	½ cup nut meats, chopped
¼ cup dates, chopped	1 teaspoon vanilla

Place the milk, water and sugar in a double boiler. When the sugar is dissolved, add the fruit and cook the filling until it is thick. Cool it and add the vanilla and the nut meats. Spread the cake, when filled, with White Icing or Chocolate Fudge Icing.

CHEESE CAKE

See Page 220.

PINEAPPLE MERINGUE CAKES

Follow the Rule for Pineapple Meringue Pie Filling—Page 216. Combine it with thin strips of cake or lady fingers in individual molds or place it in small hollow sponge cakes. Cover the tops with Meringue—Page 215, and bake the meringue as directed.

RICH LAYER CAKE

1 cup butter	3 teaspoons baking powder
2 cups sugar	(optional)
4 egg yolks	1 teaspoon vanilla
1 cup milk	4 egg whites
3 cups flour	

Cream the butter and the sugar, beat in the egg yolks and add the flour that has been sifted with the baking powder, alternately with the milk. Add the flavoring and beat the batter well. Fold in the stiffly beaten egg whites last. Bake the cake in eight layers in a moderate oven 375°. Spread Pineapple Filling or some other filling between the layers and ice the cake.

EIGHT LAYER CAKE

This cake was once the pièce de résistance of the American hostess:

Follow the rule for Layer Cake. Bake it in eight layers, spread jelly or chocolate filling between the layers and sprinkle the top with powdered sugar.

PLAIN LAYER CAKE

¼ cup butter
1 cup sugar
2 eggs, well beaten
1⅔ cups cake flour

2½ teaspoons baking
powder
½ cup milk

Cream the butter and the sugar, beat in the eggs, and add the flour that has been sifted with the baking powder, alternately with the milk. Bake the cake in two greased layer pans in a moderate oven 375° for about 25 minutes.

ORANGE CREAM CAKE

4 egg yolks
1 cup sugar
3 tablespoons cold water
⅔ teaspoon grated orange
rind
1 cup cake flour

1¼ teaspoons baking
powder
½ teaspoon vanilla
¼ teaspoon salt
4 egg whites

Beat the yolks until they are light. Add the sugar gradually and continue beating. Add the water, orange rind and the flour, which has been sifted with the baking powder and the salt. Beat the batter well, add the vanilla and fold in the stiffly beaten egg whites. Bake the cake in two greased layer pans in a moderate oven 325° for about ½ hour. When the cake is cool, spread the following filling between the layers:

Orange Cream Filling:

2 tablespoons cornstarch
2 tablespoons flour
½ cup sugar
½ cup water
¼ teaspoon salt
¾ teaspoon orange rind
½ cup orange juice

1 tablespoon lemon juice
1 tablespoon butter
2 egg yolks
1 tablespoon gelatine,
soaked in
1 tablespoon cold water
½ cup cream, whipped

Cook and stir the first eight ingredients in a double boiler until they are thick and smooth. Add the butter, pour part of the filling over the beaten egg yolks, return it to the double boiler and permit the eggs to thicken slightly. Stir in the soaked gelatine. Cool the filling and fold in the whipped cream. Chill the filling for one hour, spread it between the layers of the cake and cover the cake with:

Orange Icing:

¾ teaspoon grated orange
  rind
3 tablespoons orange juice
1 tablespoon lemon juice

1 tablespoon of butter
Powdered sugar to make the
  icing the consistency of
  heavy cream

Place the first four ingredients over a low flame and when the butter is melted, stir in the sugar. Permit the icing to stand for 10 minutes before spreading it.

ORANGE CAKE

Follow the rule for Orange Cream Cake, or for Plain Layer Cake. Place the following filling between the layers:

Orange Filling:

1 orange, juice and rind
1 teaspoon lemon juice
¼ cup sugar
1 teaspoon flour

1 teaspoon cornstarch
⅛ teaspoon salt
1 egg yolk
1 egg white

Reserve the egg white. Cook the remaining ingredients in a double boiler, stirring them until they are thick and smooth. Cool the filling. Fold in the stiffly beaten egg white and spread the filling between the cake layers. Sprinkle the cake with powdered sugar, or ice it with uncooked Orange Icing.

GERMAN APPLE CAKE—Apple Paradise
6 Servings

This is the best dessert imaginable when made with good cooking apples. It is a very indifferent one made with poor ones:

3 pounds of tart apples (7
  or 8 medium sized apples)
1 cup bread flour

1 cup brown sugar
½ cup soft butter
⅛ teaspoon salt

Peel and slice the apples into a 7 x 7 pan. (If you wish to serve the cake at table, use a pyrex pie dish). The apple layer when cooked, should be about ¾ of an inch thick. Work the other ingredients very lightly like pastry, and spread them over the apples. If the apples are dry and sweet, dot them with butter and sprinkle them with lemon juice. The success of this dish depends upon the flavor of the apples, which should be tart. A good apple needs no additional ingredients. Bake the cake in a moderate oven 375° for about 30 minutes, or until the apples are done. Serve it hot or cold, with or without cream.

GRANDMOTHER'S APPLE CAKE
Serves 12 People or more

This dish is always referred to as "Apfelkuchen" but it is really a "Torte." When properly made it might be classed as a soufflé, but no matter what it is called, or how it is made, it is a remarkably good dessert:

5 cups tart apples, peeled
  and thinly sliced
¼ cup butter
1 lemon, rind and juice
½ cup sour cream
1 cup sugar, scant, unless
  the apples are very tart

2 tablespoons bread flour
8 egg yolks
¾ cup or less blanched,
  shredded almonds
⅛ teaspoon salt
8 egg whites

Melt the butter in a skillet, add the apples and cook them covered over a very low fire, stirring them from time to time until they are tender. Combine the cream, the egg yolks and the flour and pour them over the apples. Stir these ingredients constantly until they thicken, then remove the skillet from the fire and cool the mixture. Add ½ cup of blanched almonds, and fold in the stiffly beaten egg whites, to which the salt has been added. Spread the soufflé to the thickness of one inch in a large pan or glass dish. Sprinkle the top with a mixture of sugar, cinnamon, bread crumbs and the remaining almonds. Bake it in a moderate oven 350° until it is firm— about 45 minutes. As all the ingredients, except the egg whites, are cooked before they are baked, the cake may be eaten at any time, but it is advisable to bake it until the egg whites are set. It may be served hot, but it is best very cold, covered with whipped cream flavored with vanilla, or served with Angel Ice Cream.

GERMAN CHERRY CAKE
8 Servings

4½ ounces Zwieback, ground
  (1½ cups)
¾ cup sugar

¾ teaspoon cinnamon
6 tablespoons melted butter

Combine these ingredients in the order given and work them lightly with the finger tips until they are well blended. Use a nine inch pyrex baking dish. Press the crumb mixture on the bottom and against the sides of the dish to form a shell ¼ inch thick. This shell may be filled at once, but it is very much better when chilled for several hours. Fill the shell with:

Cherry Custard:

¾ cup sour cream
½ cup sugar
3 eggs, whole

2 cups cherries, fresh or
canned, drained

Combine the ingredients in the order given. (The original recipe calls for 4 tablespoons flour dissolved in cherry juice, but the filling is far more delicate without the flour. If you like heft, however, use the flour). Bake the cake in a moderate oven 325° until the custard is firm. Serve it hot, or very cold.

JELLY ROLL

4 egg yolks
¾ cup sugar
1 teaspoon vanilla
¾ cup cake flour

¾ teaspoon baking powder
¼ teaspoon salt
4 egg whites

Cream the egg yolks with the sugar. Add the flavoring, and the flour that has been sifted with the baking powder and the salt. Last fold in the stiffly beaten egg whites. Line a 15 x 10 pan with heavy buttered paper. Spread the dough in it and bake it in a moderate oven 375° for about 13 minutes. While it is hot, cut the hard edges, spread the cake with jelly and roll it. Wrap the roll in wax paper. Before serving it, sprinkle it with powdered sugar.

NUT ROLL WITH WHIPPED CREAM

Follow the rule for Jelly Roll. Invert the cake on a towel sprinkled with powdered sugar. Roll the cake while it is hot and cover it with a damp cloth. When ready to serve it unroll it and spread it with whipped cream, flavored, to which ground nuts have been added. Roll the cake and serve it with Caramel Sauce.

CHOCOLATE FILLED ROLL

Follow the rule for Jelly Roll. Spread the cake with Chocolate Filling and serve it with whipped cream.

Chocolate Filling:

2½ ounces chocolate
1 cup powdered sugar
3 tablespoons milk

1 egg yolk
½ teaspoon vanilla

Melt the chocolate over hot water, add one-half the sugar and the milk. Add the remaining sugar beaten with the egg yolk. Cook the custard in a double boiler, stirring it constantly until it is thick and smooth. Cook it slightly, add the flavoring and spread it on the cake. Roll it like a jelly roll and serve it with whipped cream.

COCOA ROLL WITH WHIPPED CREAM
AND CHOCOLATE SAUCE

2 tablespoons cocoa	½ cup sugar
2 tablespoons flour	3 egg whites
⅛ teaspoon salt	½ teaspoon cream of tartar
1 teaspoon vanilla	½ pint whipping cream,
3 egg yolks	(1 cup)

Sift the cocoa, flour and salt. Beat the egg yolks in a separate bowl until they are light and lemon colored. Add the sugar gradually, beating constantly, and the vanilla. Combine this mixture with the dry ingredients. Beat the whites and the cream of tartar to a stiff froth and fold them lightly into the batter. Line a shallow pan with heavy oiled paper and spread the dough in this to the thickness of ¼ inch. Bake the cake in a moderate oven 325° until done. Let it cool in the pan for five minutes, then invert the contents onto a moist hot cloth. Trim off the hard edges of the cake and spread it with the cream, which as been whipped (sweetened with powdered sugar, if desired) and flavored with ¼ teaspoonful of vanilla. Roll the cake in the cloth like a jelly roll and chill it for one hour. Remove the cloth, place the cake on a platter and cut it into slices. Cover them with Chocolate Sauce— Page 324.

MOCHA TART

1 cup sugar	6 tablespoons flour
2 tablespoons coffee essence	2 teaspoons baking powder
or very strong coffee	6 egg whites
1 teaspoon vanilla	6 egg yolks

Cream the yolks and the sugar, and when they are well blended, add the coffee essence and the vanilla. Combine the flour with the baking powder and add them to the egg mixture. Beat the egg whites until they are stiff and fold them lightly into the batter. Bake the cake in two layer pan tins, in a moderate oven 350° for about 15 minutes. Serve the cake with the following filling, spread between the layers and over the top:

Filling:

1 pint cream whipped	3 tablespoons coffee essence
½ cup powdered sugar	or strong coffee

WHITE LAYER CAKE WITH CREAM NUT FILLING

2 cups powdered sugar
1/2 cup butter
3 1/2 cups cake flour
2 teaspoons baking powder
1 cup milk
1 teaspoon vanilla
6 egg whites

Cream the butter and the sugar. Add the flour, sifted with the baking powder, alternately with the milk. Add the flavoring and fold in the stiffly beaten egg whites. Bake the cake in 2 greased layer pans in a moderate oven 375°.

Nut Filling:

2 cups heavy cream, slightly soured. Beat this well, add 4 tablespoons powdered sugar, and fold in 1/2 pound blanched, ground almonds, or hazel nuts. 1 teaspoon vanilla may be added.

ALMOND AND DATE CAKE

Follow the rule for Almond and Date Bars on Page 269. Cut the cake into squares and serve them topped with whipped cream, or ice cream.

NUT LAYER CAKE WITH JAM FILLING

It is always a pleasure to serve this good little cake:

6 egg yolks
1 cup sugar
3/4 cup cake flour
1/2 teaspoon baking powder
1/2 cup nut meats, finely chopped
1 teaspoon vanilla
6 egg whites

Cream the yolks and the sugar and add the flour that has been sifted with the baking powder. Add the vanilla and the nuts and last fold in the stiffly beaten egg whites. Bake the cake in two layers in a moderate oven 350°. Spread jam between the layers and ice the top and the sides of the cake with White Icing or serve it un-iced with whipped cream.

CHOCOLATE WALNUT TORTE

1 pound English Walnuts
1 1/2 ounces chocolate, grated
9 egg yolks
1 cup sugar
1/2 cup dry bread crumbs
9 egg whites

Reserve 24 nut halves for decorating the top. Chop the remaining nuts and combine them with the chocolate. Beat the yolks in a separate bowl add the sugar and beat until it is dissolved. Add the nuts and the crumbs and fold in the stiffly beaten whites last. Bake the cake in an ungreased tin with a removable rim, in a moderate oven 350° for 45 minutes. Cover the cake with Boiled Chocolate Icing and decorate it with nut meats.

HAZELNUT TORTE

12 egg yolks
1 cup sugar
¼ pound hazelnut meats,
ground

¼ pound pecans or walnut
meats, ground
8 egg whites, stiffly beaten

Combine the ingredients in the order given. Bake the cake in layers. Place sweetened, flavored, whipped cream between the layers and ice the cake with Coffee, or Caramel Icing.

ALMOND CAKE

The following recipe is the well known German "Mandel Torte". In order to have the right result, the almonds should be put through an almond grinder (not a meat grinder). This recipe must be starred as "the" nut cake my friends so frequently ask for:

6 egg yolks
1 cup sugar
1 cup almonds, ground
(unblanched)
½ cup toasted white
bread crumbs

1 lemon or 1 small orange,
(rind and juice)
1 teaspoon cinnamon
½ teaspoon almond extract,
(optional)
6 egg whites

Cream the yolks and the sugar, and add the lemon, cinnamon, flavoring, nuts and bread crumbs. Last fold in the well beaten whites. This will make a small cake. When a larger cake is desired, double or treble the recipe and bake it in thick layers in pans with removable rims. Place Lemon or Orange filling between the layers and spread the cake with White Icing. If the cake is small and the filling is omitted, it is good with uncooked Chocolate Icing.

Lemon Filling for Cake:

Rind of 1 lemon
Juice of 2 lemons
3 egg yolks

⅓ cup water
¾ cup sugar
1½ tablespoons flour

Cook the filling over a low flame, stirring it constantly, until it is thick. A delicious flavor may be gained by adding ½ cup of apricot pulp (dried fruit stewed, sweetened and strained).

BREAD TORTE I.

In the following recipe for the well known Brod-Torte, the ingredients differ only slightly from those in the foregoing Mandel Torte, but the result, thanks to the wine bath, are amazingly different:

12 egg yolks	2⅓ cups bread crumbs
2 cups sugar	¼ pound citron, cut fine
2 lemons, rind and juice	1 teaspoon cinnamon
2 cups almonds, ground	1 teaspoon baking powder
(unblanched)	12 egg whites

Combine the bread crumbs and the baking powder. Cream the yolks and the sugar and add the other ingredients. Fold in the beaten egg whites last. Bake the cake for 1 hour or more in a pan with a removable rim. When the cake is removed from the oven, pour over it at once the following mixture, strained:

1½ cups Sherry wine	1 stick of cinnamon
¼ cup water	½ cup sugar
4 whole cloves	

(White grape juice, or other fruit juice may be substituted for Sherry and sweetened to taste).

Heat this, but do not let it boil. Ice the cake with:

Chocolate Icing:

1 cup sugar	3 tablespoons milk
3 squares chocolate	1 egg yolk

Melt chocolate in a double boiler, add the sugar and the milk, when the icing begins to thicken add the yolk of 1 egg. Cook it for 1 minute longer, stirring it constantly, and spread it over the cake.

YAEGER TORTE

This is an almond cake—heavy with bread crumbs soaked in wine, served with jelly and a meringue.

1 cup dry bread crumbs	1 cup blanched shredded
2 tablespoons Sherry	almonds
3 tablespoons lemon juice	1½ teaspoons baking
5 egg yolks	powder
1 cup sugar	5 egg whites, stiffly beaten

Soak the bread crumbs in the wine and lemon juice. Cream the yolks with the sugar, add the soaked bread crumbs, ¾ cup of the almonds and the baking powder, and fold in the egg whites. Bake the cake in a shallow pan in a moderate oven 350°, cool it and spread it with jam and pile a meringue made of two egg whites—Page 215, on top of it. Sprinkle the meringue with the remaining almonds, return the cake to the oven and bake it in a slow oven 300° for 12 minutes to set the meringue.

LINZER TORTE

The following recipe is for a delicious German "company" cake. It looks like an open jam pie, and being rich, is usually served in thin wedges.

⅞ cup butter
1 cup sugar
1 teaspoon grated lemon
  rind
2 eggs
1 cup flour

1 cup almonds, (unblanch-
  ed) ground
½ teaspoon cinnamon
¼ teaspoon cloves
1 tablespoon cocoa

Combine the ingredients in the order given and stir them well. Roll the dough like pastry until it is ⅛ of an inch in thickness. Line the bottom of a pyrex dish with the dough and full on an edge ¾ of an inch thick. Cover the bottom of the cake with a layer of preserves ½ inch thick. Roll the remaining dough and cut it into strips to make a lattice over the preserves. If the dough is warm, this can be done with a pastry tube. Bake the cake in a hot oven—400°.

CREAM PUFFS—6 large Puffs or Eclairs

½ cup water or milk
¼ cup butter
½ cup flour

⅛ teaspoon salt
2 eggs

Heat the milk, add the butter and let it come to the boiling point. Add the flour and the salt and stir the batter over heat until it leaves the sides of the pan and forms a ball. Remove it from the fire, cool it slightly and add the eggs, one at a time, beating them in well. Place spoonfuls of batter in 2 inch rounds on a greased tin, heaping them well in the center. Allow two inches between the puffs. Bake them in a moderate oven 350 to 375 degrees for thirty minutes, or more. Test the puffs by removing one from the oven. If it does not fall, it is thoroughly done. When the puffs are cool, cut a gash into the side of each puff and fill them with sweetened and flavored whipped cream, or with custard filling.

Custard Filling:

3 tablespoons sugar
1 tablespoon cornstarch
⅛ teaspoon salt

1 cup milk, scalded
2 egg yolks, slightly beaten
½ teaspoon vanilla

Combine the sugar, the salt and the cornstarch. Add the scalded milk and pour this slowly over the egg yolks. Cook the custard in a double boiler, or over a low flame, stirring constantly until it is thick. Cool it and add the vanilla.

Chocolate Custard Filling:

Following the rule for Custard Filling, adding 1 square of melted chocolate to the hot milk and 3 tablespoons sugar.

Chocolate Icing:

½ square chocolate
½ teaspoon butter
3 tablespoons boiling water

¾ cup powdered sugar
¼ teaspoon vanilla

Melt the chocolate, add the butter and the boiling water, and stir these ingredients until they are smooth. Add the vanilla and the sifted powdered sugar. Add more water, or more sugar, if needed to make the icing the right consistency to spread.

CHOCOLATE ECLAIRS

Follow the rule for Cream Puffs. Shape the batter with a tube into oblongs, heaping it in the centers. Fill the eclairs with whipped cream, with Custard, or with Chocolate Custard Filling, and cover them with the Chocolate Icing given above.

MERINGUES

7 egg whites
Pinch of salt
1½ cups sugar

1 teaspoon vanilla
¾ cup sugar

Add the salt to the egg whites and beat them until they will hold a point — See Page 295. Add 1½ cups of sugar very, very slowly, beating the eggs constantly. Add the vanilla, and then *fold in* ¾ cup of sugar. Place large spoonfuls of this mixture on a baking sheet, or shape the meringues with a pastry bag into ovals. Bake them in a very slow oven 225° from 45 to 60 minutes. Remove them from the sheet when they are cold. If they are to be filled, crush the smooth side with the thumb, while the meringues are fresh and fill the hollows with sweetened and flavored whipped cream, or with a frozen mixture.

MERINGUE TART—Pinch Pie

3 egg whites	1 teaspoon vanilla
1/8 teaspoon salt	1 teaspoon vinegar
1/2 teaspoon baking powder	1 teaspoon water
1 cup sugar	

Add the salt and the baking powder to the egg whites and whip them until they are stiff. See Page 295. Add the sugar very slowly, beating constantly and from time to time add a few drops of the combined liquids. When the meringue is stiff, heap it upon the platter from which it is to be served. Shape it like a pie or tart with a heavy edge, using a spatula or knife. Bake it in a very slow oven 225° for about one hour. When it is cool, fill the center with fruit of various kinds — canned or fresh — and top it with sweetened and flavored whipped cream, fill it with Orange Ice, or some other ice and top it with whipped cream, or fill it with any good frozen mixture.

CHOCOLATE ALMOND SHELLS

8 egg whites	1/4 teaspoon cloves
1/4 teaspoon salt	Grated rind and juice of 1
2 cups sugar	lemon
1 pound almonds, ground	5 ounces chocolate grated
3 teaspoons cinnamon	

Add the salt to the egg whites and beat them to a stiff froth. Add the sugar very slowly, beating the eggs constantly, and fold in the remaining ingredients in the order given. Permit this batter to stand in a cold place for 12 hours. Shape it into balls. Prepare muffin tins or molds by dredging them with a mixture of sugar and flour. Press the balls into them and bake them in a moderate oven — 350°. Serve them with whipped or ice cream.

CREAM TART

The following recipe deserves a chapter to itself. It serves from eight to ten people, is delicate and delicious and is not at all difficult to make. The result is an optical as well as a gastronomic treat. It is a de luxe dessert, complete in itself and comparatively inexpensive. The cake batter and the meringue are baked at the same time.

1/2 cup sugar	2 teaspoons baking powder
1/4 cup butter	5 tablespoons cream
4 egg yolks	1/2 teaspoon vanilla
1 cup cake flour	

Cream the butter and sugar, add the egg yolks, lightly beaten, and the flour sifted with the baking powder alternately

with the cream. Spread the butter in two greased layer pans
8 or 9 inches in diameter, and cover it with the following
meringue:

Meringue for Cream Tart:

4 egg whites	1 teaspoon vanilla
1 cup sugar	1/3 cup almonds, (optional)
1/8 teaspoon salt	

Blanch the almonds—Page II and cut them into long shreds.
See Rule for Meringue—Page 215 and follow it. Spread the
meringue lightly over the cake batter in both pans. Stud one
meringue with the almonds, placing the shreds very close together. Bake the layers in a moderate oven for 25 to 35
minutes — 350°. Remove the layers from the oven and cool them
before removing them from the pans. Shortly before serving the
cake, place one layer, meringue side down, on a cake plate.
Spread one of the following cream fillings over it, reserving 4
tablespoonsful for the top. Place the almond studded layer,
meringue side up, on the cream filling and place the reserved
filling in the center.

Fillings for Meringue Tart

Pineapple Cream Filling:

1 cup whipping cream	1 cup crushed pineapple,
1 1/2 tablespoons powdered	(drained)
sugar	1/4 teaspoon vanilla

Apricot Cream Filling:

1 cup whipping cream	3/4 cup apricot pulp

(1 1/4 pounds dried apricots soaked for 12 hours in 3/4 cup of
water and boiled for 10 minutes with 1/2 cup of sugar, cooled
and put through a ricer).

Plain Filling:

1 cup whipping cream	sugar
1 1/2 tablespoons powdered	1/2 teaspoon vanilla

Fresh Fruit Cream Filling:

1 cup whipping cream	1 cup crushed, sweetened
	fruit pulp

Banana, peach, apricot, etc., or sweetened berries may be
used for the sweetened fruit pulp. The berries or fruit may
be combined with the cream, or placed on the lower layer of
cake, and covered with plain cream filling.

Ice Box Cakes

To be made with Lady Fingers, Sponge Cake, or Angel Food and Custard. Line a bowl with wax paper. Place lady fingers (or slices of cake) around the sides and over the bottom. Put part of the custard into the bowl, then a layer of cake, then custard and last cake. Place the bowl in the refrigerator for 12 hours, or more. Invert the contents of the bowl onto a plate, cover the cake with whipped cream and serve it.

Fillings for Ice Box Cakes

Lemon Custard:

½ cup butter	4 eggs
1 cup sugar	1 lemon, juice and rind

Grate the lemon over the sugar. Cream the sugar and butter, add the egg yolks and lemon juice, and fold in the beaten whites. 4 tablespoons stewed apricot pulp may be added to the custard, if desired, or 4 tablespoons of crushed, drained pineapple.

Chocolate Custard:

⅜ pound sweet chocolate	4 eggs
3 tablespoons sugar	1 teaspoon vanilla
3 tablespoons water	⅛ teaspoon salt

Melt the chocolate, add the sugar, water and egg yolks. Cook this mixture over hot water or over a low flame until it is smooth, stirring it constantly over hot water, or over a low flame. Cool the mixture and fold in the stiffly beaten egg whites.

Cocoa Custard:

A substitute seldom compares favorably with an original recipe, but this acceptable cocoa custard may be used when sweet chocolate is not available:

2 tablespoons cocoa	1 teaspoon vanilla
⅓ cup water	⅛ teaspoon salt
½ cup sugar	4 egg whites
4 egg yolks	

Cook the first four ingredients over hot water, stirring them constantly until they are thick. Cool them, add the vanilla and the egg whites, to which the salt has been added and which have been whipped until they are stiff.

Small Cakes and Cookies

Cup Cakes

RULE FOR CUP CAKES

Cup cakes are both easy to bake and serve. They may be baked in muffin tins, but a more attractive way to make them is to fill paper baking cups about one-third full and place them on a sheet or pan in the oven. When the cakes are done, they will have risen to within a quarter of an inch of the frilled edge. They may be sprinkled with powdered sugar after baking, or they may be iced to within 1/4 inch of the edge with butter icing or boiled icing and garnished with half a nut meat, three almonds, a cherry, raisins, etc. The recipes given for layer and loaf cakes may be used for cup cakes.

CUP CAKES WITH NUTS, RAISINS OR CURRANTS
28 cakes 2 1/4 inches across

1/3 to 1/2 cup butter
1 cup sugar
2 eggs
1 2/3 cups cake flour
1 1/2 teaspoons baking
  powder
1/2 cup milk

1 teaspoon vanilla
1/2 teaspoon almond
  extract, (optional)
1 cup nut meats, chopped or
  broken
1 cup raisins or 1 cup currants, washed and dried

Cream the butter and the sugar. Add the eggs, unbeaten, one at a time and beat the batter well. Flour the nuts and the fruit in a little of the flour. Sift the flour with the baking powder and add these ingredients to the batter alternately with the milk. Beat the dough after each addition and add the flavoring and the nuts or fruit. Bake the cakes in a moderate oven 350° for about 25 minutes.

ANGEL CUP CAKES

Follow the Rule for Angel Cakes I., using one-half the amount given.

COCOA CUP CAKES

4 tablespoons butter
1 cup sugar
1 egg
1/2 cup milk
1 5/8 cups cake flour

2 teaspoons baking powder
1/2 cup cocoa
1 teaspoon vanilla
1/4 teaspoon salt

Cream the butter and sugar and add the beaten egg. Sift the dry ingredients and add them to the butter mixture alternately with the milk. Add the vanilla and beat the batter well. Bake the cakes in a moderate oven 375°.

BLACK WALNUT SPONGE CUP CAKES

3 egg yolks	chopped
1½ cups powdered sugar	3 egg whites
½ teaspoon vanilla	1 tablespoon flour
1 cup black walnuts,	½ teaspoon baking powder

Beat the yolks, add the sugar slowly and the vanilla, continuing to beat. Fold in the nuts. Beat the whites in a separate bowl until they are stiff, fold in the flour and the baking powder, then fold them into the yolk mixture. Bake the cakes in muffin tins, or paper cups in a slow oven 350°.

MOLASSES NUT CUP CAKES
14 Cakes

⅓ cup butter	1¼ cups cake flour, scant
⅓ cup sugar	measure
1 egg	⅓ teaspoon soda
⅓ cup molasses	1 cup nut meats, broken
½ teaspoon vanilla	

Cream the butter and the sugar, add the egg and beat the batter well. Add the remaining ingredients in the order given, the soda being sifted with the flour. Bake the cakes in a moderate oven—375°.

SPICE CUP CAKES

These very good spice cakes call for little butter and no eggs:

1 cup seeded raisins	2 cups flour
1½ cups water	1½ teaspoons baking powder
½ teaspoon soda	½ teaspoon cinnamon
1 tablespoon butter	½ teaspoon allspice
1 cup sugar	½ teaspoon nutmeg

Boil 1 cup of the water and the raisins for 10 minutes. Add the soda and ½ cup of cold water. Cream the butter with the sugar, add the raisin mixture and the flour, sifted with the baking powder and spices. Bake the cakes in a moderate oven 350°.

Squares and Bars

QUICK CARAMEL SQUARES

Follow the rule for Caramel Layer Cake II. Spread the dough
¾ of an inch thick in a shallow, greased pan. Bake, ice and
decorate the cake as directed and cut it into small squares.

ALMOND AND DATE SQUARES

These squares, or bars, are very light and good. They may
be topped with whipped cream or ice cream.

⅞ cup sugar	chopped
5 egg yolks	1 teaspoon grated lemon
1¾ cups almonds, un-	rind
blanched, ground	1 teaspoon baking powder
7 ounces dates, finely	5 egg whites

Cream the butter and the yolks and add the remaining ingredients, folding in the stiffly beaten egg whites last. Place
the batter in a shallow pan lined with waxed paper. The pan
should be filled to the depth of 1 inch. Bake the cake in a
moderate oven 350° for about 30 minutes. Cut it into squares
and sprinkle them with powdered sugar.

BROWNIES OR FUDGE SQUARES

¾ cup butter	1 cup flour
4 squares of chocolate	1 teaspoon vanilla
4 eggs beaten	1 cup nuts
2 cups sugar	

Melt the butter and the chocolate. Beat the eggs, add the
sugar, flour, vanilla and the melted mixture. Beat the batter
well and add the nuts. Spread it to the thickness of 1 inch in
a shallow tin lined with waxed paper. Bake the cake in a
slow oven 350° for about 30 minutes. Cut it into oblongs.

CHOCOLATE ALMOND BARS

3 egg whites	¾ cup almonds, blanched
1⅙ cups powdered sugar	and shredded or other
1½ squares of chocolate,	nuts, chopped
melted and cooled	

Beat the egg whites until they are stiff, add the sifted sugar
very slowly, continuing to beat them, fold in the chocolate and
½ cup of the nuts. Spread the dough to the thickness of ¼
inch in a pan lined with buttered paper. Sprinkle the remaining almonds on the top. Bake the cake in a slow oven 325°
for about 45 minutes. Cut it into oblongs with a hot knife.

Date Bars

Follow the same rule for combining Date Bars I. and II. Their ingredients differ, as the first is made with white sugar, the second with brown sugar and spices.

DATE BARS I.

3 eggs
1 cup sugar
1 package dates

1 cup nut meats
1 cup bread flour (scant)
1 teaspoon baking powder

DATE BARS II.

4 eggs
2 cups brown sugar
1¼ cups chopped dates
1¼ cups nut meats
1¾ cups bread flour

½ teaspoon cloves
½ teaspoon cinnamon
⅛ teaspoon salt
2 teaspoons baking powder

Cream the eggs and the sugar and add the nuts and dates. Sift the dry ingredients and combine them with the egg mixture. Pour the batter into a shallow pan lined with wax paper and bake it in a moderate oven 325°. Cut the cake into bars and roll them in powdered sugar.

Cookies

PLAIN COOKIES

1 cup sugar
2 tablespoons butter
1 egg, beaten
½ cup milk

1 teaspoon vanilla
3 cups flour
1 teaspoon baking powder

Cream the butter and the sugar. Combine the egg, the milk and the vanilla and sift the flour with the baking powder. Work these ingredients into a smooth dough. Roll it, cut it into shapes and bake the cookies in a hot oven — 375°.

SAND TARTS

1¼ cups sugar
¾ cup butter
⅛ teaspoon salt
2 egg yolks
1 egg white

1 teaspoon vanilla
Flour to make a soft dough
Granulated sugar
Almonds, blanched and split

Cream the butter and the sugar, add the eggs, salt, vanilla and flour and mix the ingredients well. Chill the dough and roll it until it is very thin. Flour the board very lightly, if necessary. Brush the dough with the yolk of an egg (optional), sprinkle it generously with sugar and cut it with a small cookie cutter. Garnish the cookies with split almonds (optional). Bake them in a quick oven 400°.

SOFT MOLASSES COOKIES
About thirty 2½ inch cookies

½ cup shortening	1 teaspoon cinnamon
½ cup brown sugar	½ teaspoon salt
1 egg beaten	1½ teaspoons baking powder
½ cup molasses	½ cup hot coffee
2 cups flour	¼ teaspoon soda
1 teaspoon ginger	½ teaspoon vinegar

Cream the shortening and the sugar. Sift the flour with the spices, salt and baking powder. Dissolve the soda in the hot coffee. Combine the ingredients in the order given. Drop the batter from a teaspoon onto a greased tin. Flatten the dough with a spatula dipped in cold water. Bake the cookies in a moderate oven 350° for 10 minutes.

CRISP MOLASSES COOKIES
About thirty 2½ inch cookies

2 tablespoons butter	1¾ cups cake flour
2 tablespoons sugar	¾ teaspoon soda
¼ cup molasses	¼ teaspoon salt
3 tablespoons water	¼ teaspoon ginger

Cream the butter and the sugar. Add the molasses and beat the batter well. Add the sifted dry ingredients alternately with the water. Toss the dough onto a floured board and roll it to the thickness of ¼ inch. Cut it with a biscuit cutter, and bake the cookies on a greased tin in a moderate oven 350° for about 8 minutes.

Ice Box Cookies

The four following recipes are for Ice Box Cookies. They are all so good that it is hard to decide upon the best. The addition of nuts, which is optional, is considered an improvement on the plain cookie, but the cookie unadorned is mighty good.

RULE FOR ICE BOX COOKIES

Combine the ingredients as directed, and shape the dough into long rolls about 2 inches in diameter. If the dough is too soft to roll, chill it until it can be easily handled. Do not use additional flour. Cover the rolls with waxed paper and place them in the refrigerator for about 24 hours, until they are thoroughly chilled. Cut the rolls into the thinnest possible slices. The whole nut meats may be combined with the dough, or they may be used to garnish the slices. Bake the cookies in a quick oven 400°.

VANILLA ICE BOX COOKIES

This delicious cookie resembles a sand tart, and is less troublesome to make:

½ cup butter	2 teaspoons baking powder
1 cup sugar	1 teaspoon vanilla
1 egg	½ cup nut meats,
1¾ cups bread flour	unbroken

Cream the butter and the sugar and add the remaining ingredients in the order given. Follow the rule for Ice box Cookies.

BUTTERSCOTCH ICE BOX COOKIES

½ cup butter	⅛ teaspoon salt
1 cup brown sugar	½ teaspoon cinnamon
1 egg	½ teaspoon vanilla
½ teaspoon soda	½ cup unbroken nut meats
1¾ cups bread flour	

Cream the butter and the sugar and beat in the egg. Sift the dry ingredients and add them to the butter mixture with the vanilla and the nuts. Follow the rule for Ice box Cookies.

CHOCOLATE ICE BOX COOKIES

½ cup butter	2½ cups bread flour
1½ cups sugar	½ teaspoon salt
1 egg	2 teaspoons baking powder
2 squares of chocolate	¼ cup milk
melted and cooled	½ cup unbroken nut meats

Cream the butter and the sugar and beat in the egg, and the melted chocolate. Add the sifted dry ingredients and the butter mixture, alternately with the milk. Add the nuts and follow the rule for Ice box Cookies.

GINGER ICE BOX COOKIES

½ cup butter	1½ teaspoons ginger, (other
½ cup sugar	spices may be substituted
1 egg	for the ginger)
¼ cup molasses	½ teaspoon soda
2¼ cups cake flour	½ teaspoon salt

Cream the butter and the sugar and add the remaining ingredients in the order given, sifting the flour with the ginger, soda and salt. Follow the rule for Ice box Cookies.

Drop Cakes

The three following recipes make very light cookies that are good to serve with rich desserts:

VANILLA WAFERS OR DROP CAKES
About thirty 2½ inch cookies

½ cup sugar	2½ tablespoons milk
½ tablespoon butter	⅛ teaspoon salt
1 egg	1 teaspoon baking powder
¾ cup flour	½ teaspoon vanilla

Drop the batter from a teaspoon onto a greased baking sheet. Place the spoonfuls well apart, as the dough spreads readily. Bake the cookies in a moderate oven 350°.

COCOA DROP CAKES

Follow the rule for Vanilla Drop Cakes, deducting 3 tablespoons of flour and substituting 3 tablespoons of cocoa.

LEMON DROP CAKES

Follow the rule for Vanilla Drop Cakes, substituting 1 teaspoon lemon juice for the vanilla and adding a grating of lemon or orange rind.

CHOCOLATE NUT DROP CAKES

½ cup butter	⅔ cup bread flour
1 cup sugar	⅛ teaspoon salt
2 eggs (whole)	1 teaspoon vanilla
2 ounces chocolate, melted	1 cup pecans or walnuts,
and cooled	(broken)

Cream the butter and the sugar. Add the remaining ingredients in the order given, and beat them well. Drop the batter from a teaspoon — well apart — on a greased baking sheet and bake the cookies in a quick oven 425°.

FIG DROP CAKES
About 40 cookies

¾ cup butter
2 cups sugar
3 eggs
3 cups bread flour
1 teaspoon cinnamon
½ teaspoon cloves

1 teaspoon nutmeg
1 teaspoon soda
1 tablespoon hot water
½ cup walnuts or pecans
12 large figs, chopped
1 cup raisins, chopped

Cream the butter and the sugar, add the eggs and beat the batter well. Sift the flour with the spices, dissolve the soda in the hot water, and add these ingredients to the butter mixture. Last add the nuts, figs and raisins. Drop the batter from a spoon onto a greased baking sheet and bake the cookies in a good oven 450°.

COLUMBIA DROP CAKES
About 30 two inch cookies

½ cup butter
¾ cup brown sugar
2 small eggs
1½ cups bread flour
½ teaspoon soda
1 teaspoon cinnamon
½ teaspoon cloves

¼ teaspoon allspice
⅛ teaspoon salt
¼ cup water
1 cup nut meats, broken
1 cup chopped dates or 1
   cup raisins

Cream the butter and the sugar, add the eggs and beat the mixture well. Sift the flour with the soda, the spices and the salt, and add them alternately with the water. Last add the nuts and dates. Drop the batter from a teaspoon onto greased tins and bake the cookies in a quick oven 450°.

HERMITS—WITH SOUR CREAM
About 40 cookies

1 cup brown sugar
½ cup butter
1 egg
½ cup sour cream
1 cup bread flour
¾ teaspoon cinnamon

½ teaspoon cloves
¼ teaspoon soda, dissolved
   in 1½ teaspoons hot water
½ cup raisins, chopped
¼ cup hickory or other nuts,
   chopped

Combine the ingredients in the order given, cream the butter and the sugar and sift the dry ingredients except the soda which is dissolved in the hot water. Drop the batter from a teaspoon onto a greased baking tin. Bake the cookies in a hot oven 450° for about 8 minutes.

OATMEAL COOKIES I.
White Sugar

2 eggs
1 cup sugar
½ teaspoon vanilla
⅔ teaspoon salt

1⅓ tablespoons melted
butter
2 cups rolled oats

Beat the eggs, add the sugar gradually and add the remaining ingredients in the order given. Drop the batter from a teaspoon, two inches apart, onto greased tins. Spread it with a knife dipped in cold water. Bake the cookies in a moderate oven 375°.

OATMEAL COOKIES II.
Brown Sugar and Spices
About 50 cookies

½ cup butter
1 cup brown sugar, sifted
1 egg
1½ cups cake flour
2 teaspoons baking powder
½ teaspoon salt
2 teaspoons cinnamon

1 teaspoon cloves
½ teaspoon ginger
1¾ cups oatmeal
⅓ cup milk
¾ cup raisins, chopped
½ cup nut meats, chopped

Cream the butter and the sugar, and beat in the egg. Sift the next six ingredients and add them alternately with the oatmeal and the milk. Add the nuts and the raisins and beat the batter well. Drop spoonfuls of batter onto a greased baking sheet and bake the cakes in a moderate oven 350° for about 20 minutes.

CORN FLAKE DROPS

3 egg whites
1½ cups sugar
4 cups corn flakes, rolled
   (measured before rolling)

1 cup nut meats or 1 cup
   shredded cocoanut
1 teaspoon vanilla

Beat the egg whites until stiff, add the sugar very slowly, then fold in the remaining ingredients. Drop the batter from a teaspoon onto greased baking sheets. Bake the cakes in a slow oven 325°.

COCOANUT DROP CAKES

¼ pound dried cocoanut
Eagle Brand Condensed
   milk (sweetened)

1 teaspoon vanilla
Pinch of salt

Chop the cocoanut, add the vanilla and the salt, and enough sweetened condensed milk to form a thick paste. Drop the paste from a teaspoon onto buttered tins about two inches apart and bake the cakes in a slow oven 250° until they are done. They may be taken from the oven when they can be removed from the tin without breaking.

CHOCOLATE COCOANUT DROP CAKES

Follow the rule for Cocoanut Drop Cakes, heating the milk and adding 2 tablespoons of cocoa, or ¾ ounce of chocolate.

Nut Wafers

The two following Drop Cakes, or Wafers are much alike in ingredients, but surprisingly different in flavor. They are both delicious and comparatively inexpensive. Follow the same rule for combining and baking them.

NO. I. PECAN WAFERS OR DROP CAKES
About 50 two and a half inch wafers

2 eggs
1⅓ cups brown sugar
5 tablespoons flour
⅛ teaspoon salt

⅛ teaspoon baking powder
1 teaspoon vanilla
1 cup broken nut meats

NO. II. MOLASSES NUT WAFERS OR DROP CAKES
About 50 two and a half inch wafers

2 eggs
1 cup dark brown sugar
1 tablespoon dark molasses
¼ teaspoon baking powder
6 tablespoons flour

⅛ teaspoon salt
1 cup walnuts (black or
English) hazelnuts or
mixed nuts

Cream the eggs and the sugar, combine the remaining ingredients in the order given and beat them well before adding the nuts. Drop the batter from a teaspoon — well apart — on a greased baking tin. Bake the cakes in a moderate oven 375°. Remove them from the tins while they are warm.

PECAN DROP CAKES WITH GROUND NUTS

These cakes are a little more troublesome than the two preceeding ones, as the nuts must be put through a nut grinder. They are well worth the additional work, as they are distinctive and exceedingly good:

| 3 egg whites | 1 cup pecan meats, ground |
| 1⅓ cups brown sugar | 1 teaspoon vanilla |

Beat the whites until they are stiff, add the sifted sugar slowly, beating constantly, and fold in the vanilla and the nuts. Drop the batter from a teaspoon, well apart, on greased tins. Bake the cakes in a slow oven 325°.

Meringue Cakes or Kisses

For large Meringues — See Page 263. For Meringue Tart (Pinch Pie) See Page 264.

RULE FOR MERINGUE CAKES OR KISSES

Meringue cakes or kisses are made with egg whites, sugar and other ingredients. A small quantity of salt is added to the egg whites and they are whipped on a platter with a flat wire egg beater until they are stiff and hold a peak, but not until they are dry. The sugar is then added very slowly during continuous beating. When the last of the sugar has been thoroughly blended, the remaining ingredients are folded in. The batter is dropped from a spoon onto a lightly greased tin, or onto waxed paper and shaped into cones. The kisses are baked in a very slow oven 225° until they are partially dry and will retain their shape. They are removed from the pan while hot.

NUT KISSES

2 egg whites	1 tablespoon flour,
⅛ teaspoon salt	(optional)
1 cup sugar	1 cup pecans, broken or
½ teaspoon vanilla	black walnuts, chopped

Follow the Rule for Meringue Cakes.

DATE AND NUT KISSES

2 egg whites	½ teaspoon vanilla
⅛ teaspoon salt	1 cup dates, chopped
1 cup powdered sugar	1 cup nuts, chopped

Follow the Rule for Meringues Cakes.

RICH CHRISTMAS KISSES

3 egg whites
⅛ teaspoon salt
⅛ teaspoon cream of tartar
1 cup sugar
Grated rind of 1 lemon
1 teaspoon vanilla

2 teaspoons cornstarch, (optional)
3 cups mixed nuts, coarsely chopped
¼ cup citron chopped

Add the salt and the cream of tartar to the egg whites. Follow the Rule for Meringue Cakes.

German Christmas Cakes

The following are various forms of German Xmas Cakes that are so good that one wonders why they are limited to one short period of the year.

CHRISTMAS CAKES WITH MOLASSES I.

½ gallon New Orleans molasses
½ cup butter
½ cup lard
¾ cup sugar
1 pound grated almonds, unblanched
¾ pound citron
¼ pound candied orange rind

¼ pound candied lemon rind
2 teaspoons baking powder
1 teaspoon mace, (scant)
2 teaspoons cloves
12 cardamon seeds, (shelled and ground)
Grated rind of two fresh lemons
Flour

Heat the molasses to the boiling point, add the shortening, the sugar and the remaining ingredients. Knead the flour into the batter until the dough is fairly stiff. (When cold it will be considerably stiffer). When it is cool add, 2 teaspoons of carbonate of ammonia dissolved in a little warm water. Permit the dough to stand for two weeks. Then roll it until it is three-fourths of an inch thick. Place the dough in shallow, greased pans in a fairly hot oven 375° to 400°. Cut the cake into squares while it is hot.

GERMAN CHRISTMAS CAKES WITH MOLASSES II.

½ cup sugar
2 tablespoons butter
2 cups New Orleans Molasses
2 teaspoons cinnamon
½ teaspoon cloves

1 teaspoon soda
1 tablespoon hot water
1 cardamon seed, pounded
1 ounce citron, chopped
½ cup almonds, blanched and shredded
Flour

Combine the ingredients in the order given, creaming the butter and the sugar and dissolving the soda in the hot water. Add enough flour to make the dough stiff enough to knead. Permit it to stand for 12 hours, or more. Roll the dough, cut it into shapes and bake the cakes in a moderate oven 375° to 400°.

Ice them with Lemon Icing (Powdered sugar and lemon juice.)

CHRISTMAS CAKES III.
With Chocolate and Spices

1½ cups sugar
2 tablespoons butter
5 eggs
1 cup New Orleans Molasses
3 cups flour
3 teaspoons baking powder
2½ teaspoons cinnamon

½ teaspoon cloves
½ teaspoon allspice
2 ounces sweet chocolate, grated
2½ tablespoons whiskey
2½ cups pecans, broken

Combine the ingredients in the order given. Cream the butter with the sugar, add the eggs and the flour which has been sifted with the baking powder and the spices. Chill the dough until it will roll. Roll it until it is ½ inch thick. Bake it in shallow greased pans in a moderate oven 375° to 400°. Cut it into oblongs and ice them with powdered sugar thinned with lemon juice or water, flavored with vanilla.

GERMAN HONEY CAKES I.

These cakes will keep for six months or longer, if placed in a closed tin:

6 pounds honey (molasses may be substituted)
1 cup butter
Flour
1 pound almonds, blanched and shredded
½ pound citron, chopped
4 cups sugar
2½ tablespoons mixed

spices, (cinnamon, cloves, nutmeg, mace, etc.)
4 teaspoons grated lemon rind
1 ounce carbonate of powdered ammonium dissolved in ½ cup water or rum

Heat the honey and the butter in a large flat tin over a low flame. When these ingredients are lukewarm, add sufficient flour to make a semi-liquid dough. Remove the dish from the fire and add all the ingredients, except the ammonium. When the dough is nearly cold, add the dissolved ammonium and sufficient flour to make a stiff dough that will not stick to the

279

hands. This dough may be baked at once, but the cakes are better when the dough has been aged. It will keep for weeks in a cool place. Roll out the dough (it may be necessary to warm it) and spread it to the thickness of one-fourth inch in shallow greased pans. Bake it in a moderate oven — 350°. Cut the cake into squares, or oblongs, and ice them with

Lemon Icing:

4 egg whites   Powdered sugar
1 lemon rind and juice

Beat the eggs until they are stiff, add the lemon and enough powdered sugar to make the icing a good consistency to spread.

GERMAN HONEY CAKES II.
With Eggs

1 quart honey	1 teaspoon cinnamon
4 cups flour	1 teaspoon cloves
4 eggs beaten	1/2 teaspoon nutmeg
1 pound almonds, blanched	1/4 teaspoon allspice
and shredded	1/4 cup brandy
1/4 pound citron, chopped	1 teaspoon hartshorn

Boil the honey, cool it slightly and add the flour and the remaining ingredients in the order given. Chill the dough for 12 hours. Roll it to the thickness of one-fourth inch. Place it in large, shallow greased pans, or on greased sheets, and bake it in a moderate oven — 350°. Cut the cake into squares, or oblongs, and ice them with Lemon Icing.

CHRISTMAS PRETZELS

1 cup butter	4 egg yolks
1 cup sugar	2 egg whites
4 tablespoons sour cream	4 cups flour

Cream the butter and the sugar, and add the remaining ingredients in the order given. Chill the dough for several hours until it is easy to handle. Shape it into long thin rolls and twist these into pretzel shape. Place the pretzels in a greased tin, brush them with the yolk of an egg and sprinkle the tops with blanched, chopped almonds and with sugar. Bake them at once in a moderate oven 375°.

CRESCENTS

1 1/2 cups butter	4 cups flour
1/2 cup powdered sugar	1 pound almonds, blanched
1 egg	and chopped

Cream the butter and the sugar, and add the remaining ingredients. Roll the dough ¼ inch thick and cut it into crescent shape. Bake the cakes on a greased tin in a moderate oven 375°. Dip them, when baked, in powdered sugar moistened with a little vanilla.

YOLK COOKIES NO. I.

1 cup butter	½ lemon, juice and rind
1 cup sugar	4 cups flour
Yolks of 8 eggs	

Cream the butter and the sugar, add the other ingredients and mix them well. Chill the dough for one hour, then roll it into sticks ¼ inch in diameter. Shape these into the letter S, brush them with the yolk of an egg, sprinkle them with sugar and bake them in a moderate oven 375°.

YOLK COOKIES NO. II. Gelbe Plaettchen

2 cups powdered sugar	Rind and juice of 1 lemon
8 egg yolks	1 cup flour
1 whole egg	

Cream the eggs and the sugar, add the lemon rind and juice and the flour. Beat the dough and drop it by the teaspoonful well apart on a greased baking sheet. Permit the cakes to dry for 12 hours, then bake them in a slow oven 325°. 1½ teaspoons aniseed rolled, may be added to the batter.

ANISE CAKES

3 eggs	1½ cups flour
1 cup sugar	1 teaspoon baking powder
1½ tablespoons aniseed	½ teaspoon vanilla

Beat the eggs, add the sugar slowly and continue beating for 1 minute. Add the flour mixed with the baking powder, the vanilla and the aniseed, which has been well crushed with a rolling pin. Mix the batter well and drop it by the half teaspoonful, at least two inches apart, on greased baking sheets. Permit the cakes to dry for twelve hours, or more, then bake them in a moderately slow oven 325°.

SPRINGERLE

This recipe is for the well-known German Anise Cakes, which are made at Christmas time and which are stamped with quaint little designs and figures. This calls for the same ingredients as the preceding Anise Cake recipe, but is much heavier in flour. If these cakes become too hard, soften them by placing an apple in the cookie jar.

2 cups sugar
4 eggs

4 cups flour (approximately)
1 tablespoon aniseed

Cream the eggs and the sugar, add the sifted flour gradually until the dough is stiff. Roll it out to the thickness of ¼ inch. Flour a Springerle board lightly, press it hard upon the dough, then lift it carefully. Separate the squares, place them on a floured board and permit them to dry for 12 hours. Butter baking sheets and sprinkle them with aniseed. Place the cakes on them and bake them in a slow oven 300° until they are a light yellow.

The two following recipes are for German nut cakes, both delicious:

CINNAMON STARS

1 pound almonds (un-blanched), ground
2 cups sugar

1 teaspoon cinnamon
6 egg whites

Beat the egg whites to a stiff froth, add the sugar slowly, continuing to beat. Add the cinnamon and reserve ⅓ of this mixture. Fold the nuts into the remainder. Roll the batter to the thickness of ⅓ inch, using powdered sugar on the board and roller, and cut it with a star shaped cutter. Glaze the stars with the reserved mixture. Bake the cakes on a greased tin in a moderate oven 325°.

HAZELNUT CAKES

Whites of 6 eggs
1 pound hulled hazelnuts — ground
2¾ cups brown sugar

1 teaspoon vanilla
Granulated sugar
2 pounds hazel nuts, unhulled

Whip the whites to a stiff froth, add the sugar slowly, continuing to beat. Add the vanilla and fold in the ground nuts. Shape the batter into small balls, roll them in granulated sugar and bake them on a greased tin in a moderate oven 325°.

NUT AND DATE COOKIES

1 cup nuts
1 cup dates
1 cup sugar
1 cup flour

1 teaspoon baking powder
⅛ teaspoon salt
2 egg whites
1 tablespoon cream

Grind the nuts and the dates. Sift the sugar, flour and baking powder, and combine them with the nuts and dates. Add the salt to the egg whites, beat them until they are stiff, fold in the cream and the other ingredients, using the hands to combine them. Grease and flour a baking tin. Place the combined ingredients on it and pat them down into a flat cake. Bake it in a moderate oven 375°. Ice the cake while it is hot with powdered sugar moistened with lemon juice until it is the right consistency to spread. Cut it while it is hot into oblongs, or squares.

WHITE ALMOND WAFERS—Mandel Plaettchen

1 cup butter	1½ teaspoons rose water
1 cup sugar	⅛ teaspoon salt
3 egg yolks	Flour to make the dough the
2 egg whites (1 if the egg	right consistency to roll
is large)	½ pound almonds, blanched
Grated rind of 1 lemon	and chopped fine

Cream the butter and the sugar, add the well beaten eggs and stir them until they are well blended. (It is not necessary to beat the eggs separately). Add the flavoring, the salt, then the almonds and last the flour. Roll the dough until it is very thin and cut it into shapes. Brush the cakes with the following mixture:

1 egg yolk, well beaten   2 tablespoons milk

Bake them on a greased tin in a moderate oven 375°.

Quick Refreshments for Tea

LADY FINGER SANDWICHES

Spread lady fingers with jam or marmalade, and place one upon the other.

ORANGE MARMALADE SANDWICHES

Spread ¼ inch slices of bread (from which the crust has been cut) with marmalade. Roll the slices and secure them with toothpicks. Toast them under a broiler, or on a toaster, turning them to brown evenly. Serve them hot.

CINNAMON TOAST

Spread thin slices of bread with a thick layer of soft butter, and sprinkle them generously with sugar and cinnamon. Place one piece on top of the other with the prepared sides to the center. Toast the slices under, or over a quick fire. Separate them and serve them at once, cinnamon side up.

Icings and Cake Fillings

Boiled Icings

RULE FOR WHITE ICING:

Boil the water and the sugar until the syrup forms a soft ball when dropped into cold water, or when it forms a thread (when dropped from a spoon) that is about three inches long. This thread should be thin enough to curl or wave. In either case the syrup will have reached about 240 degrees of heat.

Add the salt to the egg whites. (Egg whites may be whipped until they are stiff, whipped until they are frothy, or they need not be whipped at all before adding the syrup).

The syrup is poured upon them while it is very hot in a very fine stream, the eggs being beaten constantly during the addition of the syrup and afterward, until the icing becomes creamy and of the right consistency to spread.

When the last of the syrup has been added ⅛ teaspoon of cream of tartar (to two egg whites), or a few drops of lemon juice may be added to keep the icing from becoming gritty.

Beat in the flavoring as the icing cools.

When the syrup has been cooked to the right stage, the icing will spread readily and stay where it is put. If it has not been boiled long enough and the icing does not thicken, beat it in strong sunlight, or near an open oven door, or place the bowl containing the icing over (not in) boiling water and beat the icing until it becomes the right consistency to spread.

If the syrup has been cooked too long and threatens to harden too soon, beat in a few drops of lemon juice, or a teaspoon or more of boiling water.

Have a bowl of very hot water in readiness before making a white icing. You are then prepared for any emergency.

Never place a thin, or doubtful icing *on* a cake. Do everything you can to thicken it *before* taking this step.

When the icing begins to thicken around the sides of the bowl, it is usually ready to be spread, but if you are in doubt about it, spread a small quantity only and see how it behaves. A little patience at this stage of the icing will save endless trouble and will insure a good looking cake.

Pile the icing on top of the cake and use a spatula, or knife in spreading it. Spread it quickly, working it toward the edges and sides of the cake. Dip the spatula in hot water as the icing thickens. Add a little hot water, if necessary, to soften the last icing in the bowl.

If raisins, nuts, or other ingredients are to be added to the icing, wait until the last moment to do so. Acid or oil is apt to thin the icing beyond repair, if the fruit is added too soon.

When icing large or small cakes, decorate them with nut meats, with candied cherries, angelica, etc.

PLAIN WHITE ICING

The following icing has the consistency of a marshmallow icing. As it serves every purpose, it is the only white icing I use:

2 cups sugar
1 cup water
1/8 teaspoon salt
2 egg whites

1/8 teaspoon cream of tartar
1 teaspoon vanilla or other flavoring

Boil the syrup as directed. Add the salt to the egg whites and beat them only until they are frothy. Follow the rule for making White Icing.

RAISIN SMASH ICING

Add one cup of chopped raisins to White Icing immediately before spreading it, or sprinkle the raisins over the icing as soon as it is spread.

COCOANUT ICING

If possible, use fresh grated cocoanut. This is delicious. Shredded cocoanut bought in jars, or packages, may be substituted. Sprinkle it lightly over freshly spread White Icing.

NUT ICING

Add 1/4 cup or more chopped nuts to White Icing. As this makes a rough surface, it is best to spread the icing and sprinkle chopped nuts over it before it hardens. Pistachio nuts are good for color and flavor.

CHOCOLATE COATING OVER WHITE ICING

Melt two squares of bitter chocolate, cool it and spread it with a spatula, or knife over White Icing as soon as it is set. Allow several hours for the chocolate to harden. In summer, or moist weather, add 1/4 teaspoon of melted paraffine to the chocolate. This coating *will* run. Transfer the cake to a fresh plate before serving it. Do not attempt to make this coating in excessively hot weather unless the cake can be put in an icebox until the chocolate hardens.

CHOCOLATE PEPPERMINT ICING

Add a few drops of peppermint extract to White icing and cover it with Chocolate coating.

DECORATIVE ICING—Twice Cooked Icing

This is a fine recipe for decorative icing. It will keep without hardening for a long time, if closely covered with waxed paper:

Boil 1 cup sugar   ½ cup water

Meanwhile add ⅛ teaspoon of salt to 2 egg whites and beat them until they are stiff and will hold a point. Add 3 tablespoons of sugar very slowly, beating constantly. When the syrup begins to fall in heavy drops from a spoon, add a small quantity of it to the eggs and sugar and continue beating. Repeat this process, adding the syrup to the eggs in four or five parts. If these additions are properly timed, the last of the syrup will have reached the thread stage. Beat the icing constantly. Have a pan ready partly filled with water placed over heat. The bowl in which the icing is being made should fit closely into this pan so that the bowl will be over, but not in the water. When the water in the pan begins to boil add ¼ teaspoon of powder (equal parts of baking powder and tartaric acid) and continue to beat the icing until it sticks to the sides and the bottom of the bowl and holds a point. Remove the icing from the heat. Place as much as is required for the decoration (usually about ⅓) in a small bowl and cover it closely with waxed paper. To the remainder add 1 teaspoon or more of hot water to thin it to the right consistency to spread. Beat it well and spread it on the cake. Decorate the cake with the reserved icing, coloring it with color paste and placing it in oblongs of baker's paper, that have been rolled into cornucopia shaped bags, secured near the point with a pin. Flatten a bag and cut a small piece from the point to make dots or stems. Cut it like this, Λ, to make leaves or petals. Fill the bags with icing, close them by doubling over the paper at the top, and force the icing through the point of the bag.

RULE FOR SEA FOAM ICING

Boil the sugar and the water (or the coffee) until the syrup forms a soft ball when dropped into cold water — 252°. Pour it in a thin stream on the partially beaten egg white and beat until the icing becomes creamy. Sea foam icing has a tendency to remain sticky for several hours. To overcome this, place the icing in a bowl over (not in) boiling water and beat the icing until it will hold a point. Add the vanilla, spread the icing and sprinkle it with nuts.

SEA FOAM ICING I.
1 Egg White

2 cups brown sugar
2/3 cup water
1 egg white

1/2 teaspoon vanilla
1/4 cup chopped nut meats
(optional)

SEA FOAM ICING II.
2 Egg Whites

2 1/2 cups brown sugar
1/2 cup water
1/8 teaspoon salt
2 egg whites

1 teaspoon vanilla
1/3 cup chopped nut meats
(optional)

MOCHA SEA FOAM ICING

2 1/2 cups brown sugar
1/2 cup strong coffee
1/8 teaspoon salt

2 egg whites
1/2 teaspoon vanilla

See Rule for Sea Foam Icing.

RULE FOR CARAMEL ICING

Boil the sugar and the liquid until the syrup forms a soft ball when dropped into cold water (238°). Add the butter, remove the icing from the fire and cool it. Add the vanilla and beat the icing until it is thick and creamy. If it is too heavy, thin the icing with a little hot cream until it is the right consistency to spread.

CARAMEL ICING I.

2 cups brown sugar
1 cup milk or cream

3 tablespoons butter
1 teaspoon vanilla

CARAMEL ICING II.—Opera Caramel

1 cup brown sugar
1/2 cup white sugar
3/4 cup thin cream

1/2 teaspoon butter
1 teaspoon vanilla

CHOCOLATE ICING—Boiled

2 cups sugar
2 ounces chocolate
2 tablespoons corn syrup
¾ cup milk
2 tablespoons butter
1 teaspoon vanilla

Cook the first four ingredients until the syrup forms a ball when dropped into cold water—238°. Remove the syrup from the fire, add the butter and place the saucepan in cold water. When the icing is lukewarm, add the vanilla and beat the icing until it is creamy and ready to spread. If the icing hardens too rapidly, add a few drops of hot water to it, or place the saucepan in hot water.

EMERGENCY ICINGS

The two following recipes are for very quick cooked icings. Being quick is their chief virtue, as they are more concentrated and coarser grained than the boiled icings given before. They are best spread as thinly as possible. They are perfectly acceptable emergency icings:

EMERGENCY CARAMEL ICING
Enough for a small cake or twelve cup cakes

1 cup brown sugar
3 tablespoons cream
½ teaspoon butter
½ teaspoon vanilla

Cook the first three ingredients to the boiling point, cool them slightly, add the vanilla and beat them until they are the right consistency to spread.

EMERGENCY CHOCOLATE ICING
Enough for a very small cake or ten cup cakes

1½ ounces chocolate grated
6 tablespoons sugar
3 tablespoons water

Stir these ingredients over a low flame until they are thick and glossy. Remove them from the fire and beat them until they are the right consistency to spread.

SOUR CREAM ICING

1 cup sugar
1 cup sour cream
1 teaspoon vanilla
½ cup nut meats, chopped

Boil the sugar and the sour cream until the syrup forms a soft ball when dropped into cold water—238°. Cool the syrup until it is lukewarm, then beat it until it is creamy. Add the vanilla and the nuts and spread the icing.

Steamed Icings

SEVEN MINUTE WHITE ICING

An icing that never fails:

For a small cake use one-half the amount given.

2 egg whites, unbeaten
1½ cups sugar
5 tablespoons cold water

¼ teaspoon cream of tartar
1 teaspoon vanilla

Place the first four ingredients in the top of a double boiler over rapidly boiling water. Beat them constantly with a rotary beater, or with a wire whisk for 7 minutes, or until the icing stands up in peaks. Remove the icing from the fire, add the vanilla and continue beating until the icing is the right consistency to spread.

NUT OR COCOANUT SEVEN MINUTE ICING

Sprinkle ½ cup of nut meats, or ½ cup grated cocoanut over seven minute icing.

SEVEN MINUTE MAPLE NUT ICING

For a small cake use one-half the amount given.

2 egg whites
2¼ cups brown sugar
5 tablespoons water

1 teaspoon vanilla
¾ cup nut meats, chopped
(optional)

Follow the rule for Seven Minute White Icing. Spread the icing and sprinkle the nuts over it before it hardens.

SEVEN MINUTE CHOCOLATE ICING

For a small cake use one-half the amount given.

2 egg whites
1½ cups sugar
¼ teaspoon cream of tartar
5 tablespoons cold water

3 squares of chocolate melted
and cooled
1 teaspoon vanilla

Place the first 4 ingredients in the top of a double boiler. Follow the rule for Seven Minute White Icing. Remove the icing from the fire and fold in the chocolate and the vanilla. Do not beat the icing after adding the chocolate and vanilla. Cool the icing until it is the right consistency to spread.

THREE MINUTE ICING

The following recipe makes a soft icing that is comparable to a meringue. It is a very good substitute for meringue or for whipped cream.

2 egg whites	1/2 cup sugar
2 tablespoons cold water	1 teaspoon vanilla

Place the ingredients in the top of a double boiler, over boiling water, and beat them with a rotary beater for three minutes.

Uncooked Icings

WHITE ICING

1 cup powdered sugar	1 tablespoons flavoring (Van-
1 1/2 tablespoons butter	illa, Rum, Sherry, Coffee,
1/8 teaspoon salt	etc.)

1 1/2 tablespoons hot cream or 1 egg yolk may be substituted for the butter. Cream the butter with the sugar, and add the salt and the flavoring. If the icing is too thin, use additional powdered sugar until it is the right consistency to spread.

ORANGE AND LEMON ICING

Follow the rule for Uncooked White Icing, flavoring it with:

1/2 tablespoon orange juice	A light grating of orange and
1/2 tablespoon lemon juice	lemon rind

CHOCOLATE ICING—Uncooked

1 ounce chocolate or 2	2 tablespoons hot water
tablespoons cocoa	1/4 teaspoon vanilla
1 teaspoon butter	Powdered sugar

Melt the chocolate over a very low flame, add the butter and the water. When these ingredients are cool, add the vanilla and enough sifted powdered sugar to make the icing the right consistency to spread.

CHOCOLATE BUTTER ICING

4 tablespoons butter	1/2 teaspoon vanilla
2 cups sifted powdered sugar	1/8 teaspoon salt
1 1/2 ounces chocolate, melted	4 tablespoons milk or cream
and cooled	

Cream the butter and add the sugar slowly. When these ingredients are well blended, add the chocolate, the vanilla and the salt, and just enough milk to make the icing a good consistency to spread.

CHOCOLATE BUTTER ICING—With Egg

3 tablespoons butter
1 cup powdered sugar
1 egg

1 ounce chocolate, melted
  and cooled
Cream, if needed

Cream the butter, add the sugar slowly, and when these ingredients are well blended, add the egg and the chocolate. If the icing is too heavy, thin it with a little cream until it is the right consistency to spread.

COFFEE ICING—French Icing

4 tablespoons butter
1⅔ cups powdered sugar,
  sifted

⅛ teaspoon salt
3 tablespoons hot coffee
1 teaspoon vanilla

Cream the butter and the sugar, add the salt and the hot coffee. Beat these ingredients for two minutes. When the icing is cool, add the vanilla. Permit it to stand for five minutes, then beat it well and spread it on the cake.

MOCHA ICING I.—With Powdered Sugar

¼ cup butter
1½ cups powdered sugar
1 tablespoon cocoa

¼ teaspoon vanilla
Hot coffee (about 3 tablespoons), or

MOCHA ICING II.—With Brown Sugar

⅓ cup butter
1½ cups light brown sugar
1 tablespoon cocoa

¼ teaspoon vanilla
Hot coffee

Cream the butter, add the sugar, which has been sifted with the cocoa, and when these ingredients are well blended, add the flavoring and enough coffee to make the icing the right consistency to spread.

APRICOT ICING

1½ cups powdered sugar
½ cup apricot pulp, (dried
  apricots stewed and

  strained)
1 tablespoon butter
½ tablespoon lemon juice

Stir the apricot pulp with the sugar until the mixture is smooth—add the soft butter and the lemon juice. Add more powdered sugar, if needed. This is a soft icing.

PINEAPPLE ICING

4 tablespoons soft butter
2 cups sifted powdered sugar
1 teaspoon lemon juice
1/2 teaspoon vanilla

1/8 teaspoon salt
1/2 cup chopped pineapple,
(drained)

Combine the ingredients in the order given. Permit them to stand for five minutes. Beat them until the icing is creamy.

ICING FOR CHRISTMAS CAKES

Powdered sugar
Lemon juice

Grated lemon rind,
(optional)

Moisten the powdered sugar with lemon juice, and beat it until it is the right consistency to spread. Flavor the icing, if desired, with grated lemon rind. Drop a small quantity from a teaspoon onto each cake and permit it to spread and harden.

GLAZE FOR CHRISTMAS CAKES AND COOKIES

2 cups powdered sugar
3 tablespoons boiling water

1 teaspoon vanilla

Moisten the sugar with the water and add the vanilla and beat the icing until it is the right consistency to spread.

Cake Fillings

CUSTARD FILLING

3 or 4 egg yolks
1/3 to 1/2 cup sugar
1 tablespoon flour

2 cups milk scalded
1 teaspoon vanilla

Beat the yolks, add the sugar and the flour. Pour the scalded milk over the egg mixture. Cook these ingredients over hot water until they are smooth and thick, stirring them constantly. When the custard is cool, add the vanilla and spread the filling between layers of cake.

BANANA CUSTARD FILLING

Follow the recipe for Custard Filling, adding four or more sliced bananas to the custard just before spreading it.

PINEAPPLE FILLING

See filling for Pineapple Meringue Pie—Page 216 or spread cake layers with drained pineapple and cover them with White Icing.

CHOCOLATE FILLING I.

1 cup white sugar
1 cup brown sugar
1 cup cream

1½ tablespoons butter
2 squares of chocolate

Cook these ingredients until they thicken. Cool the filling and spread it between layers of cake.

CHOCOLATE FILLING II.

2 cups sugar
4 egg yolks
1 cup milk
2 teaspoons butter

1 square of chocolate, grated
or chopped
1 teaspoon vanilla

Beat the eggs with the sugar, and add the milk slowly, the butter and the chocolate. Cook these ingredients over hot water until they are thick. Cool the filling, add the vanilla and spread the filling between layers of cake.

ALMOND FILLING WITH SOUR CREAM

1 cup sour cream
1 cup sugar
½ teaspoon vanilla

½ cup blanched shredded
almonds

Whip the cream until it is stiff, add the sugar gradually, beat in the vanilla and fold in the nuts.

ALMOND OR HAZELNUT CUSTARD FILLING
With Sour Cream

1 cup sour cream
1 cup sugar
1 tablespoon flour
1 egg

1 cup almonds, (blanched
or unblanched) ground
½ teaspoon vanilla

Heat the first three ingredients over a very slow fire. Pour them over the beaten egg and return them to the fire. When the custard is thick and smooth, add the nuts. When it is cool, add the vanilla.

FIG FILLING

½ pound figs, chopped
⅓ cup sugar
⅓ cup boiling water
1 tablespoon lemon juice

¾ teaspoon grated lemon
rind, or orange
1 tablespoon cornstarch,
(optional)

Combine the ingredients in the order given and cook them over a low flame, or in a double boiler until they are thick. Spread the filling between layers of cake.

LADY BALTIMORE FILLING—See Page 252

FRUIT FILLING FOR CAKE

3/4 cup condensed milk
1/4 cup water
3/4 cup sugar
1/4 cup dates, chopped

1/4 cup figs, chopped
1/4 cup raisins, chopped
1/2 cup nuts, chopped
1 teaspoon vanilla

Heat the first three ingredients in a double boiler. When they are smooth, add the next four ingredients and cook the filling until it is thick. Cool it, add the vanilla and spread the filling between layers of cake.

LEMON, ORANGE AND APRICOT FILLING

1 lemon or orange, grated
2 lemons or oranges, juiced
1/3 cup water
3/4 cup sugar
2 tablespoons flour

3 egg yolks
1/2 to 2/3 cup thick, stewed
    strained apricot pulp,
    (optional)

Cook the ingredients in a double boiler, or over a very low flame, stirring them constantly until they are smooth and thick. For other Lemon and Orange Fillings, see Pages 254 and 255.

Puddings

Custard sauces and puddings are prepared over boiling water, or over a very low flame. They must be stirred constantly while they are cooking and they must not be permitted to boil at any time. A high degree of heat destroys their delicate flavor and solidifies the eggs, causing them to curdle or separate. Should a custard sauce separate, remove it at once from the fire, dump it quickly into a cold bowl and whip it with a spiral wire whisk. Beat it well and it may become smooth. A spiral wire whisk is helpful when making custards and pudding mixtures.

RULE FOR WHIPPING EGGS

Use a flat wire egg beater for whipping the whites of eggs. Place the eggs on a platter, add the salt and whip them until they are stiff and will hold a point.

RULE FOR WHIPPING CREAM

Use a heavy wire beater for whipping cream. Cream cannot be very stiffly whipped as it will turn to butter. It may be sweetened with powdered or granulated sugar and flavored in any way desired. Fold in the sugar and the flavoring.

RULE FOR GELATINE

Gelatine must be soaked in a cold liquid for five minutes before it is dissolved. Dissolve it by placing it in a hot liquid — water, milk, custard, etc., or dissolve it by placing the receptacle holding it in boiling water, or over a low flame. If a mold is to be used for gelatine puddings, wet it before filling it. This will prevent the pudding from sticking to the mold. To set a gelatine dish rapidly, place the receptacle containing it in a bowl of ice water.

Custards

A family I know had a colored cook who always urged them, when they were children, to eat sparingly of the meat course and to leave a little room for the "hereafter". I have prepared so many, many "hereafters" for children and grown-ups, that I feel like Christopher Morley's heroine, who made an anthology of the loaves of bread she had baked.

The majority of the following recipes are simple, require only staple articles, and are very quickly made:

CUP CUSTARD

2 cups milk
1/4 to 1/2 cup sugar
1/8 teaspoon salt
3 egg yolks

1/2 teaspoon vanilla
1/8 teaspoon nutmeg
    (optional)

Scald the milk with the sugar, salt and nutmeg. Pour it over the beaten yolks, add the vanilla and pour the custard into a baking dish, or into individual molds. Place the molds in a pan of hot water in a moderate oven 325° until set. To test, insert a silver knife or spoon. If the custard does not adhere to it, it is ready to be removed from the oven. Chill and serve it with: Caramel Sauce—Page 323.

CARAMEL CUSTARD

1/2 cup sugar
1 tablespoon hot water
2 cups milk

1/8 teaspoon salt
3 egg yolks
1/2 teaspoon vanilla

Put the sugar in a small skillet and stir it over a quick fire until it is melted. Add the hot water and stir it until the sugar is dissolved. Heat the milk until it is scalded, and add the melted sugar. Beat the eggs, add the vanilla and pour the milk and sugar slowly over them. Place the custard in a mold set in a dish of hot water and bake it in a moderate oven 325° until it is set.

CARAMELIZED DISHES

To caramelize a mold, put ½ cup of sugar in it and place it over heat. As the sugar melts and browns, turn the mold so that the caramel will spread—push it with a spoon until the entire surface of the mold is covered, then pour a custard, or pudding mixture, into the mold and follow the directions given for cooking the custard or pudding.

DANISH CUSTARD—Quick Caramelized Custard

3 eggs
¼ cup white sugar
⅛ teaspoon salt
2 cups milk, scalded

½ teaspoon vanilla or ¼
  teaspoon nutmeg
½ cup light brown sugar

Beat the eggs, add the white sugar, salt, milk and vanilla. Roll the brown sugar with a rolling pin, or sift it. Place it in the bottom of a baking dish or mold, and pour the custard on top of it. Place the baking dish in a pan of hot water in a moderate oven and bake the custard until it is firm. Cool it and invert the contents of the dish onto a platter. The brown sugar will form a caramel sauce.

MAPLE CUSTARD
7 or 8 Servings

4 egg yolks
¾ cup maple syrup
⅛ teaspoon salt

3 cups milk
4 egg whites

Beat the yolks and the syrup. Add the milk and the salt and fold in the stiffly beaten egg whites. Fill individual custard cups, place them in a pan of hot water and bake them in a moderate oven 325° until the custard is firm.

BOILED CUSTARD OR CUSTARD SAUCE

This custard is badly named, as it must not boil at any time:

3 egg yolks
¼ cup sugar
2 cups hot milk

⅛ teaspoon salt
½ teaspoon vanilla

Beat the yolks slightly and add the sugar, and the salt. Stir in the hot milk gradually. Place the custard over a very slow fire and stir it constantly, taking care that it does not boil— or cook it over hot water until it begins to thicken. Strain and cool the custard, add the vanilla and chill it thoroughly. This is not a firm custard, it is really a custard sauce.

BAKED CHOCOLATE CUSTARD WITH MERINGUE
6 Servings

This good pudding may be served hot or cold:

1 tablespoon cornstarch	1¾ ounces chocolate
2 cups milk	4 egg yolks
1 cup sugar	

Dissolve the cornstarch in ¼ cup of milk. Scald the remaining milk, add the sugar and the chocolate, and when they are dissolved, add the milk and cornstarch. Permit this to thicken over a very low fire, stirring it constantly. Remove it from the fire and pour it over the lightly beaten egg yolks. Place the custard in a baking dish, cool it and cover it with:

Meringue:

4 egg whites	½ cup sugar
⅛ teaspoon salt	1 teaspoon vanilla

See the rule for Meringue, on Page 215. Place the baking dish in a pan of hot water and bake the custard in a moderate oven 325° until the meringue is set.

Cereal Puddings
FARINA PUDDING—Boiled

This is a good recipe for children:

2 cups milk	2 egg yolks
¼ cup sugar	1 teaspoon vanilla
½ cup farina	Pinch of salt
1 tablespoon butter	2 egg whites

Boil the milk with the sugar, add the farina and stir these ingredients until the farina is well cooked and thick. Add the butter and when it is melted, remove the pan from the fire. Beat in the egg yolks, cool the mixture and add the vanilla. Add the salt to the egg whites and whip them until they are stiff. Fold them into the farina mixture and chill the pudding thoroughly. Serve it with cream, with fruit juice, or with stewed fruits or crushed berries.

FARINA PUDDING—Baked

Follow the rule for Farina Pudding—Boiled. Grate the rind of 1 lemon into the sugar and use 3 eggs instead of 2. Place the pudding in a greased pan, spreading it to the thickness of 1 inch and bake it in a moderate oven 350° until the edges are crisp. Serve it hot with Raspberry or Loganberry juice.

TAPIOCA CREAM

2 tablespoons pearl tapioca
2 cups milk
2 egg yolks
1/4 cup sugar

1/4 teaspoon salt
2 egg whites
1/2 teaspoon vanilla

Soak the tapioca in boiling water to cover. When the water has been absorbed, add the milk. Cook the tapioca in a double boiler until it is soft and transparent. Beat the egg yolks with the sugar, pour part of the hot tapioca over them, add this mixture to the tapioca in the boiler and cook it for two or three minutes longer to permit the yolks to thicken. Stir the pudding constantly. Remove it from the fire, cool it, add the flavoring and fold in the stiffly beaten egg whites, to which the salt has been added. Serve the pudding very cold with cream.

CARAMEL TAPIOCA

1/2 cup minute tapioca
2 cups brown sugar

3 cups boiling water
2 teaspoons vanilla

Combine the ingredients and place them in a baking dish. Cook them covered in a very slow oven until the tapioca is transparent. Serve the pudding with cream.

Bread Puddings Baked

BREAD PUDDING WITH MERINGUE

6 Servings

Well made bread pudding is an excellent dish, particularly if one is clever about "jazzing up" the hard sauce that accompanies it:

2 to 3 cups bread
3 cups milk
1/4 teaspoon salt
1/3 to 1/2 cup sugar
3 egg yolks

1 teaspoon vanilla
1/2 teaspoon nutmeg
   (optional)
1/4 cup raisins

Cut the crusts from the bread and pull the bread apart. Cover it with 1 cup of milk, to which the salt has been added. Permit this to soak for 15 minutes.

Combine the egg yolks, sugar, vanilla and nutmeg with 2 cups of milk. Beat this well, add the raisins and pour the mixture over the soaked bread. Stir it with a fork until it is well blended. Place it in a baking dish and cover it with meringue.

Meringue:

⅛ teaspoon salt   6 tablespoons sugar
3 egg whites   ½ teaspoon vanilla

See the rule for Meringue—Page 215. Bake the pudding in a moderate oven 300° until the meringue is set. Serve it hot with Hard Sauce—Page 322.

BREAD PUDDING WITH NUTS AND RAISINS
6 Servings

3 or 4 egg yolks   ½ pound raisins, chopped
½ cup sugar   1 cup dry bread crumbs
½ teaspoon vanilla   ⅛ teaspoon salt
½ pound nut meats, broken   3 egg whites
  (optional)

Beat the yolks until they are light, add the sugar and beat them until they are creamy. Add the vanilla, nuts, raisins and bread crumbs. Add the salt to the egg whites and beat them to a stiff froth. Fold them lightly into the first mixture. Bake the pudding in a greased baking dish in a moderate oven 325°. Serve it hot or cold with cream or with whipped cream.

QUEEN OF PUDDINGS

2 cups milk   Grated rind of ½ lemon
½ cup sugar   2 egg yolks
⅛ teaspoon salt   ½ teaspoon vanilla
1 tablespoon butter   1 cup bread crumbs

Scald the milk, add the sugar, salt, butter and lemon rind. Pour this mixture over the egg yolks and beat them well. Add the vanilla and the bread crumbs and place these ingredients in a buttered baking dish set in a pan of hot water. Bake the pudding in a moderate oven 325° until it is firm. Cool it slightly, cover the top with dabs of jelly and a meringue made with 2 egg whites. See Page 215. Bake the pudding in a moderate oven 300° until the meringue is set.

Rice Puddings

MILK RICE

See Milk Rice—Page 44. Serve the rice with cinnamon, sugar and cream, or with Caramel Sauce—Page 323.

RICE PUDDING

2 cups boiled rice
1⅓ cups milk
2 eggs
⅛ teaspoon salt
¼ cup sugar (scant)
1 tablespoon soft butter

1 teaspoon vanilla
⅓ cup raisins (optional)
1 teaspoon lemon juice,
  (optional)
Lemon rind (optional)

Cook the rice—Page 44, (2nd method). Combine the milk, with the rest of the ingredients and pour them over the rice. Mix them well with a fork. Grease a baking dish and cover the bottom and sides with bread crumbs. Put the rice in it and cover the top with bread crumbs. Bake the pudding in a moderate oven 325° until it is set. Serve it hot or cold.

CARAMEL RICE PUDDING

2 egg yolks
1⅓ cups milk
1 cup brown sugar
⅛ teaspoon salt

2 cups cooked rice—See
  Page 44, (2nd Method)
1 teaspoon vanilla

Beat the yolks and combine them with the other ingredients in the order given. Place them in a buttered baking dish and bake the pudding set in a dish of hot water in a moderate oven 325° until it is firm. If desired, cool the pudding and top it with a Meringue—Page 215.

RICE BUTTERSCOTCH—Without Eggs

⅓ cup rice

2 cups scalded milk

Place these ingredients in a double boiler and cook them until the rice is nearly tender, stirring them several times.

Prepare a syrup of:
1 cup brown sugar

¼ teaspoon salt
2 tablespoons butter

Cook these ingredients until they are thick. Add them to the rice and cook it until it is tender. Place the pudding in individual molds, chill, unmold them and serve them with cream.

Cornstarch Puddings

CORNSTARCH BLANC MANGE

When carefully prepared and thoroughly chilled, this simple pudding is delicious:

3 cups milk
4 tablespoons cornstarch
4 tablespoons sugar

1 egg
¼ teaspoon salt
½ teaspoon vanilla

Reserve ¾ cup of the milk and scald the remaining milk. To the reserved milk add 2 tablespoons of sugar, the salt and the cornstarch. Combine this with the hot milk, stirring it constantly over a very low fire, or in a double boiler, until it thickens. Beat the egg with 2 tablespoons of sugar. Pour the hot mixture over the egg and return it to the fire for a minute or two, stirring it constantly until the egg thickens, then remove it from the fire. When cool, add the vanilla and chill the pudding. Serve it with crushed fruit, or fruit sauce, preferably a good brand of canned loganberries, strained.

CARAMEL PUDDING

1 cup sugar	⅛ teaspoon salt
2 cups milk	2 egg yolks
2 tablespoons cornstarch	1 teaspoon vanilla
1 tablespoon butter	

Place the sugar in a skillet over a quick fire. Permit it to melt and to burn slightly. Heat 1¾ cups of the milk and add it to the sugar. Stir this until the sugar is dissolved, then add the cornstarch, which has been stirred until smooth with ¼ cup of the milk. Reduce the heat to a low flame, or place the liquid in a double boiler. Stir it constantly until it boils and thickens, then add the salt and the butter. Pour this over the lightly beaten egg yolks, return it to the fire and cook it very slowly, stirring it constantly until it thickens, for about 2 minutes. Do not let it boil. Cool the pudding, add the vanilla, then chill it well, or cover the pudding with Meringue—Page 215 and bake it in a moderate oven 300° until the meringue is set. Serve it with cream. The egg whites, whipped until they are stiff, may be folded into the pudding after the vanilla has been added. This makes a very creamy pudding that freezes well in a refrigerator tray.

ROTHE GRUETZE
Fruit and Farina or Cornstarch Pudding

This good German pudding is usually made with raspberry juice, but other fruit juices may be substituted:

2 cups fruit juice, sweetened	½ cup farina
⅛ teaspoon salt	

Boil the fruit juice and add the salt. Add the farina and stir it until it thickens, or if using cornstarch instead of farina, take:

2 cups fruit juice, sweetened	2 tablespoons cornstarch
⅛ teaspoon salt	

Moisten the cornstarch with a little cold fruit juice. Boil the remaining fruit juice, add the salt and the dissolved cornstarch and cook this until it thickens. Serve the pudding made either with farina, or cornstarch, very cold with cream.

Fruit Puddings

APPLE SAUCE PUDDING

The following recipe calls for fresh or canned apple sauce. Canned apple sauce is recommended, thanks to which the pudding is very quickly made.

3 cups sweetened apple
  sauce
3 egg yolks

¼ teaspoon almond extract
  (optional)

Meringue:

3 egg whites
⅛ teaspoon salt

6 tablespoons sugar
½ teaspoon vanilla

Beat the egg yolks, add the apple sauce and the flavoring and beat the mixture well. Place it in the bottom of a baking dish. Make the Meringue—Page 215, and pile it on top of the pudding. Set the dish in a pan of hot water and bake the pudding in a slow oven 300° until the meringue is set. Serve the pudding hot, or chill it thoroughly and serve it with cream.

APPLE PUDDING

1 egg
¾ cup sugar
1 tablespoon flour
1 tablespoon baking powder

½ cup nut meats, chopped
4 medium sized tart apples,
  peeled and diced
1 teaspoon vanilla

Cream the egg and the sugar and combine the remaining ingredients in the order given. Bake the pudding in a moderate oven 325° until the apples are done (about ½ hour). Serve it cold with cream.

BROWN BETTY
6 Servings

1 teaspoon grated lemon rind
¾ cup brown sugar
¼ teaspoon cinnamon
¼ teaspoon nutmeg
¼ teaspoon salt
1½ cups bread crumbs
2½ cups pared, cored and

diced apples
¾ cup currants, washed
  and drained
2 tablespoons or more butter
3 tablespoons lemon juice
¼ cup water

Grate the lemon rind onto the sugar. Combine the sugar, the spices and the salt. Arrange the bread crumbs, the apples, the currants and the sugar in alternate layers, beginning in the order given and reserving some crumbs for the top. Dot each layer with butter and pour the combined liquids over the whole. Cover the top with the reserved crumbs and dot them with butter. Bake the pudding in a moderate oven 375°.

DATE PUDDING
8 Servings

3 egg whites	1 cup dates seeded and
1/8 teaspoon salt	chopped
3 egg yolks	1 teaspoon vanilla
1 cup sugar	2 tablespoons milk
1 cup pecan meats, chopped	1/2 teaspoon baking powder
1/4 cup black walnut meats,	1/2 teaspoon flour
chopped	

Add the salt to the egg whites and whip them until they are stiff. Fold in the remaining ingredients. Bake the pudding in a greased baking dish, set in a pan of hot water in a slow oven 325° for one-half hour. Serve it with whipped cream.

Baked Puddings

COTTAGE PUDDING

1/4 cup butter	2 teaspoons baking powder
1/2 cup sugar	1/4 teaspoon salt
1 egg	1/2 cup milk
1 1/2 cups bread flour	

Cream the butter and the sugar, beat in the egg, and add the flour that has been sifted with the baking powder and the salt, alternately with the milk. Beat the batter well and pour it into a greased shallow pan. Bake it in a hot oven 400° for 25 minutes, cut it into squares and serve it with crushed fruit, stewed fruit, or hard sauce.

INDIAN PUDDING
8 Servings

4 cups milk	1 teaspoon salt
1/3 cup cornmeal	1 teaspoon ginger
1/3 cup dark molasses	1 cup of milk
1/4 cup sugar	

Cook four cups of milk and the cornmeal in a double boiler for 20 minutes, then add the next five ingredients. Place them in a greased baking dish and cook them in a slow oven—325° for three hours. After two hours' cooking, stir in 1 cup of milk. Serve the pudding hot with cream.

Sweet Soufflés

CHOCOLATE SOUFFLÉ

1 cup milk	3 egg yolks
1 square chocolate	1 teaspoon vanilla
2 tablespoons butter	3 egg whites
1 tablespoon flour	1/8 teaspoon salt
1/3 cup sugar	

Heat the milk, but do not boil it. Cut the chocolate into pieces, melt it in the milk, and remove it from the fire. Melt the butter in a pan, add the flour, stir it until it is blended, then add the hot milk and chocolate mixture. When this is smooth, add the sugar, stir it until it is dissolved, then pour part of the hot liquid over the lightly beaten egg yolks. Reduce the heat to a low flame and return all the sauce to the pan. Permit it to thicken for about two minutes, stirring it constantly. Cool the sauce and add the vanilla. Add the salt to the egg whites and beat them until they are stiff. Fold them lightly into the chocolate mixture and pour the soufflé into a buttered baking dish. Place the dish in a pan of hot water in a moderate oven —325°—for about 30 minutes, or until the soufflé is set. Serve the soufflé hot with cream, or with Vanilla Sauce—Page 325.

LEMON SOUFFLÉ

4 egg yolks	1/2 cup nut meats, chopped, (optional)
1 cup sugar	1/8 teaspoon salt
Grated rind and juice of 1 lemon	4 egg whites

Beat the yolks until they are light, add the sugar slowly and beat them until they are creamy. Add the lemon juice and rind and the nut meats. Place the egg whites in a separate bowl, add the salt and beat them until they are stiff. Fold them lightly into the yolk mixture and place the batter in a baking dish set in a pan of hot water. Bake the soufflé in a moderate oven 325° until it is firm—about 30 minutes.

VANILLA NUT SOUFFLÉ

3 egg yolks
¾ cup sugar
½ cup pecans or almonds,
  ground

1 teaspoon vanilla
3 egg whites
⅛ teaspoon salt

Add the sugar to the yolks and cream them well. Add the vanilla and the pecans. Add the salt to the egg whites, beat them until they are stiff and fold them into the yolk mixture. Bake the soufflé set in a pan of hot water in a moderate oven — 325° — until it is firm. Serve it hot or cold with cream, or whipped cream.

PINEAPPLE SOUFFLÉ

6 Servings

1 cup sugar
½ cup butter
5 egg yolks
4 tablespoons bread crumbs

1 cup crushed pineapple,
  drained
⅛ teaspoon salt
3 egg whites

Cream the butter and the sugar and add the remaining ingredients in the order given, adding the salt to the egg whites and whipping them until they are stiff.

Place the soufflé in a baking dish and cover it with a meringue made with two egg whites — See Page 215. Bake the soufflé set in a pan of hot water in a moderate oven 325° for about 30 minutes. Serve it with cream, whipped cream or Pineapple Cream Sauce — Page 207.

PRUNE SOUFFLÉ

4 to 6 Servings

1 cup of thick prune pulp,
  (stewed, sweetened prunes,
  strained)
5 egg whites

⅛ teaspoon salt
¼ teaspoon cream of tartar
½ cup nut meats, broken or
  chopped (optional)

If there are no stewed, sweetened prunes on hand, soak and stew ½ pound of prunes. ½ cup of sugar may be added to the prunes, or it may be folded into the beaten whites. Remove the seeds from the stewed prunes and strain the pulp. Add the salt to the egg whites and beat them until they are mushy, add the cream of tartar and beat them until they are stiff. Fold in the prune pulp and the nuts. Bake the whip in a baking dish set in a pan of hot water in a slow oven — 275° — until it is firm (about one hour). Serve it hot or cold, preferably the former, with cream, or with custard sauce. 1/2 teaspoonful of lemon juice may be used in place of the cream of tartar. Add it to the prune pulp.

APRICOT SOUFFLÉ

Follow the recipe and rule for Prune Soufflé, substituting 1 cup of apricot pulp (stewed, sweetened apricots that have been put through a strainer, or ricer) for the prune pulp.

DATE SOUFFLÉ

Soak 1/2 pound of dates in water to cover, for two hours. Stew them until they are soft. Remove the seeds and put the dates through a ricer. There should be about 1 cup of pulp. Add 1/2 cup of sugar to the pulp, or fold it into the stiffly beaten egg whites. Follow the rule for Prune Soufflé.

MACAROON SOUFFLÉ

12 macaroons	1/2 teaspoon vanilla
1 cup milk	1/8 teaspoon salt
3 egg yolks	3 egg whites

Scald the milk and pour it slowly over the macaroons. Beat the egg yolks, combine them with the soaked macaroons and cook the mixture in a double boiler until it is thick. Cool it and add the vanilla. Add the salt to the egg whites, whip them until they are stiff and fold them into the custard. Place the soufflé in a buttered baking dish set in a pan of hot water in a moderate oven 325° for about 35 minutes. Serve it hot from the baking dish with cream, or invert the contents of the dish onto a plate, garnish the soufflé with candied fruit and serve it hot with whipped cream.

ENGLISH ALMOND SOUFFLÉ
8 Servings

8 egg yolks	1/2 pound almonds, blanched
2/3 cup sugar	and ground
2 teaspoons grated lemon	8 egg whites
rind	1/8 teaspoon salt

Beat the yolks until they are light, add the sugar slowly and beat the mixture well. Fold in the lemon rind and the almonds. Add the salt to the egg whites and beat them until they are stiff. Fold them into the yolk mixture. Place the batter in a greased baking dish set in a pan of hot water and bake it in a slow oven 325° until it is firm. Serve it hot or cold with the following:

Sauce:

½ cup sugar	2 teaspoons lemon juice
2 teaspoons grated lemon rind	½ cup water
	3 eggs well beaten

Cook these ingredients in a double boiler until they are thick and frothy, stirring them with a wire whisk. ½ cup of wine may be substituted for the water.

Sweet Omelets

OMELET SOUFFLÉ

2 egg yolks	4 egg whites
¼ cup powdered sugar	⅛ teaspoon salt
½ teaspoon vanilla	

Beat the yolks and add the sugar slowly. Beat this well and add the vanilla. Add the salt to the egg whites and beat them until they are stiff, then fold the yolk mixture into them. Melt ½ tablespoon of butter in an omelet pan over a slow fire. Pour the omelet into the pan, cover it with a lid and cook it over a slow fire until it is done underneath. Slash across it several times with a knife, permitting the heat to penetrate the slight crust at the bottom. Fold over the omelet, which should be soft to the inside, and sprinkle it with powdered sugar. It may be served with jelly or preserves.

RUM SOUFFLÉ

Follow the rule for Omelet Soufflé, adding one tablespoon of rum to the yolk mixture.

CARAMEL ALMOND OMELET

3 egg yolks	3 egg whites
3 tablespoons caramel sauce	¼ cup blanched, shredded almonds
½ teaspoon vanilla	
⅛ teaspoon salt	

Beat the yolks and add the caramel sauce and the vanilla. Add the salt to the egg whites, beat them to a stiff froth and fold the yolk mixture into them. Melt 2 teaspoons of butter in a skillet over a low flame. Cover the bottom of the pan with the almonds and pour the omelet over them. Follow the rule for cooking Omelet Soufflé. Serve the omelet with:

Caramel Sauce:

1 cup sugar   ¾ cup hot water

Melt the sugar in an iron skillet, add the hot water and let the syrup simmer for 10 minutes.

Steamed Puddings

RULE FOR STEAMING PUDDINGS

Place the pudding in a well greased pudding mold, in individual cups made for this purpose, or in a tin receptacle having a tightly fitted lid. (A baking powder can may be used). Fill the mold or molds two-thirds full. Place the receptacle in a steamer over boiling water, or place it on a rack in a kettle of boiling water. Keep the water boiling and do not jar the kettle. Do not permit the water to diminish to any great extent. Add boiling water so that more than one-half of the mold is immersed all the time. This will insure a light, well cooked pudding.

STEAMED RAISIN PUFF

½ cup butter   3 teaspoons baking powder
3 tablespoons sugar   1 cup milk
2 eggs   1 cup chopped raisins
2 cups flour

Combine the ingredients in the order given, cream the butter and the sugar, beat in the egg, sift the flour with the baking powder and add it alternately with the milk. Add the raisins last. Steam the pudding for one hour. See the rule for Steaming Puddings—Page 309. Serve it hot with Hard Sauce or Lemon Sauce—Page 322 or 324.

STEAMED BREAD PUDDING

½ cup bread soaked in water   1 egg
    (enough water to make   ½ teaspoon cloves
    it moist)   ¼ teaspoon cinnamon
¼ cup sour milk   ½ teaspoon soda
¼ cup butter (scant)   Flour to make a stiff batter
½ cup sugar   1 teaspoon baking powder,
½ cup seeded raisins   sifted with the flour
½ cup currants

Cream the butter and the sugar and beat in the egg. Sift the flour with the baking powder and soda and add it alternately with the sour milk. Then add the bread and the other ingredients. Steam the pudding for one hour. See rule for Steaming Puddings — Page 309. Serve it hot with hard sauce, or other pudding sauce.

STEAMED DATE PUDDING

1 cup chopped dates	1¼ cups flour
¼ cup butter	4 teaspoons baking powder
1 cup brown sugar	½ teaspoon salt
1 egg beaten	1 cup milk
½ teaspoon vanilla	1 cup broken nut meats

Cream the butter and the sugar, add the beaten egg, the vanilla and then the combined and sifted dry ingredients, alternately with the milk, last add the nut meats and dates. Steam the pudding in a mold for two hours and serve it hot with Foamy Sauce — Page 323.

STEAMED APPLE PUDDING—English Bachelor's Pudding

2 apples, pared, cored and chopped	4 tablespoons sugar
¼ cup bread crumbs	3 egg yolks
4 tablespoons currants, washed and dried	1 teaspoon lemon juice
	⅛ teaspoon salt
	3 egg whites

Combine the ingredients in the order given, adding the salt to the egg whites and beating them until they are stiff. Place the batter in a buttered, closely covered mold and steam the pudding for 3 hours. Serve it with Hard or Lemon Sauce — Page 322 or 324.

STEAMED CHOCOLATE PUDDING

1 egg	2 ounces chocolate, melted and cooled
½ cup sugar	⅛ teaspoon salt
½ cup milk	1 tablespoon butter, melted and cooled
1 cup flour	
1 teaspoon baking powder	
1 tablespoon jelly	

Beat the egg and add the remaining ingredients in the order given. Mix them thoroughly and beat them well. Pour the batter into a greased pudding mold and steam the pudding in boiling water for 1 hour. See Rule for Steaming Puddings — Page 309. Serve the pudding hot with Hard Sauce — Page 322.

STEAMED CARAMEL PUDDING

This is a delicious company pudding:

7 tablespoons sugar	1 cup almonds, ground
1 cup hot milk	(unblanched)
1/4 cup butter	1 teaspoon vanilla
1 tablespoon flour	1/8 teaspoon salt
6 egg yolks	6 egg whites

Melt the sugar in an iron skillet, when it is light brown add the milk very slowly. Cool this mixture. Cream the butter, add the egg yolks, the flour, the vanilla and the almonds. Fold in the whites of the eggs, to which the salt has been added and which have been whipped until they are stiff. Butter a mold and sprinkle it with sugar. Pour in the batter, cover it closely and steam it for 1 hour. Serve the pudding with whipped cream.

PLUM PUDDING

1 pound suet, chopped	1/2 tablespoon mace
1 pound seeded raisins	1 teaspoon salt
1 pound currants, washed	7 egg yolks
and dried	6 tablespoons sugar
1/2 pound citron, chopped	4 tablespoons cream
1 cup flour	1/2 cup brandy or sherry
1 nutmeg, grated	3 cups grated bread crumbs
1 tablespoon cinnamon	7 egg whites, stiffly beaten

1/2 cup orange juice and 2 tablespoons grated orange rind may be substituted for the brandy.

Prepare the first four ingredients and dredge them with the flour. And the remaining ingredients in the order given. Place the batter in a greased mold and steam the pudding for 6 hours. Serve it with:

Sauce:

1 cup sugar	1/8 teaspoon salt
1/2 cup butter	5 tablespoons wine
2 eggs	

Cook these ingredients in a double boiler until they are thick.

Gelatine Puddings

LEMON JELLY
4 Servings

Follow the same rule for making Lemon and Orange Jelly:

1½ tablespoons gelatine
¼ cup cold water
2 cups boiling water
¾ cup sugar

¼ teaspoon salt
½ cup lemon juice
Grated rind of 1 lemon,
(optional)

ORANGE JELLY
4 Servings

1½ tablespoons gelatine
¼ cup cold water
½ cup boiling water
½ cup sugar
¼ teaspoon salt

6 tablespoons lemon juice
1½ cups orange juice
Grated rind of 1 orange,
(optional)

Soak the gelatine in the cold water for five minutes. Dissolve it in the boiling water, add the remaining ingredients and chill the jelly until it is firm.

LEMON OR ORANGE JELLY WITH FRUIT

To mold fruits into lemon or orange jelly, chill the gelatine until it is nearly set (when it falls in sheets from a spoon). Combine it with 3 cups of cooked or raw fruits that have been well drained.

Note: Fresh pineapple must be boiled before it is added to a gelatine mixture.

PINEAPPLE JELLY
8 Servings

2 tablespoons gelatine
1 cup cold water
1½ cups hot pineapple juice
1 cup boiling water
¾ cup sugar

3 tablespoons lemon juice
1 large can shredded pineapple (No. 2), drained
⅛ teaspoon salt

Soak the gelatine in the cold water for five minutes, add the hot pineapple juice, the boiling water and the sugar and stir these ingredients until the gelatine and the sugar are dissolved. Chill the gelatine and when it is about to set (when it falls in sheets from a spoon), add the pineapple and the lemon juice. Chill the jelly and serve it with cream, or custard sauce.

FRUIT GELATINE
12 Servings

2 tablespoons gelatine
2 bananas, riced
1 cup canned apricots, (No. 2½) riced
2 oranges, rind and juice

2 lemons, rind and juice
2 cups water (part apricot juice)
1 cup sugar

Grate the orange and lemon rind onto the sugar. Soak the gelatine in ½ cup of the cold water. Make a syrup of the remaining water and the sugar. Dissolve the soaked gelatine in it and combine all the ingredients. Chill them until they are set, and serve them with cream. For invalids, omit the banana. This same recipe is used for Fruit Ice. Follow the recipe if the ice is to be placed in an electric refrigerator. Omit the gelatine, if it is to be frozen in an ice cream freezer.

Fruit Whips

FRUIT WHIP—Gelatine
6 to 8 Servings

1 scant tablespoon gelatine
¼ cup cold water
¼ cup boiling water
1 scant cup sugar

1 lemon, rind and juice
1 cup crushed or riced fruit
⅛ teaspoon salt
4 egg whites

Grate the lemon rind into the sugar. Soak the gelatine for five minutes in the cold water, dissolve it in the boiling water, add the sugar and when it is dissolved remove the gelatine from the fire. Add the lemon juice and the crushed fruit. Place the saucepan in ice water and when the gelatine is cool, whip it with a wire whisk until it is frothy. Add the salt to the egg whites and beat them until they are stiff. Combine them with the gelatine mixture and whip the sponge until it holds its shape. Chill it and serve it with cream. Use cooked prunes, apricots, apples, crushed strawberries, raspberries, canned pineapple, etc. alone, or combined with other fruits. If used alone, add 1 teaspoon of vanilla.

CHERRY WHIP

1 quart cherries, stoned
1 cup sugar

⅓ cup water

Make a syrup of the sugar and water. Drop the cherries into it and cook them until they are soft (about 3 minutes). Drain the cherries, keeping the juice:

| 1 tablespoon gelatine | ⅛ teaspoon salt |
| 2 tablespoons cold water | 3 egg whites |

Soak the gelatine in the water and dissolve it in 1 cup of hot cherry juice. Place this mixture in a bowl and set the bowl in ice water. When the mixture is cool, whip it until it is fluffy. Add the salt to the egg whites, whip them until they are stiff and fold them into the gelatine mixture. Pour this into a mold, alternating it wth layers of cooked and drained cherries. Chill the pudding until it is set, and serve it with cream, or cherry sauce.

ORANGE WHIP

The following recipe is a delicious winter dessert. As it is light and refreshing it is good after a heavy meat course. It varies with the quality of the orange juice used.

1½ tablespoons gelatine	5 egg whites
¼ cup cold water	⅛ teaspoon salt
¼ cup boiling water	¾ cup sugar
1½ tablespoons lemon juice	5 egg yolks
¾ cup orange juice	

Soak the gelatine in the cold water for five minutes. Dissolve it in the boiling water. Add the fruit juice and chill this mixture until it is about to set. Add the salt to the egg whites and whip them to a stiff froth. Add the gelatine slowly and then the sugar, one-half the amount at a time, beating the eggs constantly. When the mixture begins to thicken, fold in the egg yolks. Chill the pudding and serve it with cream.

EGGLESS PRUNE WHIP

The following dish has the double barreled virtue of being both good and cheap:

2 tablespoons gelatine	1 cup sugar
½ pound prunes, stewed	½ lemon sliced, (optional)
and riced	1 stick cinnamon (optional)

Soak the prunes in 2 cups of cold water for 12 hours. Add the sugar, the lemon and the cinnamon and stew the prunes gently until they are tender. Drain them, saving the juice. Remove the seeds and put the prunes through a ricer. Soak the gelatine in ½ cup of cold prune juice for five minutes, dissolve it in 1 cup of hot prune juice. Chill the gelatine mixture. When it is cold, whip it with a wire whisk until it is fluffy. Fold in the prune pulp and place the whip on ice until it is well chilled. Serve it with cream, whipped cream or Custard Sauce—Page 323.

EGGLESS APRICOT WHIP

Follow the Rule for Eggless Prune Whip, omit the cinnamon and substitute dried apricots for the prunes.

Sponge Puddings

SNOW PUDDING

A Fine Summer Dessert

1 tablespoon gelatine	1/4 cup sugar
1/4 cup cold water	1/4 teaspoon salt
1 cup boiling water	3 egg whites
1/4 cup lemon juice	

Soak the gelatine in the cold water for five minutes, and dissolve it in the boiling water, add the lemon juice and the sugar and chill this mixture until it is about to set. Add the salt to the egg whites, beat them to a stiff froth and combine them with the lemon jelly. Continue beating until the pudding holds its shape, then place it on ice and serve it very cold with:

Custard Sauce:

2 cups milk	2 or 3 egg yolks
1/4 cup sugar	1 teaspoon vanilla
1/8 teaspoon salt	

Follow the rule for Boiled Custard—Page 297.

MARSHMALLOW PUDDING
6 to 8 Servings

The following pudding named for its marshmallow-like consistency is very quickly made:

1 1/2 tablespoons gelatine	4 egg whites
1/2 cup cold water	1 teaspoon vanilla
1/2 cup boiling water	1 cup sugar
1/8 teaspoon salt	

Soak the gelatine for five minutes in the cold water and dissolve it in the boiling water. Add the salt to the egg whites and whip them until they hold a point, then add the first mixture, which has been cooled, in a slow stream. Add the sugar one-half a cup at a time, beating constantly. Add the vanilla and beat the pudding until it thickens. Chill it and serve it with Custard Sauce—Page 315, to which a little Sherry may be added, or with crushed fruit.

APRICOT SPONGE

½ pound apricots	2 cups cold water

Wash the apricots, cover them with the water and permit them to soak for 12 hours or more. Bring them slowly to the boiling point and simmer them until tender. Drain the fruit and put it through a ricer. Save the juice, but do not combine the pulp and the juice:

1 cup apricot pulp	3 tablespoons lemon juice
1 cup apricot juice	⅛ teaspoon salt
1½ tablespoons gelatine	4 egg whites
¼ cup sugar	

Soak the gelatine for five minutes in one-half of the apricot juice. Boil the other half of the apricot juice with the sugar and the lemon juice. When the sugar is dissolved, add the soaked gelatine. When the gelatine is dissolved, add this liquid to the apricot pulp. Chill the mixture until it is about to set. Add the salt to the egg whites and whip them to a stiff froth, then fold in the apricot jelly. Chill the pudding well and serve it with cream, or Boiled Custard — Page 297.

CHOCOLATE SPONGE

1 tablespoon gelatine	⅛ teaspoon salt
¼ cup cold water	1 teaspoon vanilla
¼ cup boiling water	2 tablespoons cocoa
⅓ cup sugar	3 egg whites

Soak the gelatine in the cold water for five minutes and dissolve it in the boiling water. Add the sugar, salt and cocoa and stir and cook them until they are dissolved. Place the saucepan containing this mixture in cold water. When the mixture is cool, add the vanilla and beat the jelly until it is fluffy. Beat the egg whites in a separate bowl until they are stiff, add them to the mixture and beat the sponge until it holds its shape. Chill the pudding well and serve it with cream, or Boiled Custard — Page 297.

MOCHA SPONGE I.

1 tablespoon gelatine	Juice of ½ lemon (small)
¼ cup cold water	⅛ teaspoon salt
1⅓ cups strong coffee	2 egg whites
¾ cup sugar	

Soak the gelatine in the cold water for five minutes. Dissolve it in the boiling coffee, add the sugar and the lemon juice and stir the mixture over heat until the sugar is dissolved. Strain this into a pan and set the pan in ice water. Cool it slightly and beat it with a wire whisk until it is fluffy. Add the salt to the egg whites and beat them (in a separate bowl) until they are stiff. Combine them with the coffee mixture and continue beating until the sponge holds its shape. Chill it well and serve it with cream.

MOCHA SPONGE II.

1 tablespoon gelatine	1/2 cup sugar (generous)
1/4 cup water	3 eggs
1 1/2 cups coffee	1/4 teaspoon salt
1/2 cup milk	1/2 teaspoon vanilla

Soak the gelatine in the water for ten minutes. Combine the coffee, the milk, one-half the sugar and the soaked gelatine. Place these ingredients in a sauce pan over a very low flame. Beat the egg yolks with the remaining sugar and add the salt. Pour part of the hot milk mixture over them, then return all of the mixture to the sauce pan, and cook and stir it for a minute longer—until the yolks are slightly thickened. Do not let it boil at any time. Remove it from the fire and chill it in ice water. When it is thick, whip the mixture with a wire whisk until it is fluffy. Then fold in the stiffly beaten whites of 3 eggs. Place the sponge in a mold and chill it well. Serve it with cream. This is delicious frozen in a refrigerator tray. If it is to be used in this way, take 3/4 cup of sugar.

Macaroon Puddings

NESSELRODE PUDDING

12 Servings

2 tablespoons gelatine	3 tablespoons ground almonds
1 cup cold water	1/4 pound ground macaroons
2 cups milk scalded	1 tablespoon brandy
2/3 cup sugar	2 teaspoons vanilla
5 egg yolks, beaten to a cream	1/8 teaspoon salt
2/3 cup raisins chopped	5 egg whites

Soak the gelatine in the cold water, for five minutes. Scald the milk in a double boiler. Stir in the sugar and the egg yolks and cook the custard for one minute, permitting the yolks to thicken. Add the soaked gelatine and the raisins, almonds and macaroons. Remove the mixture from the fire and cool it. When it is cool, add the flavoring and fold in the whites of eggs, to which the salt has been added, and which have been whipped to a stiff froth. Place the pudding in a wet mold, chill it well, invert the contents of the mold onto a platter and garnish the pudding with cherries (optional) and whipped cream.

CABINET PUDDING
6 Servings

1 tablespoon gelatine	1/8 teaspoon salt
1/4 cup cold water	1 teaspoon vanilla
2 cups milk, scalded	1 tablespoon brandy
1/3 cup sugar	6 lady fingers
3 egg yolks	6 macaroons

Soak the gelatine in the water for five minutes. Dissolve it in the hot milk, and add the sugar. Pour this over the beaten egg yolks and beat the ingredients until they are well blended. Place the custard over a very low flame and cook it, stirring it constantly until it is thick and smooth. Cool it, add the salt, the vanilla and the brandy, and chill it. Soak the macaroons in a little brandy. Line a mold with lady fingers, bits of candied cherry, angelica and pineapple (optional). As the custard begins to stiffen, place a layer of custard in the mold, add a few broken macaroons and continue this process, until all the custard and the macaroons have been used. Chill the pudding until it is firm and invert the contents onto a platter, or plate. Serve the pudding with whipped cream, or Cream Sauce:

3/4 cup thick cream	1/2 teaspoon vanilla
1/3 cup powdered sugar	

PEACH PUDDING WITH MACAROONS

1 1/2 tablespoons gelatine	1 cup sugar
1/2 cup cold peach juice	4 egg yolks
1/2 cup boiling peach juice	3/4 pound macaroons, broken
1/8 teaspoon salt	into quarters
4 egg whites	1 cup sliced peaches

Soak the gelatine in the cold peach juice, dissolve it in the boiling peach juice, and cool this mixture. Add the salt to the egg whites and beat them until they are stiff. Add the gelatine in a thin stream, beating the eggs constantly. Add the sugar 1/2 a cup at a time and continue beating until the pudding will holds its shape. Then fold in the egg yolks. Place a layer of pudding in the bottom of a dish, add a layer of macaroons and peaches and cover them with a layer of pudding, continue this process until the ingredients have been used. Chill the pudding well. The pudding may be molded in individual dishes, or placed in sherbet cups. Serve it with whipped cream. The macaroons may be soaked in wine.

Charlottes

CHARLOTTE RUSSE
10 to 12 Servings

2 tablespoons gelatine
1/4 cup cold water
2 cups milk
1/2 cup sugar
2 to 4 egg yolks

1 teaspoon vanilla, or 1
   tablespoon brandy
1/8 teaspoon salt
2 to 4 egg whites
2 cups cream, whipped

Soak the gelatine in the cold water. Scald the milk and pour it over the yolks, which have been beaten with the sugar, add the dissolved gelatine and stir the custard over a very low flame until it begins to thicken. Cool it and add the flavoring. Add the salt to the egg whites, beat them until they are stiff and fold them into the custard. Beat the cream until it is stiff and fold it into the custard. Line a mold with lady fingers, fill it with the custard and chill the pudding thoroughly. Invert the contents of the mold onto a platter and serve the pudding garnished with cherries and whipped cream (optional).

CHOCOLATE CHARLOTTE
6 Servings

1 tablespoon gelatine
1/4 cup cold water
3/4 cup milk
1 ounce chocolate

1 pint double cream
1 egg white
1 cup sugar (scant)
1 tablespoon vanilla

No I. Soak the gelatine in the cold water for five minutes. Heat the milk to the scalding point and dissolve the gelatine and the chocolate in it. Chill the milk mixture and when it begins to thicken fold it into No. II.

No. II. Beat the cream until it is stiff, add the stiffly beaten egg white, the sugar and the vanilla. Combine this with No. I. and pour the mousse into a mold.

Chill, unmold and serve it with cream, or whipped cream.

Uncooked Puddings

DATE LOAF

1/2 pound graham wafers
1/2 pound marshmallows
1/2 pound dates

1/4 pound nut meats, chopped
1/2 cup cream
1 cup whipping cream

Roll the crackers until the crumbs are fine. Cut the dates

and the marshmallows into small pieces. Combine the first five ingredients, shape them into a roll and wrap the roll in waxed paper. Chill it for 12 hours. Serve it cut into slices with whipped cream.

CHOCOLATE WAFERS AND CREAM
4 Servings

5 ounces very thin Chocolate Wafers (Famous Wafers)
1 cup cream, whipped

1/2 teaspoon vanilla
1/2 cup chopped nuts
Chocolate shot (optional)

Place alternate layers of chocolate wafers and whipped cream, flavored with vanilla, and combined with chopped nuts, in a bowl. Chill the mixture well for several hours, invert it onto a platter and cover the whole with chocolate shot (decorettes).

FRENCH CHEESE CREAM
Fromage À la Crème

This very simple dessert is as good as any elaborate concoction I know:

1 cup whipping cream
1/8 teaspoon salt

1 pound cheese (Philadelphia, or other soft cream cheese)

Whip the cream. Soften the cheese, add 2 tablespoonsful of the cream and beat the mixture well, add the salt and fold the mixture into the remaining cream. Line a bowl, or mold, with a piece of cheese cloth, place the cream in it and chill it for several hours until it is the consistency of a soft gelatine pudding. Invert the contents of the mold onto a platter and surround the cream with fresh strawberries, raspberries, or other raw fruit. Serve the cream with powdered sugar to be sprinkled over the fruit.

MACAROON CHARLOTTE
6 Servings

The following white pudding is appropriate at Christmas time garnished with candied cherries:

12 macaroons
1/8 teaspoon salt
2 egg whites
1/4 cup powdered sugar
1/2 teaspoon vanilla

1/4 teaspoon almond extract
1 cup heavy cream
12 lady fingers, or 2 cups of shredded sponge cake

Roll the macaroons until the crumbs are very fine. Add the salt to the egg whites and whip them until they are stiff. Fold in the powdered sugar, the flavoring and the rolled macaroons. Whip the cream and fold it in. Line a mold with the lady fingers, or sponge cake, fill it with the cream and chill the charlotte for 2 hours or more. Invert the contents of the mold onto a plate and garnish the pudding with cherries. This pudding may be made in individual molds, or in paper cups.

STUFFED PEACHES—Fresh or Canned

Peel and halve large firm peaches. Remove the stones and fill the cavities with pieces of marshmallow and with shredded almonds. Chill the fruit and serve it with cream. (If fresh fruit is prepared in advance, wrap it in oiled paper until it is to be served.)

Pudding Sauces

HARD SAUCE

Hard sauce is given different flavors, but its basis is always the same, although its proportions may differ:

2 tablespoons to ¼ cup butter
1 cup powdered sugar, sifted
⅛ teaspoon salt

Flavoring — 1 teaspoon or more vanilla, lemon, orange, coffee, whiskey, brandy, etc.
1 egg (optional)

Cream the butter until it is very soft. Add the sugar gradually, then the salt and beat these ingredients until they have a smooth, soft consistency. Beat in the flavoring and the egg (if desired) and chill the sauce thoroughly.

BROWN SUGAR HARD SAUCE

½ cup butter
1 cup brown sugar
4 tablespoons cream
2 tablespoons wine or 1

teaspoon vanilla
4 tablespoons chopped nuts (optional)

Cream the butter, add the sugar slowly and add the cream and the wine drop by drop in order to prevent the ingredients from separating. Beat the sauce constantly. When it is done, chill it thoroughly.

STRAWBERRY HARD SAUCE

⅓ cup butter
1 cup powdered sugar

⅔ cup strawberries, crushed

Follow the rule for Hard Sauce.

RASPBERRY HARD SAUCE

Follow the rule for Strawberry Hard Sauce, substituting ½ cup crushed raspberries.

BANANA HARD SAUCE

Follow the rule for Strawberry Hard Sauce, substituting ½ cup crushed bananas and adding 1 teaspoon vanilla.

FOAMY SAUCE

5 tablespoons to ½ cup
  butter
1 cup powdered sugar
1 egg yolk

1 teaspoon vanilla, or 2
  tablespoons wine
⅛ teaspoon salt
1 egg white

Cream the butter, add the sugar slowly, the vanilla and the egg yolk. Beat the sauce over hot water until it is smooth, then fold in the stiffly beaten egg white, to which the salt has been added.

CUSTARD SAUCE

Follow the Rule for Boiled Custard — Page 297.

CARAMEL SYRUP

Place 3 cups of sugar in an iron skillet and melt it over a very slow fire. If a strong caramel flavor is desired, the sugar may be burned slightly. Add 3 cups of boiling water gradually to the melted sugar and cook these ingredients until they are the consistency of maple syrup. This syrup may be kept indefinitely in a closed jar.

CARAMEL SAUCE

1 part caramel syrup
2 parts cream or top milk

Vanilla, as desired
⅛ teaspoon salt

HOT CARAMEL SAUCE

1¼ cups sugar
⅓ cup hot cream

½ teaspoon vanilla

Melt the sugar in an iron skillet over a very low fire, stirring it constantly. When it is melted, add the cream very slowly, and stir the sauce until it is smooth. Remove it from the fire and add the vanilla. To keep the sauce hot, place it over hot water. Chopped nuts, or pieces of marshmallow may be added to it.

HOT BROWN SUGAR SAUCE

1 cup brown sugar
½ cup water
1 egg beaten

3 tablespoons lemon juice
⅛ teaspoon salt

Cook the sugar and the water for five minutes and pour the syrup in a fine stream over the egg, beating it constantly. Cook the sauce over hot water for 2 minutes, add the lemon juice and salt, and serve it.

BUTTERSCOTCH SAUCE

1¼ cups brown sugar
⅔ cup corn syrup
4 tablespoons butter

½ cup cream
¼ cup milk

Boil the sugar, syrup and butter to the soft ball stage, then add the cream and milk. Serve the sauce either hot or cold.

GRATED CHOCOLATE OR CHOCOLATE SHOT

Sprinkle grated sweet chocolate, or chocolate shot over desserts, whipped cream or ice cream.

CHOCOLATE SAUCE
6 Servings

1 cup boiling water
½ cup sugar
1 ounce bitter chocolate

⅛ teaspoon salt
½ teaspoon vanilla (added when sauce is cooked)

Cook the sauce slowly until it is the consistency of thin syrup. Cool it slightly and add the vanilla. Do not stir it while it is cooking. Serve either hot or cold. This sauce may be made in a large quantity and kept in the icebox for days ready for use.

CHOCOLATE SAUCE WITH BROWN SUGAR

4 ounces chocolate grated
1 cup brown sugar

½ cup cream

Combine the ingredients and boil them until they are smooth and thick, beating them constantly with a rotary beater, or a wire whisk.

LEMON SAUCE—With Eggs

⅓ cup butter
1 cup sugar
3 egg yolks, beaten

⅓ cup boiling water
3 tablespoons lemon juice
1 teaspoon grated lemon rind

Cream the butter, add the sugar slowly, and the egg yolks. Add the water gradually and cook the sauce over a very low flame, or in a double boiler until it thickens, stirring it constantly. Remove it from the fire and add the lemon rind and juice.

LEMON SAUCE WITH CORNSTARCH

½ cup sugar
1 tablespoon cornstarch
1 cup boiling water
2 tablespoons butter

1½ tablespoons lemon juice
⅛ teaspoon nutmeg
⅛ teaspoon salt

Combine the sugar and the cornstarch and add the water slowly, stirring the sauce constantly. Boil it over a low flame until it thickens (for about five minutes) remove it from the fire and add the remaining ingredients.

VANILLA SAUCE

Follow the rule for Lemon Sauce with cornstarch, substituting 1 teaspoon vanilla for the lemon juice.

ORANGE SAUCE

1 teaspoon grated lemon
   rind
1½ teaspoons lemon juice
½ cup orange juice
5 tablespoons sugar

2 egg yolks, slightly beaten
⅛ teaspoon salt
2 egg whites
1 teaspoon vanilla

Combine the first five ingredients, place them over a low flame and stir them constantly until they are smooth and thick. Remove the sauce from the fire. Add the salt to the egg whites, beat them until they are stiff, fold them into the sauce, cool it and add the vanilla.

FLUFFY STRAWBERRY SAUCE

2 cups ripe strawberries
½ cup powdered sugar

1 teaspoon lemon juice
1 egg white (unbeaten)

Hull the berries and mash them with a silver fork, add the sugar, the lemon juice and the egg white. Whip the sauce with a wire whisk until it is light and fluffy.

FRUIT SAUCE

½ cup sugar
3 tablespoons flour
⅛ teaspoon salt
1 cup sliced peaches, crushed
   fruit, or fruit juice

1 cup water
2 tablespoons butter
1 tablespoon lemon juice
⅛ teaspoon cinnamon or
   nutmeg

Combine the sugar, flour and salt and add the remaining ingredients. Cook them over hot water, stirring them constantly until they are thick and smooth. Serve the sauce hot or cold.

LOGANBERRY OR RASPBERRY JUICE

Add   1 quart of berries and
1 cup of sugar to   2 tablespoons of water

Cook the berries until they are soft. Then strain the juice from them.

CANNED LOGANBERRY OR RASPBERRY JUICE

Strain the juice from canned loganberries, or raspberries.

Ice Creams, Ices and Frozen Desserts

Ice Creams and Ices to be Frozen in an Ice Cream Freezer

RULES FOR MAKING ICE CREAM AND ICES IN A FREEZER

Use cream that is twenty-four hours old, as it makes a finer grain than fresh cream. When it is possible to do so, dissolve the sugar in liquid over heat before adding it to the cream.

Add $\frac{1}{8}$ teaspoonful, or more, of salt to the syrup. Cool the syrup before adding it to the cream. Chill the mixture to be frozen before placing it in the ice cream container.

Fill the ice cream container only three-fourths full to allow for the expansion of the frozen cream.

Allow from three to six measures of ice to one measure of coarse (rock) salt, according to the rapidity with which you wish to freeze the cream. The larger proportion of salt will bring quicker results, but the cream is finer grained when it is frozen slowly. Pack the freezer one-third full of ice before adding any salt, then add the salt and the remaining ice and salt in alternate layers around the container until the freezer is filled.

Turn the cream slowly at first until a slight pull is felt, then turn it rapidly.

If the ice cream is to be used at once, turn it until it is very stiff. If the ice cream is to be packed, turn it only until it is the consistency of thick sauce.

Pour off the salt water in the freezer. Wipe the lid carefully, remove it, remove the dasher, scrape it and pack the cream down with a spoon. Place a heavy piece of waxed paper over the top of the container. Place a cork in the lid, fit it closely on the container and repack the ice cream in additional salt and ice. Cover the freezer with newspapers and a piece of carpet, or other heavy material.

VANILLA ICE CREAM I.

1 quart cream
3/4 cup to 1 cup sugar

1 1/2 teaspoons vanilla
1/8 teaspoon salt

Heat one cup of the cream and dissolve the sugar in it. Cool it, add the remaining ingredients and freeze the cream.

VANILLA ICE CREAM WITH EGGS

3/4 cup sugar
1 1/2 cups milk
2 to 3 egg yolks

1/8 teaspoon salt
1 tablespoon vanilla
2 cups cream, whipped

Dissolve the sugar in the milk over a low flame. When the milk is scalded, pour it over the egg yolks, beat the mixture well and cook it slowly, stirring it constantly until it is thick and smooth, or cook it in a double boiler. Chill the custard, add the salt, the vanilla and the whipped cream and freeze it.

CARAMEL ICE CREAM

See the Rule for Caramel Syrup—Page 323. Add 2 tablespoons or more of caramel syrup to every quart of Vanilla Ice Cream mixture and freeze the cream.

CHOCOLATE ICE CREAM

1 1/2 squares chocolate, or
  1/4 cup cocoa
1 cup sugar
1/2 cup hot water

1/4 teaspoon salt
1 tablespoon vanilla
1 quart thin cream

Melt the chocolate and add the sugar, the salt and the hot water. Chill this mixture, flavor it, add it to the cream and freeze it.

COFFEE ICE CREAM

3 cups milk
1 1/2 cups sugar
2 eggs beaten
3 tablespoons very strong

boiled coffee
1/2 teaspoon salt
1 cup cream—beaten

328

Scald the milk, add the sugar and pour this mixture over the eggs. Cook the custard over a very slow fire, or cook it in a double boiler, stirring it constantly until it is thick. Add the coffee and the salt. Cool the mixture, add the beaten cream and freeze it.

PISTACHIO ICE CREAM

This makes a pretty Christmas dessert served with a meringue tart, whipped cream and cherries:

Vanilla Ice Cream
4 ounces pistachio nuts
1/4 cup sugar
1/4 cup cream

A few drops of rose water
1 teaspoon vanilla
1/2 teaspoon almond extract

Shell the nuts and blanch them like almonds. Pound them in a mortar with the rose water, and add the cream and the sugar. Follow the rule for Vanilla Ice Cream, using 1/4 cup of sugar less than the recipe calls for, and add the pistachio mixture. Color the ice cream pale green and freeze it.

MOCK PISTACHIO ICE CREAM

Add 1 tablespoon vanilla, 1 teaspoon almond extract and green coloring to Vanilla Ice Cream.

PEPPERMINT ICE CREAM

1/2 pound peppermint sticks
2 cups milk

2 cups cream

Grind or crush the candy and soak it in the milk for 12 hours. Combine the milk and the cream and freeze the mixture.

STRAWBERRY ICE CREAM I.

7/8 cup sugar
1 quart strawberries

1 quart cream

Hull the berries, crush them, add the sugar and chill them thoroughly. Combine them with the cream and freeze the mixture.

PEACH ICE CREAM

4 pounds ripe peaches
1 cup sugar

1 quart cream
1 teaspoon vanilla

Pare, slice and mash the peaches. Add 1/2 of the sugar, cover the peaches and permit them to stand until the sugar is dissolved. Add the vanilla and the remaining half of the sugar to the cream. Half freeze this mixture, then add the sweetened peach pulp and freeze the cream.

APRICOT ICE CREAM

For fresh Apricot Ice Cream follow the rule for Peach Ice Cream, substituting apricots for peaches.

DRIED APRICOT ICE CREAM

2 cups apricot pulp (½
  pound apricots)
1 to 1¼ cups sugar

2 tablespoons lemon juice
1 quart cream

Cook the apricots as directed on Page 163. Put them through a ricer. Cool the pulp, add the lemon juice and the cream and freeze the mixture.

BANANA ICE CREAM

Partially freeze Vanilla Ice Cream and add:

1 cup banana pulp
½ cup lemon juice

⅛ teaspoon salt

Stir these ingredients until they are blended with the cream and freeze the mixture.

ANGELICA I.

1 cup sugar
¾ cup water
3 egg whites

1 pint heavy cream
1 teaspoon vanilla

Boil the sugar and the water until the syrup threads—See Page 323. Pour it slowly over the stiffly beaten egg whites and continue to beat the mixture until it is cool. Fold in the stiffly beaten cream and the vanilla and freeze the mixture. This recipe may be made with only 1 cup of cream.

MACAROON ICE CREAM

1 cup crushed macaroons
  (12 macaroons)
1 cup cream
¼ teaspoon salt

¾ cup sugar
1 tablespoon vanilla
3 cups cream

Combine the macaroons with the cup of cream, add the salt

and the sugar and heat these ingredients until the sugar is dissolved. Chill them, add the remaining ingredients and freeze the cream.

FROZEN EGG NOG

2 cups milk	1 teaspoon vanilla
1 cup sugar	1 pint double cream
4 egg yolks	

Cook the milk with the sugar over a slow fire until it is scalded. Pour it over the beaten egg yolks, beat the mixture well and return it to the fire. Stir it constantly until it is smooth and thick, but do not let it boil. Chill the custard, add the vanilla and partially freeze the mixture. Remove the dasher, add the whipped cream and finish freezing the mixture. See Page 327 for packing the ice cream. When ready to serve it make a funnel shaped hole in the center, fill it with several tablespoons of whiskey, brandy, or rum and stir it into the ice cream.

MARSHMALLOW NUT MOUSSE

1 pint double cream	flavoring
⅔ cup powdered sugar	½ cup pecans
(scant)	¼ pound marshmallows
2 teaspoons vanilla	cut in pieces
2 tablespoons caramel	

Whip the cream, fold in the sugar, the vanilla and the caramel flavoring. See Page 323. Partly freeze this mixture, then beat in the nuts and the marshmallows and freeze the cream until it holds its shape.

PEANUT BRITTLE MOUSSE

¾ pound peanut brittle, crushed	1 pint cream, whipped

Combine the ingredients and freeze them. Serve the mousse with Chocolate Sauce — Page 324.

LEMON ICE

Lemon or Orange Ice served in a Pinch Pie, or in Meringues topped with cream makes a good dessert:

2 teaspoons grated lemon rind	4 cups water
2 cups sugar	¼ teaspoon salt
	¾ cup lemon juice

331

Grate the rind into the sugar. Combine the sugar, water and salt and boil them for five minutes. Add the lemon juice, chill the mixture and freeze it.

ORANGE AND LEMON ICE

The following is delicious served with a good dash of rum. It then becomes Roman Punch:

2 teaspoons grated orange
   rind
2 cups sugar
4 cups water

1/4 teaspoon salt
2 cups orange juice
1/4 cup lemon juice

Follow the rule for Lemon Ice.

MINT SHERBET

2 cups sugar
2 cups water
2 lemons, grated and juiced
2 oranges, grated and juiced

12 sprigs of fresh mint,
   chopped
1 egg white
Green coloring

Boil the sugar and the water for five minutes. Pour the syrup over the mint leaves and permit them to steep for 1 hour. Strain the syrup, add the fruit juice and rind and the green coloring and freeze the mixture. When it is partially frozen add the stiffly beaten egg white and freeze it until it is firm. Garnish the ice with mint leaves.

PINEAPPLE ICE

1 cup sugar
4 cups water
1/8 teaspoon salt

1 cup crushed pineapple
6 tablespoons lemon juice

Boil the water with the sugar for five minutes. Cool the syrup, add the remaining ingredients and freeze the ice.

RASPBERRY ICE I.

Follow the proportions given for Raspberry or Loganberry Ice, Page 340, omitting the gelatine. Freeze the mixture.

STRAWBERRY ICE

2 cups riced or strained
   strawberries
1 1/2 cups sugar

4 cups water
1 tablespoon lemon juice

Boil the sugar and the water for five minutes. Cool the syrup, add it to the remaining ingredients and freeze the mixture.

FRUIT ICE WITH BANANA I.

Banana gives a pleasant flavor to fruit ices:

3 lemons, rind and juice
3 oranges, rind and juice
2 cups sugar
3 cups water

2 bananas, riced
1/2 can apricots (No. 2 can)
Fruit and juice

Grate a part of the rind of the oranges and lemons into the sugar. Add the water and boil the syrup for five minutes. Add the remaining ingredients, chill the mixture and freeze it.

LEMON, ORANGE OR PINEAPPLE SHERBET

Follow the rule for Lemon, Orange, or Pineapple Ice, using only two cups of water. When the mixture is frozen to a mush, add the stiffly beaten whites of two eggs. Combine them well with the cold mixture, then freeze the sherbet until it is firm. Pack it in ice and salt for at least one hour before using it.

PINEAPPLE MILK SHERBET

1 cup milk
1/2 cup cream
1 cup sugar
1/8 teaspoon salt

1 cup water
2 tablespoons lemon juice
2 1/2 cups crushed pineapple

Pour the chilled milk and cream in the ice cream container. Combine the remaining ingredients. Stir them well, chill them, add them to the cold milk and cream, and freeze the mixture.

LEMON MILK SHERBET
1 1/2 Quarts

7 tablespoons lemon juice
1 1/3 cups sugar

3 1/3 cups milk or milk and cream

Dissolve the sugar in the lemon juice and add it gradually to the milk. If the milk curdles slightly, it will not matter after it is frozen. Freeze and pack the sherbet and permit it to stand for three hours before using it.

Ice Creams, Ices and Desserts
To be frozen in
Refrigerator Trays or in Molds

RULES FOR MAKING FROZEN DESSERTS WITH
MECHANICAL REFRIGERATION:

In order to freeze ices and ice creams successfully in a mechanical refrigerator, or in a mold packed in ice and salt, it is advisable to add some thickening substance to the mixture to be frozen. This substance may be dissolved gelatine, flour or cornstarch, egg yolks in custard or hot syrup poured over egg yolks or egg whites.

When cream or condensed milk is used in creams or mousses it must be stiffly whipped and folded into the other ingredients just before the mixture is put into a refrigerator tray or mold.

Mechanically frozen ice creams and ices have not the light consistency characteristic of churned ice creams and ices, but in the case of mousses and bombes, excellent results are obtained.

In the case of ices and sherbets vigorous beating at intervals during the freezing time will give the ice the quality of a frappé, (coarsely frozen water ice.)

Corn syrup added to water ice, ice cream or mousse, helps to prevent an icy consistency—a good proportion being one part corn syrup to two parts sugar.

Combinations that are too sweet will not freeze in a mechanical refrigerator. A good proportion is one part sugar to four parts of liquid.

Sherbets are water ices to which a small amount of dissolved gelatine is added. When partially frozen the ice is combined with stiffly beaten egg whites.

Parfaits are stiffly beaten egg whites over which a thick hot syrup is poured. When the mixture is cool it is combined with stiffly whipped cream.

Mousses are heavy cream whipped and combined with flavors of different kinds, eggs, fruit pulp, chocolate gelatine, macaroons, etc.

Bombes are Mousses frozen into various shapes.

The length of time for freezing ices and ice creams depends upon the refrigerator used. Companies manufacturing refrigerators issue time charts for freezing desserts. The period varies but is usually from four to six hours.

TO BEAT CREAM

Place thoroughly chilled cream in a mixing bowl. Beat it with a spiral wire whisk, or a rotary beater, until it begins to stiffen. Be careful not to beat it too long, as it will turn to butter.

TO BEAT CONDENSED MILK

Place the milk in a double boiler. When it is scalded, add gelatine, which has been soaked in cold water, and dissolve it well. Allow one-half teaspoonful of gelatine soaked in two teaspoonfuls of cold water to one and one-fourth cups of scalded condensed milk. Chill the milk thoroughly, then beat it like cream.

RULE FOR SEALING AND PACKING MOLDS

Molds fitted with tightly closing lids are made for freezing creams and ices. If there is no mold available—a baking powder can, or other tin receptacle that will close tightly, may be used.

Fill the mold with any desired mixture suited to the purpose of still freezing, cover the top of the can with a piece of heavy waxed paper and adjust the lid. Let the waxed paper protrude for an inch or more. Lift the paper and spread a generous coating of lard around the container under the paper, then plaster the paper down firmly and spread lard around the edge of the lid. This will keep the salt water from penetrating.

Have ice ready that has been pounded into small pieces, and set the mold in a bed of ice. Allow from two to six portions of ice to one of salt, and cover the mold completely. A bucket or pail is best that will allow for about a three inch packing. Freeze the cream from four to six hours.

VANILLA ICE CREAM II.

2 teaspoons gelatine	¾ to 1 cup sugar
2 tablespoons cold milk	⅛ teaspoon salt
1 cup cream	3 cups cream, whipped

Soak the gelatine in the milk for five minutes. Heat the cream, dissolve the sugar in it and add the gelatine. Cool this mixture and add the salt and the vanilla. Place it in refrigerator trays and when it is thoroughly chilled, whip it with a spiral wire whisk. Whip the cream until it is stiff and fold it into the chilled and beaten mixture. Freeze the cream until it will hold its shape.

335

DELMONICO ICE CREAM
6 to 7 Servings

2 egg yolks
4 tablespoons cream
3½ tablespoons powdered
   sugar

1 teaspoon vanilla, or
1 tablespoon Sherry
1 cup cream, whipped
2 egg whites, whipped

Beat the yolks with the sugar, add the 4 tablespoons of cream and beat this mixture well. Place it in a double boiler and cook it until it is smooth and slightly thickened, stirring it constantly. Remove it from the fire and cool it. Add the vanilla and chill it. Whip the cream and the egg whites in separate bowls until they are very stiff. Combine them lightly and fold in the custard.

CARAMEL ICE CREAM II.

See Caramel Syrup on Page 323. Follow the rule for Vanilla Ice Cream and add 2 or more tablespoons of caramel syrup.

STRAWBERRY ICE CREAM II.
4 Servings

1 scant pint strawberries
Powdered sugar

1 cup double cream

Wash the berries, drain them well and stir them with sufficient powdered sugar to sweeten them thoroughly. Whip the cream and fold it into the berries.

ANGELICA II.
2 quarts

1½ cups sugar
½ cup water
2 egg whites
1 teaspoon vanilla, or 1

tablespoon or more of
Sherry
3 cups double cream,
   (1½ pints)

Boil the sugar and the water until the syrup threads, see Page 323. Pour the syrup slowly over the beaten egg whites. Beat this mixture until it is cool and add the vanilla. Beat the cream in a separate bowl until it is stiff, and combine it lightly with the egg mixture.

PINEAPPLE AND MARSHMALLOW MOUSSE

1 cup heavy cream, whipped
3 tablespoons powdered
   sugar
1 teaspoon vanilla
10 marshmallows

1 cup crushed pineapple,
   drained
¼ cup almonds, blanched
   and shredded

Whip the cream until it is stiff, add the sugar and the vanilla. Cut the marshmallows into fourths and add them to the cream. Last fold in the crushed pineapple and the nuts.

RASPBERRY PARFAIT

1 cup sugar
¾ cup water
¼ teaspoon salt
3 egg whites

2 cups cream, whipped
1 quart raspberries,
mashed

Boil the water and the sugar until it threads—Page 323. Add the salt to the eggs and whip them to a stiff froth. Pour the syrup over them in a thin stream, beating them constantly until they are cool. Whip the cream to a stiff froth and combine it lightly with the eggs and the crushed raspberries.

MAPLE PARFAIT

6 egg yolks
¾ cup maple syrup

1 pint whipping cream,
(2 cups)

Place the yolks and the syrup over boiling water and cook them until they are thick and smooth, stirring them constantly. The custard is ready to be taken from the fire when it will coat a spoon. Poor the custard into a bowl and beat it with a wire whisk until it is cold. Combine it lightly with the whipped cream.

CARAMEL PARFAIT

1½ teaspoons gelatine
½ cup cold water
½ cup sugar
½ cup boiling water
2 egg yolks

½ cup sugar
2 teaspoons vanilla
2 cups cream, whipped
(1 pint)

Soak the gelatine in the cold water for five minutes. Melt the sugar until it browns, stirring it constantly, and burn it slightly. Add the boiling water and cook the caramel for 1 minute. Add the second half cup of sugar to the egg yolks and beat them well, add the caramel slowly and cook this mixture over a slow fire, or in a double boiler, stirring it constantly. Add the soaked gelatine and dissolve it. When the custard is thick and smooth, remove it from the fire, add the vanilla and chill it until it is nearly set. Fold it into the stiffly beaten cream.

Bombes, Mousses

The three following Bombes, or Mousses, are old treasured family recipes. These mixtures were placed in molds, packed in ice and salt and served on "occasions."

Today similar recipes are to be found in any book on Iceless Refrigeration. Modern equipment has made these dishes commonplace, but for me they retain a certain glamor associated with distinguished company, conviviality and the easy flow of intellectual conversation.

CHOCOLATE BOMBE

1 teaspoon gelatine	2 tablespoons cocoa
1 cup cold water	1 teaspoon vanilla
1 cup milk	1 pint double cream,
1½ cups sugar	(2 cups)

Soak the gelatine in the water for five minutes. Boil the milk with the sugar and the cocoa, dissolve the gelatine in this mixture and cool it. Add the vanilla and chill the mixture until it is about to set. Fold it lightly into the stiffly beaten cream.

VANILLA BOMBE

1 teaspoon gelatine	2 egg whites
¼ cup water	1 quart double cream,
2 cups milk	(4 cups)
1½ cups sugar	18 macaroons, soaked in
2 egg yolks	wine and spread with
1 teaspoon vanilla	tart jelly

Soak the gelatine in the water for five minutes. Boil the milk with the sugar and dissolve the gelatine in the liquid. Add the egg yolks, beat the mixture for 1 minute over a low fire, permitting the eggs to thicken slightly, then remove it from the fire, cool it, add the vanilla and chill it. Beat the egg whites to a stiff froth. Place the cream in a separate bowl and beat it to a stiff froth. When the custard mixture is about to set, fold it into the egg whites, and combine this lightly with the cream. Place alternate layers of the cream and the macaroons in a refrigerator tray, or in a mold, and freeze the bombe.

APRICOT BOMBE

1 teaspoon gelatine
¼ cup cold water
2 cups apricot pulp and
juice, (dried apricots,
cooked and put through

a ricer, see Page 163)
Juice of 1 lemon
1 cup sugar
1 pint double cream

Soak the gelatine in the cold water. Boil the apricot juice, add the sugar, dissolve it and dissolve the soaked gelatine in the syrup. Add the apricot pulp and chill this mixture until it is about to set. Whip the cream until it is stiff and lightly fold in the gelatine mixture.

STRAWBERRY, OR RASPBERRY BOMBE

1¼ tablespoons gelatine
2 tablespoons cold water
3 tablespoons hot water

1 quart berries
1 cup sugar
1 pint cream (2 cups)

Wash the berries and combine them with the sugar. Chill them for 1 hour and rub them through a sieve. Soak the gelatine in the cold water for five minutes, dissolve it in the boiling water and add it to the fruit juice. Chill the juice and when it is nearly set, fold it into the stiffly whipped cream.

PEANUT BRITTLE BOMBE

2 eggs
½ cup hot maple syrup
1 cup whipping cream

½ cup peanut brittle,
crushed with a rolling pin

Beat the eggs slightly, add the maple syrup and cook these ingredients over hot water. Beat them from time to time with a wire whisk until they are thick, then cool them. Whip the cream, add the peanut brittle and fold in the egg mixture.

PEPPERMINT BOMBE

1 pint cream, whipped
(2 cups)
6 ounces thin peppermint

sticks
Chocolate decorettes

Whip the cream until it is stiff. Crush the peppermint sticks with a rolling pin. Combine them with the cream and place the mixture in a mold, or in a refrigerator tray. Place several tablespoons of chocolate decorettes in the center of the cream and freeze it.

ORANGE ICE AND FROZEN WHIPPED CREAM

The juice of 6 oranges   1 pint cream, whipped,
Sugar   ½ cup nut meats

Sweeten the orange juice, if the oranges are acid. Whip the cream until it is stiff and combine it with the nuts. Put the orange juice in the bottom of a mold, or in a refrigerator tray, and pile the cream on top of it.

RASPBERRY ICE II.

To be used as a lining for a bombe, or in the bottom of a refrigerator tray.

1 teaspoon gelatine   ½ cup sugar
1 tablespoon cold water   1 cup water
1 quart red raspberries,   Juice of ½ lemon
   fresh or canned

Soak the gelatine in the cold water for five minutes. Crush the berries and put them through a fine strainer, or a doubled piece of cheese cloth. Strain ½ cup of water through the raspberry pulp. Add ½ cup of water to the sugar and boil the syrup for 3 minutes. Dissolve the soaked gelatine in it and chill it. Combine the syrup and the raspberry and lemon juice. Place the mixture in a chilled mold, or in a refrigerator tray. Fill the mold or the tray with sweetened flavored whipped cream and freeze it. The gelatine may be omitted and the ice may be frozen in a freezer. Line a chilled mold with the ice and fill the center with Angelica, whipped cream, etc.

If raspberries are not available, substitute canned Loganberries. They have character and a delicious flavor.

LOGANBERRY ICE

2 teaspoons gelatine   2 cups water
¼ cup cold water   3 cups loganberry juice,
2 cups sugar   (Contents of a No. 2½
¼ teaspoon salt   can, strained)

Soak the gelatine in the cold water. Boil the sugar, the salt and the water for five minutes. Dissolve the gelatine in the syrup, cool it and add it to the loganberry juice.

FOUNDATION RECIPE FOR SHERBET
Still frozen

2 teaspoons gelatine   1 cup fruit juice
¼ cup cold water   2 egg whites
¾ cup sugar   ⅛ teaspoon salt
1¾ cups water

Additional fruit juice, or fruit pulp, may be substituted for part of the water. This applies to all fruit juices, except lemon and orange. For Lemon Sherbet, substitute ¾ cup of lemon juice and ¼ cup of water for the fruit juice and add grated lemon rind. For Orange Sherbet, substitute 1½ cups of orange juice and ¼ cup of lemon juice for the fruit juice and add grated orange rind. Soak the gelatine in ¼ cup of cold water for five minutes. Boil the sugar and 1¾ cups water for 10 minutes. Dissolve the gelatine in the boiling syrup. Cool this mixture, add the fruit juices, or fruit pulp, and place the sherbet in the refrigerator tray for three quarters of an hour. Turn it into a chilled bowl and beat it thoroughly. Place the egg whites in a separate bowl, add the salt and beat them until they are stiff. Fold them into the sherbet and return the sherbet to the refrigerator tray. At half hour intervals, stir the sherbet from the back to the front. Stir it just before serving it, after at least four hours of freezing.

FRUIT ICE WITH BANANAS II.

Follow the rule for Fruit Ice — Page 332, adding 2 tablespoons of gelatine. Soak the gelatine for five minutes in ¼ cup of fruit juice, and dissolve it over heat. Combine it with the other ingredients.

CANNED FRUIT
Still frozen

Freeze a can of fruit, following the Rule for Packing a mold — Page 335. When it is frozen, place it horizontally and open it with a can opener by running the opener around the side of the can near the top. Invert the contents of the can and slice the iced fruit and juice, serving each slice topped with whipped cream. Fruit may be placed in a refrigerator tray, but it must not be frozen too long. Two hours is usually sufficient.

The following recipes, made with condensed milk in the place of cream, are acceptable and good:

VANILLA ICE CREAM WITH CONDENSED MILK
4 Servings, still frozen

⅓ to ½ cup sugar
¼ cup cream
1½ teaspoons vanilla

1¼ cups condensed milk, (unsweetened)

Heat the cream and dissolve the sugar in it. Chill this mixture and add the vanilla. Prepare and beat the condensed milk

—See Page 335. Combine it lightly with the sugar mixture, and freeze the cream in a refrigerator tray.

CARAMEL ICE CREAM WITH CONDENSED MILK

Add 2 tablespoons of Caramel Syrup—See Page 323 to Vanilla Ice Cream, using the smaller amount of sugar.

MACAROON BISQUE WITH CONDENSED MILK

Add 2 tablespoons of Caramel Syrup—See Page 323 and ¾ cup crushed macaroons (about 10 macaroons) to Vanilla Ice Cream, using only ¼ cup of sugar.

APRICOT MOUSSE WITH CONDENSED MILK

6 Servings, still frozen

This is undoubtedly the best of the condensed milk recipes:

¼ pound dried apricots,
  (1 scant cup)
1 cup water
½ cup sugar
1 teaspoon gelatine

1¼ cups condensed milk,
  (unsweetened)
½ teaspoon vanilla
⅛ teaspoon salt

Soak the apricots in the water for 12 hours. Bring them very slowly to the boiling point, add the sugar and cook them for two minutes. Cool them and put them through a sieve or ricer. There should be about ¾ cup of pulp and ¼ cup of juice. Soak the gelatine in 2 tablespoons of cold juice. Dissolve it in 2 tablespoons of hot juice, and add the juice to the pulp. Prepare the milk—See Page 335, chill it and whip it to a stiff froth. When the apricot pulp is about to set, fold it in lightly and freeze the mixture by packing it in a mold, or putting it in refrigerator trays.

SAUCES FOR FROZEN DESSERTS

See Pudding Sauces—Page 322.

CARAMELIZED NUT OR PEANUT BRITTLE

Crush or grind caramelized nuts. Serve them sprinkled over ice cream.

CHOPPED NUTS

Serve chopped nuts over ice cream, or over frozen desserts.

DECORETTES

Serve decorettes sprinkled over frozen desserts.

Jellies, Jams, Preserves and Marmalades

Jellies, Jams, and Marmalades are made by boiling fruit juice and sugar, or fruit and sugar, until these ingredients reach a stage when they will form a jelly.

RULE FOR MAKING JELLY, JAM, ETC.

Fruit:

The best results are obtained by using fruit that is slightly under-ripe, when its pectin content is highest. Fruit that is ripe, or over-ripe does not form a jelly readily.

Some fruits contain so little pectin (raspberries, pineapple, cherries, strawberries), that the addition of another fruit rich in pectin is needed to make their juices thicken. Apples, crab-apples, currants, grapes, gooseberries, plums and cranberries are added measure for measure to the fruits lacking the necessary amount of pectin.

Commercially prepared pectin is on sale at all groceries, and is in favor with many people. No recipes for jellies and jams made with commercially prepared pectin are given, as special instructions invariably accompany the purchase of this product.

Water:

Water is added to fruit in varying quantities. Strawberries and some other berries may be preserved without the addition of water. Apples, plums and pears require it.

Water may be added to fruit until it can be seen through the top layer, but the fruit must never float in water.

Juice for Jelly:

When the fruit has been cooked until it is soft, extract the juice by putting it through a jelly bag. If the jelly is to be clear and sparkling, do not squeeze the bag.

Special racks are sold for jelly making — a bag accompanying them. If there is no available jelly rack and bag, make a jelly bag of a material that is heavy enough to hold back the particles that will cause the jelly to be cloudy. The bag may be of flannel, or heavy muslin, or three or four layers of cheese cloth. Sew the bag well so that it will be strong. The top may be bound with tape and loops of tape may be sewed to it from which to hang it.

After using the bag, rinse it in boiling water.

The strained juice may be reheated, poured boiling hot into sterilized jars, and covered tightly with screw tops. It will keep indefinitely and can be made into jelly at your convenience.

Sugar:

Use ¾ cup of sugar to every cup of juice, or fruit, except in cases where the fruit is extremely acid. Then use 1 cup of sugar to 1 cup of fruit, or juice.

A jelly that contains too little sugar will not thicken, but a jelly that contains too much sugar will become syrupy and will not thicken either.

To Boil Jelly:

The best jelly is made by cooking a small quantity of juice at a time — from 4 to 6 cups. Measure the juice and place it in a deep kettle that will allow for the boiling up of the liquid.

Boil the juice rapidly for five minutes and skim it, if necessary. Add the sugar, stir it until it is dissolved, and continue to boil the juice rapidly, without stirring it, until it is ready to be removed from the fire.

To Test Jelly:

Begin to test the juice five minutes after the sugar has been added. Place a small amount of jelly in a metal spoon, cool it slightly and let it drop back into the pan from the side of the spoon. As the syrup thickens, two large drops will form along the edge of the spoon, one on either side. When these two drops come together and fall as one drop—the "sheeting stage" has been reached—220° (The jelly may be tested by placing a small amount on ice).

The jelly is then ready to be taken from the fire. The time for cooking required will probably be between 12 and 20 minutes, dependent upon the kind of fruit and the amount of sugar used.

Place the jelly at once in sterilized glasses.

Do not boil jelly unnecessarily. Quick, short cooking preserves both its color and its flavor.

To Sterilize Glasses or Jars:

Fill glasses or jars ¼ full of water and place them well apart, in a shallow pan partly filled with water. Heat them in the oven until the water simmers. If the lids are placed lightly upon the glasses, they will be sterilized at the same time.

Paraffine:

Melt paraffine over a very low flame, or over hot water. Pour it from a small teapot, or pitcher. Cover the jelly, as soon as it is cold, with a very thin coating of paraffine. On the second day, cover the jelly again with a thin film of paraffine, tilting the glass to permit the paraffine to cover every bit of the surface. The two coatings should not be more than one-eighth inch thick. A heavy coating of paraffine is apt to pull away from the sides of the glass.

Cover the jelly glasses with tin lids and store the jelly in a cool, dark place. If placed in a warm, light place, it may "weep" (ooze from the glass.)

Preserves:

Preserves are fruits cooked with sugar until the syrup thickens—the fruit being permitted to remain whole.

Apply the test given for jelly. If you like a "loose" quality in preserves, cook them until two heavy drops form on the edge of the spoon and not until the two drops combine and fall together.

346

Jam:

Jam is fruit cooked with sugar until the ingredients thicken and the fruit loses its shape.

Jellies

CURRANT JELLY

Currant jelly may be made with, or without, the addition of water. Wash the currants, but do not stem them. If no water is desired (and this is a matter of taste), crush the bottom layer of currants and pile the rest on top of them. If water is used, allow about one-fourth as much water as there is fruit. Cook the currants until they are soft and colorless. Follow the Rule for Making Jelly — Page 344.

CURRANT AND RED RASPBERRY JELLY

This is the most delicate of jellies:

Prepare the currants as for currant jelly. Crush the raspberries and add them to the currants. Cook the fruit until the currants are soft and colorless. Strain the fruit through a jelly bag. Equal parts of raspberries and currants may be used — or 2 parts raspberries to 3 parts currants, and even 1 part raspberries to 3 parts currants will impart a delicious flavor to the jelly. Use ¾ cup of sugar or 1 cup of sugar to every cup of juice. Follow the Rule for Making Jelly — Page 344.

CURRANT AND BLACK RASPBERRY JELLY

1 quart currants 2 cups water
2 cups black raspberries Sugar

Follow the rule for Currant and Red Raspberry Jelly.

BLACK RASPBERRY AND GOOSEBERRY JELLY

2 quarts black raspberries Water
4 quarts green gooseberries Sugar

Place the fruit in separate saucepans. Add ¼ cup of water to the raspberries and 1 cup of water to the gooseberries. Cook the fruit until it is soft, combine it and strain it through a bag. Allow ¾ cup to 1 cup of sugar for every cup of the combined juices. Follow the Rule for Making Jelly — Page 344.

APPLE JELLY

Wipe tart apples, quarter them and remove the stem and blossom ends. Put the apples in a saucepan and add water until it can be seen through the top layer of apples. Cover the pan and cook the apples until they are soft. Drain them through a coarse sieve. Put the juice through a jelly bag, taking care not to press the bag. Boil the juice in small quantities (4 to 6 cups of juice) for 20 minutes. Add ¾ to 1 cup of sugar for every cup of juice and continue to boil the syrup. Follow the Rule for Making Jelly — Page 344.

MINT JELLY

Follow the rule for Apple Jelly. Before removing the jelly from the fire, bruise the leaves of a bunch of fresh mint, hold the stems in the hand and pass the leaves through the jelly until the desired strength of mint flavor is obtained. Add a small quantity of green coloring.

ROSE GERANIUM JELLY

Follow the rule for Mint Jelly, substituting two or three sprays of rose geranium leaves and a small amount of red coloring.

CRAB-APPLE JELLY

Follow the rule for Apple Jelly. Do not quarter the crab-apples, cut them in half.

QUINCE JELLY

Scrub the quinces and cut them into quarters. Remove the seeds and follow the rule for Apple Jelly. See the rule for Quince Jam — Page 351.

PARADISE JELLY

20 medium sized apples   1 quart cranberries
10 medium sized quinces

Cut the apples, unpeeled, into quarters. Peel the quinces, cut them in quarters and remove the seeds. Combine the apples and cranberries, barely cover them with water and boil them until they are soft. Barely cover the quinces with water and boil them until they are soft. Follow the Rule for Making Jelly—Page 344, combining the juices. Boil the juices for 12 minutes before adding the sugar. Allow 1 cup of sugar to each cup of juice. Boil the jelly in small quantities—4 to 6 cups at a time.

GRAPE JELLY

Wash grapes that are under-ripe and remove them from their stems. Place them in a kettle with a small quantity of water, about ½ cup of water to 4 cups of grapes. A quartered apple may be added to this amount of grapes (but the addition is optional). It is supposed to keep grape jelly from sugaring. Boil the grapes until they are soft and strain them through a bag. Follow the Rule for making Jelly—Page 344.

SPICED GRAPES

15 pounds of concord grapes	4 two inch sticks of
2 tablespoons whole cloves	cinnamon
2 cups vinegar	Sugar

Wash the grapes, remove them from the stems and drain them. Place one-half of the grapes in a kettle, add the other ingredients and cover them with the remaining grapes. Cook them until they are soft and strain the juice through a jelly bag. Follow the Rule for Making Jelly Page 344, allowing a cup of sugar for every cup of juice.

PLUM JELLY

Goose plums make a delicious jelly or jam.

Put small red plums in a saucepan and add water to them until it can be seen through the top layer. Boil the plums until they are soft, then strain them through a coarse strainer and put the juice through a jelly bag. Follow the Rule for Making Jelly—Page 344, allowing ¾ to 1 cup of sugar to 1 cup of juice, according to the acidity of the fruit. See the rule for Plum Jam —Page 351.

Preserves
STRAWBERRY PRESERVES I.
Without water

Wipe, pick over and hull strawberries. Place them in a bowl and sprinkle them with sugar—allowing ¾ to 1 cup of sugar to every pound of berries. Permit them to stand for

12 hours. Cook no more than 4 cups of sugared berries at a time. Bring them quickly to the boiling point and cook them quickly for 15 minutes.

STRAWBERRY PRESERVES II.
With water

2 pounds of berries (whole)   7/8 cup water
3 cups sugar

Place the sugar and the water in a pan over a quick flame. Stir these ingredients until the sugar is dissolved, bring the syrup to the boiling point and when it is boiling rapidly, add the unwashed berries. Cook them eleven minutes and permit the preserves to cool slowly.

STRAWBERRY AND RHUBARB PRESERVES

2 quarts berries, hulled   1 quart rhubarb cut into
8 cups sugar   small pieces

Pour the sugar over the rhubarb and permit these ingredients to soak for 12 hours. Bring them quickly to the boiling point, add the berries and boil the preserves until they are thick (about 15 minutes).

GOOSEBERRY PRESERVES

This is good with a meat course, as it is tart and has character.

4 cups gooseberries   1/2 cup water
3 to 4 cups sugar

Wash the gooseberries and remove the stem and blossom ends. Add the water and the sugar and place these ingredients over a quick fire. Boil them quickly until the berries are clear and the juice is thick (about 15 minutes).

Jams

RASPBERRY OR BLACKBERRY JAM

Cook raspberries, or blackberries (crushing a few of them) with an equal amount of sugar, or a little less, over a quick fire, stirring them frequently from the bottom to keep them from sticking. Boil them until they are thick.

QUINCE JAM

After making Quince Jelly—Page 348, strain the quince pulp left in the strainer and jelly bag, through a fine sieve. Add 1 cup of quince juice to 3 cups of pulp and ¾ cup to 1 cup of sugar for every cup of pulp and juice. Cook the jam in small quantities for about 20 minutes—until it is thick and smooth, stirring it frequently from the bottom, as it is apt to stick.

PLUM JAM

Follow the rule for Quince Jam, substituting plum pulp and plum juice.

FIVE FRUITS JAM

The following is an "A I." blend:

Strawberries	Raspberries
Cherries	Gooseberries, in equal
Currants	amounts

Hull the berries, seed the cherries, stem the currants, pick over the raspberries and head and stem the gooseberries. Place as much sugar as you have strawberries in a porcelain lined dish and soak them for twelve hours. Bring them quickly to the boiling point and boil them with as little stirring as possible until the juice thickens (for about 15 minutes). As strawberries are apt to come a little in advance of the other fruits, these preserves may be set aside until the other fruits are available. Boil the remaining fruits over a quick fire separately, or together, adding a small amount of water and ¾ as much sugar as there is fruit. When the jam is thick (in about 20 minutes) combine it with the strawberries.

Marmalades

ORANGE MARMALADE

2 large oranges	11 cups water
2 large lemons, or	8 cups sugar
3 small ones	

Cut the fruit into halves and remove the seeds. Soak the fruit in 11 cups of water for 24 hours, then cut it into very fine shreds with a sharp knife. Boil it in the water in which it was soaked for 1 hour. Add 8 cups of sugar and boil the marmalade until it forms a jelly when tested. Follow the Rule for Making Jelly—Page 344.

ORANGE, LEMON AND GRAPEFRUIT MARMALADE

1 grapefruit   3 lemons
3 oranges

Remove the seeds, and slice the fruit into small pieces with a sharp knife. Measure the fruit and juice and add three times the amount of water. Soak the fruit for 12 hours, boil it for 20 minutes and permit it to stand again for 12 hours. Add ¾ cup of sugar for every cup of fruit and juice and cook these ingredients in small quantities, from 4 to 6 cups at a time, until they form a jelly when tested. Follow the Rule for Making Jelly — Page 344.

APRICOT AND PINEAPPLE MARMALADE
WITH ORANGES

1 pound dried apricots   1 No. 2 can crushed
2 oranges   pineapple
1 lemon   7 cups sugar

Wash the apricots and soak them for 12 hours in water to cover. Drain them, keeping the water, and put them through a grinder into a large bowl. Cut the oranges and the lemon in halves, add the juice to the ground apricots and grind the orange halves into the small bowl. Add the apricot water, the pineapple and the sugar and boil these ingredients until they thicken.

APRICOT AND PINEAPPLE MARMALADE

1 pound dried apricots   Juice of 1 lemon
1 No. 2 can of crushed   Sugar
  pineapple

Wash the apricots and soak them for 12 hours in water to cover. Bring them slowly to the boiling point, strain them, reserving the juice, and put them through a ricer. Drain the pineapple, add it to the apricot pulp and add the juice to the apricot water. Measure the pulp and the juices, but keep them separate. Allow ¾ cup of sugar for every cup of pulp and juice. Boil the juices rapidly for 5 minutes, add the sugar and when it is dissolved and the syrup is boiling, add the combined pulp and the lemon juice. Boil the marmalade for 10 minutes, or until it thickens.

SEEDLESS WHITE GRAPES AND ORANGE MARMALADE

1 small orange very finely sliced	2 cups seedless grapes
3/4 cup water	1 1/2 cups sugar
	1 tablespoon lemon juice

Soak the orange in the water for 3 hours. Add the grapes and soak them for 30 minutes. Bring the fruit slowly to the boiling point and boil it quickly for 5 minutes. Add the sugar and the lemon juice and boil the marmalade for 6 minutes.

Conserves

BLACK CHERRY CONSERVE

2 oranges	Juice of 2 lemons
Water	3 1/2 cups sugar
1 quart black cherries, seeded	

Wash the oranges and slice them into very thin slices removing the seeds. Barely cover the slices with water and cook them until they are tender. Add the remaining ingredients and cook the conserve until it is thick and clear.

SPICED RHUBARB CONSERVE

1 orange	1/2 cup water
1 lemon	1/4 cup vinegar
1 ounce ginger root	1 1/2 cups strawberry rhubarb
1/8 pound cinnamon candy, (red hots)	3 cups sugar
1 blade mace	1/4 cup white raisins, (optional)
2 whole cloves	

Wash the orange and the lemon and cut them into very small pieces, taking out the seeds. Tie the spices in a small bag. Place the fruit, the candy, the spices and the water in a pan and boil them until the fruit is tender. Add the rhubarb, the sugar and the raisins and cook the marmalade until it is thick.

TUTTI FRUTTI

The following conserve was a tradition in our family until it became impossible, or difficult rather, to secure brandy. It is unusually good served with a meat course, or as a sauce over puddings and ices.

1 pint brandy	Sugar
Fruits of various kinds	

Place the brandy in a stone crock and add fruit as it comes into season. Strawberries, cherries, currants, raspberries, apricots, peaches, pineapple, etc. With each addition of fruit, add the same amount of sugar. Stir the Tutti Frutti every day until the last of the fruit has been added. Cover the crock well and keep it in a cool place.

Pickles

BRINE

Brine is a solution of salt and water. Use one part common salt to nine parts water. Combine the salt with a little water, dissolve it and add the remaining water.

MUSTARD PICKLE

Since making the following mild and palatable pickle for the first time, I have abandoned all other mixed pickles and have clung to this one, as it meets with general and enthusiastic approval:

4 quarts green vegetables,
   (cucumbers, green tomatoes, green beans, etc.)
1 large cauliflower

2 dozen small onions
2 dozen or more small
   gherkins

Slice the cucumbers (unpeeled, if they are tender) and cover them with brine—Page 355. After 12 hours drain them well. Slice the tomatoes, beans, gherkins, etc., peel and slice the onions and break the cauliflower into small flowerets. Pour boiling, salted water (1 teaspoon salt to 1 quart water) over these vegetables, bring them to the boiling point, drain them well and add them to the drained cucumbers. Prepare the following mustard sauce:

Mustard Sauce:

1½ cups flour
6 tablespoons dry mustard
1½ tablespoons tumeric
2½ quarts mild cider
  vinegar

2½ cups sugar
3 tablespoons celery seed
Salt, if needed

Combine the flour, the mustard and the tumeric and rub them to a smooth paste with 2 cups or more of the vinegar. Bring the remaining ingredients to the boiling point, add the mustard mixture slowly, stirring the sauce constantly. When the sauce is smooth and boiling, pour it over the drained vegetables. Place the pickle in jars and seal them.

SOUR-SWEET GREEN TOMATO PICKLE

1 peck green tomatoes
2 cups salt
6 white onions, sliced
4 pints vinegar, (8 cups)
2 pounds brown sugar
2 tablespoons ground
  mustard

1 cup flour
1 tablespoon tumeric
2 cups vinegar
1 tablespoon whole cloves
1 tablespoon stick cinnamon

Cut the tomatoes in half crosswise. Sprinkle them with salt and permit them to stand for 3 hours. Drain them for 12 hours. Wash the tomatoes in clear water. Put them in a kettle with the onions and 4 pints of vinegar and bring them to the boiling point. Make a paste of the sugar, mustard, flour, tumeric and 2 cups of vinegar. Add this paste to the boiling tomatoes and onions, add the spices and cook the tomatoes until they are transparent.

YELLOW CUCUMBER PICKLE
Senf Gurken

These large, firm, luscious slices are served very cold with meat:

Allow 1½ gallons of vinegar to 1 bushel of cucumbers . This recipe will make about 14 quarts of pickle.

Cut large yellow cucumbers into strips, pare and seed them. The strips should be about 1½ x 2½ inches in size. Soak them for 12 hours in brine — Page 355, and drain them well.

Prepare quart fruit jars in the following manner:

Sterilize the jars and place in each one:

A slice of horseradish, 1½ inches long, ⅓ inch wide, ⅓ inch thick. A piece of long, hot, red pepper, ½ inch long, 4 sprigs of dill blossom, 1 tablespoon white mustard seed. Use one-half of this amount in pint jars.

Prepare the following vinegar mixture, and bring it to the boiling point:

1 gallon vinegar	2 cups water
¾ cup sugar	

Taste it to be sure that it is palatable, as the strength of vinegar varies: Immerse a few strips of cucumber in it at a time. Boil them for 1 minute only, then pack them into a jar. When the jar is full of cucumber strips, cover them with boiling vinegar and seal the jar. Permit the pickle to ripen for 6 weeks before serving it.

SWEET-SOUR SPICED CUCUMBER PICKLE

20 pounds of small cucumbers	1 cup salt
	12 cups water, (3 quarts)

Scrub the cucumbers and soak them for 24 hours in brine made of the salt and water. Remove them from the brine and pour boiling water over them. Drain them in a colander and place them while hot in sterilized fruit jars. Fill the jars with the following vinegar mixture, pouring it into them while it is hot:

1 gallon vinegar	1 ounce stick cinnamon
11 cups of sugar	1 tablespoon cloves
2 ounces mixed whole spices	1 teaspoon alum
Seal the jars at once.	

OLIVE OIL PICKLE

Yield 3 quarts

24 cucumbers, 3 to 4 inches long	1 cup white mustard seed
	1 tablespoon celery seed
½ cup salt	½ cup olive oil
2 small onions	4 cups vinegar

Wash the cucumbers and cut them, unpeeled, into very thin slices. Sprinkle them with the salt and permit them to stand for 3 hours. Drain them well and add the very finely sliced onions. Add the remaining ingredients, mix them thoroughly and let the pickle ripen for 3 weeks before using it.

Mid-Winter Pickles

MID-WINTER PICKLE IN MUSTARD SAUCE

2 onions
2 dozen large, sour pickles
4 cups vinegar
1 cup sugar (brown or
    white)
1 tablespoon mustard

2 tablespoons cornstarch
1 teaspoon tumeric
Salt
2 teaspoons celery seed
½ teaspoon paprika
A few grains of cayenne

Slice the onions and pickles. Dissolve the cornstarch, mustard and tumeric in 1 cup of vinegar. Combine the remaining vinegar with the sugar, seasoning and celery seed and bring it to the boiling point. Add the dissolved cornstarch and boil the mixture until it thickens, stirring it constantly. Add the sliced onions and pickles to the boiling dressing. Place the pickle in jars.

MID-WINTER PICKLE—SOUR-SWEET

With or without spices

12 large cucumber pickles
3 cups sugar (brown or
    white)
3 tablespoons mustard seed

3 tablespoons celery seed,
    or 6 tablespoons mixed
    spices in place of the
    mustard and celery seed

Cut the pickles into one inch slices, cover them with the other ingredients and permit them to stand in an earthen receptacle for three days, or more, until the sugar is dissolved. They are then ready to be bottled. The crock may be rubbed with garlic, or 1 clove of garlic sliced may be added to the pickle.

MID-WINTER GARLIC PICKLE

1 dozen cloves of garlic
50 cucumber pickles
⅔ cup olive oil
6 cups vinegar

½ cup whole spices
2 tablespoons black pepper
1 cup taragon vinegar
8 pounds brown sugar

Cut the cucumbers into one inch slices and place them with the garlic in a stone jar. Pour the olive oil over them. Bring the vinegar, spices and sugar to the boiling point and boil them for 10 minutes. Pour them over the cucumbers and permit the pickle to ripen for three weeks before using it.

MID-WINTER PICKLED ONIONS

Save the liquid from any kind of pickle. Add small onions, or medium sized dry onions cut in two. Permit them to stand for one week before serving them.

UNCOOKED, SPICED CABBAGE PICKLE

1 gallon of shredded
  cabbage
Salt
1 pound sugar
½ ounce cinnamon
½ ounce cloves
½ ounce allspice

3 tablespoons ground
  mustard
1 tablespoon white mustard
  seed
1 ounce ground horseradish
Vinegar

Shred the cabbage, place it in layers in a stone jar, sprinkling each layer generously with common salt. Permit it to stand for 12 hours. Wash off the salt, drain the cabbage well and place it in layers in jars, sprinkling each layer with the combined sugar and spices. Cover the cabbage with cold vinegar.

Relishes

CHILLI SAUCE

½ bushel tomatoes,
  (16 quarts)
14 large green peppers,
  finely chopped
1 dozen large white onions,
  finely chopped

1 cup sugar
¼ cup salt
1 teaspoon ground cloves
2 cups vinegar

Scald, peel and slice the tomatoes. Bring them to the boiling point, then add the remaining ingredients. Boil the sauce until it is thick—for about 3 hours. Taste it before bottling it, add additional salt, if it is needed, and bottle the sauce.

VEGETABLE RELISH
Yield 3 quarts

This relish can be used to advantage in salad dressings and salads:

2 large carrots
1 small head of cabbage
4 white onions

4 large red sweet peppers
4 large green sweet peppers
¼ cup of salt

Chop the vegetables until they are very fine, add the salt and let them stand for three hours. Drain them well and add:

3 cups vinegar
2 cups sugar
1 tablespoon celery seed

1 tablespoon mustard seed
1/8 teaspoon red pepper

Mix the ingredients well and can them. (No heating or cooking is required). Pack the jars well and keep the pickle covered with vinegar. If there is more liquid than necessary, pour off the surplus.

INDIAN RELISH
Yield about 4 quarts

12 green tomatoes
12 tart apples (peeled)

3 onions (peeled)

Put these ingredients through a food chopper, or cut them very fine.

Boil 5 cups vinegar
5 cups sugar
1 teaspoon red pepper

3 teaspoons ginger
1 teaspoon tumeric
1 teaspoon salt

Add the chopped ingredients and cook them until they are thick, about 30 minutes.

Pickled Rind and Fruit

WATERMELON PICKLE
Yield about 4 quarts

7 pounds of rind
8 cups sugar, (white or
 brown)
3 cups vinegar
2 sticks cinnamon

1 lemon, finely sliced
1 orange, finely sliced
1/4 pound preserved ginger,
 or 1 ounce ginger root
6 drops oil of cloves

Cut all the red meat and the green peel from the rind. Weigh the rind and soak it for 12 hours in 13 quarts of water, to which 3 cups of salt have been added. Drain the rind, cover it with fresh water, soak it for 2 hours and drain it well. Boil the vinegar, sugar, cinnamon, orange and lemon until the syrup is clear (about 15 minutes). If ginger root is used, it is added at this time. Add the watermelon rind and boil it until it is tender, but not soft (test it with a straw). Remove the rind, using a skimmer, and place it in sterilized jars. Boil the syrup until it thickens. Remove it from the fire, cool it slightly and add the preserved ginger and the oil of cloves. Pour it over the rind and seal the jars. Tighten the lids after several hours.

PICKLED PEACHES

7 pounds peaches	2 tablespoons cloves,
8 cups sugar	(remove heads)
2 cups cider vinegar	2 sticks cinnamon, broken
1 cup water	into small pieces

Peel clingstone peaches and weigh them. Make a syrup of the vinegar, sugar and spices (tied in a bag) and boil this until it is clear (about 15 minutes). Add enough peaches for one jar and cook them until they are tender. Test them with a straw and remove them before they become soft. Place the peaches in a sterilized jar and cover it to keep them hot. Continue in this way until all the peaches are cooked. Cook the syrup for about ten minutes longer and pour it boiling hot over the peaches. Seal the jars at once.

SPICED PEARS

8 or 10 pounds winter	6 cups brown sugar
pears (Kiefer) cut into	2 teaspoons cloves
quarters, peeled and cored	1 long stick cinnamon
2½ cups vinegar	

Boil the last four ingredients, add the pears and cook them until they are tender (about 3 hours). Place them in jars, cover them well with the syrup, and seal the jars. The syrup may be saved and used a second time.

Candies and Confections

RULE FOR MAKING CANDY

Use a granite or porcelain lined saucepan and a wooden spoon. Cook the ingredients very slowly at first, stirring them constantly, until they are dissolved, then boil them rapidly (unless cream is used, then bring the ingredients quickly to the boiling point to prevent them from separating).

Wipe the crystals from the side of the pan with a wet cloth wrapped around the tines of a fork.

It is essential in candy making to cook the syrup to the right degree. This can be accurately determined by the use of a candy thermometer, or by testing it in the following manner:

Have a cup of cold water in readiness. Drop a little of the boiled syrup into it. If the syrup can be gathered up with the fingers into a soft ball, it has reached the soft ball stage 236-238 degrees. If the syrup can be gathered up with the fingers into a firm ball, it has reached the firm ball stage 246-248 degrees. If the syrup becomes hard and cracks when knocked against the side of the cup, it has reached the crack stage 290-310 degrees.

When pulling candy, dip the hands frequently in cold water. If gloves are used, grease them lightly and dip them in flour.

Place the thermometer in the syrup when heavy bubbles begin to form. Watch it closely and remove the candy from the fire as soon as the thermometer reaches the right degree. Place the thermometer in hot water to clean it.

PLAIN WHITE PULL CANDY

3 cups white sugar
1 cup water
1/8 teaspoon soda

1 tablespoon vinegar
1/2 teaspoon butter

Cook these ingredients to the crack state—290-310 degrees. Pour the candy onto an oiled platter, or onto a marble slab and let it cool until a dent can be made in it when pressed with a finger. Gather it into a lump and pull it with the finger tips until it is light and porous. Pull any desired flavoring or coloring into the candy, shape it into long thin strips and cut them into one inch pieces. Place the candy in a tightly covered tin, if you wish it to become creamy.

CHOCOLATE PULLED CANDY

Spread an oiled dish with grated chocolate. Follow the rule for Plain White Candy and pour it onto the chocolate. Pull the chocolate into the candy.

CREAM CANDY

2 1/2 cups sugar
1/2 cup water
1/8 teaspoon salt

1/2 cup cream
1/2 teaspoon vanilla

Boil the first 3 ingredients for 6 minutes. Skim them, then pour in the cream so slowly that the boiling is not disturbed. Cook the syrup to the crack stage 290-310 degrees, add the vanilla and follow the rule for Plain White Candy.

BROWN SUGAR TAFFY

3 cups brown sugar
1 cup cream, or milk
1 tablespoon vinegar

1/2 teaspoon soda
1/4 cup butter

Cook these ingredients, stirring them very gently from the bottom to keep them from burning, to the crack stage 290-310 degrees. Follow the rule for Plain White Candy.

MOLASSES CANDY

1 teaspoon butter
1 cup dark molasses
1/2 cup sugar

1 tablespoon water
1/4 teaspoon soda

Melt the butter in an iron receptacle, add the molasses, water and sugar and stir these ingredients until they are dissolved. Boil them to the crack stage — 290-310 degrees — stirring them constantly toward the end. Add the soda, stir it in well, and follow the rule for Plain White Candy.

CHOCOLATE FUDGE

2 ounces chocolate
2 cups sugar
1/8 teaspoon salt
1/4 cup milk

1 tablespoon butter
1 teaspoon vanilla
1/3 cup nuts broken
(optional)

Cook the first four ingredients to the soft ball stage 238°. Remove the syrup from the fire and add the butter. Beat the candy while it is cooking and while it is cooling. Add the vanilla and the nuts, and pour the candy on an oiled platter. Cut it into squares before it hardens.

COCOA FUDGE

2 cups sugar
4 tablespoons butter
2 tablespoons cocoa
1/2 cup milk

1/3 cup light corn syrup, (scant)
1 teaspoon vanilla
1/2 cup nuts (optional)

Cream the butter and the sugar. Add the cocoa, the corn syrup and the milk and cook these ingredients to the soft ball stage — 238°. Remove the syrup from the fire, cool it slightly, add the vanilla and beat the candy well until it is creamy. Add the nuts just before it begins to harden. Pour the candy onto an oiled platter, and cut it into squares while it is hot.

BROWN SUGAR FUDGE

2 cups brown sugar
1/4 cup cream
1/8 teaspoon salt

1/3 cup nuts (optional)
1 teaspoon vanilla

Cook the first three ingredients to the soft ball stage — 238° — and remove them from the fire. Beat the candy while it is cooking and while it is cooling. Add the nuts and the vanilla and pour the candy onto an oiled plate. Before it hardens, cut it into squares.

CANDY PUDDING

5 cups light brown sugar
¾ cup light corn syrup
1 tablespoon butter

¼ teaspoon salt
1 cup cream
¼ cup water

Cook these ingredients, stirring them constantly, to the soft ball stage 238°. Add:

1 pound almonds, blanched
    and shredded

¼ pound chopped figs
1 pound raisins, chopped

Stir the candy well, remove it from the fire and beat it hard until it begins to cream. Roll it in a damp cloth. When it is cold and firm, cut it into pieces.

TRUFFLES

6 ounces Baker's Dot sweet
    chocolate
½ teaspoon cinnamon
½ tablespoon butter

½ can (7½ ounces) Bor-
    dens Eagle Brand sweet-
    ened condensed milk
½ teaspoon vanilla

Melt the chocolate over hot water and add the cinnamon and the butter. When the butter is melted, add the milk and the vanilla. Stir these ingredients until they are thoroughly blended. Pour the mixture onto a shallow platter and chill it for two hours, or more. Form it into balls and roll the balls in decorettes (chocolate shot), or chopped nuts. Chill the candy until it is hard.

CHOCOLATE BALLS WITH NUTS

1 egg yolk
¼ cup sugar
2 tablespoons flour

1 cup milk
⅛ teaspoon salt
½ pound sweet chocolate

Cook the first five ingredients over a slow fire, stirring them constantly. When they are thick, remove them from the fire. Melt the chocolate in a separate saucepan, cool it and combine it with the egg mixture. Shape the candy into small balls and roll them in powdered sugar. Place each ball between two walnut or pecan halves.

DIVINITY

2 cups sugar
⅔ cup water
⅔ cup light corn syrup
2 egg whites
⅛ teaspoon salt

1½ teaspoons vanilla
1 cup nut meats
½ cup candied pineapple
    and cherries (optional)

Cook the sugar, the water and the corn syrup to the soft ball stage — 238°. Add the salt to the egg whites and beat them until they are stiff. Pour the syrup over them in a thin stream, beating them constantly. When the syrup has been added, place the bowl containing the candy over hot water and beat it until it sticks to the bottom and the sides of the bowl and stands up in peaks. Remove it from the fire, add the flavoring and the nuts and spread the candy upon an oiled plate. Cut it into squares.

SEA FOAM

3 cups light brown sugar	2 egg whites, stiffly beaten
1 cup water (½ cup of this may be corn syrup)	1 teaspoon vanilla
	1 cup nut meats
1 tablespoon vinegar	

Boil the sugar, water and vinegar to the soft ball stage — 238°. Pour the syrup in a thin stream over the stiffly beaten egg whites, beating them constantly. Place the bowl containing the candy over, not in, boiling water and beat the candy until it is thick and creamy. Add the vanilla and the nuts and pour it onto a shallow, oiled platter. Cut it into squares while it is hot.

CHOCOLATE CARAMELS

40 Caramels

1 cup sugar	¼ teaspoon salt
¾ cup light corn syrup	1½ cups cream
3 squares chocolate	

Stir this candy constantly while it is cooking. Combine the first four ingredients and ½ cup of cream. Cook them to the soft ball stage — 238°. Add ½ cup of the cream and again cook the candy to the soft ball stage — 238°. Add the last ½ cup of cream and cook the candy to the firm ball stage 248°. Remove the candy from the fire and pour it into an 8 x 4 tin that has been lightly oiled. Do not scrape the pan. When the candy is cold mark it with a knife into squares, invert it onto a slab, turn it right side up and cut the squares with a long sharp knife. Permit it to dry for 3 or 4 hours. Wrap each piece of candy in waxed paper.

CREAM CARAMELS

2 cups sugar   1 tablespoon butter
1 cup cream

Cook these ingredients, stirring them constantly, to the soft ball stage — 238°. Beat the candy until it is creamy, pour it into an oiled pan and cut it into squares.

MAPLE CARAMELS

2 cups brown sugar   ½ cup cream
1½ cups maple syrup   1 tablespoon butter

Cook the first three ingredients to the soft ball stage 238°. Try out a few drops on the edge of a saucer, if they harden add the butter and pour the candy into an oiled tin. Cut it into squares as it hardens. Nuts may be added to the candy just before removing it from the fire, or they may be sprinkled on the greased tin.

GUM DROPS

2 tablespoons gelatine   1 tablespoon lemon juice
½ cup cold water   Flavoring
2 cups sugar   Coloring
¾ cup boiling water

Soak the gelatine for 5 minutes in the cold water. Pour the boiling water over the sugar, stir the sugar over a slow fire until it is dissolved, and add the soaked gelatine. Bring these ingredients to the boiling point and boil them for 10 minutes. Remove the syrup from the fire and add the lemon juice and the flavoring. (It is well to taste the candy to see that it is sufficiently flavored). Pour it into a pan that has been dipped in cold water and permit the syrup to harden for 12 hours. Cut it into squares, or oblongs, with a hot knife and roll the pieces in powdered sugar, or in granulated sugar.

GINGER GUM DROPS

Follow the rule for Gum Drops, adding ½ cup of crystalized ginger, chopped, to the syrup after removing it from the fire.

GINGER CANDY

2 cups white sugar   2 tablespoons butter
1 cup brown sugar   ¼ pound preserved ginger,
¾ cup milk   chopped
2 tablespoons white corn   1 teaspoon vanilla
  syrup

(If preserved ginger is used, drain it well. If candied ginger is used, wash the sugar from it in the milk, dry the ginger and chop it.)

Cook the sugar, milk and syrup to the soft ball stage — 238° — add the butter and remove the syrup from the fire. When it begins to cool, beat it until it begins to thicken. Add the vanilla and the ginger. Pour the candy onto a greased platter and cut it into squares before it hardens. These candy squares may be dipped in bitter chocolate — See Page 370.

CARAMEL CREAMS WITH NUTS

This makes a delicious rich cream or fondant:

1½ cups sugar	½ cup sugar
7 tablespoons cream	6 tablespoons butter
⅛ teaspoon salt	12 or more marshmallows

Bring the first three ingredients to the boiling point. Place the sugar in an iron skillet, melt it, and if a strong caramel flavor is desired, burn it slightly. Pour the boiling syrup very slowly into the caramelized sugar, stir the mixture until the caramel is dissolved and cook it to the soft ball stage — 238°. Add the butter and remove the candy from the fire. Beat in one dozen or more marshmallows, one at a time. Beat the candy until it is smooth and creamy. Drop it by the teaspoonful onto waxed paper and garnish each drop with half a nut meat.

RICH PRALINES

1⅞ cups powdered sugar	2 cups nut meats, (hickory
1 cup maple syrup	nuts, or pecans)
½ cup cream	

Cook the sugar, syrup and cream to the soft ball stage 238°. Remove the candy from the fire, beat it until it is creamy and stir in the nuts. Shape the candy into small balls.

PRALINES

2 cups brown sugar	1 teaspoon vanilla
1 cup water, or milk	1 cup pecan meats
1 tablespoon butter	

Boil the sugar and the water to the soft ball stage — 238°. (If the candy is to be used at once, it may boil a little beyond this stage — 248°). If milk is used, stir the syrup to keep it from curdling. Add the butter and when it is melted, place the saucepan containing the candy in cold water. When the bottom of the saucepan is cool, begin to beat the candy. Beat it until it is smooth and creamy, then add the vanilla and the nuts. Pour the candy onto an oiled surface. Before it is hard, break it into pieces. If the candy refuses to sugar after being spread, work it with a spatula, or knife.

NUT BRITTLE

Peanut, almond, etc.

This candy ground or crushed is delicious over ice cream and other desserts:

1 cup sugar   1 cup nuts

Melt the sugar in a skillet until it is light brown, stirring it constantly. Add the nuts, stir them in the syrup until they are well coated, then pour the candy on an oiled platter. When it is cold, break it into pieces.

SUGARED ALMONDS

2 cups sugar   1/2 cup water
1 teaspoon cinnamon, or   1 pound almonds,
   more   unblanched

Stir this candy constantly. Cook the first 3 ingredients until the syrup is clear and falls in heavy drops from a spoon. Add the almonds and stir them until they are well coated. Remove the candy from the fire and stir it until the nuts are dry. Sift them to remove the superfluous sugar. Add a very little water to the sifted sugar, a few drops of red coloring and as much additional cinnamon as is desired. Boil the syrup until it is clear, then add the almonds and stir them until they are well coated.

SALTED NUTS

1 pound almonds, or other   2 tablespoons butter
   nuts   Salt

Place the almonds in a skillet, add the butter and cook them over a slow fire, or place them on a broiler under a slow fire, leaving the oven door open. Shake the skillet from time to time. Cook the almonds until they are a light brown, sprinkle them generously with salt and drain them on brown paper, changing the paper after the first 3 minutes.

ORANGE PASTE WITH NUTS

¼ cup cold water
2 cups sugar
½ cup water
½ pound nut meats, very
    finely chopped

1 lemon, rind and juice
1 orange, rind and juice
½ teaspoon vanilla
6 drops rose water,
    (optional)

Soak the gelatine in the cold water for 5 minutes. Boil the sugar and the half cup of water and add the soaked gelatine. Boil the syrup for ten minutes over a quick flame, using an asbestos plate under the saucepan to keep the syrup from burning, or cook it in a double boiler for 20 minutes. Meanwhile, chop the nuts, place them on a platter, grate the fruit rind over them, cover them with the fruit juice and add the rosewater. Add a few drops of coloring if desired. Pour the syrup over these ingredients. The paste should be about ¼ inch thick. Chill the paste for 6 hours, or more, then cut it into squares and roll them in powdered sugar. This candy will soften readily in very hot weather.

CHOCOLATE COATING

4 ounces bitter chocolate
2 tablespoons butter

1 square inch of paraffine
5 drops vanilla

Place these ingredients in a small shallow pan over hot water until they are well blended. Remove them from the fire and when they are nearly cool, put the food to be dipped in the coating on a fork, dip it quickly and place it on a piece of waxed paper to dry.

STUFFED DATES OR FIGS

Soak the fruit in a little wine, lemon or orange juice, or place it in a colander over steam for ten minutes. Remove the date seeds and fill the cavities with pieces of marshmallow and nut meats. Shape the fruit in its original form and roll it in powdered sugar. The fruit may be stuffed with candied ginger, candied fruit, nuts, or fondant.

Candied Fruit Peel

Here are two recipes for grapefruit or orange peel—both very good. The first can be made in an hour or two—the second requires 24 hours soaking. The first is a moist peel. The second has a more sugared quality.

CANDIED GRAPEFRUIT OR ORANGE PEEL I.

Cut the peel into narrow strips, cover it with cold water and bring it slowly to the boiling point. Remove it from the fire and drain it well. Repeat this process, boiling the peel in five waters in all. Drain it well each time. Make a syrup allowing 1/4 cup of water and 1/2 cup of sugar to the peel of 1 grapefruit. Add the peel and boil it until all the syrup is absorbed, then roll it in sugar and spread it to dry. The sugared peel, when thoroughly dry, may be dipped in Chocolate Coating—See Page 370.

CANDIED GRAPEFRUIT OR ORANGE PEEL II.

Cut the peel into strips and soak it in salt water to cover for 24 hours, (1 tablespoon of salt to 4 cups of water.) Drain the peel, rinse it and soak it for 20 minutes in fresh water. Drain it, cover it with fresh water and boil it for 20 minutes and drain it again. Measure as much sugar as you have peel. Cook the peel (adding a very little water only if necessary), until it has absorbed the sugar. Shake the pot as the syrup diminishes so that the peel will not burn. This method does not necessitate rolling the peel in additional sugar.

STUFFED APRICOTS

The following recipe makes a delicious confection·

1 pound dried apricots	10 ounces marshmallows
Syrup	Sugar

Wash and scrub 1 pound of dried apricots in hot water. Steam them over hot water in a covered colander for 20 minutes. Make a syrup of:

1 cup sugar   1/2 cup water

and boil it until it spins a thread. Place the apricots in this and stir them about gently with a fork. Permit them to drain on a board for a few minutes. Place a piece of marshmallow in the center of each apricot and roll the fruit in sugar.

Beverages

Hot Beverages

COFFEE

Coffee to be good must be freshly ground. Buy only a small quantity at a time and keep it in an air-tight container. It is best made in a granite or porcelain lined pot.

BOILED COFFEE
8 Servings

1 cup ground coffee
1 egg white, slightly beaten

1 cup cold water
4 cups freshly boiled water

Combine the first 3 ingredients. The egg shell may be added to this mixture. Pour the boiling water over the coffee grounds and boil the coffee for 3 or 4 minutes. Stop the spout of the coffee pot with paper. Set the pot on the back of the stove, cut down the grounds from the sides, add ¼ cup of cold water and permit the coffee to stand for 10 minutes before serving it.

DRIP COFFEE

Place very finely ground coffee in a strainer. Allow 1 heaping tablespoon of coffee to every cup of water. Place the coffee pot where it will be hot. Boil the water and pour it slowly into the strainer, a cupful at a time. The coffee is ready to be served when the water has dripped through. It may be refiltered if it is not strong enough.

PERCOLATED COFFEE

Allow 1 heaping tablespoon of ground coffee for every cup of water. Place the water, hot or cold, in the bottom of the coffee pot, place the coffee in the strainer and boil the water, permitting it to boil up and percolate the coffee grounds for 5 minutes, or until the desired strength of coffee is obtained. Permit the coffee to stand for 5 minutes before serving it.

TEA

Bring cold, fresh water to the boiling point. Make the tea in a china or earthenware pot. (A metal pot is apt to spoil its flavor.) Scald the pot. Allow 1 teaspoon of tea for every cup, and place it in the scalded pot. Pour a small quantity of boiling water over the tea. Permit it to steep 1 minute, add the rest of the boiling water, stir the tea and permit it to steep in a warm place for two minutes before serving it. It may then be strained, if desired.

COCOA

1 cup milk
2 teaspoons cocoa
2 teaspoons sugar

1/8 teaspoon salt
1 cup boiling water

Scald the milk. Combine the cocoa, sugar, salt and boiling water. Boil these ingredients for 1 minute and add them to the scalded milk.

CHOCOLATE

1½ ounces chocolate
¼ cup sugar
¼ teaspoon salt

1 cup boiling water
3 cups milk, scalded
½ teaspoon vanilla

Melt the chocolate over hot water. Add the sugar, the salt and the boiling water slowly. When these ingredients are smooth, combine them with the scalded milk. Boil them for 1 minute, beat them with a wire whisk, add the vanilla and serve the chocolate.

MULLED WINE

This is fine for an after the theater party, served with Pecan Nut Cakes, or other good cookies:

Water
Sugar
Stick cinnamon
Cloves
Wine

Orange juice and rind
Lemon juice and rind
Pineapple juice
Grape juice, or other fruit
   juices

Make a syrup of 1 part water and 2 parts sugar. Add the spices and boil the syrup for 5 minutes, then strain it. Combine the remaining ingredients in any quantity desired. Use anything that is palatable. Add the syrup gradually, until the desired degree of sweetness is obtained. Heat the wine, but do not boil it. Color it with red coloring. Serve it very hot with slices of pineapple and lemon.

Cold Beverages

ICED COFFEE

Prepare boiled or percolated coffee, add sugar and chill it. Just before serving it add 2 tablespoons of cream to every cup of coffee. Serve it over crushed ice, or pour chilled and sweetened coffee into glasses and top the coffee with whipped cream or vanilla ice cream.

ICED TEA

Prepare hot tea, strain it and pour it over crushed ice. Serve it with lemon slices and sugar.

ICED TEA WITH COLD WATER

Add 2 tablespoons of tea to a quart fruit jar of cold water. Place it in the sun for 2 hours, strain it at once, replace it in the fruit jar and keep it in the refrigerator ready for use.

ICED TEA WITH MINT LEAVES

Leaves of 4 mint sprigs,
   bruised

2 large lemons, juiced
6 cups tea

Combine the mint leaves and the lemon juice. Pour the hot tea over them. Permit this mixture to steep for one-half hour. Strain it and chill it. Serve it over crushed ice, garnished with mint leaves. Add sugar as desired.

ICED CHOCOLATE

Prepare hot chocolate, chill it and serve it over crushed ice. Top it with whipped cream, or ice cream.

LEMONADE

Allow the juice of 1/2 lemon and from 3 to 4 teaspoons of sugar to every cup of water. A few grains of salt may be added. The sugar and water need not be boiled, but the quality of the lemonade is improved if they are. Boil the sugar and the water for two minutes. Chill the syrup and add the lemon juice. Orange, pineapple, raspberry, loganberry, white grape juice and other fruit juices may be combined with lemonade. Chilled tea may be added to these combinations in any quantity desired.

ORANGEADE

Pure undiluted orange juice served over crushed ice is best. Water, lemon juice and sugar may be added in any quantity desired.

MINT CUP

4 stalks of mint	1/4 teaspoon salt
2 cups sugar	Green coloring
2 cups water	1 quart gingerale
12 lemons, juiced	

Remove the tips of the mint and the leaves. Combine the mint, the sugar and the water and boil them for five minutes. Strain the syrup, add the lemon juice, the salt and the coloring. Chill the mixture well and combine it with the chilled gingerale.

GINGER ALE CUP

1 cup sugar	Juice of 6 lemons
1 cup water	1 quart gingerale
Juice of 6 oranges	

Combine the sugar and the water and boil them for five minutes. Cool the syrup and add it to the fruit juice. Chill it and combine it with the ginger ale just before serving it. Serve it over crushed ice.

FRUIT PUNCH

1 cup sugar
1 cup water
2 cups hot tea
2 cups strawberry juice, or
other lightly sweetened
fruit juice

¾ cup crushed pineapple
Juice of 5 lemons
Juice of 5 oranges
1 cup maraschino cherries
1 quart carbonated water

Boil the sugar and the water for 10 minutes. Add the hot tea and cool the mixture slightly. Then add the pineapple and the fruit juices. Chill this for 1 hour, then add sufficient ice water to make a gallon (4 quarts) of liquid. Add the carbonated water and the cherries just before serving the punch.

EGG NOG
1 Serving

1 egg yolk
1 tablespoon sugar
¼ cup cream

⅛ to ¼ cup rum or brandy
1 egg white beaten

Beat the yolk with a wire whisk and add the sugar and the cream. Beat these ingredients well, add the rum and fold in the well beaten egg white.

EGG NOG WITH MILK

6 egg yolks
½ cup sugar
4 cups milk

1 cup brandy
½ teaspoon, or more, nutmeg
6 egg whites

Beat the yolks with a wire whisk and add the sugar slowly. Beat this mixture until it is light and lemon colored. Add the milk, the nutmeg and the brandy. Last fold in the stiffly beaten egg whites.

RHUBARB WINE

Cut rhubarb into pieces and soak it in water to cover for 3 days. Drain the fruit, save the juice and put the fruit through a press to extract the remaining juice. Add 2 gallons of water to every gallon of juice. Add 3 pounds of sugar to every gallon of liquid. Permit the juice to ferment for 6 weeks in hot weather, and longer in cold weather. Bottle it tightly and let it age.

APRICOT CORDIAL

2½ cups water
1 cup sugar
1 tablespoon vinegar
1½ cups alcohol

1 quart bottle of Apricot
Cordial (Le Jung Wolf
& Co.)

Boil the water for 5 minutes. Dissolve the sugar in it, but do not boil it. Add the vinegar and cool the liquid. Add the alcohol and the apricot cordial.

QUINCE LIQUEUR

The formula for this delicious and unusual liqueur was given by a French Priest to his friends.

2 quarts of quinces
1½ gallons whiskey
2 ounces cardamon seed
¼ ounce mace

½ ounce aniseed
½ vanilla bean
½ ounce nutmeg, grated

Wash the quinces, core them, put them through a food chopper and combine them with the other ingredients. Put this mixture in a stone jar and let it remain there for three weeks. Strain it through a jelly bag and sweeten it to taste with a syrup made with granulated sugar and a very little water. If whiskey is not available 2 quarts of alcohol and 4 quarts of distilled water may be substituted for the whiskey.

Miscellany

The spice of life is also to be found in cook books. During my extensive delvings I have come across the following gems: The first two are French, the third is German and the fourth and fifth may be nationally classed as "Gemixte Pickles."

I.

"The hare demands to be flayed alive, the rabbit prefers waiting."

II.

"*Pigs Feet*. Take your feet, wash them, scratch them, put them on the griddle, cook them to a turn and serve them."

III.

"Take twelve eggs, if you have them."

IV.

"*Butter Dumplings*. Take butter the size of an egg, as much butter as eggs, stir. Add eggs and enough flour, but not too much. Drop with spoon into broth."

V.

DANDELION BLOSSOM WINE

6 quarts of blossom	1 orange
4 pounds sugar	2 lemons (slice rind and all,
1 gallon water	only take out seeds)

Water must be hot; let all boil for ten minutes, then let cool to luke warm and put in two tablespoons of yeast (dry); let stand for one week, then press out the juice as dry as you can, of the bloom; then put in jug, but do not cork until it quits working. It will sizzle a fine mist, and until it stops do not cork. It is ready for use then, or age will improve it. For best results, leave in jug until fall, then bottle for use. This is for one gallon. I make a gallon at a time and boil then another and so on; then put in a big stone crock for the week and stir it once in a while, for everything will come to the top, then press and put in the jug.

Favors for Children's Parties

Candlestick:

A flat, soft gum drop, two Life Savers, (one nicked), and a very small candle.

Turtle:

One-half of an English walnut shell, a soft gum drop pressed into it and raisins on toothpicks.

Fig and Raisin Man:

A marshmallow partly dipped in chocolate, a pulled fig, raisins on toothpicks for arms and legs, and almonds for the extremities. Icing for the features.

Gum Drop Man:

Two flat gum drops, four long gum drops and toothpicks. Icing for the features.

Fig and Raisin Cat:

Two pulled figs joined with toothpicks, split almonds for ears, raisins on toothpicks for legs, icing for mouth and eyes, straws for whiskers and a ribbon bow around the neck.

379

RECIPES AND SUGGESTIONS FOR LEFT-OVER FOOD

Tomato Cases—Page 66, Pepper Cases—Page 69, Onion Cases —Page 72, Cucumber Cases—Page 73, Pimentoes—Page 74, Baked Potato Cases—Page 75 and Carrots—Page 73, may be filled with left-over meat, fish, potatoes, rice or vegetables, alone or in some good combination. Moisten these ingredients with gravy, cream sauce, butter, eggs, bacon fat, milk or cream and combine them with dry bread, bread crumbs, onions, nut meats, etc. Prepare and fill the cases and cook them as directed.

Waffles combine well with meat, fish or vegetables.

Add ¾ to 1 cup of finely minced or ground left-over food to waffle batter—Page 206, cook the waffles and serve them with cream sauce or gravy.

Deep custard cups are useful for serving small amounts of left-overs. Fill them with moistened seasoned food, cover the tops with pieces of buttered paper secured with string or rubber bands, and place the cups in a pan partly filled with boiling water. Steam the food on top of the stove or in the oven until it is thoroughly heated. Remove the papers. If desired, the tops may be sprinkled with bread crumbs dotted with butter or sprinkled with cheese and browned under a broiler.

Other suggestions for serving left-over food may be found on Page 33.

To utilize the following articles of food, try the recipes suggested.

Apple Sauce:
Pudding—Page 302, Cake—Page 238.

Bacon Drippings:
Bacon drippings will keep indefinitely. Use them for sautéing meats, potatoes, mushrooms, eggs, etc.

Bones:
Chicken Bone Soup—Page 22.

Ham Bone—Split Pea or Bean Soup—Page 22.

Ham Bone Stock—Split Pea or Bean Soup—Page 23.

Left-over Soup—Page 21.

Turkey Soup—Page 21.

Bread:

Bread Egg and Cheese Dish—Page 61.
Croutons—Page 31.
Bread Dressing—Page 152.
In Tomato Cases, etc.—See first paragraph of this chapter.
Steamed Bread Pudding—Page 309.
Queen of Puddings—Page 300.
Bread Pudding—Page 299.
Bread Pudding with Nuts and Raisins—Page 300.

Bread Crumbs:

Place stale bread in a slow oven. When it is dry, crush it with a rolling pin and place the crumbs in a covered fruit jar. Use them for breaded dishes, oysters, cutlets, etc.

Cheese:

Macaroni—Page 41.
Rarebit—Page 59.
Croquettes—Page 54.
Popovers—Page 191.
Noodle Ring—Page 43.
Rice—Page 45.
Tomato Rice—Page 46.
Ramekins—Page 47.
Welsh Rarebit over Grilled Tomatoes—Page 59.

Chicken Fat:

Use chicken fat like bacon drippings or as a substitute for butter in baking.

Coffee:

Coffee Flavored Layer Cake—Page 233.
Soft Ginger Cookies—Page 271.
Mocha Sea Foam Icing—Page 287.
Mocha Tart—Page 258.
Mocha Sponge—Pages 316-317.

Cream Sauce:

Creamed Potatoes—Page 99.
Soufflés—Page 80.
Creamed Eggs—Page 38.
Waffles—See second paragraph of this article.

Egg Yolks:

Scrambled in Tomato Soup—Page 35.
Scrambled—Page 35.
Mayonnaise—Page 183.
Hollandaise Sauce—Page 158.
Sponge Cake—Page 225.
Yellow Loaf or Layer Cake—Page 231.
Yolk Cookies—Page 281.
Cup Custards—Page 296.
Caramel Custard—Page 296.
Boiled Custard Sauce—Page 297.
Drop yolks into simmering water, cook them under the boiling point until they are firm. Rice them and use them as a garnish for salads, etc.
Add egg yolks to Cream Sauce—Page 154. Do not boil the sauce after adding them.

Egg Whites:

Angel Cup Cakes—Page 267.
Angel Cake—Pages 266–267.
Angel Cake (Chocolate)—Page 234.
Cinnamon Stars—Page 282.
Corn Flake Drops—Page 275.
Chocolate Almond Bars—Page 269.
Hazelnut Cakes—Page 282.
Kisses—Page 277.
Lady Cake—Page 228.
Meringue Tart—Page 264.
Meringues—Page 263.
Nut and Date Drop Cookies—Page 282.
Pecan Drop Cakes—Page 276.
Pound Cake—Page 229.
White Cake—Pages 227-228.
Marshmallow Pudding—Page 315.
Sea Foam Candy—Page 366.
Divinity—Page 361.
White Icing—Page 285.

Fish:

Fish and Nut Timbals—Page 49.
Molded Fish Salad—Page 17.
Fish Soufflé—Page 83.
Steamed Fish Pudding—Page 91.
Rice Ramekins—Page 47.

In Tomato Cases, etc.—See first paragraph of this chapter.
Aspic Salad—Page 13.
Sandwich (Mock Chicken)—Page 11.
Fish Salad with Celery and Mayonnaise.
Eggs Stuffed with Fish—Page 16.
¾ to 1 cup flaked fish added to Waffles—See first paragraph of this chapter.

Fruit Juices:

Cocktails—Page 1.
Fruit Gelatine—use proportions for Orange Jelly—Page 312.
Sherbet—Page 341.
Fruit Sauce for Custards or Puddings.
Fruit Salad Dressing—Page 185.
Lemonade—Page 375.

Gravy:

Combine gravy with cooked rice, spaghetti, etc., adding chopped onions, celery, carrots or peppers.
Serve gravy with Waffles—See first paragraph of this chapter.

Grapefruit and Orange Peel—Page 370.

Hash—Page 56.

In Biscuit or Pie Dough—Page 56.
In Pie Shells—Page 211.
In Tomato Cases, etc.—See first paragraph of this chapter.
With Celery—Page 56.
With Waffles—Page 206.
Meat Roll—Page 56.
Shepherd's Pie—Page 55.

Jellies:

Dissolve bits of jelly and jam with a small quantity of boiling water and use them for pudding sauce.
Use jelly in place of apple sauce in Turnovers—Page 215.
Lady Finger Sandwiches—Page 283.

Meat:

Aspic Salad—Page 13.
Bacon Left-overs—Page 55.
Chicken and Ham Creamed—Page 52.
Chicken Croquettes—Page 53.

Chicken Salad with Celery and Mayonnaise.
Chicken or Veal Force Meat—Page 32.
Chicken—In Tomato cases, etc.—See first paragraph of this chapter.
Eggs in a Nest—Page 39.
Ham Cakes with Eggs—Page 52.
Ham in Tomato Cases, etc.—See first paragraph of this chapter.
Ham, Jellied Mousse—Page 52.
Ham Left-overs—Page 140.
Ham Sandwich Spread—Page 12.
Ham Soufflé—Page 83.
Minced Ham in Baked Potatoes—Page 75.
Scalloped Meat with Rice and Tomatoes—Page 55.
Meat Pie Roll—Page 56.
Meat scraps, cooked or uncooked—Soup—Page 21.
Meat Salad with Celery and Mayonnaise.
Meat Soufflé—Page 84.
Meat Loaf in Pastry—Page 55.
Meat in Tomato Aspic—Page 173.

Meat and Vegetable Scraps:

Economy Soufflé—Page 84.
In Tomato Cases, etc.—See first paragraph of this chapter.
$3/4$ to 1 cup of finely minced solids added to the recipe for Waffles—See second paragraph of this chapter.
Pastry—Page 55.
Meat Roll—Page 56.
Soup—Page 20.
Shepherd's Pie—Page 55.
Vegetable Dish—Page 65.
Bacon Left-overs—Page 55.

Pickle Vinegar:

Pickled Onions—Page 359.

Potatoes:

Potatoes au Gratin—Page 99.
Baked Mashed Potatoes—Page 101.
Creamed Potatoes—Page 99.
Eggs in a Nest—Page 39.
Hashed Brown—Page 100.
O'Brien—Page 100.
Mashed Potato Puffs—Page 101.

Potato Cakes — Page 100.
Potato Cheese Puffs — Page 54.
Potato Soufflé — Page 81.
Sautéd Potatoes — Page 100.
Shepherd's Pie — Page 55.
Mashed Potato Pie — Page 54.

Prunes or Apricots:

Eggless Apricot Whip — Page 315.
Eggless Prune Whip — Page 314.
Soufflé — Page 306.

Rice:

Cheese Rice Boiled — Page 45.
Cheese Rice Baked — Page 45.
Eggs with Rice and Tomato Sauce — Page 36.
Rice Ramekins — Page 36.
In Tomato Cases, etc. — See first paragraph of this chapter.
Rice Pudding — Page 301.
Caramel Rice Pudding — Page 301.
Rice Muffins — Page 190.
Rice served with cinnamon, sugar and cream or fruit juice.

Sausage:

Liver Sausage Sandwiches — Page 7.

Soup:

Aspic Salad — Pages 13-16.
Dumplings — Page 150.
Brown Sauce — Page 155.
Gravy — Pages 153-154.

Sour Milk:

Biscuit — Page 188.
Bran Muffins I — Page 190.
Cottage Cheese — (Sour milk thickened and placed in a cheese cloth bag on ice until the whey has dripped from it).
Doughnuts — Page 202.
Gravy — Pages 153-154.
Gingerbread Waffles — Page 206.
Griddle Cakes — Page 214.
Mock Venison — Page 137.

Pancakes — Page 205.
Spoon Bread — Page 189.
Velvet Spice Cake — Page 238.

Sour Cream:

Almond Cake Filling — Page 293.
Cream Sauce for Mulled Cucumbers and other Vegetables —
Page 120.
Gravy — Page 153-154.
Sour Cream Cake — Page 231.
Coffee Cake — Page 293.
German Cherry Cake — Page 257.
In Ice Cream with soda added to cut the acid.
Grandmother's Apple Cake — Page 256.
Salad Dressing — Page 184.
Sour Cream and Horseradish Sauce — Page 159.
Sour Cream Icing — Page 288.
Waffles — Page 206.

Tomato Juice:

Aspic — Page 173.
Cocktail — Page 1.

Vegetables:

Vegetable Bisque — Page 24.
Vegetable Dish — Page 65.
Vegetable Parings — See Soups — Page 20.
Vegetables in Tomato Cases, etc. — See first paragraph of this
chapter.
Vegetable Soufflé — Page 81.
Vegetable Stock — Page 154.

Corn:

Corn Oysters — Page 66.

Spinach:

Eggs in Spinach with Cheese — Page 39.
Oysters in Spinach — Page 18.

Tomatoes:

Tomato Pancakes — Page 63.
Tomatoes and Corn — Page 64.
Vegetable Stock — Page 154.
Soup — Page 20.

MENUS

Building menus is so largely a matter of standards, traditions, budgets, diet restrictions and individual taste that it is difficult to plan them for people one does not know.

BREAKFAST MENUS

To balance the New Englander's codfish balls and baked beans, the Southerner's grits and bacon and the Northerner's fried cakes and doughnuts, there is the modern trend to make the first meal of the day as light as possible. Today the average woman's breakfast is probably—

FRUIT   DRY TOAST
            A BEVERAGE

and the average man's is—

            FRUIT   CEREAL
        EGGS WITH HAM OR BACON
        HOT BREAD AND A BEVERAGE

The following suggestions are offered to vary the monotony of these menus:

I

A delicious and complete breakfast that requires no pot scouring:

ORANGE JUICE   BACON CORNMEAL WAFFLES
                        COFFEE

II

APPLES STUFFED WITH SAUSAGES OR SAUSAGE MEAT
        MUFFINS   JELLY
            A HOT BEVERAGE

III

        FRUIT   SOFT COOKED EGGS
    TOMATO PANCAKES   A HOT BEVERAGE

IV

GRAPEFRUIT   HAM CAKES WITH EGGS
        BISCUIT   HONEY
            A HOT BEVERAGE

TOMATO COCKTAIL   BACON LEFT-OVERS
POPOVERS   MARMALADE

A HOT BEVERAGE

Interest may be added to the breakfast menu by serving one of the following dishes:

Baked Bananas and Crisp Bacon
Apple Pancakes
Blueberry Pancakes
Potato Pancakes
Blueberry Muffins
Bacon Muffins
Pineapple Waffles
Orange Waffles
Graham Popovers
Brown Sugar Roll
Crumb or Sour Cream Coffee Cake
Date Muffins

See the Index for further suggestions.

LUNCHEON MENUS

The luncheon menu is usually determined by the breakfast that has preceded it and the dinner that is to follow it. As the main dish of a simple luncheon try one of the following:

Egg poached in Tomato Soup
Creamed Eggs on Toast
Bread, Egg and Cheese Dish
Emergency Soups
Oysters and Bacon
Tomatoes or Melons, Stuffed with Cottage Cheese
Baked Tomatoes Stuffed with Onions, Creamed Food, Corn, Stuffed Olives, etc.
Onion Soup
Peppers stuffed with Rice, Hash, Oysters, etc.
Poached Eggs on Rice with Tomato Sauce
Eggs in Mustard Sauce
Scrambled Eggs with Onions
Boiled Green Onions on Toast
Onion Soufflé
Tomato Soup Soufflé
Left-over Soufflé
Creamed Crab, Tuna, etc.
Creamed Eggs and Asparagus
Toasted Braunschweiger Sandwiches

Egg and Bacon Sandwich
Cheese Rice, Boiled
Shrimp Wiggle
Welsh Rarebit on Tomatoes
Tomato Rarebit
Wood Chuck
Lunchettes
Baked Cucumbers Filled with Dressing or Hash
Baked Potatoes Filled with Minced Ham, Hash or Creamed
  food
Broiled Tomatoes and Onions
Baked Egg Plant
Eggs and Cheese in Bread Cases
Cheese Custard Pie
Egg Timbals
Oyster Soufflé
Oyster Omelet
Mushrooms and Bacon
Curried Rice

Some of the breakfast menus offer suggestions applicable to
luncheon menus.

J

HONEYDEW MELON OR CANTALOUPE FILLED
          WITH COTTAGE CHEESE, GARNISHED WITH
                    SEEDLESS GREEN GRAPES AND MAYONNAISE
          NUT BREAD   A BEVERAGE
          ANGEL CUP CAKES WITH CHOCOLATE ICING

II

CABBAGE, APPLE AND NUT SALAD WITH
                    BOILED DRESSING, OR SOME OTHER SALAD
     CREAM CHEESE SANDWICHES   A BEVERAGE
                    SPICE CUP CAKES

III

COLD SLICED MEAT
          TOMATOES STUFFED WITH ASPARAGUS,
                    ALMONDS AND MAYONNAISE ON LETTUCE
     BISCUIT OR CORN BREAD   A BEVERAGE
CARAMEL PUDDING   CHOCOLATE ICE BOX COOKIES

IV

OMELET WITH CREAMED OYSTERS OR SAUTÉD MUSHROOMS
GRAPEFRUIT SALAD ON LETTUCE WITH FRENCH DRESSING
          PIMENTO LUNCHEON CHEESE   HARD CRACKERS
A BEVERAGE   CHOCOLATE CAKE WITH FRUIT FILLING

V

TOASTED MUSHROOM SANDWICHES ON DARK BREAD
HEAD LETTUCE SALAD WITH FRENCH DRESSING
APPLE SAUCE PUDDING   SAND TARTS
A BEVERAGE
(If Toasted Mushroom Sandwiches on White Bread are substituted, serve
Quick Caramel Squares in the place of Sand Tarts.

VI

CORNMEAL SOUFFLÉ   SLICED HAM
CUCUMBER SALAD OR MOLDED VEGETABLE SALAD
A BEVERAGE   FRESH OR STEWED FRUIT
MERINGUE KISSES

VII

VEGETABLE DISH WITH BACON   SPOON BREAD
PINEAPPLE GELATINE   COCOA DROP CAKES
A BEVERAGE

VIII

CRACKERS   BOUILLON   RADISHES
BACON, SWEET POTATO AND PINEAPPLE DISH   A BEVERAGE
GREEN SALAD WITH FRENCH DRESSING   TOAST
CHOCOLATE OR MACAROON SOUFFLÉ

IX

WAFFLES AND CREAMED CHICKEN   TOMATO SALAD
MOLASSES NUT WAFERS   PINEAPPLE SHERBET
A BEVERAGE

X

MUSHROOM OR OYSTER SOUP
FRUIT SALAD   RUSKS
NUT LAYER CAKE WITH JAM FILLING
A BEVERAGE

XI

TOMATOES FILLED WITH PINEAPPLE AND CELERY
SPINACH RING WITH MUSHROOMS
CHANTILLY POTATOES   POPOVERS
CHOCOLATE FILLED ROLL OR COCOA ROLL
COFFEE

XII

HOT TOMATO CHEESE CANAPÉ
SWEETBREADS AND OYSTERS ON SKEWERS
STUFFED SWEET POTATOES   STRING BEANS I
SOUR MILK BISCUIT   JAM
JAPANESE PERSIMMON SALAD WITH FRENCH DRESSING
CHOCOLATE BOMBE
ANGEL CAKE III WITH BLACK WALNUTS
COFFEE

XIII

PINEAPPLE BOATS OR COCKTAIL
MUSHROOM SOUFFLÉ   GRILLED TOMATOES AND ONIONS
NEW POTATOES   CORN STICKS
PEAR SALAD AND WATERCRESS
CARAMEL OR MAPLE PARFAIT
CINNAMON STARS   COFFEE

XIV

GRAPEFRUIT COCKTAIL WITH SHERRY   PASTRY SNAILS
BROILED SWEETBREADS, LAMB CHOPS OR CENTURY STEAKS
CHEESE POTATO PUFFS GREEN PEAS OR ARTICHOKES
PARKER HOUSE ROLLS   JELLY
RASPBERRY ICE AND ANGELICA BOMBE
TRUFFLES   COFFEE

XV

CLAM BROTH   ASPARAGUS CANAPÉ
RAGOUT FIN IN INDIVIDUAL RICE RINGS
MOULDED PINEAPPLE AND CUCUMBER SALAD
MARSHMALLOW NUT MOUSSE   PRUNE CAKE
COFFEE

MEATLESS LUNCHEON

GRILLED TOMATOES AND MAYONNAISE
STEAMED FISH PUDDING
GREEN BEANS   CREAM SAUCE WITH CAPERS
FRENCH FRIED POTATOES
MALAGA GRAPE SALAD ON LETTUCE
PECAN CAKES   CHOCOLATE OR PEACH ICE CREAM
COFFEE

PLATE LUNCHEONS

I

CREAMED EGGS AND ASPARAGUS IN
RAMEKINS, OR ON RUSKS
GINGER ALE SALAD OR
TOMATO ASPIC ON LETTUCE WITH MAYONNAISE
HOT BUTTERED BISCUIT (Mock Rolls)   A BEVERAGE
PEPPERMINT ICE CREAM
COCOA OR MOLASSES CUP CAKES

II

CROQUETTES OR MOLDED MEAT OR FISH IN
ASPIC ON LETTUCE WITH MAYONNAISE
OLIVES   GREEN PEAS   POTATO CHIPS OR POTATO BOATS
HOT BUTTERED MUFFINS
MERINGUES FILLED WITH APRICOT ICE CREAM
CHOCOLATE BALLS   BEVERAGE

391

III

BOUILLON   CAVIAR CANAPÉS
INDIVIDUAL NOODLE RINGS WITH CHICKEN À LA KING
FROZEN TOMATO ASPIC
HOT BUTTERED ROLLS
ALMOND AND DATE SQUARES WITH WHIPPED CREAM
COFFEE

DINNER MENUS

I

SPARE RIBS AND SAUERKRAUT   MASHED POTATOES
CARAMEL BANANA CAKE
COFFEE

II

HAMBURGER AND ONIONS
BAKED EGG PLANT   POTATO BOATS
TOMATO ASPIC ON LETTUCE
MARSHMALLOW PUDDING   SOFT MOLASSES COOKIES
COFFEE

III

BREADED VEAL STEAK
BUTTERED BEETS   RICED POTATOES
COLE SLAW
BAKED CHOCOLATE PUDDING OR APPLE PIE
COFFEE

IV

HASH
CREAMED ONIONS   GLAZED SWEET POTATOES
LETTUCE WITH THOUSAND ISLAND DRESSING
BLUEBERRY PIE
COFFEE

V

BEEF ROLLS
SQUASH   BAKED RICE
MUFFINS
LEMON SOUFFLÉ OR APRICOT MOUSSE WITH
CONDENSED MILK
CHOCOLATE DROP CAKES
COFFEE

VI

VEAL SOUFFLÉ OR BEEF LOAF   SCALLOPED POTATOES
PARSLEY CARROTS   WHOLE WHEAT MUFFINS
CELERY SALAD
CHIFFON LEMON PIE OR FAIRY TART
COFFEE

392

VII

TOMATO COCKTAIL
BROILED STEAK
CREAMED CELERY AND GREEN PEPPERS   FRIED POTATOES
CHOCOLATE WAFFLES AND CHOCOLATE SAUCE
COFFEE

VIII

LAMB CHOPS   PEAS AND PARSLEY
MASHED POTATOES   WILTED LETTUCE
BRAN MUFFINS I
SNOW PUDDING
BLITZKUCHEN   COFFEE

IX

POT ROAST   DUMPLINGS
TURNIPS, OYSTERPLANT OR MULLED CUCUMBERS
SHREDDED GREEN PEPPERS ON LETTUCE
CARAMEL CUSTARD   VANILLA ICE BOX COOKIES
COFFEE

X

STUFFED PORK CHOPS OR PORK CHOPS AND APPLES
CREAMED CABBAGE   SOUTHERN SWEET POTATO PUDDING
TOMATO SALAD
PINEAPPLE MERINGUE CAKES
COFFEE

XI

TOMATOES FILLED WITH STUFFED OLIVES
CHICKEN OR RABBIT POT PIE
GREEN BEANS   MUSTARD PICKLE
FRUIT WHIP OR GELATINE   CHOCOLATE ALMOND BARS
COFFEE

XII

TOMATO CANAPÉ WITH BACON
STEWED CHICKEN
CREAMED SPINACH   BOILED RICE OR DUMPLINGS
APPLE PARADISE
COFFEE

XIII

FRUIT COCKTAIL
ROAST BEEF
ZUCCHINI   TOMATO PUDDING
BROWNED POTATOES   RICE MUFFINS
BROD TORTE WITH CHOCOLATE ICING OR
ENGLISH ALMOND PUDDING
COFFEE

XIV

TOMATO AND CAVIAR CANAPÉS

ROAST VEAL OR KIDNEY ROAST

BROCCOLI, WITH HOLLANDAISE SAUCE

NOODLES OR SPAETZEN   PICKLED PEACHES

CHOCOLATE CAKE WITH CHOCOLATE COATED WHITE ICING

ORANGE PUDDING   COFFEE

XV

WHITE GRAPE COCKTAIL

CROWN ROAST OF LAMB, GRAVY AND MINT SAUCE

NEW POTATOES AND PARSLEY

BOILED CAULIFLOWER AND SAUTÉD

MUSHROOMS WITH DRAWN BUTTER

CORNSTICKS   CURRANT JELLY

PECAN DROP CAKES   CHOCOLATE BOMBE

COFFEE

XVI

PINEAPPLE AND ORANGE MINT COCKTAIL

FROG LEGS   BRUSSELS SPROUTS

HOT POTATO SALAD   ROLLS

FROMAGE À LA CRÉME WITH STRAWBERRIES

COFFEE

XVII

TOMATO CANAPÉ WITH CREAM CHEESE AND

ANCHOVY PASTE

CELERY   CLEAR SOUP   OLIVES

SQUAB STUFFED WITH RICE   BRAISED ENDIVE

AVOCADO PEAR SLICES ON LETTUCE

FRENCH DRESSING

SUNSHINE CAKE   STRAWBERRY ICE CREAM

COFFEE

XVIII

CELERY ASPIC ON TOMATO AND LETTUCE

FILET OF BEEF WITH MUSHROOM GRAVY

NEW POTATOES   CREAMED SPINACH

SPICED PRUNES   SCONES

GRANDMOTHER'S APPLE CAKE WITH ANGELICA ICE CREAM

COFFEE   PRALINES

XIX

DEVILED EGGS DE LUXE

BROILED CHICKEN   GREEN PEAS AND MUSHROOMS

PEAR POTATOES   CORN OYSTERS

ICE BOX ROLLS   JELLY

AVOCADO, GRAPEFRUIT AND ORANGE SALAD ON

LETTUCE, FRENCH DRESSING

CHEESE CARROTS   CRACKERS

MERINGUE CREAM TART WITH APRICOT FILLING

COFFEE   TURKISH PASTE

XX

CLEAR SOUP

BROILED LOBSTER   TARTAR SAUCE

GREEN ASPARAGUS WITH DRAWN BUTTER

POTATOES AND PARSLEY

ENDIVE SALAD

LOGANBERRY OR PINEAPPLE ICE   VELVET SPICE CAKE

XXI

COFFEE

ONION SOUP

BAKED STUFFED FISH GARNISHED WITH

MASHED POTATOES IN TOMATOES,

LEMON SLICES AND PARSLEY

BISCUIT   ARTICHOKES

CUCUMBER AND LETTUCE SALAD

GERMAN CHERRY CAKE

COFFEE

XXII

CREAMED OYSTER CANAPÉS   TOMATO JUICE COCKTAIL

BAKED HAM GARNISHED WITH PINEAPPLE SLICES

BAKED MACARONI   WHITE ASPARAGUS

CLOVER LEAF ROLLS   JELLY

MERINGUE TART FILLED WITH

LEMON AND ORANGE ICE, FLAVORED WITH RUM,

TOPPED WITH WHIPPED CREAM

COFFEE

XXIII

OYSTERS IN GRAPEFRUIT

CLEAR SOUP WITH MARROW BALLS

CRACKERS   CELERY

TURKEY OR GOOSE, DRESSED WITH

SWEET POTATOES AND APPLES

BRUSSELS SPROUTS   GNOCCHI

HOT BREAD

NUT CAKE (Mandel Torte)   APRICOT BOMBE

COFFEE

Born in St. Louis in October 1877 of German stock, Irma von Starkloff Rombauer grew up and married, never expecting to earn her own living. But after her husband's sudden death in 1930, this celebrated hostess became a cookbook author. With the publication of the first *Joy of Cooking* in 1931, she began a family tradition that was passed to her daughter Marion Rombauer Becker in the 1950s and to Marion's son Ethan Becker in 1976.